The Commercial Offices Handbook

Tim Battle (Ed.)

D1513897

RIBA Enterprises

© RIBA Enterprises, 2003

Published by RIBA Enterprises Ltd, 1–3 Dufferin Street, London EC1Y 8NA

ISBN 1 85946 109 3

Product Code: 25000

The right of Tim Battle *et al* to be identified as the Authors of this work has been asserted in accordance with the Copyright, Designs and Patents Act 1988.

British Library Cataloguing in Publication Data
A catalogue record of this book is available from the British Library.

Editor: Tim Battle
Publisher: Geoff Denner
Commissioning Editor: Matthew Thompson
Project Editor: Katy Banyard
Copy-Editor: Ramona Lamport
Typeset, printed and bound by Hobbs the Printers, Hampshire

Every effort was made by the Publisher to seek copyright permission for the use and reproduction of images in this book at the time of Publication.

While every effort has been made to check the accuracy of the information given in this book, readers should always make their own checks. Neither the Authors nor the Publisher accept any responsibility for mis-statements made in it or misunderstandings arising from it.

Front cover: Canon HQ, Reigate. David Richmond Architects.
        Photographer: Nathan Willock, VIEW.

Contents

Forewords

Lord Rogers of Riverside

The Urban Task Force Report, *Towards an Urban Renaissance* was published in 1999 and stated that 'towns and cities should be well designed . . . [and] support a range of diverse uses within a sustainable urban environment'. Clearly, commercial offices, a key feature of modern towns and cities have an important role in improving the quality of both our daily working lives and environment.

Sustainable urban regeneration should be founded on principles of design excellence, social well-being and environmental responsibility within a viable and legislative framework. This Handbook's strength lies in the persuasive case it makes for a sustainable development cycle for commercial offices, from an initial investment standpoint right through to the occupation by the workforce.

In my mind, there is little doubt that there is a growing awareness of the benefits of sustainable development amongst the community at large. By highlighting this issue, the publication of The Commercial Offices Handbook is indeed timely.

David Steventon, President British Council for Offices

Commercial offices – prominent in the built environment of every city in the UK – are a diverse class of buildings, varying, both externally and internally, in shape, size and facilities. A handbook targeted at the creators, builders, and occupiers of office space is a tool which has been necessary for some time.

Founded upon the expertise of many of Britain's best designers, developers and providers of commercial office space, this text provides the reader with clear guidance on the creation and procurement of commercial offices, together with an overview of the office industry at large.

The text adopts a systematic approach to the subject in focus. Starting with commercial office space in a global context, and moves steadily forward from the questions of finance at the start of an office development to the issues which arise when an office becomes an occupied, living building. The breadth of material covered will mean that this book becomes a vital support for all professionals and students of the built environment.

The Commercial Offices Handbook comfortably supports the move towards research and development which the office industry has now begun to follow, seeking to define and illustrate best practice for the improvement of both the physical form of offices and the operational efficiency of office space.

The apparent easy scope of this text hides the considerable effort and energy which went into its production. I trust that the industry at large will take note of its comments and conclusions and use it as a working document, lending support to their own goals and targets whilst incorporating into their daily activities the best practice outlined within these pages.

Introduction

Tim Battle, Editor
Timothy Battle and Associates

The role of the Master Builder in Medieval times was clear and concise. His success lay in successfully interpreting the grand vision of his Patron, and having the technical and management skills to deliver within the money that was available.

Now, at the turn of the Millennium, procuring commercial offices reflects the way in which society has since evolved. There is no longer a single point of responsibility; rather there are many competing interests that seek to influence the outcome. There is an increasing awareness that macro issues such as global warming and the globalisation of business activity are coming in to conflict with the needs of society as a whole, and of the individual, which in turn has fuelled the debate on sustainability.

Everything is becoming more complicated.

In 1998 I took on the role of Editor for the third revision of the *British Council for Offices Guide to Best Practice in the Specification for Offices*, and which was published as the BCO Guide 2000.

What quickly became apparent was that as an industry we were too focused on the process of procuring commercial offices as a product. We judged success when we had achieved practical completion and could move on to the next development project. This was aptly summed up by Sir Stuart Lipton, of Stanhope Plc, who when asked what was his definition of an intelligent building, replied that it was one let to a blue chip client on an upwards only, 25 year lease.

I decided that the revised *British Council for Offices Guide* should lay greater emphasis on reviewing a series of options in the design and procurement of commercial office space rather than opt for a 'one fits all solution'. The eventual end user of the workspace should have a far greater influence on understanding the outcomes that were to be achieved, and by recognising the complexity of the process, we had to look at the broader aspects of the procurement cycle.

But recognising the complexity and many layered aspects of the procurement of commercial offices enabled a fresh approach to providing a more detailed analysis, which in turn became the genesis of *The Commercial Offices Handbook*.

This presented an opportunity to review in much greater depth the multiple facets of sustainability in the procurement of commercial offices, whilst identifying one major conundrum in the sustainability debate, that of the factors that can be identified, and then measured, as enhancing workplace productivity. There are no shortage of subjective comments that pleasant working surroundings *must* enhance workplace productivity, regrettably there is a complete dearth of hard fact to show that £x spent on 'pleasant surroundings' can give £y improvement in workplace productivity, and so attract a £z premium rent.

The authors for each chapter were selected because of their acknowledged expertise in their particular field of activity, as indeed was the subsequent peer group reviewer for each chapter. Whilst no account of the many, varied and complicated issues that go into the procurement of commercial offices can be wholly complete, we have identified, or given a reference, to what is currently considered to be best practice in this field at the current time.

In addition the authors have been encouraged to indulge in some 'future gazing' to see how their particular discipline might evolve over the coming decade.

I owe a great debt to all the contributors who have generously put up with my cajoling over the past year as we worked up the concept through to the completed chapters in the Handbook, and I am particularly grateful to Bob Dalziel for his never flagging encouragement and enthusiasm. Finally, I would like to thank the peer group review panel for their wise and measured comments and Katy Banyard for keeping us all in line.

Tim Battle
January 2003

Timothy Battle, Editor
Timothy Battle & Associates

Tim Battle has spent over forty years of his life working in the construction industry.

His experience ranges from that of a services contractor, Towco, followed by a services consultant, Rybka Battle, through to his current role of enabling conferences, Timothy Battle & Associates. His three sons are all involved in the construction industry.

He now measures success by his ability to attract a platform of speakers to speak on a topical theme, who are recognised for their expertise in a particular field of construction procurement activity, and can engage with an audience. Conferences run with Architects' Journal/Emap have included: skyscrapers *Tall Storeys?* on shopping centres, *Cities Fight Back*, on hotels, *Hip or Hype?* and *The Time Line,* dealing with PFI/PPP procurement issues.

He has enabled the British Council for Offices Spring Conferences at the RIBA as well as initiating the first Future Project Seminars at MIPIM, Cannes for The Architectural Review. He has organised BCO technical tours to Chicago, Frankfurt, Paris, Brussels and Berlin to see how property professionals in other countries carry out their business activities.

Tim is on the Board of Management of the British Council for Offices, was Editor of the *BCO 2000 Best Practice Guide* and is enabling the BCO Fitting Out Guide 2003 as well as an update of the BCO Best Practice Guide to be issued in 2004.

Acknowledgements

We would like to thank the following individuals for their sound advice as part of our peer group review panel:

Andrew Lett	Aukett Ltd
Bill Gloyn	A O N Group Ltd
Chris Liddle	HLM
David Ainsworth	Greycoat
David Turrent	E C D Architects & Energy Consultants
Francis Ives	Cyril Sweett
Gerald Kaye	Helical Bar plc
Ian Liddel	Buro Happold Engineers Ltd
Jack Pringle	Pringle Brandon
John Spanswick	Bovis Construction Ltd
Keith MacKenzie	Betty Siddel Gibson
Mark Whitby	Whitby Bird & Partners
Martin Quicke	Denton Wilde Sapte
Neil Pennell	Land Securities Properties Ltd
Richard Saxon	Building Design Partnership
Rob Bold	Grimley International Ltd
Sam Cassels	ISGC
Stephen Mudie	Davis Langdon Everest

Thanks also to Duncan Mactear and colleagues at 4Projects for the construction and maintenance of the RIBA Enterprises-Commercial Offices Handbook extranet site.

1 The global office

Francis Duffy
DEGW

The global office – a personal perspective

To understand where office design is going it may help to reflect on where it has come from. Because the design of the working environment is such a complex subject with so many contradictory trends, readers of this deliberately practical handbook have every right to expect some kind of a global roadmap to explain not just how office design has developed over the last four decades but also why things have happened in the way they have. Having been an interpreter of the field for so long and having worked for so many international businesses in so many parts of the world, I may have some kind of qualification as a cartographer. However, since office design is a relatively recent phenomenon that has attracted little formal attention from historians, everyone should be aware that this very sketchy map is personal, not fully validated and still developing.

However, I must admit, I have seen over the years a lot of offices. With this dubious advantage, is it still possible to discern the big picture? I believe it is, especially given the consistency with which four fundamental questions about office design have turned up again and again over the last 40 years, admittedly in many different forms:

- What impact, if any, does the design of the office have upon organisational success?
- Should offices be made more consistent or more diverse?
- How is office space best procured – by owners, developers or others?
- As businesses and information technology change, is the office still a stable building type?

All four questions can be traced back to the tensions created by a single conflict of interests. Each question is an aspect of the ongoing, and probably never-to-be-resolved, argument between two diametrically opposed schools of thought. The position of the first of these schools is that of the developer and even more of the financial institutions that fund them, i.e. the supply side of the big economic equation that connects office users with office space. To most developers – despite a few honourable exceptions – property is merely a commodity. If exchange matters more than beneficial use, as it certainly does to most institutions, landlords and developers, it makes sense if all office space is more or less the same. Moreover, in a market in which developers take so many risks – not least because of the ups and downs of economic cycles – stability as well as homogeneity is thought to be a good thing. The position of the second school is that of the demand side. This is the point of view of corporate clients – more precisely of *enlightened* and *user orientated* corporate clients – for whom office space is less a commodity than a business tool. New ideas about office design are valuable to businesses to the extent that they can be used to enhance competitive advantage. It also makes sense for such clients to consult office users about what kind of space will help them do their work better, although they also readily acknowledge that whatever users say they want is certain to mutate and evolve. For such clients, change and diversity are more likely to be evidence of vitality rather than risk.

The purpose of this chapter is to examine the practical consequences of these fundamental differences in a way that sheds light upon the reasons for the complex and contradictory ways in which office design has developed, and probably will continue to develop.

Important steps in the development of the office

The office is a relatively new building type. Office work became important only towards the end of the 19th century when governments discovered the need to be supported by a large bureaucratic apparatus, and commerce began to demand equivalent machinery for steering, controlling and recording the ever more complex activities of burgeoning enterprises. Earlier in the 19th century, office activities, such as they were at that time, were accommodated in buildings the form of which was generally derived, depending on culture and circumstances, either from the grand architecture of palaces (*see* Figure 1: Sir William Chambers's Somerset House in London) or from the utilitarian model of the mill (e.g. Peter Ellis's Oriel Chambers in Liverpool). A minor – and much older, and still surviving – pattern is the college-like design of the Inns of Court, a reminder of how the form of the office might have remained had bureaucracy never been invented and if the Industrial Revolution had never occurred.

That office architecture should have a characteristic form of its own is a late 19th century idea. The office building, as we know it today, especially in its high-rise manifestations, is, as is well known, an American innovation, created out of necessity in the extraordinary circumstances of the explosion of the US economy after the Civil War. Not surprisingly, given its immense geographical advantages, Chicago, in the last two decades of the 19th century became the archetype of a new kind of city where the huge scale of enterprise, commercial advantage, technological vision, real estate ingenuity, constructional imagination and architectural invention combined to create the new, high-rise office architecture that has become the model to which all cities everywhere continue to aspire (*see* Figure 3).

Figure 1: The prestigious Somerset House (William Chambers, c.1776–1801)

Figure 2: 'The icon for the open plan'*: Interior Larkin Building, Buffalo (Frank Lloyd Wright, 1904)

Figure 3: Frankfurt Cityscape showing the impact of the popular 'Chicago model'

*Quoted from Juriaan van Meel, *The European Office*, Rotterdam, 010 Publishers (2001)

What is curious is that the Chicago model of the office, magnificent as it is, has been copied so much, has lasted so long, and has been challenged so little. Perhaps the reason is that this model of the office was so deeply grounded in what was an entirely new kind of economy. The skyscraper office is the product not just of the startlingly innovative constructional and information technologies that have attracted so much attention from commentators, it has also been shaped by two other factors: new forms of organisational culture and new methods of real estate procurement. The cultural values implicit in the iconography of the high-rise office remain those of the dominant business ideology of the time of the skyscraper's invention – a mechanistic view of office workers as so many individual units of production in a great machine directed from on high by all seeing, all knowing leaders (*see* Figure 2). From the very beginning of the Chicago model to this day, the dominant mode of real estate delivery is that the developer as entrepreneur is the essential intermediary between the users of buildings and those whose business it is to supply them. The landlord has, as Louis Sullivan noted somewhat bitterly at the very end of the 19th century, 'the right to build as he chooses'. In contrast, in post Second World War northern Europe, an attempt was made to create a democratic office architecture, the form and procurement of which were intended to be more responsive to the demands of end users and to the culture of different kinds of business. But it is strikingly obvious that the northern European model of the office has been far less widely exported than the original and still globally dominant North American model.

Office design, of course, has not been static. In each of the four decades of development that I have observed, office design has reflected quite specific crises and opportunities. These have given each decade of office design its own special characteristics.

The 1960s: the office as a communications system

Innovative office design of the 60s was dominated by the idea of the office as a cybernetic system. This led to:

- The recognition, originally in northern Europe and somewhat later in North America, that the office interior can be thought of as a informational device which can be designed in a systematic way to enhance communications within businesses.
- The invention of forms of office layout (e.g. *bürolandschaft* or office landscaping) (*see* Chapter 7) and office furniture systems (e.g. Herman Miller's Action Office) that were intended to respond to the idea of the office as a dynamic, informational network. Most of these new work styles were predicated on the open plan.
- A growing acceptance that not all the components of anything as large, complex and long lasting as an office building should be designed with the same degree of longevity. Some elements (such as office furniture) can be more useful and flexible if they are given a much shorter life span than 'stiffer', longer-term elements such as environmental and informational infrastructures and, of course, the even longer-term skin and structure of the building itself.

- As soon as this division made on the basis of temporality was recognised, two powerful axes of common interest were created. The longer-term one is between the architect and the landlord or developer. The shorter-term axis is the shared professional interests of the space planner (or interior designer) and the tenant.

The 1970s: the office as a social system

In the 70s the idea that the office is a social and informational system developed in two very different ways in North America and northern Europe:

- The rapid migration continued in North America of functional and problem solving from the long-term building shell to the shorter-term elements of the interior.
- North American architects, with their eyes firmly on developer clients, left the design of the interior to specialist space planners and interior designers who studied how best to accommodate changing tenant requirements.
- In northern Europe this functional division of responsibilities was slowed down by the relative weakness of developers combined with rise of the power of end users who, with statutory protection from Workers' Councils, began to demand and indeed get from architects, office environments much more specifically designed to respond to end user interests – privacy, acoustic control, individual office rooms equipped with personally responsive environmental controls.
- The consequence was a divergence that widened for the rest of the century between northern European offices – increasingly narrow and highly articulated in plan form, elaborate and particular in design, more and more environmentally responsible and social democratic in their underlying value system – and North American offices which tended in exactly the opposite direction to become deeper and simpler in plan form, much more generic in design, environmentally unresponsive and, above all, predominantly corporate, rather than social, in their iconography.
- The former kind of office architecture, shaped as it has been by popular priorities, can be described as 'bottom up'. The latter kind has been shaped by 'top down' priorities that stem from board room and shareholder priorities. While users are more interested in building features that add value to their working lives, employers in the end have been far more interested in cutting costs.

The 1980s: facilities management and distributed intelligence

In the 80s the rapid diffusion of distributed intelligence led to new challenges for those responsible for accommodating rapidly changing business practices:

- The legitimisation in 1981 by IBM of the Personal Computer and the consequent escape of the computer from specialised computer rooms into the general office – distributed intelligence – which immediately strained all building systems physically and placed an equivalent managerial strain on everyone responsible for managing office space.

- The rapid professionalisation, initially in North America and somewhat later in northern Europe, of corporate real estate (CRE) and facilities management, the two initially in-house, later extensively out-sourced, groups responsible respectively for the procurement of office buildings and their day-to-day management.

- Information technology coupled with deregulation accelerated the globalisation of certain industries – e.g. financial and professional services – which enormously increased the demand for consistent worldwide guidelines to regularise patterns of space use everywhere.

- Financial centres – London and Tokyo first, then Paris and Frankfurt – began to import North American office design practices in order to compete in an increasingly global market place. Other sectors, especially information technology, the media, and the pharmaceutical industry followed.

- Much interest in – and rather less success in achieving – 'intelligent buildings', i.e. buildings that are integrated in terms of their systems, that provide a robust infrastructure for increasingly ubiquitous information technology, that are consequently capable of being managed – or even of becoming self-managing – in a much more responsive way, and that are designed to anticipate and to respond to changing user demands.

The 1990s: new ways of working change the office

Throughout the 90s it became increasingly clear that office technology, office processes, office buildings, office interiors and, above all, office culture were all about to change.

- The realisation in many sectors of office activity that information technology has the power to challenge and transform all the conventions – social, cultural, technological, constructional – that have shaped office culture and office design for 100 years.

- The creation of virtual organisations linked across time and space by electronic means and the questioning of conventional ways of working, including the value of place.

- The end of synchrony – i.e. the new ability for people to work via electronic networks without being co-located and without the need to adhere to the same timetable.

- More sophisticated ways of mapping how office activities are changing, particularly patterns of communication and interaction and, perhaps even more importantly, of investigating how intensively (or intermittently) office space is actually used through time.

- The discovery that conventional office space is a grossly underused resource – especially when its use is measured over time.

- Increasing pressure from management to drive down office occupancy costs (e.g. by minimising work place standards – for example, by workplace sharing, 'hotelling', hot-desking and home working), as well as searching for better ways of using the working environment to add value to office work.

- The parallel growth of high street service providers, such as Kinko's, responding to the needs of the increasing number of home-based, or partially home-based, mobile office workers.

- The subsequent realisation that in an increasingly virtual and mobile world, the role of the physical office environment is likely to become not less but much more important, particularly as a means of fostering and supporting interactive and collective activities. Evidence of this shift towards the office becoming a more social place is the gradual decline of the importance of individual workplaces within the overall space budget.

- The realisation that the physical design of the office provides the opportunity for organisations to transform office culture radically.

- The corollary is that change management and design are interdependent – change management is facilitated by design and thus the importance of design is considerably enhanced.

What these changes cumulatively amount to is the erosion, if not dissolution, of most of the conventions that have shaped the cities of the 20th century. The eventual impact will be enormous – not least because in the developed world at least half the working population already works in offices with an even more rapidly growing proportion in the developing world. Change will affect those who supply office space as much as those who demand it.

How has corporate real estate (CRE) practice developed?

- What impact do CREs think that the design of the office has upon organisational success?
- Do they believe that offices should become more consistent or more diverse?
- How do they think office space is best procured?
- As businesses and information technology change, how much do CREs believe the office should change?

In the 1950s, office design – both architecture and interiors – was already being used extensively by globalising businesses to establish their brands internationally. Office design was also being used to reinforce corporate values and to buttress corporate discipline. From the 50s right through to the 70s, commercial imperatives – external branding and internal discipline – shaped the classic design programmes of such exemplary patrons of international design services as IBM and Olivetti. Corporate real estate departments imposed the highest design standards on acquiescent, international branch offices, standards that were vetted by designers of the calibre of Eliot Noyes and Ettore Sottsas, and maintained by elite teams of highly skilled, in-house project managers.

Ambitious corporate design management, although it continues (an excellent contemporary example is Ericsson), is highly visible but has always been exceptional. Cost control and variety reduction, following a logistical, quasi-military model, have been much more important determinants of the quality of international corporate real estate. The chief instrument by which this much more humdrum objective of international corporate control was achieved was by 'corporate standards', rules, specifications and procedures, written locally in Chicago or New York and rolled out everywhere, without discrimination or choice. On the whole, since the beginning of the 80s, corporate standards have tended to be less design influenced and more cost driven. The tendency towards distancing corporate real estate from strategic business considerations has been encouraged by the increasing professionalisation of facilities management and subsequently by the increasingly popular corporate habit of outsourcing non-core service functions, including real estate and facilities management. Deterioration in design quality seems to be an inevitable consequence of stripping property assets off company balance sheets in order to concentrate energy and capital on what are generally thought to be more essential business objectives.

The day-to-day practice of corporate real estate has changed a lot. Centralised control, whether by design gurus or on the military model, is vulnerable because it is so labour intensive and expensive. Today everyone on the international circuit in corporate real estate seems to be overstretched. Where once hundreds of project managers serviced large corporations' properties spread across a large territory such as the whole of Europe, the same workload is now handled by a handful of over-worked people, frequently buttonholed, constantly on the run. In these circumstances, and especially in periods of rapid growth or decline in office head count, attempts to manage corporate real estate globally are increasingly liable to be subverted by local practices in brokering, design and construction.

A related crisis is the increasingly obvious tension between corporate real estate and user interests. Real estate management structures, under the severe pressures described above to cut costs and to outsource wherever possible, are finding it extremely difficult to cope with increasingly empowered users. Economic, demographic and technological changes are creating a new kind of office workforce, with an entirely different economic, social and educational profile, whose expectations of the working environment are rising and whose potential to demand attention, to create trouble, and to want change, is very much on the increase.

And yet it is strange how strongly the homogenisation of international real estate portfolios persists despite these factors and despite major cultural differences. European businesses operating in the US have been generally much more reluctant to import their own standards and procedures and are far more likely to adopt the customs of the country than their US counterparts operating in Europe. The reason may be simply economic. North American office workers are prepared to accept environmental conditions that are much poorer than those to which ordinary Europeans have become accustomed in the last two or three decades, particularly in Scandinavia, Germany and the Netherlands. Despite the Federal system and a vast geography, 200 years of a common culture and 100 years of the mechanistic view of organisational culture (often called 'Taylorism' or 'Fordism' after its most famous exponents), have made all US offices – not to mention much of the rest of the paraphernalia of American life – look very much the same wherever they happen to be. Americans, perhaps without realising it, tend to assume that uniform office design standards *ought* to prevail everywhere in the world, just as they do at home. If they do not find consistency, they impose it. Europeans, from long experience of cultural and linguistic differences, are more tolerant of diversity – but only at home.

All this may change. In both North America and northern Europe, a new and very different argument has begun to be heard which may influence international real estate practice as profoundly as any of the factors discussed above, as the knowledge economy develops and grows. A growing number of leading businesses, especially those whose success depends upon motivating knowledge workers, have begun to realise that workplace design can be helpful in change management, thus re-connecting design with corporate strategy. The design of buildings and interiors is being used to facilitate technological and cultural change because the physical environment conveys information about corporate values powerfully, persistently and pervasively. Of course, this information can be negative as well as positive – which merely serves to stress the importance of design. The big current paradox is this: as the working environment is discovered to have the potential to become more and more useful and central to advanced businesses at the strategic level, operational day-to-day corporate management of real estate in most ordinary enterprises is in practical terms totally detached from strategic intent. In many businesses the use of design for strategic business purposes has effectively been ruled out, not least by outsourcing, formulaic space standards and cost cutting.

To address the four questions directly:

- *What impact do CREs think that the design of the office has upon organisational success?*

Depending on the kind of company they work for, CRE attitudes to design and business success have changed over the last four decades. The most ambitious have thought of the office as a symbol of the brand. More have tried to use office design in a military way as a means of achieving central discipline and control. However, the CRE function itself has changed more than CRE attitudes. CREs, despite (and perhaps even because of) their increasing professionalisation, have experienced a substantial decline in their power within corporations over the last four decades. This decline has been accompanied by an understandable, if regrettable, tendency for CREs to behave as if they belonged to the supply side rather than the demand side of our equation – i.e. tending to be more sympathetic to issues of project management and delivery than to using quality design to serve business and user interests. This tendency has been exacerbated by the increasingly common corporate practice of outsourcing their role altogether. It is only in very

9

recent times that issues related to cultural change has made the CRE role potentially strategic once again – but so far only in advanced organisations that are beginning to understand the value of design to knowledge work and knowledge workers.

• *Do CREs believe that offices should become more consistent or more diverse?*

Supply side pressures towards cost cutting and efficiency have tended to force even the most well-intentioned and user sensitive CREs into adopting easily replicable and formulaic design solutions. The so-called 'universal plan', i.e. providing exactly the same type and size of workplaces for everyone everywhere is an example. The intention is to cut the costs of churn (reallocating workplaces because of organisational changes), and to make the relocation of staff easier. The operational conclusion is that people are easier and cheaper to move than workplaces – i.e. furniture matters more than people. Dealing with diversity has often been daunting for conventionally trained CREs. The problem of combining efficiency with user choice is very real and not at all easy to solve. New ways of working, based on the premise that people should be free to choose not only their timetable but also their entire work style, are presenting CREs with an unprecedented challenge.

• *How do they think office space is best procured?*

The general shift has been from labour intensive, top-down control of office design projects by powerful and well equipped in-house CRE departments to the devolution of executive responsibility for the provision of design solutions and the management of office space to outsourced suppliers. In more advanced, knowledge-based organisations, there is some evidence of a reverse trend as some CREs are being asked to become involved in using the design of office space to manage change.

• *As businesses and information technology change, how much do CREs believe the office should change?*

The underlying pressure for embracing change is being stimulated by increasingly ubiquitous, powerful and reliable information technology. To take advantage of this important opportunity, CREs are being asked to establish working relationships between themselves and their peers in human relations and information technology and, at the same time, to achieve equivalently open and friendly relationships with user departments. Such discourse is surprisingly difficult to achieve in most businesses, a dysfunctional state of affairs that client organisations, committed to knowledge management, quite simply cannot allow to persist.

How has development practice changed?

Unlike corporate real estate executives, the attitudes of office developers to the buildings they promote, finance, construct, manage and exchange have changed relatively little since the 50s – especially in the US. This is not to say that there have been no new ideas in real estate. For example, on the financial front many innovations have occurred, such as the American REITs (Real Estate Investment Trusts – that make the value inherent in property into tradable instruments) to the very different, but in some ways analogous, British PFIs (Private Finance Initiatives – a way of allowing Government to reduce the burden of taxation by, in effect, selling its office properties to the private sector and then leasing them back). Moreover, a number of other important initiatives have emerged in the market such as serviced offices, enriched by understanding the ways in which hotel and business centres make most of their money – i.e. by selling services by the second rather than square feet by the year. Such office space, managed by hybrid service cum real estate companies such as HQ (now alas no longer with us) and Regus (still struggling for profitability) is available, at a cost, on very short leases. However, in terms of the quality of office building, especially in relation to user priorities, as opposed to the more macro level ways in which office development is financed and marketed, evidence of innovation and improvement is much harder to find.

The three main functional divisions that characterise North American development and are generally taken for granted (the separation of building development from building use, the separation of landlord from tenant, and the separation of long-term architectural design from shorter-term interior design) are not in the longer term likely to continue to be in the consumer's interest. This is despite the economic benefits for the developer inherent in the division of labour, the managerial logic of distinguishing between the differing time horizons of building owners and tenants, and the constructional convenience of separating long-term design elements from short-term features. Granted that each strategy taken separately is eminently sensible. However, in combination the consequence of these essentially mechanistic and Taylorist divisions of responsibility is a user-unfriendly array of increasingly conservative products and services that are, by all accounts, impossible to change.

This is not to claim that the northern European system of procuring office space, biased as it is towards building ownership rather than tenancy, has solved the problem of accommodating change any better. Indeed, the result of the ownership of offices by user organisations is one-off, purpose-made, uniquely briefed office buildings that are arguably even more vulnerable to change than rent slabs. However, one virtue of the northern European system is that the inherent quality of design specification and construction of such buildings has remained higher than comparable North American offices. In Scandinavia what is undoubtedly the highest quality of office environment in the world is almost entirely the product of a continuing tradition of intelligent and well directed pressure from users on suppliers.

A distinguishing feature of office design in northern Europe, with its higher concentration of owner-occupiers, is the much higher level of interest in designing office buildings in an environmentally friendly and sustainable way. It is interesting that in the UK, which like the US has a predominantly developer-led office design culture, there is some evidence in advanced development practice, of an intermediate condition reconciling some of the better features of the more easily exchanged North American office buildings with some of the attention to natural environment and other user-friendly features that is characteristic of many northern European buildings. For

11

Figure 4: Typical open plan office layout

Figure 5: A different approach to providing work areas

example, elaborated facades designed to permit aspect and daylight while preventing heat gain and glare from sunlight are now not uncommon – perhaps through the influence of bodies such as the British Council for Offices. It is also striking that US architects tend to design to a much higher specification when they work in the UK and elsewhere in Europe.

Overall in Europe, because of the relatively high incidence of owner-occupation and also end user pressure often exerted via the statutory influence of Workers' Councils, environmental, ergonomic and design standards, both in purpose built and developer buildings, are undeniably higher. Innovation continues to be possible – for example, throughout Europe displacement air conditioning, i.e. using the volume beneath the access floor as a plenum, is common and the use of photovoltaic panels is becoming a feature of office architecture. In North America, even the use of access floors for cabling is very rare because developers are working within a fiscal regime that gives them zero incentive to relate costs in use to capital costs. To the North American developer cutting costs means cutting capital costs – only possible either by exploiting economies of scale or by reducing the inherent quality of the specification.

What has happened in North America, as noted above, has been a shift in the problem-solving load from architecture to interior design – for example, in environmental services, data and electrical transmission, and acoustics. One result is increasingly elementary office space, as deep as possible to minimise the ratio of the relatively expensive perimeter to floor area, with minimal circulation, noisy and unzonable air conditioning, undersized and under-ducted cores, and minimal aspect. Another result is relatively complicated, elaborated and expensive office furniture, usually in the form of cubicles, laid out following a 'troglodytitic' interior design logic without reference to orientation, aspect, work processes or, oddly enough, even to economy – so huge are the workplace footprints by European standards.

Again to address our four questions directly:

- *What impact do developers think that the design of the office has upon organisational success?*

It is abundantly clear that North American developers have very little interest in the organisational success of their tenants – or even in how efficiently space is used or in the comfort of the users. These considerations simply do not come within their remit. While there is no reason to believe that European developers, given the same fiscal framework, would not operate in exactly the same way, the experiences in the UK of Stockley Park, Broadgate and Chiswick where tenant research was part of the developers' briefing process, demonstrate that user feedback can dramatically reshape development practice, provided the incentive exists. In these cases the context was global change and the poor quality of the existing product. The incentive was stiff competition for tenants, both locally and internationally.

- *Do they believe that offices should become more consistent or more diverse?*

There is no current reward for developers working in the North American mode – and that means anywhere in the world – that can be gained by introducing novelty or diversity into their product range. Designing for diversity means choice, choice means complexity, complexity means higher capital costs. Only in Europe, and to a lesser extent in Japan, is the persistence of owner-occupier choice possible.

- *How do they think office space is best procured?*

Divisions of responsibility, as described above, are deeply embedded in the North American system. A pointer for change is the growing market for serviced offices which, in theory, should both open up developers to informed user pressure and increase the potential returns. Another possibility is the growth of pre-lets in a currently softening market in which developers may be forced by competitive pressure to respond more attentively to user needs.

- *As businesses and information technology change, how much do developers believe the office should change?*

The current situation is that, incredibly in a period of massive change in office technology and culture, there appears to be no incentive for developers operating within the tight margins of the highly prescriptive North American system, to acknowledge that anything is changing at all, let alone initiate innovations themselves. Perhaps the most ironic example is what has been called the 'Silicon Valley Mystery', the desperately poor operational and environmental quality of the vast majority of office architecture in the place where, throughout the 90s, many of the most entrepreneurial and technologically advanced companies in the world were concentrated. Contrast this with the invention that is so very evident in custom built (but still ultimately institutionally financed) projects for Ericsson in the US, for BA at Waterside in the UK, or for Commerzbank in Germany.

New ways of working, sustainability and productivity

What neither business clients nor developers, in both Europe nor North America, have still not fully grasped are the implications of reinventing office architecture to take advantage of the potential of office space to be designed in ways that (a) respond to the opportunities offered by new ways of working, (b) stimulate greater productivity in office work and (c) maximise the chances of a creating environments that will be sustainable through the first decades of the 21st century.

The last issue is in theory the simplest but in practice the most intractable. Users and developers, corporate tenants and institutional owners all, in theory, stand to benefit from office buildings that do not guzzle gas, in which costs in use are kept to a minimum, that are not only easy to run but do not harm people in the process, that inflict the smallest amount of damage on the environment, and that can be adapted and improved through time. In practice, achieving these self-evidently desirable goals is more difficult than it ought to be. For example, in the US the fiscal convention of disengaging capital budgets from annual running costs discourages both developers and the procurers of buildings in both private and public sectors from spending money up front on building features designed to drive down occupancy costs. In contrast, the more sharply directed energy policy of the European Union has resulted in a direct and innovative architectural responses – new kinds of building skin, shading devices, photovoltaic cells, mixing natural ventilation with artificial cooling systems, displacement air conditioning, and chilled ceilings. However, even the most advanced European architects admit that there is a long way to go before office buildings consume zero energy, emit zero carbon and cause zero environmental impact.

The first issue, the introduction of new ways of working, is the most encouraging on both sides of the Atlantic. There are now a substantial number of projects where not only have new ways of working been demonstrated to be more efficient and effective working environments than conventional offices, but also where the projects themselves have been used as the means of broadcasting and strengthening business aspirations – transparency, agility, responsiveness to change, greater interaction, more interconnectedness, more autonomy, greater empowerment, less supervision, less hierarchy. Such projects are examples of what is becoming management's most powerful engine for achieving cultural change. Enough practical experience has been accumulated of the conditions under which such change management processes can be successfully conducted – strong and sustained leadership; a systemic approach that gives equal weight to the design of information technology, the design of human resources and the design of the working environment; good data about how emerging working patterns can be best supported by architecture and interior design; and last, but not least, the carefully planned and well-timed involvement of users throughout the design process. And yet there is tremendous room for improvement. The legacy of decades of mechanistic and divisive management styles lives on in millions of square feet of Dilbertville (the office world so ruthlessly satirised by cartoonist Scott Adams), cubicles in North America and under-populated labyrinths of cellular offices in northern Europe.

Change on the largest scale will only come when the second of our three issues is addressed – i.e. when the contribution of office design to productivity is routinely measured.

There are no real barriers to measurement of the relation between the working environment and productivity. It is relatively easy to measure the *efficiency* with which office space is used over time. For example, the financial benefits that wireless environments can bring in permitting more intense and beneficial occupancy of a given amount of office space can be calculated from observations of how people actually use the space over time. Such measures are direct – every square metre saved in accommodating a team brings a financial benefit. The *effectiveness* with which office space is used, i.e. not how much money is saved but what value does design add to business performance, can also be measured – however, in a fundamentally different way. Measures of *effectiveness* are inherently indirect. This means that the relationship between the working environment and individual and business performance is filtered by many intervening variables. Moreover, the physical environment cannot be studied on its own. How well space performs is closely related to and, to some extent dependent on, the performance of information technology as well as on the well-being of the office as an organised community. What is measured in such situations is the opinions and feelings of the people involved – what they think is important, what works well and what does not, whether the goals set have been achieved or not.

Incidentally, it should be pointed out that this methodological problem is not unique to the measurement of the performance of office space. As office work becomes more complex, plural and interactive there is scarcely any aspect of business performance that can be measured directly. Indicators there are in plenty. The eventual metric is commercial success. But exactly how success is achieved – in the development of a new product, the creation of valuable intellectual property, the creation of a successful marketing campaign, the conduct of a legal case – depends upon skilful management, i.e. the experience of fine judgement and the manipulation of many variables, just as it does in the measurement of the value added to a business by office design.

There is a third dimension of the performance of office space that is also measurable but which has been very much neglected: the success with which office environments broadcast and support the messages that organisations want to transmit to customers and to staff. This is the enormous, long term, omnipresent and sustained *expressive* capacity of office space. Since this is the realm of branding and communications, similar market research techniques to those used in marketing and advertising to measure the success of any programme of communications can be used equally powerfully in this respect: what message was intended, how successfully was it communicated and to whom?

All three dimensions – efficiency, effectiveness and expression – must be taken into account when assessing the productivity of building use and the added value that design can bring to business – when used intelligently and purposefully. It is chastening to reflect on the continuing better performance of the US economy, despite a building stock that has deteriorated in quality over the last four decades. That the economy of the European Union, despite its generally more user-friendly office stock, is less productive than the US is merely a reminder of two iron economic laws: first, that efficiency can never be neglected in office design and, second, that the office design's latent capacity to generate greater effectiveness and to express corporate values powerfully has to be *directed and managed* before its full potential can be released. Design, on its own, however good, can do nothing.

Measurement of the impact of design on business performance has been neglected not because it is particularly difficult but because marginalised architects and outsourced procurers have lost any sense of the connection between business purpose and the working environment. Those who do not understand strategic purpose cannot possibly know what to measure. The saddest aspect of this failure to connect business purpose to design is that when the question of the measurement of this relationship is raised (as it sometimes is), spuriously high levels of proof are demanded which are far more stringent than those used in any other part of the business.

The future

Let us reiterate the four questions addressed in this Chapter:

- *What impact, if any, should the design of the office have upon organisational success?*
- *Should offices be made more consistent or more diverse?*
- *How is office space best procured – by owners, developers or others?*
- *As businesses and information technology change, should the office continue to be a stable building type?*

These questions have been examined from the viewpoint of both sides of the supply and demand equation – the points of view and the attitudes of both the suppliers and the procurers of office space. More important than the separate problems of each side is the overriding fact that today the equation hardly exists. Users and suppliers, for a whole variety of complex reasons, have almost lost contact with each other.

Users have been cut off from thinking about office space in a purposeful way. Corporate real estate and development have become dangerously self-sufficient and inward looking. Cost-cutting has become it own reward. The convenience of the supply side (developers and architects included), has been allowed to carry too much weight.

Fortunately the way forward is obvious. The signs are propitious. There have been many innovations recently in information technology, work processes, and organisational culture as well as in corporate real estate and facilities management practice and in design – wherever, that is, where the old conventions of design and procurement have been abandoned and fresh thinking has been allowed to flourish. So much so that there are considerable grounds for hope for a reconciliation of the conflicting perspectives described at the beginning of this chapter. It is by no means inevitable that developers and clients should be at odds – just a freak of the history of a particular part of the economy at a particular time, admittedly of longer duration than one would have wished.

Innovative projects, still mostly in northern Europe, demonstrate that office design, if intelligently managed, can have a significant impact on organisational success. Diverse forms of practice and new ways of working together have demonstrated that differences *can* be legitimate; innovation *is* possible. The supply chain can be improved. New ways of working are likely to lead to further disintermediation in procurement and to the opening up and democratisation of the design and delivery process. In this new atmosphere of change, which just at present can be felt somewhat more easily in Europe than in North America, neither the cookie cutter approach of old fashioned corporate real estate nor the narrow conventions of developer's products are likely to be relevant for very much longer.

More feedback is the key. Feedback between users and suppliers is an essential component of business success. It implies the infinite possibility for change and improvement and it depends upon measurement. Measures of how well buildings perform in relation to business strategy are critical because they address the fundamental issue of what office buildings are intended to achieve.

The answers to the four questions posed throughout this chapter, and the logic that underpins the partial answers sketched above, expose a false dichotomy. Office space is perfectly capable of becoming both an essential business tool as well as a most valuable and exchangeable commodity, but this will happen if – and only if – we think about solving problems in a way that brings back purpose into office design. And then finally we will know the definitive answer to the fourth and last question – whether the office will continue to be a viable building type. It will all depend on what we all, individually and collectively, decide is the kind of world we want to live and work within.

Author profile

Dr Francis Duffy CBE PPRIBA
(Founder) DEGW

Francis Duffy founded the DEGW partnership with John Worthington and Luigi Giffone in 1974. In Spring 2001 he was seconded to DEGW's North America office and is currently based in New York, supporting an increasingly important branch of the practice, developing relationships with North American clients and running a graduate workshop at MIT which is researching innovation in workplace design.

His work in DEGW falls into three main streams. The first is relating changes in organisational situations and information technology to office and other kinds of design. Francis Duffy is particularly interested not only in change management but also in measuring how effectively and efficiently buildings are being used to meet clients' changing goals.

The second stream is developing DEGW research. This has been built up through projects such as a pioneering study of the relevance of open office planning in four European countries for IBM; the ORBIT studies on the impact of information technology on the office building, first in the UK and then in the United States and Japan.

The third is developing the theory and practice of design through writing for a wide audience at a number of different levels – theoretical and research papers, technical information for architects, founding and editing *Facilities* newsletter for facilities managers, and articles and reviews for the professional and general press. He is also the author of a number of books including *Office Landscaping, Planning Office Space* (with Cave and Worthington), and *The Changing City* (with Henney), *The Changing Workplace* (ed. Hannay) and *The Responsible Workplace* (with Crisp and Laing).

2 Investment – the institutional perspective

Paul McNamara and Martin Moore
Prudential Property Investment Managers Ltd

Introduction

It is rather too easy for those who are involved on a day-to-day basis in property investment and development to fall into the trap of taking property's position in investment portfolios for granted. The decision to invest in commercial property is neither inevitable nor a simple decision to make. There is no automatic right for property to have a place in the investor's portfolio; it has to earn its place.

For many (probably the majority of) investment funds, property is simply not appropriate as an asset in which to invest. If investment funds are small in size, then it is not easy to contemplate investing in single assets with lot sizes of £1 million and above. Similarly, if the aim of a fund is to be dynamic and to be managed actively and aggressively to take advantage of opportunities in asset markets when they arise, then the length of time it takes to buy and sell property militates against it having a major role in a portfolio. In this respect, even the most 'liquid' of commercial properties can take, on average, nearly two months to transact. The opportunity cost implied in this illiquidity (i.e. the chance to profit or avoid losses by transacting into or out of other more liquid markets) is, for many, a deterrent to getting involved in property.

However, for larger, more long-term investors like pension funds and life insurance companies, property is a real alternative to domestic and non-domestic equities, and to sovereign and corporate bonds. But, even here, property has to earn its place. In this respect, property has varied in its attractiveness to UK institutional investors over time.

The DTZ Research report, *Money into Property* (2002), shows that insurance company and pension fund property holdings have risen steadily over the last 30 years to a current figure in the region of approximately £80 billion. The Investment Property Databank (IPD) – the independent performance measurers for the industry – estimates the investible universe for commercial property to be in the region of £140 billion. The BPF has recently published an Office of National Statistics estimate of the total size of the UK commercial property investment market (including commercial, industrial and 'other' non-residential properties) at approximately £625 billion.

In terms of the institutions, Figure 1 shows that property represented ten per cent and three per cent of total investment portfolio asset values respectively for insurance companies and pension funds in 1963. Through steady growth, pension fund exposure peaked in 1974 at just over 15 per cent and stayed at around that level until the early 1980s. For insurance companies, the peak came in the early 1980s with overall exposures to property of around 21 per cent of total institutional assets. Since that time, property has drifted steadily lower in its importance to the major institutional investors. Following a brief recovery in interest in the boom years of the late 1980s, property has continued to drift lower in institutional portfolios to a point where it now constitutes only 5 per cent of pension fund investment portfolios. Insurance company exposures were only marginally higher at six to seven per cent.

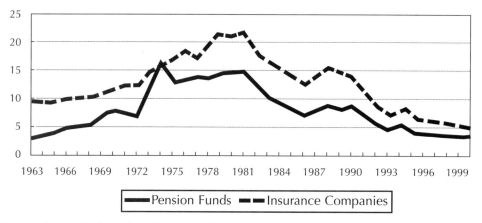

Figure 1: Property's share of total institutional assets

However, even these figures mask an underlying reality, namely that it is the larger pension funds and insurance companies that tend to hold the biggest exposures to property. Many smaller funds have abandoned property altogether in the belief that it is hardly worth holding a two or three per cent exposure to property given the extra work and effort it then entails to keep such a small portion of the portfolio in operation.

So, with the above in mind, it does appear that property has proven better at earning its place in the institutional portfolio in some periods than others.

However, these are clearly not the only important players in the market. In aggregate, property companies are an important force in the UK property market with assets in the region of £35 billion between them. Similarly, UK property holds no fears for overseas investors. In 2001, DTZ Research showed that gross purchases by non-UK investors have been running at approximately £3.2 billion per annum through the 1990s with subsequent sales running at less than half this figure. Investors from all corners of the globe have invested in the UK market.

The remainder of this chapter will explore the case for holding property in an investment portfolio. It will then present a case study of how that justification for property is regularly reviewed at one of the UK's largest property investment organisations.

How investing institutions think about investment

The pressures that affect the nature and composition of the investment portfolios of long term financial institutions vary over time. Different types of institution service, different forms of clients. Insurance and assurance companies have responsibilities to policy holders. Depending on whether they are public companies or mutual companies, they may also have responsibilities to shareholders.

Similarly, pension funds have responsibilities to provide for existing and prospective pension holders. In the implementation of their investment policy, they also have responsibilities to current employers and employees in terms of minimising the level of extra contributions required to meet promised pension commitments.

Given these constituencies, long term financial institutions should not be seen as entirely free agents in terms of the investments they can make. They are restricted in their ability to take risks. They must select assets which not only produce returns in a manner that broadly matches the incidence of the liabilities to which they are exposed, but there are also strict legislative controls in place to ensure they are secure from the risks of insolvency. It is imprudent and, in some instances, illegal for such institutions to expose themselves to undue risk.

In the case of life insurance companies, they clearly compete with each other for market share in the same way that companies do in any other industry. The performance of investments will influence both the scale of eventual policy or savings products' payouts and, in the case of non-mutualised funds, the level of dividends paid to shareholders. To perform poorly would risk losing customers to other companies and generating poor share performance. As such, investors are concerned with not only the absolute level of their investment portfolios but they are also interested in their relative performance. Customers require security. They would not thank their investment manager for performing spectacularly well in some years and spectacularly badly in others as it would make their own financial planning precarious.

There are, therefore, two major concerns that face long term financial institutions when building investment portfolios. Competitive levels of return to those available from other investment organisations must be provided. However, undue risk has to be avoided. Long term financial institutions are under a duty to respect these parameters.

In the equity markets, this can be taken to an extreme whereby the investor can offer its clients an index tracked fund where the constitution of the investment portfolio is identical to that of the index for that asset type. Because one ICI share is the same as any other ICI share, the performance of the fund can be guaranteed to mirror that of the underlying index (with some minor differences relating to fees and swapping around exposures to companies in a timely way so as to match changes in the index). However, in the absence of a truly securitised market in property, the portfolios of properties put together and the index are unlikely to behave identically. But still, as we shall see below, there are ways in which the property investor can control risk in a property portfolio.

How assets get priced

Increasing flows of information, improving technology and liberalisation in terms of the movement of capital across international boundaries all mean that financial institutions now have a very broad array of assets in which they can invest. A simple classification of investment types open to institutional investors in the UK would identify company shares, derivatives (options and futures), government and corporate bonds, and property. There is the opportunity to invest in any or all of these, across the world.

Each of these different forms of investment asset has a unique potential for income return or capital return, or both. Each has a unique profile of risk attached to it. In short, each can be characterised by a different 'risk-reward' profile. Investors will regularly review the risk-reward profile of this universe of assets and calibrate the price it is willing to pay for each different asset. This calibration will be done in a manner that reflects the risks perceived to pertain to each asset type.

Without seeking to enter a detailed debate about investment theory, this idea can be explored a little further by way of example. The Government in the UK periodically raises money by issuing bonds. Investors purchasing such bonds usually receive a steady income and a final lump sum payment. Returns on the bonds are guaranteed by the funds raised by the Government through taxation and other means. If the income from investing in bonds is fixed (i.e. they are the same each year), then unanticipated bouts of inflation will undermine the value of those assets. Because of this risk, a level of compensation gets built into the pricing of those bonds to cover for the chance that inflation might be higher than expected. Hence, ordinary 'gilts' are said to carry an inflation risk premium. However, if returns from such bonds have increases in their returns linked to inflation, then the investor has a doubly secure investment. In some ways, such an asset could almost be considered 'risk free'.

The concept of a risk free asset is an important foundation to how investors review how to set the prices for other, risk-bearing asset types. Clearly, on a like for like basis, an investor would pay more for an asset that is guaranteed against inflation than one that is not. This is because there is no risk that income and final payments will be eroded by unanticipated inflation. A rational investor would always demand a premium return/lower price for investing in an asset that has risks attached to it. This will come in the form of a higher rate of required return, which in turn will be achieved by reducing the price for the asset until it gives a sufficient return to compensate for the perceived risks of the subject asset.

Risk, in this context, can be viewed as the chance of receiving less reward from an investment than was anticipated from the asset.

The vast majority of investment opportunities exhibit risks of one form or another. Manifestly, returns from company shares depend significantly on how a company will perform. If economic conditions have been poor or the management of the company has taken bad decisions – or both – company dividend payouts and corresponding returns from such investments will be poor.

Investors therefore have to carry a view as to the price at which they will invest in a company that will generate them the level of return which they believe is commensurate with the risks attached to that company. If the price is higher than that which the investor has identified as giving 'fair value' (i.e. will deliver the required levels of return), then the investor is being inadequately rewarded for the risks being taken and the investment is dear and to be avoided. If the price is lower, then excess returns can be generated and the investment is cheap.

Explicitly or implicitly, investors considering investment in commercial property as a whole or individual properties in particular, should similarly derive a central view of the returns they require from making the investment. In the light of expected levels of income growth from the asset, it is possible to derive a 'fair price' at which a property might be invested in (or disinvested from). In doing this, the reward demanded for the perceived risks of an investment (otherwise called the 'risk premium') will be adjusted to take account of the many different forms of risk to which properties are exposed. As with company shares, economic conditions may prove worse than anticipated, making rental growth from properties less easy to achieve; tenants may even go bankrupt leaving a period of no income. More longstanding risks exist for commercial property. For example, new work practices or technological advances may render certain types of property obsolete.

Interestingly, the overall return of a portfolio of assets is equivalent to the weighted average of their individual returns. However, the riskiness of a portfolio of assets is not. Clearly the risks of individual assets do require consideration and this is usually reviewed by reference to how volatile, how unpredictable, how risky the returns from that asset have been and are likely to be in the future.

However, in a form of 'not placing all one's eggs in one basket', the volatility in overall portfolio returns can be reduced if assets that perform differently over time can be bunched together in a portfolio. Presuming equal weights of both in a two-asset portfolio, if returns to Asset A generally go up when returns to Asset B go down, then the combined portfolio will see stable returns year on year. Assets A and B are said to be negatively correlated. If they were perfectly positively correlated (i.e. their returns both went up and down together over time), then combining them would do nothing to reduce risk at the portfolio level.

Hence, one can take two unpredictable/risky individual assets and, by combining them in a portfolio, make the returns to the portfolio more predictable/less risky. By judicious selection of assets, risk can be reduced at the portfolio level. This is called 'diversifying' risk. In what follows, we will see if property has any of these benefits to offer to investors putting together multi-asset portfolios.

Hence, in summary, when considering investing in a given asset, a financial institution will want to consider what it will contribute not only by way of returns but also what it will do to the risk profile of the fund. When considering commercial property, investors will add a risk premium to the expected returns from risk free assets to establish a 'target' rate of return that will compensate them for the perceived risks of owning property. When combined with a view about how the income from the asset might grow, this helps to determine the price that the investor will pay for that asset.

The following section will examine the sorts of returns that property might be expected to return and how they compare with the returns expected from other asset classes. It will also review the extent to which property has (or more pertinently has not) delivered these required returns. Finally, it will review the sort of diversification benefits property can deliver to the multi-asset portfolio.

The case for property

As stated, the case for investing in any asset should be based on the effects that it has on both the return and the risk profile of a portfolio. What follows is a brief review of the troublesome (but improving) history of property returns. This is followed by a review of the contribution that property makes to risk reduction in the investment fund.

Property returns

As things stand currently (summer 2002) property has been the best performing investment asset over the last one, three and five years. However, this should not blind us in the property industry from remembering that the long run history of property returns has been unequivocally poor.

In order to have confidence in investing a proportion of the multi-asset portfolio in property in the future, investors need to understand what it was that went so badly wrong for property from the 1960s to the 90s and which caused it to generate such poor returns. Second, they would have to gain comfort that property has 'learnt its lessons' such that history is unlikely to repeat itself with respect to the property returns of the future.

With respect to the sorts of returns that property should deliver over the long term (meaning decades), PruPIM believes that property should deliver returns marginally lower than equities (or 'shares') but well in excess of Government bonds (or 'gilts').

This is because property, like equities, is a 'real asset', it houses economic activity and should see its performance dominated by the fundamentals of the real economy, mitigated to a certain extent by the availability of land to supply the needs of the economy. As such, property and equities are subject to the same economic vicissitudes and uncertainties.

However, UK property, with its currently dominant mode of long leases with upwards only rent reviews, provides investors with cash flows that are, for the periods between rent reviews, fixed in nominal terms – like gilts. Hence, property has both equity and bond-like characteristics and should be expected to exhibit long run returns between the higher returning, unpredictable/risky equities and the more stable, predictable/less risky gilts.

Depending on the time period chosen, the historical record broadly confirms these relative performance ratings. Table 1 shows data from the three decades between 1971 and 2001.

Table 1: Real returns for the main UK asset classes, 1971 – 2001 inclusive

UK asset class	Total return (net of inflation)
UK equities	c7%
UK gilts	c4%
UK property	c5%

Table 1 also shows that the absolute level of property returns has been substantially below those of equities over this very long period. On this basis, the multi-asset allocator is entitled to ask – given the labour intensity of investing in property and the illiquidity that surrounds property – why one should bother including property in the investment portfolio when one could invest in equities.

The required return an investor would set for property would be a very individualised number – there is no rule that says it must be a given level of return. At PruPIM, we believe that we should receive approximately 5.75 per cent returns after inflation has been accounted for. On this basis, property has failed to deliver its required returns over recent decades. And, in reviewing the numbers in Table 1, we must remember that the property returns number only looks that good because of the excellent performance of property in recent times. A similar analysis in the mid-1990s would have shown property having produced closer to 3.5 per cent real return – a suggestion of clear discrepancy between required and delivered returns.

Close examination of historic property returns does reveal that the property market has proven severely dysfunctional for much of the post-war period. However, on the presumption that yesterday's investors were not stupid and would not have invested in such a risk bearing asset as property for the sorts of returns delivered (at least up until the mid-1990s), something must have surprised and disappointed investors. Only by understanding what surprises ambushed investors in the past and by gaining some comfort that similar surprises are not waiting in store in the future, can the asset allocator allocate funds with a clear conscience to property for the long term.

We would identify at least four reasons why property-disappointed investors over the post-war period might have been surprised and disappointed by way of returns.

(a) **'Boom-bust' development cycles** have caused periodic collapses in rental levels for UK property. This was especially the case in the early 1970s and early 90s and affected the central London office market most of all. In terms of our earlier discussion about how investors price assets, these collapses in rents resulted in delivered income growth being far lower than had been assumed by purchasers in their original investment appraisals. As such, the level of returns delivered were far lower than those which any rational investor should have been demanding. Hence, this is one source of historic disappointment for investors in UK property.

(b) **A lax land use planning system** that did not adequately control the supply of new development was a significant contributor to the particularly savage development boom-bust that occurred at the beginning of the 1990s. In a period where political philosophy was very dominated by the notion that the market should decide, there was a general reduction in the involvement of the state in many aspects of life in the UK. The ability of planning to control and direct development was reduced through much of the 1980s and, as a result, there was no ready constraint to the flood of development proposals, in both retail and offices, which emerged at the end of the 1980s. The ready availability of finance for development, coupled with the ready availability of sites upon which to develop, facilitates a surfeit of development. This fuelled the sort of boom-bust described above, leaving investors with lower than their required returns from property investment.

(c) **The rate at which the utility of new buildings depreciates was inadequately factored into asset appraisals in the 1960s and 1970s.** Strange though it may seem, the first academic reviews of the appropriate amortised cost of building depreciation were seen in the mid- to late-1980s. Whether or not it was that, at this time, many of the buildings developed in the early and mid 1960s on 25-year leases were coming to the end of their lease terms and needed re-positioning in the marketplace, it does seem that the cost of building depreciation became a hot topic in the late 1980s. Clearly, if the cost of positioning and re-positioning buildings to attract tenants is underestimated then, a bit like overestimating rental growth, these unexpectedly high costs will lead to less than expected returns.

(d) The higher than anticipated inflation seen in the post-war period substantially eroded the real value of property income. As mentioned earlier, property income follows a stepped profile over the term of a property lease, with rents being set for pre-determined periods and then re-set at rent review (after five or more years). In those periods when the rent is fixed in nominal terms, an unexpectedly high inflation will erode the real value of rents and reduce the real returns to the asset. For much of the 1960s and 70s, inflation was extremely and unexpectedly high. This, coupled with the generally longer periods between rent reviews (14 years was common), decimated the real returns from property.

Looking forward, how comfortable can we feel that these factors will not re-appear to cause yet further negative surprises for investors. We will consider each in turn.

It would clearly be foolish to believe that the apparently universal phenomenon of property cycles might have been banished in the future. However, we at PruPIM believe that the information upon which decisions to develop and invest are made is much improved now, compared with times past. There are now ten times the number of researchers actively involved in the property market than there were ten years ago. We also believe that the evaluation techniques now available to property investors and lenders mean they have a far clearer view of prospective market performance than in the past. This should all lead to investor and developer behaviour that reduces the amplitude of property cycles. The discipline shown by the market in the late 1990s is, we believe, the first signs of this.

Turning to land-use planning, the currently existing cross-party support for a return to tighter, more 'sustainable' planning controls in the 1990s should further help constrain the worst excesses of property developers. The fact that banks also seem to be much more disciplined in their lending regimes also gives comfort in this respect.

With respect to depreciation, all professional investors now build in asset depreciation rates into their valuations, adjusting the price they are willing to pay for an asset to adequately account for depreciation and achieve the rates of return they require. The industry debate today is not so much about whether or not compensation is required for depreciation, rather it is about the appropriate rate for different types of asset in different locations. That this oversight has now been rectified means there is far less scope for investors to make mistakes in this regard than they appear to have done in the past.

Finally, inflation control is clearly at the very heart of Government policy, not just in the UK but around the world. With this cross-party support for the control of inflation, it seems unlikely that 'runaway inflation' will return to harm the real value of property income in the future in the way that it did in the 1960s and 70s. We should also note that the emerging new forms of flexible lease mean that the impact of excess inflation is lessened since rents will get 'marked to market' more regularly in the future and would, therefore, more quickly absorb the impact of higher than expected inflation.

So, given the above, property should be better able to deliver in the region of 5.75 per cent going forward. This should still be beaten by equities and, therefore, there is still some reasoning to be examined as to why a rational investor would bother to invest in property when s/he could obtain higher returns (and greater liquidity) by investing in equities. The answer, of course, has to lie in what property offers by way of risk reduction in the multi-asset portfolio.

Property and portfolio diversification

As can be seen from Table 2, the returns from direct property show low positive correlations with those from equities and gilts. Importantly, they also show a lower level of correlation than exists between equities and gilts. This means that property returns, at least as measured on a year-by-year basis, are delivered relatively independently from those from the other main UK asset classes.

Following on from what was said above, this means that property investments help to damp down the year-on-year variability in the returns to the overall investment fund. In short, property appears to be particularly helpful in reducing risk in the multi-asset portfolio.

Table 2: Asset to asset performance correlations – 25 years to 1999

Asset class	UK equities	Overseas equities	UK gilts	Direct property	Property shares
UK equities	**1.00**	0.42	0.62	0.29	0.70
Overseas equities		**1.00**	0.12	-0.07	0.00
UK gilts			**1.00**	0.22	0.53
Direct property				**1.00**	0.60*
Property shares					**1.00**

*28 year figure is 0.45

This 'diversification' benefit probably occurs because changes in the real economy take time to manifest themselves in property returns. For example, increased demands for space from a growing economy take time to manifest themselves in rental growth. Firms 'make do' with increasing their utilisation of current space until the pressures become such that additional premises are required. As these aggregate, economy-wide, pressures for space mount, the needed new space then takes time to deliver. Similarly, in a downturn, staff are made redundant but lease commitments remain in place. These and other factors illustrate that property cycles and returns are less immediately linked to the economic cycles that might drive equity and gilt markets more contemporaneously.

It should also be noted from Table 2 that property shares have a very high positive correlation with equities in general. This means that investing in property shares does much less to diversify returns in the multi-asset portfolio than investment in direct property.

Conclusion

Property does not have an automatic right to a place in a multi-asset investment portfolio. It has to earn that place. It does so by virtue of its potential to deliver near equity returns and to make a noticeable contribution to risk diversification. No better example of both these traits is the performance of property in the latter part of the 1990s and into the new millennium. Property has been the best performing asset over the five years from 1997 to 2001. When equity values plummeted in 2000 and 2001, it was those investors who had a noticeable allocation to property that had a safety net in place for overall portfolio returns.

Historically, the repeated occurrence of boom-bust development cycles, the existence of a relatively lax land use planning system, the failure to properly understand the rate and magnitude at which property assets depreciate over time, and the incidence of savage bouts of unexpectedly high inflation, have all harmed property performance. PruPIM believes that, because of developments in the market, in the information that it now has at its disposal and the increased sophistication that now exists amongst property investment practitioners, these factors will be much less likely to lead to disappointment amongst investors with respect to property returns.

There is currently no real significant alternative to direct property for investors attempting to capture property market-type returns. Property shares are not an appropriate substitute, traded as they are as part of most investors' equity portfolios. However, the industry presses on to try and establish tax-transparent securitised property markets and, increasingly interestingly, index-based property derivative instruments.

Author profiles

Martin Moore, Managing Director
Prudential Property Investment Managers Ltd (PruPIM)

Martin Moore was appointed Managing Director of PruPIM in 1996, having previously held the position of Investment Director from 1990.

In April, Martin was appointed a Crown Estate Commissioner. He is the immediate past chairman of the Investment Property Forum and Westminster Property Owners Association and has worked on various property related panels for both the Association of British Insurers and the Royal Institution of Chartered Surveyors. He is a member of both the General Council and Policy Committee of the British Property Federation. At the beginning of 2001 he was also invited to join the design review committee of CABE.

Prudential Property Investment Managers Limited is part of M&G, the investment management arm of Prudential plc. It is one of the most active organisations in the UK property market, managing around £12bn invested in a number of different portfolios ranging in size from under £50m to over £8bn.

The London based team comprise around 300 people, many of whom are Chartered Surveyors specialising in the fields of management, development, leasing, investment and valuation.

Paul McNamara, Director, Head of Property Research
Prudential Property Investment Managers Limited (PruPIM)

Paul McNamara joined PruPIM in 1987. As head of the Property Research Team, he is responsible for the overall direction, progress and quality of property research within Prudential Property Investment Managers Ltd. Paul is also a Director and a member of the Executive Management Team of PruPIM

Paul has a first class honours degree in Geography from the University of St Andrews and a PhD in Geography from the University of Edinburgh. In 1992, he became an Associate of the Institute of Investment Management and Research.

Paul is a member of the Property Advisory Group advising the Office of the Deputy Prime Minister on property market related issues. He is the Chairman of the Property Finance and Economics Research Network, Chairman of the IPF Education Strategy Group, a member of the Management Board of the Investment Property Forum and the Honorary President and a past Chairman of the Society of Property Researchers.

3 The developer

Julian Barwick, Development Securities Plc
Alistair Elliott, Knight Frank

Introduction: what makes you get out of bed in the morning?

About ten years ago I, (Julian Barwick), accompanied Paul Stickney of Lesley Jones Architects on a day's tour of retail warehouse parks. Paul has a lively and engaging intellect – an excellent antidote to the dreary topic of our tour and I suggested to him at lunch what a good developer he would have been had he chosen a different career. 'You couldn't be more wrong,' he said, 'I haven't the right attitude.' 'What do you mean?' I replied. 'As a professionally trained architect,' he said, 'if someone comes to me with a problem, I try to solve it for them the best I can. If you, however, as a developer are similarly presented with someone's problem you have a different instinct; you see how you can turn the situation to your advantage.'

In these days of customer focus, I am only too aware how politically incorrect it is to dwell on what it is that makes us suppliers tick – for, in the end, that is all any of us are, even the mighty Prudential. And, of course, there is no doubt that occupier needs in the long run are paramount. But a brief insight into the motivation of the development team members should help to bring alive the process of design and construction of the commercial office building, and explain why so many of us who are engaged in this endeavour, do it again and again and again.

This chapter follows the structure of the development process – a fluid and non-sequential course of events. There is a developer's first evaluation of an opportunity, or an idea which becomes a proposal. But at the same time the developer must be considering financing such a proposal and the kind of team that may be needed. He or she must then secure the finance, put the team together and consider the economic context within which commercial office buildings are procured, often all concurrently and certainly in no set order. These elements are covered in the first half of the chapter. Then, in more detail, it considers the specifics of the occupier and the product itself.

Risk and reward: where does the money come from?

So let us (as developers like to do) leap to a few assumptions: we have found the land, and it is in a part of the country where demand is strong; the planning is straightforward, access is good and the site is easy to develop. We have had a session with the design team and we know what we want to build.

But where do we go to get the money?

Perhaps the most obvious solution is by borrowing some or all of the money needed to develop from the bank. However, bank loans for development are not easy to come by, particularly where a development is speculative and the market uncertain. What is the bank's security? If it is possible to persuade the bank to advance a loan, the return to the developer apparently increases.

Table 1: A successful project

	Without the loan	With the loan
Total cost	100	100
Loan		– 70
Developer's equity outlaid	100	30
Sale proceeds	120	120
Loan repayment		– 70
	120	50
Surplus at completion	20	20
Return on equity	20%	67%

However, the developer is now much more exposed to risk than previously, because whether the development is successful or not he will still have to pay the bank the same amount – and this indeed was the root cause of the property crash in the 1990s.

Table 2: A failure

	Without the loan	With the loan
Total cost	100	100
Loan		– 70
Developer's equity outlaid	100	30
Sale proceeds	90	90
Loan repayment		– 70
	90	20
Surplus at completion	(10)	(10)
Return on equity outlaid	(10%)	(33%)

So, whilst this can be an acceptable method of generating cash flow to finance a development, it does not really affect the overall level of returns required from the development. The more you borrow, the bigger the return required on your equity.

The second way to obtain the funding is through procuring an investor to put up the money. Every investor has a choice: a choice of sector and, if he or she should choose property, a choice of developers and properties. The process starts with deciding whether or not to leave their money in, say, a building society (where it should be safe as houses). For the professional investor, this risk free option is usually represented by an investment in government stock (or gilts). Beyond that, the professional investor focusing on the UK has a range of choices, of which the most important ones are equities (say the FTSE 500) and then commercial property (shops, industrial and offices).

Both equity and property are more risky than gilts, and consequently demand a higher return. So after the building society, the next safest option is gilts, but if you really want to make money, you will need to take risk. How much is up to you, and depends upon the amount of money you want to make. Different shares have different risk and consequently the extra return (the risk premium) is very variable. But for low risk, conventional property investment, the risk premium would appear to be about 500 basis points (or five per cent to you and me).

Table 3: Typical expected returns in 2001

	Building society	Gilts (10 year bond)	Equities (FTSE 500)	Commercial property
Income	4%	5%	3%	7%
Capital	0%	0%	6%	3%
Total	4%	5%	9%	10%

For property development, there are additional and different risks, over and above normal investment risks, which increase the return required by investors to a range of 15-20 per cent pa. (depending on the risk involved). If the development is speculative, for example, the return will need to be greater than 20 per cent. If the development is entirely pre-let, the required return will be considerably less.

To see how the risks and rewards are calculated, it is best to take some semi-theoretical figures of the costs and value of the building.

Costs

1	**Land**	1600
	inclusive of agents and legal fees	
2	**Design**	350
	at 12% of construction	
3	**Construction**	3000
	30,000 sq ft gross at 100 per sq ft	
4	**Leasing**	100
	at 20% rent	
5	**Interest**	390
	as calculated on a cash flow	
6	**Void**	510
	at 1 year's rent	
	TOTAL COST	**5950**

Value

7	25,500 sq ft net (85% net to gross) at £20 per sq ft	510 pa
8	Investment yield	7%
	therefore multiplier	14
	TOTAL VALUE	**7140**

Surplus

9	Value less cost	1190
	Surplus as % cost	20%

First of all, it is no coincidence that the surplus is 20 per cent exactly: the numbers are worked backwards. This has not been done to aid the readers of this *Handbook*, this is what actually happens in practice. The developer will decide what profit margin he requires first, and then work with the rest of the variables to see if he can mould together a set of numbers that makes sense of the land price and the construction cost, when compared with the likely value of the completed product.

So which of these numbers really matter? Well, they all do of course, but which are the most important variables and which have the most profound affect on the developer's bottom line?

Most important
- The investment yield.
- The rental rate per square foot.
- The net to gross ratio.
- The void cost.

Important
- Construction cost.
- Interest.

Least important
- Design fees.
- Leasing fees.

Hunting in packs: leadership and teamwork

At the same time as securing the funding, putting together the right development team is crucial. This team represents the pooling of a range of different, and often highly specialised talents, all for the purpose of creation: the creation of buildings, assets and work places. Some of the team's talents are better suited to one aim or the other: an architect has qualified longer than a surgeon to operate on buildings – an education that has perhaps paralysed the architect by information overload. However, each member of the development team can derive satisfaction from the same or different aspects of the myriad of processes that go into the development of corporate offices. Indeed, the size, style, quality and construction of a development will demand a unique balance within a team. Fundamentally, the process of development is highly satisfying, because it is a tangible business: the fruits of labour are left imprinted on the landscape, and indeed the creation of that building is in turn the motor for a far greater contribution to the economy throughout its lifetime – a fact that does not escape the notice of the infamous egos of the development team. The common threads of creativity, profitability and, to a large extent, the sociability and variety of the industry drive all members of the team to a greater or lesser extent. So how does this team, all aiming for the same point, yet each approaching from different directions, pull together to achieve their aim?

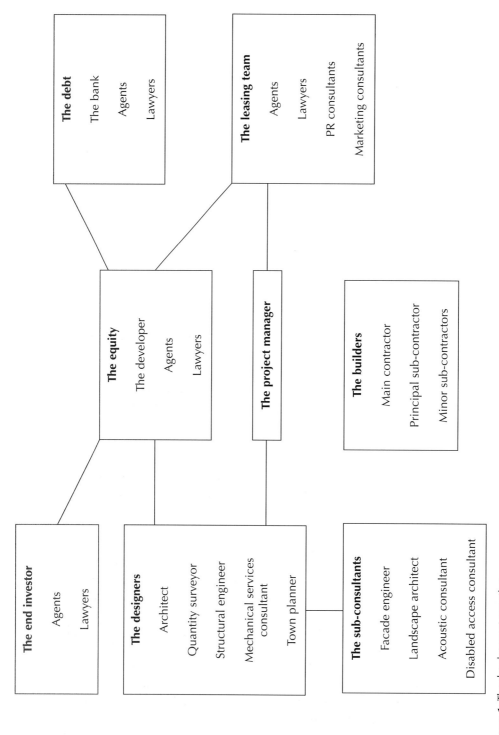

Figure 1: The development equation

Teamwork

The development team is essentially divided into interrelated areas of expertise; finance, development management and marketing/leasing (*see* Figure 1). Most members of the development team are keen to demonstrate their experience of all aspects, in a bid to emphasise their own indispensability and high value – and the lower value of everyone else's contribution. In overall control, the developer reins in this ambition and ensures each member excels without extending their remit to the disadvantage of the project, or indeed himself.

In many respects, the developer is most at risk from the avarice of his colleagues, as each attempts to multiply their share of the dividends, and therefore reducing the developer's final 'pot'. Indeed, complication of the brief becomes an intellectual game as the addition of layers and layers of contractors and consultants obscures who holds actual responsibility from the developer.

The key to management, therefore, lies in the division of risk amongst the team. In practice, this means that the developer must commit to a minimum number of promises he cannot fulfil; the quantity surveyor must be able to calculate accurately the ability of the developer to fulfil the promises he has committed to; the surveyor must actually be able to convert the pipe dream of the architect into a realistic proposition with market credibility; and the 'other contractors' must be held accountable for the multiple sub-contractors.

This principle becomes even more critical when the developer acts as a long-term landlord. His involvement with the occupier will consequently be more prolonged and hence, much closer – their endeavours to please the end user do not end at the time of moving in. However, this is a key opportunity to continue to add value and ensure that the working environment continues to be better than the competition, and the tenant can continue to retain optimum productivity. Occupiers' requirements and expectations are increasingly high – not for opulence but for flexibility, efficiency and functionality.

The niche of the agent

Every member of the team must have a persuasive sales message. From the developer with his initial proposal to the architect selling his design above his competitors. However, if there is one member of the team who wholeheartedly thrives on the marketing side of the marketing/leasing split, it is the agent. Paid for securing the opportunity, not for creating a profit, the agent is not really concerned by the minutiae of the building. Although infected by his team-mates' compulsion to interfere in everyone else's business, in reality he would rather be given a product and tout it on the market. The agent tires of the artistic warblings of the architect or the delusions of the developer about ensuring each project is the one he shall be remembered by, because soon he shall have moved on to another deal. The sooner he moves onto the next product, the greater the recompense. The ability of the agent to do this, however, depends on a favourable market context or his ability to operate successfully, even when market conditions are more testing. It is important to remember the agent may be advising the occupier, fund or developer, and on occasions more than one of these! Nevertheless, the agent that shines will be as good in a poor market: he adds real value when translating market experiences from a range of deals and developments into the team such that the product benefits.

Market context: statistics v gut instinct

In addition to the financing deal they have secured, and the team they have assembled, a third major influence on the financial viability of a project is the market context in which they are operating. In the property market, the highs are legendary and the lows devastating. When the market is booming, no one can put a foot wrong – even inexperienced amateurs can wow their cronies with glorious success. When the market is in recession, it hits *everyone*. The ability to divine those property professionals who genuinely add value to a project is only really possible in the intervening periods, when the market is reasonably stable. It is then that an exceptional development team will not simply spot an opportunity, but maximise the potential of that opportunity, through research, collaboration and innovation.

The market, however, is not a static concept and there have been significant changes over the past ten years. The development industry has learnt several important lessons from the era of boom and bust, the most important of which is to approach development with as much flexibility as possible. It has also appreciated the importance of creating structures which win the hearts and minds of those both in and outside the industry.

Today there is a greater understanding of the business from those inside it. This enables developers to understand better exactly what it is that occupiers want, and to predict more accurately trends further in advance. This more dynamic market environment is also the result of stronger relationships between members of the development team, due at least in part to the greater risks and rewards increasingly on offer. The stakes are greater, but this makes for a stronger team more committed to each product and more determined to get it right.

In line with this increased market complexity, property development relies increasingly heavily on research as well as intuition and experience. The building must be suited to the land, to the demand and to the occupier, and the team must be the right one to develop the building. A combination of vision, market knowledge, an awareness of one's contemporaries and, above all, an understanding of what the occupier wants, are the qualities that divide the exceptional from the ordinary.

The planning process

However well the team works together and however accurately the market is read, it is the planning process that is such a crucial element in determining the success or failure of a scheme. Often highly politicised, bureaucratic, costly and risky, the planning process can be a battle of dogma and ideology, fought through council meetings, residents' associations, the press and even central government.

Perhaps, for obvious reasons, the key issues relating to the planning process is what a building does, what it looks like and, increasingly, the demands it will place on the local infrastructure. Is it too tall? Is it too ugly? Does it fit into its context? Beauty may be in the eye of the beholder, but planning authorities are the arbiters of taste in this case. Indeed this may be no bad thing. As guardians of our nation's fabric, it is the planning authority's role to protect us from what can often be better described as scars than works of art.

There are a range of pushes and pulls. Perhaps a generalisation, but occupiers want car parking, planners do not. Buildings and office parks need critical mass, which often does not conform to the relevant local plan. Pressures on local infrastructure may dictate external funding, which the development equation will not allow. Requirements for impact and observations on design may not fit with the need for efficient, flexible and functional buildings. The planning process uses a range of issues, and highlights the differing agendas, but each ego must ultimately feel recompensed and vindicated.

The occupier rules

It is a great, and invaluable skill to be able to read the market trends and optimise opportunities: to look at demand both currently and in the future; to predict geographical trends; to spot the downturns and upturns in property value; and to link these to political developments concerning, transport, planning, landlord and tenant matters, land use legislation and the like. Not to mention economic circumstances and global events, the background to which has now changed attitudes forever. Ultimately if you do not let the building, there is no deal, and indeed no point! All these factors can be condensed into one key concept: the needs of the occupier are paramount. Creating a building which is attractive to the occupier must constantly be the primary concern of the team, no matter how much they think they know better (and they usually do). Although not physically a part of the team in the speculative development process, the occupier must exist permanently in the minds of each team member. The size of buildings, the location, the amenities, transport, flexibility of tenure, mix of uses, specification and the mechanical and electrical installation, are the overriding concerns of any occupier, and therefore transfer to the overriding concerns of the developer, agent, architect and all members of the development team. Whilst we cannot predict the market with absolute certainty, what is possible is to ensure that developments are sustainable and resilient to market fluctuations – in short, offices where people want to work and can do so efficiently.

There are a range of other unavoidable issues which must be embraced by the team, and which retain significant importance in the occupier's mind. Not only is it the flexibility of initial occupation which concerns the occupier, but also flexibility in the event that a disposal is necessary. 'Exit strategies' must be considered and viable by way of lease assignment, sub-letting of floors and part-floors.

Cost in use is an unavoidable concern, not just rent but the rates payable, plus the level of service charge and, if appropriate, other payments for the estate management. What is the level of cost, what does it cover, and is it good value? Business is competitive, margins are permanently under review and benchmarking is now commonplace.

Whilst not influenced directly by the development team, there are other factors which must be clarified and presented as part of the package, including demographics, amenities, retailing, business infrastructure, communications (transport and telecoms) and general utilities.

Therefore, no matter how hard the financier tries to place himself on a pedestal away from the perceived grubbiness of the various development processes, and no matter how hard the architect tries to immerse himself in the creativity of development, away from the street fighting of the market place, the team must, in fact, gel as a holistic unit in order to be able to convert their individual skills and expertise into a rounded development that satisfies the needs of the occupier.

The product: bricks not clicks

This chapter illustrates that each member of the development team, no matter what their motivation for working in the property industry, is intrinsically linked to the product: a building. The range of products on offer to the tenant extends from single workstations in business centres to large freehold HQ offices. In the spectrum are flexible multi-let buildings or those on standard full repairing and insuring terms on a 25-year basis and subject to five yearly upwards only rent reviews. There is a growing acceptance that a building cannot be built and let by one person, and with such large sums of money to be made and lost, it is essential that behind the usual turf warfare, each team member has the respect of the others.

The final product of this complicated team interaction is a landmark that will remain in place for many years, and in many cases can define the local environment. In many cases this is a supreme achievement and, whether the result is admired or scorned, it is a tangible testament to the work put in. However, a building should not be judged simply as an object of art: the actual form of the building must be considered in many contexts: how it looks, how it works, and what it costs.

The appearance of the building informs, and is informed by, how the building works. Perhaps surprisingly, the decisions about how the building works can inform a great deal of the other development decisions. Safety has, unsurprisingly following recent terrorist activity, become a key concern of occupiers – how can the workforce get out of the building, and how can the fire risk be minimised? The quality of the goods access might not win a building any awards, but it may win it tenants. The same applies with ease of cleaning, environmental credentials, M&E, air conditioning, and so on. However, much more than this, it is the developer's responsibility to look at how the building contributes to its surrounding area, both in an aesthetic way and in the opportunities it creates – both through its usage and through the atmosphere it creates. Mixed-use developments have seen a recent boom in their popularity for these very reasons – they help to remove the need for such extensive travel to and from work and make steps towards the creation of a rounded community.

Finally, what the whole development process boils down to is the cost of the product: to build, to buy, to let, to run and to sell. Is the initial investment in the building going to be substantial in order that the running costs are low and/or environmentally friendly? How long is the building designed to last for? How much rent is needed to make the project viable, and is this a realistic expectation? And are the staff housed in the building optimising their economic potential?

So why?

It is easy to ask question after question and come up with few answers, but in essence that is the joy of the development process. There is no rulebook: for each project the area is different, the requirements are different, the market is different, and most importantly of all, the team will be different. So what does make us get out of bed in the morning? It is the challenge of turning the situation to our own advantage; it is the servicing of the needs of unique occupiers; it is the creativity of the industry; and it is the constant job of selling. But incorporating all of these elements is the notion that each day we have the chance to be a pioneer, and fulfilling that role is a lifelong challenge.

Author profiles

Alistair Elliott BSc MRICS, Proprietary Partner Business Space
Knight Frank

Alistair Elliott has been actively involved in the office agency arena for 19 years. His experience spans a range of projects large and small ranging from Cardiff to Canary Wharf. Whilst there has been an emphasis towards advising landlords, he has been involved in a variety of occupier work particularly for Reckitt Benckiser Plc, Pharmacia & Upjohn, CSC Computer Sciences, Readers Digest, Xerox and others. A past chairman of the Office Agents Society, Alistair's interests within the profession extend to 'green buildings', office design and specification.

Major clients include: Reckitt Benckiser Plc, Hermes, PruPIM, Aberdeen Property Investment Managers, Brixton Plc, Slough Estates Plc, AXA Sun Life Properties, Argent Plc, CSC Computer Sciences Ltd, and Akeler.

Julian Barwick, Joint Managing Director
Development Securities Plc

Julian Barwick spent two years in private practice with Daniel Smith before joining MEPC in 1978. He left in 1998 to join the Board of Development Securities Plc, where he was appointed Joint Managing Director in 2000. He also sits on the Board of the British Council of Offices, is Chairman of the Paddington Regeneration Partnership and property advisor to the Bedford Estates.

As well as the enviable reputation Development Securities Plc has – quite justifiably – earnt following the success of the award winning 2 million sq ft Paddington Central scheme, Julian is also proud of the company's Business Parks programme in London and the south, where they have buildings currently under construction at Cambourne (Cambridgeshire, and another prize winner) and the Royal Docks, London.

In 2002, Development Securities is probably the most highly regarded developer of offices and business parks in the United Kingdom.

4 The cost management process – designing and procuring for value

Paul Morrell
Davis Langdon & Everest

'Price is what you pay. Value is what you get'.
Warren Buffett, Investment Guru and billionaire.

Introduction

Quantity surveyors should enjoy commercial office developments above all others. Their business is numbers, and few construction endeavours are so singularly focused on getting the numbers right as commercial offices: net area, rent and investment yield for gross value; gross area, design fees, land and construction costs and interest rates for gross cost; and the difference between those two, the developer's margin for profit and risk, is the whole purpose of the exercise. There is no point in saying to a commercial developer on completion 'shame about the cost escalation, but at least it's a good building'. Developers should, of course, be concerned about building good buildings, even beautiful buildings, but this is a means to an end. The end is the securing of funds, tenants and a purchaser; and, in the longer term, creating value in their own brand so they can repeat the exercise.

This is not a new phenomenon. Writing 80 years ago, American Cass Gilbert, the architect of the Woolworth Tower, described offices as 'a machine that makes the land pay',[1] and more recently SOM's Gordon Bunshaft echoed this in saying, 'I am not sure that office buildings are even architecture. They are really a mathematical calculation, just three-dimensional investments'.[2] The first quotation perhaps comes from an age when architecture was more comfortably settled amongst the beaux arts, and it certainly pays inadequate respect to what architecture is and does now; but it remains a fact that office buildings are as much a built equation as 'frozen music' – and if the numbers of the equation and the notes of the music are in discord, then the tune will justifiably be called by he who pays the piper.

It follows that the success of commercial office development depends absolutely upon effective cost management, and this chapter of the handbook looks at the elements of an effective service designed to deliver this. This is addressed from the point of view

---

1 Quoted by Carol Willis in *Form Follows Finance,* Princeton Architectural Press, Princeton (1999).
2 Ibid.

not of the quantity surveyor, but of the rest of the team, showing what they should expect to contribute and to receive as part of the process. And their contribution is key, for if there is just one message that should be taken away from this chapter, it is that cost control is the function of the whole project team. Short of physical violence (which only a very small minority of clients regard as an appropriate part of the process), the quantity surveyor has no means of preventing designers from putting pen to paper in a way that will violate the budget. The quantity surveyor's job is therefore the constant provision of information and ideas – about the estimated cost of design proposals as they are developed, and about the alternative cost of different ways of achieving the same objective.

Before any of this can begin, however, there needs to be created an environment within which a successful outcome can first be defined and then be achieved. In this, the client has a critical role to play, and for any project the necessary pre-conditions to such success are:

- a clear set of realistic objectives, suited to the purposes of the client;
- the assembly of a team of people with the experience, skills and instincts necessary to meet those objectives;
- the establishment of an effective management and procurement regime, with clear lines of authority, responsibility and communication between all of those involved.

All of these words are heavily loaded, and each is worthy of an essay in its own right. If things are going to run right on a project, then they have to start right; and if they do not, then they can only be put right thereafter by superhuman effort or supernatural luck. As both are in short supply, clients owe it to themselves not to be in too much of a hurry at the commencement of a project, and to get these three fundamentals right. To them, and embracing all three, there can be added a fourth – which is the stimulation of an appropriate project culture. The essentials of this are realism rather than unfeasible expectation; teamwork rather than egocentricity; mutual accountability rather than a cycle of default and blame; co-operation rather than confrontation; and, throughout, a concentration on the positive and on the celebration of success. This in turn calls for leadership – and ideally strong client leadership (as many of the worst examples of cost escalation have occurred on projects where the client is hardly identifiable, let alone inspirational).

Of course, there is a 'chicken and egg' problem here, because the process by which some of the key decisions are made needs to be reiterative. For example, the team that is assembled for a project needs to comprise the people most suited to the specific objectives of that project. However, defining realistic objectives (what should be built, how long it should take, and how much it should cost) are themselves matters for advice, and the team therefore needs to be in place before the objectives can be fully defined. Herein lies the competitive advantage of experience, and those who lack it (whose own competitive advantage is a fresh point of view and a sense of optimism unclouded by experience) would be well advised to buy some in.

The definition of objectives will, of course, vary substantially from client to client, and project to project. Nonetheless, all clients will have value for money as a key objective. The difficulty is that this term has become de-valued as a cliché, whilst rarely being so well defined as to be a hard measure of performance. This in turn rests on the difficulty of having a fixed definition for such a variable measure, as this too will vary from client to client, and project to project. There are plenty of generalised definitions of value for money but a version that will do as well as any is: 'the optimum combination of whole life costs and quality, in order to meet the users' requirements.'

The problem is that this begs many questions: How is an 'optimum combination' recognised, and how are the benefits to be measured? Which users? And so forth. These questions therefore relate to terminology, to methods of measurement, and to the identity of the decision makers; and all of this needs to be worked out for each project. Without it, there is no clear objective and it will consequently be a matter of random chance as to whether or not it is achieved – and yet little time is spent on this vital issue, as people are keen to get on with the less abstract (and therefore more tractable) matters of the shape of the building, the number of floors and so on.

For all clients, there is also the potential for a problem (if not a crisis) of identity, in the split personality of the paymaster (who has the control of budgets as a priority) and the users (who obviously want the best building that they can get). This schizophrenia can then be either mediated or further complicated by the addition of a facilities management resource. In commercial property development, there is then still another complication added to this in the frequent separation of design, development, occupation and ownership. Typically, because it is an investment medium, a commercial office building is owned by an individual or institution whose primary interest is in the income that it can produce. That income is provided by the payment of rent by a tenant, and the tenant normally occupies by virtue of a lease which makes him responsible for paying virtually all of the costs of maintaining and operating the building. Furthermore, property investors frequently do not have the resources or the inclination to develop the buildings in which they invest, and there consequently enters a third party, the developer, who recognises opportunity, puts together the deal, and assembles and manages the team of people necessary to design and construct the building.

Each of these three parties therefore has a different interest in the building, and that interest operates over a different time horizon.

- The occupier regards the building as a means of production, and his interest is in being able to operate efficiently within his chosen business. His maximum interest will be for the length of lease (typically 25 years), but the reality is that few businesses can think more than five years ahead – and precious few can see that far.

- The owner's interest should extend over the whole life of the building – which in theory might be 50 or 60 years, but which in practice (and even if he does not trade the building in the interim) is frequently no more than 25 years, as the rate at which office buildings become obsolescent is no longer than the term of a typical occupational lease. He will have some interest in the durability of the building, on the grounds that there may not be a need to redevelop after 25 years, and because a tenant's default might mean that he has to re-let the building at some time during its life. Apart from that, however, and the need to maintain a reputation as a good landlord, he will have no detailed interest in the cost of maintaining and operating the building.

- Put simply, the developer's interest really runs for no longer than the time it takes to identify and fulfil the opportunity, whereupon his stake (if any) will be sold to the long-term owner. Again with the exception of those developers who have a sophisticated view of the potential value of their own brand, his interest in the cost of maintaining and operating the building, or in its real suitability for the business purposes of the tenant, would extend no further than the point at which he is confident that he can dispose of his stake.

Just how wide the implications of these differences of time horizon can be is illustrated by Figures 1 and 2.

Figure 1 shows the cost of developing, owning and operating a typical office building over the 25 years of an occupational lease, all reduced to present value at a discount rate of 6 per cent. It shows that, excluding land (a major variable, of course), 52 per cent of the total goes on creating the investment (the completed building, furnished),

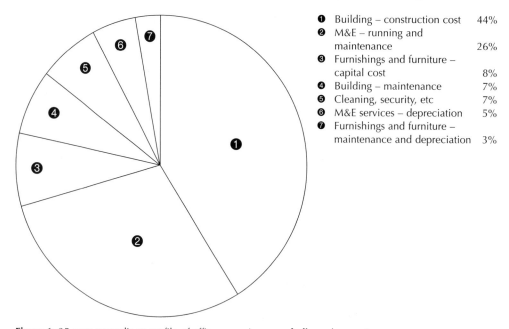

❶	Building – construction cost	44%
❷	M&E – running and maintenance	26%
❸	Furnishings and furniture – capital cost	8%
❹	Building – maintenance	7%
❺	Cleaning, security, etc	7%
❻	M&E services – depreciation	5%
❼	Furnishings and furniture – maintenance and depreciation	3%

Figure 1: 25-year expenditure profile of office occupiers – **excluding** salary costs

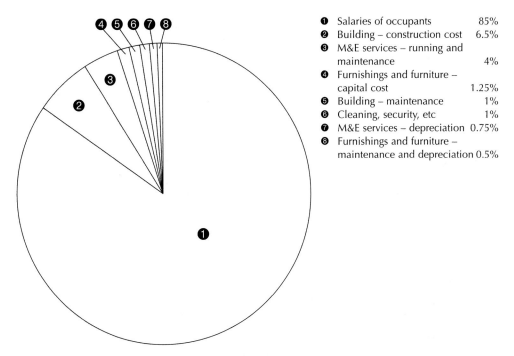

❶	Salaries of occupants	85%
❷	Building – construction cost	6.5%
❸	M&E services – running and maintenance	4%
❹	Furnishings and furniture – capital cost	1.25%
❺	Building – maintenance	1%
❻	Cleaning, security, etc	1%
❼	M&E services – depreciation	0.75%
❽	Furnishings and furniture – maintenance and depreciation	0.5%

Figure 2: 25-year expenditure profile of office occupiers – **including** salary costs

and the balance of 48 per cent goes on owning and operating the facility. This excludes the costs of the salaries of those who work in the building.

Figure 2 then repeats the calculation, but includes in the equation the present value of salaries that the occupier will pay to his staff. The effect is dramatic. Just 7.75 per cent of the total cost now goes on creating the investment, 7.25 per cent goes on maintaining and operating the facility, and 85 per cent goes on salary costs.

These figures, although rounded, are based on the analysis of a real building, and, whilst the figures will vary depending upon the specification of the building, and its location, occupational density, etc the general lesson of the proportions will remain the same. For most service businesses, the high proportion of the total business costs that go to salaries is fairly typical – and it is clearly the most important budget head. It follows that a very small movement in the productivity of their people, or in the quality of the work that they produce, would be far more significant than a major movement in the cost of the building. In simple terms, a 7.5 per cent improvement in output would justify spending virtually twice as much on the building.

Unfortunately, evidence about the effect of office design on output is largely unscientific, and is beset by too many external factors to say that any change for the better is the result of the quality of space alone (as management style, corporate culture, new technology, market conditions and many other things will have an equal or greater effect). Nevertheless, few business leaders or managers would regard the effect of space upon the spirit and productivity of their people as negligible – and practically nobody who has moved from an old building to a new one would. The dramatic difference between salaries and property as a proportion of building costs also demonstrates that the arguments do not need to be very powerful to be compelling. The leverage between capital cost and occupational cost is so high that a substantial increase in the former is repaid by only a marginal improvement in the latter – and the client can therefore reasonably ask whether it is feasible that the improvement in performance can be expected to be so small that the initial capital investment is unjustified.

Amongst the factors most likely to affect productivity in office work are:

- the workstation itself – individual space allowances, the furniture system, technological support, relationship between workstations and so forth;
- air quality – fresh air, thermal comfort and the ability to exercise some individual control over both;
- the quality of natural and artificial light, including the control of glare;
- noise and acoustic conditions generally;
- the general organisation of space within and between departments;
- he location and type of support facilities;
- the general creation of a positive mood through the creation of an environment that 'lifts the spirits'.

In addition, in an example of where so-called 'hard' and 'soft' issues might touch, case studies published by the Rocky Mountain Institute[3] have shown a connection (albeit an inadvertent one) between staff productivity and drives to increase the energy efficiency of buildings. Part of this may be because of a sympathetic response to a business that is addressing an issue of popular concern. More of it, however, is probably the consequence of such programmes also paying attention to the more fundamental factors outlined above – particularly the quality of air and light.

And yet, however dramatic the figures are, the truth is that they do little to influence office design, and the way that office buildings are created. This can be attributed in part to the disconnection between commissioning and occupying a building referred to above, with the consequent difference of interests – but it is also possible to exaggerate the extent to which this causes a real problem in the quality or suitability of office premises.

This exaggeration usually starts by casting the developer as the villain (interested only in the short term, and in cutting cost in order to maximise development profit), and the occupier as the injured party (invariably an enlightened employer, with a long-term interest in office space as a staff amenity, and as an aid to creative thought and operational efficiency). In reality, though, no suppliers operating in a competitive

---

3 *Greening the Building and the Bottom Line*, Rocky Mountain Institute, Colorado (1994) available at www.rmi.org.

market can afford to omit from their offer features that are valued by their customers. The problem is that the features which one might expect to be valued (character, environmental responsibility, genuine flexibility and so forth) are only rarely so valued that occupiers will demand them in preference to a benchmark building delivered for a benchmark rent. Too often, enlightened developers seek to provide something above the lowest common denominator, only to see it rejected – either by virtue of a lack of tenant interest in the building, or in the tenant reversing the enlightened choice (of which the arch example is probably an insistence upon adding full air-conditioning to buildings that have been designed to work perfectly well with natural ventilation or in mixed mode).

This too, however, can be seen as a supply side problem. One instinctively knows that the quality of office space must be a significant influence on the output of those who occupy it, and the connection to the occupier's own value chain must therefore be a powerful one. The problem is that this is known only at an instinctive or anecdotal level, and the argument for moving above the lowest common denominator is consequently therefore persuasive only to the already converted. What is needed, therefore, is real evidence of the connection between quality of space and productivity. The problems of this are manyfold. Firstly, how is productivity measured within the context of office work (where one blinding, creative thought can outweigh tons of paper-based transactions)? Secondly, how does one isolate what economists call externalities – facts beyond those which are being studied, which may have an equal or greater influence? These are tough questions, and in the face of them it is easy enough to say that there cannot be a scientific answer, and that it is consequently not even worth starting the exercise. In a knowledge-based economy, however, there can be few more important questions, and it should therefore be a matter of national priority to research this issue – looking at the speed of production, the incidence of errors, absenteeism, staff retention, etc – and get at least some answers.

In the meantime, and in the absence of occupiers valuing features that depart from the 'plain vanilla' of comparatively deep plan, rectangular, air-conditioned space behind a sealed facade, it should be no surprise that that is what is consistently provided. Developers and investors cannot rely upon the occasional tenant who values features beyond this being in the marketplace at the same time as the development becomes available – and then another such tenant being around if or when there is a need to re-let. This may be the real disconnection: that for an occupier nothing should be more important than the suitability of office space to his business operations; whilst for the developer, nothing is more important than timing; and for the investor there is nothing more important than the ability of the building to generate income and growth.

Within this context, the reality may be that there is no level of specification that will shift a building when there are no tenants in the market, and similarly none that is so bad that a building will stick when there is a shortage of stock and a strength of demand; and there are only limited times when the balance of supply and demand is such that buildings in a given location are competing with each other on specification.

Notwithstanding the above, nobody would say that the nastiest, cheapest building is the one to build, and practically all developers will invest in quality above the lowest common denominator. Just as in advertising, however (where it is said that half of all expenditure is wasted – but there is no way of knowing which half), some of this additional expenditure will play no part in adding to the developer's bottom line.

The cost and value management process

With the proper environment established, and with a settled view as to the outcome that would represent value, the journey through the cost and value management process can commence. The key elements of that process are:

- cost modelling and cost drivers;
- cost planning;
- benchmarking;
- value analysis;
- life cycle costing;
- risk management;
- procurement;
- post-contract cost management.

Each of these is considered separately in this chapter, once again with the caveat that the process is reiterative and that, under some procurement arrangements, parts of the project may still be at (say) cost planning stage whilst others have already moved into the post-contract phase. There should, however, be clear pauses at defined stages of design (as in, for example, the RIBA Plan of Work), at which the client confirms that the design gives him what he wants. Without this, subsequent change will be expensive and at the cost of abortive work.

Cost modelling and key cost drivers

Many of the calculations involved in development economics are run backwards – finishing with the desired result and then modelling how the other components of the calculation need to come together to produce that result. In theory, the calculation of site value that will underlie most decisions to commit to a commercial development is a straightforward one: the gross value of the completed development, less all of the costs of designing, constructing and disposing of it (including rolled up interest charges), less a margin for risk and profit, equals the amount that can be paid for the site. In practice, the client and his agents will have an idea from comparable deals of what has to be paid for the site to secure it – and so the game commences.

The challenge is to balance the entrepreneurial ambition of the developer with the realities of what can be achieved on the site in terms of the quantity, quality and cost of accommodation. At the risk of being accused of cynicism (described by George

Bernard Shaw as the power of accurate observation as perceived by those who have not got it), one might add that dispassionate advice about such realities may not always be so easy to find amongst those whose livelihood depends upon transactions proceeding.

At this inception stage of the project, therefore, the role of cost modelling is twofold. Firstly, it needs to be a reference point for realism. Developers will have their own ideas about what an office building should cost, and only last week the agent was probably told by somebody (somebody else) that offices (on a different site, and possibly of a quite different type) could be built for less. Buildings are, however, made up of bits, and so are their costs. So, as a blinding glimpse of the obvious, if an office building is going to cost (say) £130/sq ft, then the quantities and prices of all of the bits need to add up to that.

The 'bits' referred to are the elements of the building (substructure, frame, upper floors, etc), and the components of each element; and these elements and components are also the constituent parts of a cost model. (The term 'cost modelling' is being used here to describe all of the initial estimating techniques that are appropriate at feasibility stage, and the fundamental thing is that the analysis has to get down to a finer grain than an overall rate per square metre.)

At this point it is worth looking at the distribution of cost for typical commercial office buildings, considering city centre offices, and low energy business park buildings separately – the latter being less constrained by the particular characteristics of the site, and therefore more easily modelled towards an optimum solution. Table 1 shows this distribution, simplified into groups of elements.

Table 1 Broad make-up of office construction costs

Element	City offices %	Business park offices %
Substructure	6	3
Frame, floors, roof, stairs	11	16
External walls, windows, doors	15	18
Internal subdivision – partitions, doors	6	7
Internal finishes, fittings	12	8
Plumbing/mechanical services	22	18
Electrical services	10	11
Lifts	4	2
External works	2	6
Preliminaries	12	11
Total (to category A finish)	100%	100%

What matters about this calculation is not so much where the big numbers are, but rather which of the big numbers can be changed – in other words where there are design or specification choices that can be made to produce a different answer. The fact is that much of the way that the design has to develop will be pre-ordained by the constraints of the site, the commercial imperatives of developers, the qualitative expectations of investors and owners, and the performance needs of occupiers. From project to project, therefore, design development tends to home in on the same handful of issues that are both cost significant and capable of being influenced.

The key cost drivers at this stage are:

- site abnormals (for urban sites in particular);
- efficiency – the target net and gross areas, including any non-office area (such as retail, storage or parking);
- shape – the disposition of those areas, floor by floor, effectively fixing the plan, height and orientation of the building;
- structure – the structural and planning grid, and floor loadings;
- the specification choice for cladding and internal fit-out;
- the degree and means of environmental control.

Site abnormals
Site abnormals are effectively the costs necessary to create a 'clean site' ready to receive the new building, and not usually picked up by reliance upon historical cost data or benchmarking exercises. The principal items include demolitions and site clearance, dealing with contamination or hazardous materials, abnormal ground conditions (poor bearing capacity, high water table, underground obstructions, etc), external influences on the site (particularly sources of noise or vibration), and work at the boundaries or to adjoining buildings.

In addition, there will be a general location factor, with the cost of construction across the UK varying by about 25 per cent as a result of regional cost differences.

Efficiency
As developers pay for gross area and get paid for net area, the difference between the two (the net to gross efficiency may also be the difference between success and failure. 'As every schoolboy knows,' net to gross should be 80 per cent or better – and achieving less than this will usually result in a response from the developer to the effect that the outcome is 'unacceptable'. In reality, however, efficiency is conditioned by the shape of the site (and therefore of the building), the size of the floor plate, building height, and means of escape strategy – as well as the ingenuity of the design. The building also has to work, and a highly efficient building may also be inflexible, for example in use or in sub-division. Building less efficiently may also make it possible to pile more space on the site, so that although each lettable square foot will cost more, the value of the building will be increased by an amount that more than compensates. Floorplates that are apparently uneconomic to construct, by comparison

with the fuller floorplates below them, may consequently add to the developer's return notwithstanding their relatively high construction cost – and the higher the land value, the truer this will be.

Achieving the optimum efficiency is therefore a question of looking at alternatives, rather than working to the mantra of a single number, and it is perhaps this fact more than any other that prevents the development of a standard solution for offices, balancing construction cost and market value. The shape of the site, the rights of adjoining owners, the requirements of the planners and many other external forces will all affect the permissible bulk of the building, and any one of these factors might drive the optimum way to arrange the office space. For example, where the planners impose an absolute limitation on height, then it may well be worth incurring the additional cost of constructing deep basements for parking, plant and other support space, leaving the maximum possible amount of above-ground space for lettable area. As a variant to this, where the height limits are particularly tight, and the construction of extensive basements is feasible, it may be worth giving up space above ground in order to get light (and therefore value – which follows the light) down to below-ground space. Exploring these possibilities, and coming up with imaginative proposals to maximise site value, is at the very core of the art and science of commercial office design at feasibility stage.

Shape
Figure 3 shows that the cost of cladding an office building is say 15 per cent to 20 per cent of total construction cost, and because it is so much influenced by specification and shape this is also the single item of cost that can be most affected by design decisions. Shape influences this cost in two principal ways: the complexity of the profile of the building in both plan and section, and the general plan shape of the building (the efficiency of shape).

Efficiency of shape is indicated by wall to floor ratio – the gross amount of external facade (elevation area) divided by the gross internal floor area. The two simple examples shown in Figure 4 illustrate this point.

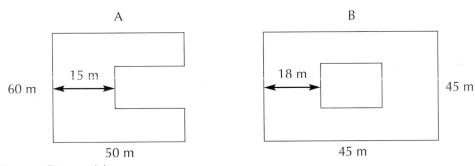

Figure 3: Efficiency of shape

Building A is a fairly conventional rectangular block, 15 m deep, without an atrium or central courtyard. Assuming a floor-to-floor height of 3.80 m, it has a wall-to-floor ratio of 0.57:1 (elevation area of 1,102 sq m divided by gross internal floor area of 1,950 sq m).

Building B is an equally conventional 'doughnut' courtyard building, which is also built to a deeper (18 m) plan, of about the same area. For this building, the wall-to-floor ratio is 0.42:1 (821 sq m of elevation area for 1,944 sq m of gross internal floor area). Building A therefore has about one-third more external wall for every square metre of floor area – and if the cladding cost is say 17.5 per cent of the total building cost, then this difference alone represents a six per cent increase in cost above Building B.

Of course, absolute freedom of choice rarely exists and there will be constraints relating to planning conditions, the configuration of the site, the rights of adjoining buildings and so on which will limit choices. Where options do exist, however, few individual decisions will have as much impact as this on total cost; and this explains why, doubtless to the frustration of many architects, the harsh light of cost review focuses so sharply and so consistently on plan depth and the specification for the cladding.

As a broad guide, a ratio of 0.40:1 or better would be good, and above 0.50:1 there would need to be some compensating benefit for the loss of efficiency of enclosure.

The other dimension to shape is height. As a rough rule of thumb, about 30 per cent of building cost is height-dependant, so a change of five per cent in floor-to-height (say up from 3.80 m to 4 m) would increase costs by about 1.5 per cent. It is not a great deal, and the saving will be eroded further (indeed, it may even become an extra) where the zone available for structure becomes so limited that inefficient beam sections need to be used. Squeezing the void between the ceiling and the floor above will also have an impact upon the design and/or installation of engineering services, and this too has a cost effect. Within the bounds of good sense, therefore, decisions about floor-to-floor height are more likely to be driven by the desire to maximise developable area within the height set by planning constraints, than by considerations of construction cost.

Structural cost
It is a truism that structural cost is primarily a function of span – and this will be compounded by an associated impact on fabric costs, as structural depth is also a function of span. For an increased span this will mean increased building height, and therefore increased costs in all of the vertical elements, unless the structure and service zones are integrated – for example by use of cellform or castellated beams.

Typical cost increases for structural grids above 6.00 x 7.50 m (probably the tightest sensible grid for offices) are set down in Table 2. This shows the effect on both the structure alone (substructure and superstructure), and on total construction cost, taking into account the effect of additional structural depth on other elements of the building.

Table 2 Comparative structure costs

Structural grid (m x m)	Cost index (structure)	Cost index (total)
6.00 x 7.50	10	1000
6.00 x 12.00	120	1003
6.00 x 15.00	130	1019
7.50 x 7.50	100	1000
7.50 x 9.00	115	1008
9.00 x 9.00	120	1003
9.00 x 12.00	130	1008
9.00 x 15.00	145	1027

Note: based on a seven-storey building, with steel structure

Clearly this is sensitive to assumptions about the specification of other vertical elements (most particularly cladding, once again – the assumption here being a medium quality curtain wall), but the figures do demonstrate that there is a significant difference in structural cost for a clear span of say 12 m or 15 m, although as a proportion of total construction cost this is not so great. Whether this represents value then depends upon the perceived benefits of column-free space. Real enthusiasts will point out that there is some marginal gain in reduced column area to deduct from the net lettable area, but this is unlikely to achieve a gain of much more than one-tenth of one per cent. Every little bit helps, of course, but the real issue is one of quality of space.

Structural cost will also be affected by the shape and general organisation of the building, with cantilevers, set-backs and transfer structures all increasing the weight of steel.

The other significant variable in structural cost relates to *floor loadings*. The debate about the proper allowance to make for superimposed loads has rumbled on for some time now (having positively raged for a while, whilst there were dramatically different points of view), and this is a prime example of a 'creep' in standards resulting from a lack of empirical data and an over-reaction to some structural failures. For 'offices for general use', the Code of Practice by which most structures are designed (BS 6399: Part 1) recommends working to a uniformly distributed imposed 'live' load of 2.5kN/sq m (50lbs/sq ft) with an additional allowance of 1kN/sq m (20lbs/sq ft) for the dead load of partitions.

More recently, the drive for flexibility, whereby an office tenant could arrange his accommodation (including filing and storage) more or less however he chose across the floor plate, and the reaction to one or two well-publicised structural failures, has led to a call for an increase in design loads. As a consequence of this, they had risen by the end of the 1980s to a fairly general standard of 4 to 5 kN/sq m (80 to 100lbs/sq ft) live load, still plus 1kN/sq m for partitions. This represented a high watermark, and one from which there was a general call for a retreat. A position paper sponsored by Stanhope in 1992 illustrated the over-provision that this standard represented. It supported the argument with research that demonstrated that loadings higher than the British Standard recommendation of 2.5kN/sq m are required only for storage or centralised filing; that this need rarely extends over more than five per cent of the floor area, and that this proportion of stronger structure will be inherent in most structural designs. It therefore proposed a new standard of 2.5kN/sq m generally, with five per cent of the floorspace designed to a higher standard. The BCO specification now takes the same line, proposing a general standard of a 2.5kN/sq m live load, with 7.5kN/sq m (150lbs/sq ft), over five per cent of the primary lettable area (having flirted briefly with a recommendation for 2.5kN/sq m throughout – which most practitioners felt to be skinning things too much).

This continuing debate has been rehearsed at some length because it is illustrative of a number of issues that arise in setting standards for modern offices:

- Firstly, it shows how standards can be talked up as a consequence of having additional layers of protection – each new benchmark becoming a minimum institutional standard (usually set or demanded by advisers acting in good faith, but with a limited understanding of its technical implications).

- Next, it shows how a proper standard should be set – which is by reference to typical use, empirically tested, with sensible allowances for flexibility around the norm.

- It then poses some questions relating to the difference between cost and value. The cost differential between different loadings obviously depends on structural system, span and ground conditions, but as an indication, the saving by reducing from a general live load of 5kN/sq m to 2.5kN/sq m would be about ten per cent of structural cost. This typically represents little more than one per cent of total construction cost. On the one hand, this is not a great contribution to the bottom line. However, so much office cost is set by external conditions that all opportunities for savings merit serious consideration: a construction cost saving of five per cent might move the developer's margin from say 15 per cent to 16.5 per cent – growth in profit and risk cover of ten per cent on the margin itself. However, for the occupier, and therefore for an investor interested in longer term flexibility, this may represent a risk for which there is no reward, and the loss of just one tenant who is advised that the design loading is inadequate could represent the difference between a successful investment and an unsuccessful one. This therefore touches once again upon the difference between cost and value, upon the different criteria for value on the part of developers and investors, each with their different time horizons of interest, and upon the need for reasoned advice, rather than 'copy cat' specification demands, based more on perception and a suspicion of change than on need.

- For all of those involved in development, there is (or should be) a further consideration –the issue of sustainability and waste. Additional floor loadings are designed-in only at the expense of additional material. Both natural resources and energy are therefore consumed in meeting a higher standard, and that consumption represents waste if it never secures a material benefit. A free market economist might say that the pricing structure should deal with this, and when society values its resources (and the fall-out from energy consumption) more highly, then this will be factored into the equation. In the meantime, concern and care will have to stand in the place of market forces, challenging the amount that should be paid (and consumed) for over-provision in the interests of future flexibility.

The final issue on structure relates to the perennial question of steel versus concrete. The technical arguments are well rehearsed. By comparison with reinforced concrete, the advantages of a steel structure are that it is lighter (which may well have implications on foundation design); it deals more effectively with longer spans (but usually at the cost of greater building height); and it is inherently flexible. The advantages of reinforced concrete, by comparison, are shallower depths for spans up to say nine metres; greater efficiency in dealing with square (rather than rectangular) grids; and the potential to use the thermal mass of the structure as a moderator of internal temperature, and therefore as part of an energy-efficient design. If there is a generalisation about cost, it is that concrete would be cheaper for those grids for which it is technically feasible, but steel would be quicker – and it would therefore be a matter of appraisal as to whether the advantages of speed (reduced time-related site establishment costs, reduced impact of inflation and interest charges, and speed to market) compensate for the additional construction costs. Span will usually be the principal determinant, though, with the structures for spans up to nine metres being 70 per cent concrete, 30 per cent steel; for nine to 12 metre spans 50/50; and for spans greater than 12 metres five per cent concrete, 95 per cent steel.

It has to be said that few of these generalisations are universal and invariable truths. The implications of the structural depth required for steel can be mitigated by integrating the design of the structure and services; the economic spans of concrete can be stretched by using post-tension slabs; and there are compensating environmental arguments for steelwork. Above all, even the arguments about cost and speed will vary according to the skills of specialist contractors and the market in which they operate. The answer therefore changes as the trade contractors with the best skills fill their order books and, in an industry where there is great inelasticity of supply, manage their workload by increasing their prices. Once again, therefore, standard solutions rarely remain standard for long, and the best way forward is established by analysis rather than by slavish pursuit of precedent.

Specification choice
Although specification choices obviously run right through the building, just two cost-significant aspects are considered here: cladding and internal finishes.

As already indicated, cladding is both a significant and significantly variable component of the construction cost of commercial offices. It therefore merits close attention – and certainly closer attention than the too-frequent tendency to deal with it at cost planning stage simply by choosing a rate to the nearest £50/sq m. Clearly the contribution that cladding makes to total cost is a function of its quantity (principally, in turn, a function of the movements in wall-to-floor ratio considered above) and of unit rate. The unit rate is then determined by complexity and by the basic specification.

Complexity is principally influenced by the plan and section of the building, which will determine the degree of repetition, and the number of corners or changes of direction – each of which carries a cost. Economy is therefore served by maximising repetition – although monotony is served by the same thing, and the designer's skill therefore lies in balancing these two factors so that the result is both affordable and distinctive.

As far as specification is concerned, the principal cost drivers are transparency (with the cost range running from brick buildings with punched windows up to fully glazed facades); and, for curtain walling in particular, the choice of system. Here the key choice is between stick and unitised systems. Looking only at base cost, stick systems will be cheaper (and with a wider choice of specialist contractors), but there are costs involved in providing access and hoisting for site assembly, and installation will be slower – probably delaying the dates for both watertightness and completion. As well as tighter quality control, therefore, the speed of installation of a unitised system may, on analysis, make it the value-led option.

Thereafter the critical cost decisions relate to pane size and the centres of mullions, as these determine glass thickness and the dimensions necessary to resist wind load.

Turning to finishes, the choice is, of course, both wide and discretionary. There remains, however, a market pressure to associate high quality with expensive materials, and this is a pressure well worth resisting. A bad building smeared with marble is still a bad building, and both economy and elegance are frequently better served by simpler tastes. Here too the job of the designer is to challenge perceived wisdom and come up with new ideas that are both imaginative and durable.

Environmental control
There is little doubt that, during the course of the 1990s, fan-coil units have become the air-conditioning system of choice. They score on high cooling capacities, adaptability (in dealing with various and changing degrees of cellularisation), and the relative reliability of a proven technology. Because of the constant pressure to

maximise net-to-gross efficiency, they also score over variable air volume (VAV) systems, because of their reduced space requirement, both in central plant and in on-floor risers.

These advantages have overcome the disadvantages of fan-coil that previously promoted VAV as the system of choice, namely in reduced air quality, higher noise levels, higher running costs and maintenance requirements, and the need to get into the occupier's space to carry out maintenance on the fan-coil units themselves.

If one had to place a bet now for the system of choice for the next cycle, it should probably be on displacement ventilation. Some early applications of this system became notorious as buildings that were slow to let, doubtless as a consequence of the natural conservatism of the market, and particularly on the part of those who advise tenants on the basis of specifications led by the feeling that there is safety in numbers; but there is now increased take-up of the displacement ventilation option – and, it seems, less market resistance.

Under this system, fresh air, cooled to just below temperature, is supplied at low velocity at floor level, with upward air movement then assisted by the heat generated by occupants and their equipment. The warm air is extracted at ceiling level, and this together with relatively high fresh air supply rates (typically 22 litres per second, compared with 15 for fan-coil units) results in much improved air quality. Heating is then provided by the addition of perimeter heating, and cooling by chilled beams or (where the required cooling capacity is lower) by chilled ceiling tiles. As well as an improvement in air quality, running and maintenance costs are reduced as a result of air being introduced at relatively higher temperatures, and the heating and cooling elements within the office space being generally static.

Against this, there is still a price premium to be paid for chilled beam/chilled ceiling installations, and they need to work in conjunction with a high performance external building envelope (to minimise peak cooling loads at the perimeter), more complex ceiling systems, deeper floor voids (potentially leading to a higher floor-to-floor height), and marginally larger plant room areas.

Table 3 shows the relative capital and recurrent cost implications of the generally used environmental control systems, on an index basis by reference to low pressure hot water heating only.

The relationship between cost and value will depend upon a detailed analysis by comparison with the alternative, looking (for example) at whether increased plant sizes actually lead to a reduced lettable area within the developable envelope, whether the increased floor-to-floor height is inevitable – and, if so, whether it too actually reduces the amount of lettable area that can be developed on the site, market reaction to different systems, and the value placed on lower recurrent costs, and so forth.

Table 3 Summary of comparative costs of different environmental control systems

System	Capital cost	Energy cost	Maintenance cost	Whole life cycle costs
LTHW heating	100	100	100	100
Four pipe fan-coil	280	550	690	260
VAV with LTHW perimeter heating	315	375	385	290
Displacement ventilation (minimum fresh air), chilled ceiling and LTHW perimeter heating	345	265	460	275
Displacement ventilation (minimum fresh air), chilled beam concealed in ceiling, LTHW perimeter heating	320	265	460	265

*Note:*capital costs include the cost of the ceiling (including the upgrade for the chilled ceiling installation) the whole life cycle costs also include the ceiling.

Source: Davis Langdon & Everest/Mott Green & Wall

The whole picture

Although each of these major cost drivers is taken individually, it is fundamental that they should be considered collectively. Structures, envelopes and environmental control systems work together, and the identification of the best option will depend upon an analysis of all of the alternatives, and the way in which each part of the desired specification impacts upon the others. All of these then work with optimising the efficiency of the building (in terms of the rent-earning floor space as a proportion of total built space), and they too, therefore, are at the core of the art and science of commercial office design.

Cost planning

During the course of sketch design (RIBA Work Stage C), the cost model needs to be developed into a detailed cost plan, itemising the approximate quantities and rates of all elements of the scheme. This is a reiterative exercise, and should not just be (as it so often is) a one-off exercise completed at the end of Stage C – when it has the potential to produce an unwelcome result. It follows that time needs to be built into the design programme to cost and re-cost the ideas as they develop, so that the cost plan can truly be what its name suggests – a plan to complete the scheme for a predicted cost.

In addition, the cost plan should not only be prepared in detail, but also published in detail. As with so many exercises in economics, the cost plan will tend to conform to Pareto's principle, with 80 per cent of the money being concentrated in about 20 per cent of the items, but detail that is held only by the quantity surveyor denies the client and the whole design team the opportunity of playing their full part in the process. Value for money is, above all, a concept that 'belongs' to the client, and the client needs to see where his money is being spent, so that he can question assumptions and satisfy himself that it is being spent in conformity with his own criteria for value.

Similarly, architects, engineers and specialist designers frequently (but sadly not invariably) have a good understanding of the cost of their own designs gathered from other projects, and only foolish pride would prevent a quantity surveyor from taking advantage of that in discussing successive drafts of the cost plan to refine the result. This process also serves one of the most important requirements of the cost plan as the scheme moves through successive design stages, which is that it secures project team 'buy-in'. This can only happen if the team has played a part in the development of the cost plan and knows, no later than the end of RIBA Work Stage C, what provisions have been made for their own work. By that time, there needs to be a clear understanding of 'what you see is what you get', so that all team members (specifically including the client) understand that what is not provided for in the cost plan cannot be provided in the scheme without compensating adjustments elsewhere in the design or to the budget.

A cost plan that provides no more than a breakdown of the total into elements therefore misses out on one of the most important, and possibly *the* most important, purposes of a cost plan; and detail should be demanded – not least to ascertain that it actually exists.

Once the client has accepted the Stage C report, and the associated cost plan, then there is something to be said for treating that cost plan exactly like a contract sum – and reporting subsequent changes as additions to or omissions from the total, balancing these, as long as is practical, by compensating adjustments to the design reserve and contingency allowances. This keeps the scheme on track to comply with the budget – or represents an early warning that the budget is threatened by the development of the brief or design. Clients and designers will always have ideas that put the cost plan under pressure, and the important thing is that the pressure is not denied, and that the cost consequences of each idea are discussed early enough to take corrective action – if that is the client's choice. That something cannot be accommodated within the budget is never exactly good news. That it cannot be accommodated, and that there is nothing that can now be done to deal with the problem, is unreservedly *bad* news. Cost management from the end of Stage C (which is really the first point at which the budget can be described as the product of a reasoned estimate) is therefore about the avoidance of unwelcome surprises – and particularly surprises that are incapable of remedy.

Client reviews of the project from this point forward should therefore include regular cost reports, just as they would in the post-contract stage, and the quantity surveyor needs to be looking not just at drawings as they are issued, but also over the shoulders of the designers as they work, and at correspondence, meeting minutes and so forth, to pick up the earliest possible signs of developments that are inconsistent with the assumptions made in setting the cost plan.

Benchmarking

Benchmarking is the comparison of a proposed scheme with other schemes of similar type and class, looking at cost and value, and the drivers of both. It has its limitations. Being based on historic norms, it is like trying to find your way by looking in the rear view mirror, and there is a danger that it will stifle innovation and drive everything back to a lowest common denominator. Also, in order to take proper account of the inevitable variables between schemes, so much discretionary adjustment may be necessary that the exercise proves no more than that nought equals nought.

However, if any building type submits to the kind of analysis which can inform a benchmarking exercise it is commercial offices, where the pressures of the marketplace and the requirements of institutional investors produce some consistency in what is built. Given this, benchmarking serves as a useful guard against complacency, posing questions as to why certain aspects of the scheme are showing a markedly different cost from the same aspect of competing schemes. Asking and answering those questions also provides a structured and comparatively objective way of discussing with the client the cost of the scheme against the range of costs demonstrated by similar projects, and our experience is that this can reinforce the client's confidence in the estimate and his sense that the answer represents value.

For commercial offices, therefore, it is worth benchmarking the scheme under development against historic data relating to:

- construction cost (£ per square metre of gross internal floor area, and £ per square metre above ground – which rules out one of the major variables, particularly for city centre developments);
- efficiency (net lettable floor area as a percentage of gross internal floor area);
- cost drivers – wall to floor ratio, weight of structural steel (or reinforcement) per square metre of gross floor area, cooling load per square metre of net lettable floor area, etc;
- speed of construction (square metres per month).

These are all pretty crude measures, and the data does not provide the means of producing an estimate. That still depends upon the detail. They do, however, assist the cost modelling process, and they provide a broad means of testing the answer.

Value analysis

Value analysis is one technique for exploring whether additional cost produces additional value. It is in danger of falling into disrepute, too often being characterised as little more than cost cutting – attributable partly to the pressures referred to above and partly to the lack of sophistication of those who practise it (too often, sadly, quantity surveyors); but if practised properly, it remains a valuable tool for identifying *unnecessary* cost – which can be defined as cost that serves neither life, nor use, nor customer need.

There is, it must be said, more than one point of view about what 'properly practised' might mean. In the United States, where the technique began, there tends to be a complete shadow team (architect, structural and services engineers, cost consultant) who pore over the design and propose alternatives. The disadvantage of this is that the process can become adversarial, and the incumbent team becomes over-defensive of 'their' proposal, and demotivated if it is changed.

In the UK, it is more usual for the incumbent team to carry out a structured review of its own work, independently facilitated (where 'independent' may mean by an individual from within one of the practices making up the team, but without a prior involvement in the project). The danger of this is that there may be insufficient challenge to the status quo, and that the team remains hostage to its own prior ideas. On balance, however, our experience is that the latter approach works best, so long as the facilitation maintains the right balance between challenge and confrontation.

The process then proceeds in two tranches, the first of which (sometimes distinguished as value management) will comprise a review of objectives – looking at *what* is to be done. The outcome of this should be an agreed statement of all project objectives (in respect of both the end product and the process by which it will be delivered), and a review of the best ways of meeting those objectives. This should be conducted as soon as possible after project inception, but with enough of the background to the site researched to identify relevant constraints.

The second session (more focussed on value engineering – on *how* things are to be done) would normally be completed at the end of sketch design (RIBA Stage C), recognising the truism that the ability to influence the outcome reduces exponentially as one moves through the design stages. In this second session, the sketch design will be reviewed at a considerable level of detail, and all alternative ways of achieving the same end should be investigated. This starts with a brainstorming session, at which ideas for alternatives are tabled – and, in order to encourage the greatest number of ideas, none should be challenged on the grounds of predictions about their practicality or cost. Once all of the ideas have been tabled, they are reviewed for practicality (and at this point it is worth stating that this is primarily a judgement for the client, and a value engineering process run without the presence of the client is therefore at best a wasted opportunity, and at worst a waste of time and money).

This produces a reduced list of ideas that are worthy of further exploration, from the point of view of technical practicality ('buildability') and their cost and time consequences, including consequences over the whole life of the project. These are quickly worked through, and the client then chooses which are to be implemented.

It is only fair to say that many design teams view this process with doubt or suspicion. Few of us like being challenged on ideas that have taken time and trouble to develop, and everyone knows that the focus will be on costs which stand out above the bare minimum. There is, however, no respectable reason why a client should be required to pay more than the bare minimum unless he can be persuaded that it produces value for him; and design teams who lead their client into greater expenditure simply by denying them the knowledge that a lower cost alternative exists deserve to forfeit their client's trust.

The corollary is that the value engineering process can help create trust, by making the client a full partner in decisions about value – decisions that he alone is able to make with a full appreciation of his own criteria. For some of those criteria will be subjective, and if a client is attracted to option B so much more than a less costly option A that he is content to pay the difference, then that is as good a test of value as any. Once every alternative has been considered, then the cumulative effect is to illustrate the lowest cost for which the challenge of the brief could be met. For the client, knowing where this point lies, and being able to make decisions to add back cost on the grounds that the difference is considered worth it, is a solid basis for a trusting working relationship thereafter, dispelling the suspicion that there is a cheaper option that nobody will reveal.

Life cycle costing

The consideration not just of initial capital cost, but also of the cost of running and maintaining a building is called life cycle costing, and there is a problem with it. In fact, there is more than one problem, but the greatest of them is getting occupiers interested. Precisely because these costs are such a low proportion of total business costs, they do not represent a boardroom issue. It follows that, although there is frequently a pro forma requirement in a client's brief for a building to be efficient in energy consumption and the other components of running and maintenance, this general aspiration is rarely backed up by a readiness to commit additional capital in order to secure recurrent savings in the future. This is particularly so when the taxation treatment of capital and revenue expenditure is seen as penalising the former – and capital expenditure is so much easier to see and comprehend (and therefore to cut).

Nonetheless, the proportions shown in Figures 1 and 2 show that occupiers should be as interested in the recurrent cost element of life cycle cost as in the initial capital cost; and if they were sufficiently interested to demand the best outcome over the whole life of the building, then many of the other problems of life cycle costing (most particularly the absence of sound data regarding component life, maintenance cycles, etc) would be addressed. Pressures which might bring this about include a move towards serviced offices (where the usual disconnection between the person committing the initial capital expenditure and the person picking up the bill for the recurrent expenditure is mended, with the same person now responsible for both – and with competition forcing him to try to optimise both); or a possible trend towards so-called 'corporate PFI', whereby, once again, the occupier buys not just so many square feet of carpet (an input), but so many square feet of fully serviced space suitable for occupation (an output).

Risk management

The estimating processes of the industry, and therefore the budgeting processes of its clients, have tended to work to a single, deterministic figure – or at least a figure that is hoped to be deterministic of the desired outcome. The reality for customers is that construction work is beset with uncertainties, and to work to a single figure is optimistic to the point of being misleading. This is so much so that doing so actually jeopardises the possibility of delivering the building at any given figure, as there is a silent assumption that that figure can be achieved, come what may. A necessary protection against this is therefore the implementation of risk management procedures.

Risk management deserves not just a chapter to itself, but a whole book. The means by which it may be carried out varies from a broad commonsense review ('what would happen if . . .') to a highly detailed analysis, with the probability and severity of each risk quantified, and the answer processed by techniques such as Monte Carlo simulation (doubtless so called because, for all the maths, the predictions remain a gamble). But at the core of all of them is the idea that every estimate, though it might be presented as a single figure, is the result of a host of assumptions. Any of these may subsequently turn out to be wrong, and if they do, then the single figure estimate will prove to be right only if, by good fortune, the differences between assumption and actuality compensate for each other.

This argues for the need to explore alternative outcomes, and detailed analysis of the risks that attend the project. Indeed, the very act of listing those risks, considering whether they can be eliminated, offloaded or managed, and identifying who is to take responsibility for whatever action is agreed is a useful step in 'taking care of business' for the developer.

Procurement

To start with the purpose of the exercise, the general objectives of the procurement process are to:

- select a competent and committed project team (including the contractor or construction manager and his trade contractors);
- introduce each team member to the process at the appropriate time;
- secure value for money – the optimum balance between the highest standards of materials and workmanship, the shortest possible programme, and the lowest possible cost;
- ensure reasonable parity of opportunity (and absolute parity where competitive tendering is a part of the process);
- create incentives for the achievement of the client's declared objectives.

Over-arching all of these, at least for those who work in and live by the industry, there should be a continuing concern to arrange things so as to promote and maintain efficiency in the industry.

Above all, though, procurement arrangements are principally about risk and value – how the former is disposed, and how the latter is secured. If there is a general rule (and there are not many relating to procurement), then I would say it is that a client should carry risk for no longer than he can create value by doing so. That value might be secured by getting a better building (however that might be defined for a specific client) or by avoiding paying too much to get rid of the risk (as risk is not shed free of charge).

Turning then to generic choices of arrangement, there are three basic types, and then an almost infinite number of hybrids. However, the three basic types are:

1. Design and build, whereby the client sets out his requirements and then invites a contractor to be responsible both for design and construction. On the face of it, this represents the maximum imposition of risk onto the contractor.
2. Construction management, whereby the client places separate contracts for the design (and normally for each separate discipline of the design) and for the trade works (again separately), and then for the management of the construction. This therefore represents the opposite extreme – the maximum retention of risk by the client.
3. The so-called 'traditional' arrangement, whereby the client places separate contracts for the design (again normally for each discipline separately) but a single contract for construction, ostensibly (and the word is used advisedly) for a fixed sum. This therefore represents a middle road on risk.

Figure 4 summarises these broad alternatives, and also illustrates that there are actually countervailing risks at work.

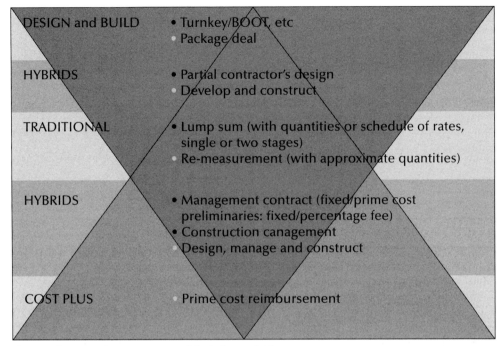

Figure 4: Contractual arrangements and the balance of risk

Risk is generally perceived as relating to cost and programme, and the red triangle indicates that maximum risk transfer in these respects, from client to contractor, resides in the Design and Build option – increasingly transferring back to the client as one runs down through the options. There is also, however, a quality and fitness for purpose risk – one that, for the reasons noted above, impacts more heavily on the users. For risk transfer to be effective, the means of controlling risk have to pass as well, and that means that the control of design development will pass to the contractor once he has been appointed. The point at which this occurs, and the quality of project definition upon which the contract is based, are therefore critical; and it follows that quality and fitness for purpose risk will tend to run in the opposite direction to cost and time risk (the green triangle) – with Design and Build representing the maximum risk to the client.

Clients choosing a procurement route are therefore faced with a wide range of possibilities across these generic types or any hybrid thereof. There will be no shortage of advice. This is a subject that tends to raise strong feelings, and the various protagonists, some of whom (including quantity surveyors, of course) speak from a point of view that is complicated by special interest, may well have a strong predisposition to work in a particular way. Frequently they find the only thing that they can agree on is that it is a case of 'horses for courses' – but if it were possible to match horses reliably to courses, then it would be the punters that are rich rather than the bookies. Once again, therefore, the way ahead is pointed by analysis rather than prejudice.

The constant strife for competitive positioning, also promotes a steady stream of 'new' arrangements holding out the prospect of particular success by comparison with the alternatives – frequently with the word 'solutions' included somewhere in the title or tag line. There is, however, a reality that must be faced, and that is that there is an unavoidable sequence of events that has to be followed in constructing anything, and particularly where a commitment is required on price or programme. That sequence is:

- the perception of need;
- a brief, or detailed statement of need;
- an outline design in response to that brief;
- a freeze of both brief and design;
- a fully defined design, worked up in detail;
- pricing and procurement;
- planning, programming and mobilisation;
- construction;
- commissioning.

To change sequence or overlap ('fast track') these stages is to increase risk, and probably to introduce waste – and any system that proclaims to be able to change or overlap the stages without cost, risk or waste is almost certainly a quack remedy.

Choosing the arrangement most appropriate for each project therefore depends upon a full analysis of the client's criteria against a range of factors, including:

- the client's priorities in respect of time, cost and quality and the point at which this trinity is balanced in his own perception of value;
- the client's attitude to risk (which may well be influenced by prior experience, possibly to the point of immovable prejudice, and by his decision-making structures);
- as an extension to this, whether certainty of cost and/or time are valued more highly by the client than being able to say in retrospect that it could not have been done with less of either;
- the particular characteristics of the project (complexity v simplicity, the way that quality impinges upon fitness for purpose – and therefore value, whether it is capable of full pre-definition, the anticipated incidence of change, etc);
- the availability of project management, design and construction skills – both generally and within the client organisation (from the point of view of risk management and the creation of value);
- the state of the market.

All of this also needs to be considered within the context of programme – as the criticality of a completion date may not always allow time to follow the logical sequence of complete design, definition, procurement and construction (that is, for the whole of the project) in a way that would otherwise best protect the client against risk.

In commercial property development, the operation of the principle of retaining risk for only so long as it can lead to value, as enunciated above, has tended to produce polarised positions – and, between them, a hybrid which has the potential to become a new standard. The polarised positions are that those developers who believe that they possess skills that run into the procurement and construction phases of a project may choose to create value by assuming some of the risk of procurement and construction. They will then seek to create value by managing out those risks at a cost that is less than would have been paid to a contractor as a premium for taking on the risk himself. Such developers will incline towards the construction management route, or a development of it.

The risks of this should not, however, be underestimated. As well as being on risk in proceeding to construction in advance of having a price for all of the work, the client under a construction management arrangement also carries all of the risk occurring at the interface – that is, he will have to pay one trade contractor who has been caused delay and/or disruption by another, and will be able to recover that expenditure only to the extent that he can prove who caused the delay and/or disruption. Without a lump sum for the work, the presumption that everything is included in the contractor's price unless the contract specifically entitles him to more is lost – and this represents the loss of a considerable protection.

Speaking on this subject at a conference on procurement, I once posited three pre-conditions for those contemplating construction management as a preferred procurement route:

- Firstly, they should make themselves fully aware of the risks they are assuming.
- Secondly, they should possess the skills, experience, resources and inclination to manage those risks.
- Thirdly, if anything does go wrong, then, at the end of the day, they must be prepared to pay up and look big.

I suggested that the last of these was the one that would cause most clients difficulty. Sharing the platform that day was Peter Rogers of Stanhope, who qualified these conditions by saying that paying 'at the end of the day' was too late – and that a developer who is truly committed to construction management must be prepared to pay as soon as a problem arises, and to buy his way out of it. Having no problem with *that* idea is a rarer quality still, and I can think of no better test question for those considering construction management as the way forward.

At the other pole are those developers who have no interest in managing the design, the procurement or the construction, and who see no great opportunities for creating value beyond identifying the opportunity in the first place, assembling the land and the team necessary to develop it, obtaining consents, and subsequently marketing the building. For these clients, the preferred procurement arrangement might well be Design and Build. For a player whose interest in fitness for purpose is less than his need to meet cost and time targets to protect the assumptions of his appraisal, this will be perceived as the option by which the maximum amount of risk is transferred to the contractor.

Given the extremes of risk represented by these two polar opposites of procurement arrangements, it is unsurprising that clients and their advisors search for a happy medium. It is perhaps too early to say that it will invariably be 'happy', but a median way has developed which has the potential to become a new tradition, as it seems to combine the best of all possible worlds (although those with longer memories will recall that the same thing was said of management contracting – a procurement arrangement which turned out to have unique risks, without unique balancing benefits beyond a degree of administrative convenience). This arrangement poses under a number of titles: Develop and Construct, Guaranteed Maximum Price (almost always a misnomer), two-stage Design and Build, and so forth. At the core, however, is a common principle – and that is that the client retains control of the design team (and therefore of the design process) up until the point of entering into a contract for the construction. In accordance with the principle that risk should be retained for only so long as value can be created by carrying it, this contract will be entered into only after the client is satisfied that he has a scheme which is sufficiently well designed to have optimised the amount and disposition of lettable area on the site, and to set standards which will maximise rent and investment yield. At that point the design consultants are novated to a contractor, who then becomes responsible for completing the design.

At this point it is necessary to look at timing – and a problem instantly arises. This is that the programme pressure under which commercial development proceeds frequently means that design and construction need to overlap – and once the work is split into separate packages (or series of packages), there is no single point at which the project passes into a post-contract phase. If the designers are to be novated, then they will find themselves working simultaneously for the contractor on those parts that have passed into contract, whilst still being retained by the client for any packages still in design development – and, of course, there are interface issues that mean that even this split is not as clean as it sounds.

If, therefore, the client does still have a preference for a fixed contract price (and most clients would, given the choice, if time and the other pressures to which construction projects are subject permit), then the procurement route that seems to meet this need runs as follows:

- The design consultants are appointed separately from the contractor for the pre-contract stages.
- A contractor (or more particularly a constructor) is also appointed early in the design stage, to provide the pre-contract services that would be typical in construction management – planning, programming (and particularly lead-in programming), advice on buildability, etc.

- If necessary, trade contractors are appointed for the 'early' packages – that is, those packages that need to get under way in advance of there being sufficient design and procurement completed on the rest of the project to ask for a lump sum, with the contractor managing them – again in an arrangement similar to construction management.
- When the great majority of the work has then been designed, a contract sum is negotiated on the basis of trade works tendered in the usual way, plus allowances for the contractor's preliminaries, overheads, profit and risk (for which purpose some principles would have been established as part of the original selection of the contractor).
- At this point, the client will enter into a lump sum contract for the whole of the works – and simultaneously arrange novation of the design consultants to the contractor, who thereafter becomes responsible for the completion of design. Any works already in progress at that point are also subsumed into this main contract, again by novation of any trade contracts placed in advance.

This route might better be called 'Design *then* Build' (or, to a contractor given to a general feeling of being hard done by, 'Dump and Build'); and its principal advantages of by comparison with the more traditional alternatives are:

- The client can choose those people whom he thinks best to design and construct the building separately, rather than hoping that they might come together in an ad hoc consortium.
- The client can work co-operatively and in continuous dialogue with his chosen designers, to develop a preferred option.
- In addition, there is an opportunity for an extended period of co-operative working between the designers and the contractor; and the early involvement of both means that firms can be selected who are known to be ready to work together – avoiding the abrupt 'shot gun marriage' that can otherwise be a feature of novation.
- By early involvement, the contractor can also contribute to the development of the cost plan – and then 'buy in' to working within it.
- It is possible, at the client's risk, to start work on site in advance of being able to agree a fixed contract sum, but with the protection of a fixed sum once it is realistic to agree one.
- Once the preferred option has been developed (to whatever degree of detail the client chooses), responsibility for completing the design (comprehensively as to scope, effectively as to function, co-ordinated with other elements, and timeously) passes to the contractor. Thereafter, the only grounds for a further adjustment to the price or programme would normally be a change requested by the client.

The principal *disadvantages* by comparison with the alternatives are:

- A general disadvantage of the use of novation in this way is that contractors' freedom to use their own design skills is constrained – indeed, widespread use would positively discourage contractors from building up their design skills.

- Because the pre-contract stages of the project take place with the contractor being part of the team, the contract sum (or a significant part of it) has to be negotiated. This can, however, be managed by joint tender action, handled on an open book basis, for much of the trade work.
- There are, nonetheless, risks in commencing on site in advance of securing a price for the whole of work, and there loss is of some competitive tension in negotiating the contract sum or GMP (for which reason the client needs to retain the right to walk away in the event of failing to agree a satisfactory contract sum, but in respect of which it is only realistic to allow a margin for risk). Of course, if it is not possible to agree a contract sum, the option remains to continue on a construction management arrangement – albeit with the new set of risks that apply for that arrangement.
- Once a design team has been novated, and a contract sum has been agreed, then there must be no ambiguity about it – the designers no longer work for the client, and there is a clear commercial difference of interest between the client and the contractor (and therefore the novated designers).
- As a consequence of this, to the extent that every detail of the building has not been settled at the point of novation/contract formation, the client will either need to accept what is given by the contractor (assuming that it is consistent with those Employer's Requirements that have been settled), or pay for any enhancement. Beyond the point of novation, therefore, this arrangement suffers from all the other disadvantages of Design and Build – principally the pressure to manage cost by managing the unresolved elements of the design (with the potential casualties being in the detail, functionality and whole life cost).

There is nothing disreputable about this: if maximum risk is passed to the contractor (and there is no denying that this arrangement is predominantly about risk transfer – and specifically about transferring the risk of that last ten per cent of the design that so frequently causes clients 90 per cent of their problems), then he has to be allowed to manage it within whatever flexibility is given by the contract. Potentially, however, the prime driver at this point becomes the ease and economy of construction, rather than the life-long purpose of the building – and it is in the latter that real value resides.

It follows that the critical requirement for a successful project (from the client's point of view) is a fully comprehensive set of requirements – drawings and specification, completed before novation as the basis of the contract sum. Exactly how this would work on a specific project can only be established by working through a design, procurement and construction programme in considerable detail. It may be that by the time a limited package of advance works is complete, the great majority of the rest of the works (say 70–80 per cent of the total project value) can have been designed and procured. If, however, the time required for design and procurement means that there is an extended period within which work is progressing on site, but it is not practical to agree a lump sum with the contractor, then the principle of negotiating a lump sum becomes less and less attractive. It is also likely to mean that there is a fairly large margin of detailed design still to complete at the point at which it would otherwise be attractive to enter into a lump sum contract, and then all of the problems of a loss of control over final quality and detail kick in – as for the basic Design and Build option.

The crux is therefore to balance the risk of the completion of the design being unsatisfactory with the risk of proceeding without the benefit of a secure contract sum – all against the pressures of a constrained programme (and, almost invariably, an equally constrained budget). Working out where this balance occurs is critical to success.

Novation

For the design team, one of the principal issues that will arise under a two-stage Design and Build arrangement, or any variant of it, is the presumption that they will be 'novated' to the contractor – which probably now happens in about half of all Design and Build contracts. Novation is essentially a tripartite agreement by which the contractor takes over the appointment of the consultants who had previously been acting for the client. Its terms will vary from project to project (and lawyer to lawyer), but it will normally provide for the client to be discharged of any continuing obligations to the consultants, whilst the consultants' obligations to the client are picked up by the contractor, and for the settlement of any outstanding fees and an agreement in respect of future fees. In addition, and in spite of a major attraction to the client being that oft-quoted 'one backside to kick', it will probably require the consultant to enter into a collateral warranty to the client, offering a continuance of a duty of care as if still appointed by him. Well, who would not go for belt and braces if both are on offer?

As a still further complication, the client no longer has a team of his own post novation – generally apart from the quantity surveyor, who will stay in direct employment to carry out the administrative functions of the contract as the employer's agent. Recognising this, the client may choose to retain exactly the same consultants under a new and separate appointment to continue to provide him with advice on the completion of the design, the contemplation of changes, and the quality of execution of the work.

Now lawyers would probably say that only architects or engineers with a death wish would put themselves in the predicament in which they owe parallel duties of care, in respect of the same matter, to two parties with quite different interests. And they would probably be right (although, on another day, they would be advising the client to put the consultants in just that predicament).

They might also say that only clients with a death wish would hand over control of the completion of a design with capacity to create or destroy value to a contractor whose interest in the project will extend only over a year or three, and that only contractors with a death wish would take responsibility for work, possibly by a designer that they have never previously met (and with an uncertain remedy against people with uncertain assets), without having been in control – or possibly even present – when that work was done.

It would be glib to say that there is at least a balanced distribution of risk here. The fact is that, contrary to the usual perception of Design and Build and its variants, there is a lot of risk – and novation probably creates as many risks as it redresses. It follows that time needs to be allowed for all involved to appraise their risk position (particularly a contractor who is asked to adopt a design developed before his involvement). Where the system is used successfully (and it is used successfully on a fairly routine basis by some clients), the critical observation is that it tends to be by clients who work regularly in this way, and who are working with people with whom they have developed successful long-term relationships. There is therefore unlikely to be a clash of personalities (for example, a contractor who is reluctant to accept the design consultants under a novation agreement); and the repeat buying power of the client will encourage all of those involved to try and solve problems rather than capitalise upon them. It follows that the further from this reasonably settled arrangement any proposition for novation might be, the more caution there should be in considering and executing it.

Partnering
At the time of writing, it is impossible to expound on the subject of procurement without reference to partnering. This term is being used to describe a host of arrangements, but all have in common the conviction that parties working together are more likely to produce the desired outcome than parties who are in confrontation or conflict. It is not difficult to agree with this – indeed, it never has been. With this agreed, though, there is then a wide range of ways in which different clients move forward. Some (and some of the most successful ones) simply work regularly with people that they find perform well for them, and do so without any formal arrangement beyond agreements relating to each separate project. Others proceed to a more strategic arrangement, with formal framework agreements that cover the basis upon which they will work with a panel of appointed firms over a whole programme of projects.

Whether written or unwritten, though, most of these arrangements will be woven around the qualities considered key to a successful partnering arrangement, which are:

- the creation of an integrated team with clearly understood, shared objectives;
- the maximum opportunity for all who are involved to make a productive contribution to the development process;
- an appropriate sharing of risk and reward;
- a commitment to continuous improvement – and, as a corollary, the measurement of performance;
- a means of resolving disputes, or potential disputes, that is as quick and constructive as it can be;

- a desire to spread these principles as far as possible up and down the supply chain – and too many companies reveal a lack of real belief in partnering by being anxious to partner with their customers (seeing it, perhaps, as shelter from the chill wind of competition) but reluctant to do so with their suppliers or subcontractors.

There are some who would take this further, and say that an essential component of partnering is the absence of any form of competitive tendering anywhere along the supply chain, and the substitution with a transparent process conducted within the context of a target price. Target pricing (setting the price for which each component and element of the building needs to be completed to meet the overall target cost) is, indeed, implicit in cost planning. There is, however, nothing specifically wrong with the operation of competition – and, indeed, the movement of prices following the deregulation of the previously nationalised utilities illustrates that there can be clear benefits. What does not work though is to ask a vague question of the marketplace, fail to provide adequate or timely information to make the requirement clear enough for delivery, and then seek to hold the contractor to a bargain which only he is required to keep. This characterises the worst kind of conflict that has dogged the industry, and it represents waste.

Where, however, the requirement is clear, and will not change, and the client and his agent are able to keep to their side of the bargain, then there is nothing wrong in putting that requirement to the market and asking for a price. Entering into alternative arrangements which make the development of the price itself a more collaborative effort will then be available at the option of those who regularly go into the marketplace for construction work, and who are therefore able to leverage their buying power and take advantage of long-term relationships with those who provide them with good service (and good prices). For them, benchmarking substitutes for the competitive tendering process in ensuring that complacency has not crept into the arrangement to a degree that has undermined competitiveness.

Summary
In summary, there is an almost infinite set of variants of the basic set of procurement options, to meet an almost infinite set of project circumstances and client criteria. The key decisions, though, relate to:

- whether there should be split or single responsibility for design and construction;
- if there is to be single responsibility, the point at which that should be fixed;
- the extent to which the contract sum should be the product of competition;
- the desire for a commitment to price and/or programme – and again the point at which this commitment should be given.

Although there can be no hard and fast values, Table 4 gives the general character of the basic procurement options by reference to these and other key issues.

Table 4 Relative strengths of alternative procurement routes

Selection criteria	Traditional lump-sum	Two-stage traditional	Construction management	Management contracting	Design and Build	Develop and Construct
Price certainty before commitment to build	5	2	1	1	5	4
Lowest construction cost	4	3	2	2	5	4
Programme commitment from contractor before entering contract	5	4	1	1	5	4
Shortest overall programme (inception to completion)	2	4	5	4	3	4
Control over design and materials	5	5	5	5	2	4
Control over choice of trade contractors and sub-contractors	2	3	5	4	1	3
Input (during design) from contractor on programming and buildability	1	3	5	5	2	3

Key:
5 = achieves criterion very well;
3 = achieves criterion to an acceptable level;
1 = does not achieve criterion.

Table 4 Relative strengths of alternative procurement routes – *continued*

Selection criteria	Traditional lump-sum	Two-stage traditional	Construction management	Management contracting	Design and Build	Develop and Construct
Control over programming/on site	2	2	5	5	1	1
Single point of responsibility for design and construct	1	1	1	1	5	4
Direct contractual relationship between employer and designers	5	5	5	5	1	3
Liquidated damages recoverable from contractor is he completes late	5	5	1	1	5	5
Ability to introduce and accommodate changes at controlled cost	4	4	5	5	2	2
Suitability for complex design	3	3	5	5	2	3

Key:
5 = achieves criterion very well;
3 = achieves criterion to an acceptable level;
1 = does not achieve criterion.

Source: adapted from table in *BCO Guide 2000: Best Practice in the Specification for Offices.*

Post-contract cost management

If we have learnt one thing, it is that there is no standard format in which post-contract cost reports should be presented to the client – and the most important thing is that the client receives the information in a way that is clear to him, and that it then fits as seamlessly as possible into his own internal reporting procedures.

In addition, what has to be tracked during the post-contract stage and the amount of detail that is necessary will depend upon the contractual arrangement, and the grounds upon which the costs for the work might need to be adjusted.

In general, however, cost reports should comprise three blocks of information:

- The benchmark against which changes are to be reported. This may be a fixed contract sum, if the project is being procured on a more traditional basis, or it may be a cost plan progressively replaced by tenders. Clients do, however, get understandably nervous if the benchmark itself changes, so it should be a comparatively settled figure – subject only to approved changes to the budget where the client has requested and agreed changes to the scope of work.
- The current status of costs against the benchmark, showing orders placed and variations instructed.
- Further changes which, although not instructed, are anticipated. This need to look ahead, and to give early warning, is perhaps one of the weakest areas of reporting, and an area where clients experience particular frustration.

As in the cost planning stage, movement in cost by comparison with the net budget will normally be balanced by a compensating adjustment to the contingency allowances – and this is probably a good point about which to say something about contingencies.

Clients do not like contingency sums. They believe that, if there is a contingency, then the design team will try to spend it – and probably succeed. The fact is, however, that there are almost always contingent events occurring in construction projects, every one of which represents a prototype with a host of variables, and these need to be budgeted for. The contingency sum is the usual way of doing that. Other clients, whilst they acknowledge this, prefer to keep a contingency in their own sock, in an amount undeclared to the design team. Whilst it may indeed be prudent for clients to keep a development contingency which is undeclared (including to the quantity surveyor), there are two good reasons why there should be a margin for contingency published in the project budget.

The first is that, because the team knows that contingent events are unavoidable, and that the client must therefore have a contingency, they may actually assume it is more than it is, and in either event will believe that managing the budget against that contingency has become a job for the client. They certainly will not believe that the figure net of contingencies is the 'real' budget.

Secondly, project teams should be expected to work to targets, and they should get their satisfaction from delivering projects in accordance with the functional specification, budget and programme agreed with the client at the outset. Completing within a cost which includes a reasoned and reasonable contingency should therefore be deemed a success – and the team should be encouraged to work with that objective in mind, and be allowed to celebrate doing so. It is a genuinely difficult thing for a project team to hit these targets, in an environment where there are many variables over which they have no direct control; and whilst it is some comfort to know that a client is not distressed by over-reaching a tight budget by a few per cent, it is not nearly as good for the soul as knowing that the job was genuinely finished for no more than the target cost.

The other aspect of contingency management that can cause tension during the post-contract stage is the point at which it is judged that the contingency is no longer adequate. Clearly, if the contingency sum is an arbitrary figure (and exactly why contract contingencies are so frequently three per cent is lost in the mists of time – but it clearly is arbitrary), there can be no scientific basis for making such adjustments. It cannot, however, make sense to draw down a disproportionate amount of the contingency in the very earliest stages of the contract, perhaps because of encountering bad ground, so that with say just ten per cent of the contract duration expired and ten per cent of the contract value expended, significantly more than ten per cent of the contingency sum has been eroded. In the absence of a proper basis for the evaluation of contingencies, therefore, I would say that the method of management should be as arbitrary as the method of establishing the sum in the first place – and that if three per cent of contract value has some logic at commencement, then the contingency should be maintained at three per cent of the outstanding expenditure, month on month. To act on this, and potentially report on extra when there is a significant amount of contingency sum left does, as noted, frequently lead to tension – but is also has the beneficial effect of serving up an early (if rather brutal) warning, and provides an opportunity of taking corrective action whilst there might still be time and scope to do it.

Avoiding this fairly crude approach to contingency management is therefore one more benefit of risk analysis. If the contingency sum is the product of a series of allowances made against specific risks, then it makes sense to release each part of the contingency when (and only when) the risk it is intended to provide for is safely in the past. In this context, contingency management is an automatic consequence of proper risk management.

Epilogue

There is a great deal of process in all of this. Following the *Rethinking Construction* report produced under the leadership of Sir John Egan, and the proper attempt to learn relevant lessons from other industries, there is a new concentration on process – and certainly, in an industry that tended to make things up as it went along, the application of logic and order could only be an improvement. Process is not, however, an end unto itself, and on its own it does not create (or necessarily even lead to) value for money. It does that only if it is regarded as a framework for *thought*.

In developed, knowledge-based economies, it is only in the quality of their thoughts that individual companies can differentiate themselves from others operating in the same market. In commercial office developments, therefore, the thought needs to extend from developers and investors (researching the needs of occupiers and the best possible ways of meeting them), through designers (looking at a proper balance between the quantum and quality of space, to maximise the developer's return whilst still meeting the need of his customers), to quantity surveyors (looking at the best way of taking the client into the market and managing the commercial relationships between the parties), to constructors (looking at the ease and economy of construction, without compromise of long-term use, and managing the supply chain to deliver). Value is therefore a chain, with all parties involved in the process seeking continuous improvement not only in the way that they do things, but also in the way they can create value for others in the chain. This is the very essence of an efficient market.

To revert to the quotation by Warren Buffett that heads this chapter, price is certainly what you pay, come what may; but only if all of the parties play their full part in doing what they do well will value truly be what you get.

Getting it right – a checklist for clients:

- Set clear, realistic objectives in respect of product, price and programme.
- Agree and publish criteria for value for money.
- Assemble the people with the best mix of skills and experience.
- Establish a project management regime with clear lines of authority, responsibility and communication, and with all team members fully aware of each other's roles.
- Invest time and effort in melding all of those appointed into a team, and establish a positive project culture.
- Recognise the importance of client leadership, and provide it.
- Set clear points at which the design is signed off as acceptable, so that subsequent work can proceed without backtracking.
- Insist on detail in cost reporting, and on all team members understanding and buying into cost targets.
- Submit the project to both benchmarking and value analysis and play a full part in the latter.
- Take time to consider the preferred procurement route by reference to clear criteria, the ability to manage risk and the constraints of programme.
- Be realistic about contingencies, and make the team responsible for managing them.

Author profile

Paul Morrell, Senior Partner
Davis Langdon & Everest

Paul Morrell is Senior Partner of Davis Langdon & Everest, where he has worked since graduating from Reading University in 1971. He is a Commissioner on the Commission for Architecture and the Built Environment, Fellow of the Royal Institution of Chartered Surveyors, an Honorary Fellow of the Royal Institute of British Architects, a Vice President of the British Council for Offices, and a member of the Construction Committee of the British Property Federation – where he also chairs the sustainability group.

For the last 25 years, Paul has worked principally in the commercial property sector, working in particular with Stanhope (Stockley Park, the ITN Headquarters, Garrard House, and many others); Greycoat (Brittanic House, 99 Gresham Street and Moor House); and Hammerson (99 Bishopsgate and Globe House).

Davis Langdon & Everest is an international firm of cost and project management consultants. In all that they do, they seek to focus on value rather than cost, and on the real objectives of the client rather than standard solutions. This leads to a constantly renewed source of ideas for the advancement of affordable office design, as displayed in projects such as

40 Grosvenor Place for Grosvenor;
Chiswick Park for CPUT, with Stanhope as Development Manager;
1 London Wall for Hammerson/Kajima.

Data gathered from the full depth and breadth of the firm's experience in commercial office development is then used as a benchmark against which to test creative development proposals for value.

5 Legal

Ann Wright, Penny Moore and James Madden
Nabarro Nathanson

Site procurement: steps to be taken prior to exchange of contracts

Background

Once a contract for the sale and purchase of land has been exchanged (and this does actually mean the swap of identical versions of the contract signed by each party), a binding commitment to sell and purchase the land is created subject only to the satisfaction of any conditions to completion which are expressed in the contract.

The second before exchange either party can withdraw, whereas the second after exchange both parties are committed. The time of exchange is documented formally by lawyers. The lawyers usually exchange contracts over the telephone and the Law Society lays down strict rules to which solicitors must adhere.

Consequently, the purchaser needs to be absolutely satisfied that they understand all of the legal aspects of the property and that all risks are identified and dealt with before exchange of contracts. This is perhaps particularly important when a site is going to be redeveloped.

Planning conditions

It is quite common for contracts for the sale of development sites to be conditional on receipt by the developer of a satisfactory planning permission. The landowner could insist on an unconditional contract but this would be unsatisfactory for the developer. First, the developer is at risk that planning permission might not be granted. Second, if contracts have not been exchanged, the developer is at risk of having obtained planning permission for the benefit of the landowner who may then seek to renegotiate the price or sell elsewhere.

The details of planning conditions to the contract are usually very complex. A developer will wish to have an absolute discretion over whether the terms of the planning permission are acceptable. The landowner will resist this because, in essence, it will create an option for the developer – giving the developer an option to withdraw on receipt of what is ostensibly an entirely satisfactory planning permission.

The parties will, therefore, have to agree in considerable detail which likely terms are to be acceptable and which will allow the developer to withdraw. This can be a very lengthy process. There is also an element of speculation involved because neither the landowner nor the developer can fully anticipate the likely requirements of the planning authority, and terms and conditions may be imposed in the planning permission which were unforeseen by either party. Once granted, the planning permission is only beyond challenge after a period of three months. In this period, the planning permission can be made the subject of a judicial review which challenges the process and basis on which the permission has been granted.

Title

Copies of the landowner's title documents will need to be produced ('deduced') to the developer's solicitor. Quite frequently a development site has been assembled and will actually consist of a number of titles brought together by the landowner over a period of time. Site assembly is complex. The lawyers, surveyors and other consultants need to be sure that all of the parts of the jigsaw puzzle, which comprise the title, fit together without any gaps, and allow the development to take place.

Boundaries

Moreover, the lawyers will need to be certain that all of the boundaries abut public highways, allowing access to the site. In some instances, access is not directly onto a public highway but via private roads or other rights of way. This can be extremely troublesome for development sites. A developer would need to be absolutely certain that the rights granted for the development site over any private roads are sufficiently clearly drawn to enable what is likely to be a significant increase in use. It is not unusual for the local planning authority to insist on the upgrading of roads as part of the development and in those circumstances, the local Highways Authority will usually agree to bring the roads under their control ('adopt' the roads).

Restrictive covenants

The title will need to be checked also to ensure that there are no obligations affecting the site ('restrictive covenants') which prevent the planned development and use of the site. Over time, a site can become burdened with obligations restricting its use, for example, for housing only or preventing certain trades. If these obligations have been imposed some time ago, the chance of enforcement becomes more remote. However, the fact that the obligations are ancient will be immaterial if, for example, the site is within a residential area which has a residential use only covenant and is proposed to be developed for offices. The adjoining home owners with the benefit of the covenant will be entitled to enforce that covenant. It is only where, say, the change of use to offices has occurred some time ago, and everyone has accepted that change, that enforcement becomes unlikely. Insurance is available to protect developers where enforcement is remote but remains a slight possibility. Insurance will generally not be available if it is clear that the development will constitute the first breach of the covenant, no matter how old.

Environmental due diligence

As a result of the introduction of new environmental legislation over the last ten years, it has become increasingly common for anyone considering acquiring an interest (whether freehold or leasehold) in a new property to undertake environmental due diligence. Concerns about potential environmental liabilities have been fuelled by the fact that there are circumstances in which owners and occupiers of land (including tenants) can become liable for the consequences of contamination which they did not originally cause.

The issues become particularly relevant in relation to sites which are being redeveloped. This is because the planning authorities are generally now required to be satisfied that a site will be 'fit' in environmental terms for its proposed use. Conditions requiring that the environmental status of a site be investigated and all necessary remediation works carried out are now commonly attached to planning consents.

The extent of due diligence to be undertaken will vary from case to case. However, a common starting point is to commission research into the historical uses of the site and its environmental setting. This may be commissioned from a search company or, more commonly in the case of redevelopments, from an environmental consultant who will also visit the site and provide an initial analysis of the level of risk associated with it. If this initial level of due diligence (known as a 'Phase I investigation') reveals potential issues of concern, the consultant is likely to recommend a further level of due diligence which involves intrusive investigations and the undertaking of an analysis of samples of soil and groundwater – this is known as a Phase II investigation.

If the results of the Phase I and Phase II investigations suggest that remediation work is going to need to be carried out, it is important to the tenant that the developer is required to procure the carrying out of those works to the satisfaction of the various environmental authorities. Additionally, consideration may be given by the parties to include express provisions in the lease of the completed development regarding responsibility for any residual risks arising from historical contamination of the site.

Rights of light

Part of the legal due diligence prior to exchange will be to identify rights of light. Neighbouring buildings may have rights over the development site to prevent the latter being built in a way which would diminish the light to existing buildings. The law relating to rights of light is very complex. Once areas of concern have been identified by the lawyer, specialist rights of light surveyors will be called upon to survey the site and identify areas within the site which are affected and also the relevant height restrictions. These specialist surveyors will also be responsible for seeking to agree compensation with the owners of affected buildings in order for the development to proceed.

Searches and enquiries

Enquiries of the landowner

The lawyer for the developer will raise detailed questions about the use of the land.

It will be important to establish that the land is not subject to ('encumbered by') third party interests such as leases, rights of way granted to adjoining owners, or any other arrangements whether formal or informal which would prevent the landowner selling the land unoccupied ('with vacant possession').

The landowner will also have to disclose any disputes relating to the land, any notices which the landowner has served or received, and the tax status of the land.

Local authority search

A search is made at the local authority. This search will (among other things) identify:

- the roads which are public highways;
- whether the drainage system is also maintained at public expense;
- whether there are any compulsory purchase orders relating to the property;
- whether there are any tree preservation orders affecting the property;
- whether any rights of light notices (notices from adjoining owners to preserve their rights of light – see above) are registered;
- the planning status of the property and its planning history.

Commons search

A search is also made of the Commons Registry. Common land is owned by the Crown and the commons search is the only way to establish that ownership. Clearly, any part of the development site which is 'common land' cannot be sold or developed.

Other searches

Depending on the area, the lawyer will also carry out more unusual searches, such as:

Chancel repair search: This is a liability imposed on landowners adjoining a church for the cost of the upkeep of its chancel. Historic as this is, the liability does continue.

Coal search: This search will reveal areas where there have been workings, any proposals to re-open the workings, and any restrictions on building over those workings.

Statutory bodies: The lawyer for the developer will also write to the water, gas and electricity statutory bodies for the area (plus the river authority, if relevant) to establish the route of the relevant services and any restrictions on moving/building over those services.

Transferring ownership

Exchange of contracts does create a binding commitment to buy and sell. However, actual transfer of legal ownership ('completion') does not necessarily take place simultaneously with exchange, although it can do.

The landowner may wish to delay completion until practical completion of the works to be carried out on the development site. This is quite common with local authorities where the 'price' for the land can include a commitment to complete works on the development site – for example, completion of a residential element on a commercial development site. Consequently, the developer will be given permission ('licence') to occupy the development site until completion.

It is also quite common for a developer never to acquire a site. The developer will contract with the landowner to carry out the works but will require the landowner to transfer ownership to an ultimate purchaser who will have provided funds to ('forward fund') the developer to enable him to carry out the works.

Tax

The principal taxes on land transactions are VAT and stamp duty. The developer will have paid VAT on all its construction costs and usually will charge VAT on the rent to be paid under the head. Stamp duty is paid on the legal documentation for both the transfer of the land to the developer and the lease granted to the tenant – and is now a significant cost.

Due diligence checklist

Title

- Does the title jigsaw fit together?
- Are there any restrictions against use?
- Are there any rights enjoyed by others?

Enquiries

- Is the landowner in dispute with a third party?
- Has the landowner served or received notices?
- Will VAT be payable?

Searches

- Land registry.
- Local authority.
- Planning history.
- Common land.
- Water, gas, electricity.
- Chancel repair.
- River authority.
- Coal.

Letting and leasing arrangements: the Agreement for Lease

Background

Put simply, the Agreement for Lease sets out all of the legal obligations of the principals ('parties') to the Agreement. The prospective landlord and the tenant will each be a party. However, if the works to the building are being carried out by a developer then the developer may be also party to the Agreement to assume full responsibility for those works and the landlord will only be a party for the purposes of granting the lease as the landowner.

For a tenant, this arrangement can be problematic. The developer will seek to be released from liability under the Agreement at the earliest possible point; usually after the defects liability period under the building contract. The landlord will resist any effort to impose any liability on it.

Define works being undertaken

It is crucial that the Agreement defines very clearly the works which are being undertaken at the building; usually by reference to plans and a specification.

On a practical note, if the plans and specification are cumbersome, it is preferable to have detailed references incorporated into the Agreement but for the Agreement to provide that full copies are held either on site or elsewhere.

It seems obvious to say that the Agreement must provide for a start and end date for the works and deal with the impact of delays. However, the start date frequently will be conditional on, for example, receipt of planning permission and the end date will certainly be subject to force majeure – this means matters beyond the control of the landlord, usually thus entitling the contractor under the building contract to an extension of time for example, delays in sourcing materials), or delays caused because the tenant has requested changes in the works.

The impact of delays will also need to be addressed. The developer is usually allowed a margin of delay without there being any recourse by the tenant. Significant delays are usually dealt with by payment of liquidated damages (a pre-agreed estimate of the cost to the tenant of delays) rather than allowing the tenant to terminate the Agreement. Only extremely long delays (likely to be delays resulting in the programme timetable being at least doubled) would allow a tenant to terminate the Agreement.

Changes made by the landlord

The Agreement will address which changes the developer (or the landlord if building the offices itself) can carry out freely and those which will require the tenant's permission. The developer will be anxious to ensure that it can substitute materials and make minor changes freely. A tenant will, of course, be equally anxious to ensure that no changes affect the tenant's ability to occupy the offices as it plans and also may have concerns about changes in colour or design which might impact on its corporate image. The extent to which the tenant will wish to be involved in changes does depend on the nature of its business and each case has to be looked at individually.

Tenant's works

In many cases, tenants prefer to take the office space when it has been completed to Category A (basically meaning built but not fitted out in any manner) and then to instruct its own contractors to carry out a full fit out. The advantage is that the tenant has control over the detail of the fit out and the timetable. There are, however, significant cost savings to be had if one building contractor carries out all the work to the space. Sometimes agreements attempt to provide for 'co-working' by the landlord's contractor simultaneously with the tenant's contractor. It is virtually impossible for the Agreement for Lease, however, to regulate this situation, particularly bearing in mind that the Agreement is entered into long before this situation actually occurs and a prescriptive language usually fetters successful arrangements. It is often best for the Agreement either to be silent on the point – leaving it for the landlord and tenant to work out any opportunity to achieve simultaneous working on a practical basis – or for the Agreement simply to acknowledge that the parties will try to work towards this goal.

UK leases usually contain stringent controls on tenant's works. Leases will not allow a tenant to carry out structural and external alterations or alterations to the mechanical and electrical systems. Tenants usually need consent even for non-structural alterations unless they can be removed easily and without damage, such as demountable partitions. Tenants do try to negotiate a more flexible regime, but largely this is resisted.

Procedure for certifying practical completion

Certification of practical completion is, or should be, of concern to the tenant. Tenants should be given the right to notification that the offices are to be inspected with a view to certifying practical completion. The tenant should be entitled to be present at that inspection and to give their views ('make representations'). Properly negotiated agreements will require the landlord to take into account the tenant's comments; if necessary postponing the certification until the issues raised by the tenant have been resolved.

Grant of Lease

At the very core of the Agreement for Lease is the arrangement for the grant of the lease itself. The tenant will usually be required to complete the lease with the landlord very shortly after practical completion has been certified. Some landlords will not grant the lease until the tenant's works have been completed, regarding this as an incentive to the tenant to complete the fit out works quickly and under the close supervision of the landlord.

Dispute resolution

The landlord will try to keep disputes to a minimum by giving the tenant little opportunity to object. The landlord will seek to avoid the need for a dispute resolution by providing that whoever is to certify practical completion, whether the architect or employer's representative, will have a duty of care through the tenant, inviting the tenant to accept that the certification will be dealt with fairly. In significant agreements the landlord may agree references to an expert, but this is relatively rare.

The lease

The lease regulates the relationship between the landlord and tenant throughout the period ('term') of the lease, but in the first few years there will be a number of provisions which are essentially carried forward from the Agreement for Lease. This is not an exhaustive review of lease terms.

Defects

Traditionally, tenants assume full repairing responsibility for their office space and shared responsibility with other tenants for the exterior and the common parts. The tenant's responsibility will be either direct or through the service charge where the landlord will carry out work him- or herself, and re-charge the cost to all of the tenants in the building.

Landlords will strongly resist any attempt by the tenant to make the landlord responsible for remedying defects. The landlord's argument will be that tenants should pursue their rights under their warranties (if any) against the landlord's building contractor and professional team. If a developer has carried out works then generally the landlord will not accept liability. However, this imposes enormous burdens on the tenant, bearing in mind that the tenant has probably had little real opportunity to review the works when they were undertaken and will, at best, have had a right to make representations on the inspection before practical completion. It is important, therefore, that tenants fight hard to be absolved from liability in meeting the cost of defects, particularly through the service charge. Clearly the bargaining strengths of the parties will be significant.

Consequently, the tenant will need to ensure that liability for defects is excluded both from its repairing liability in relation to the space it occupies and also from its liability to contribute towards the service charge.

It is unlikely that the landlord will accept this arrangement for the life of the lease and usually tenants will only succeed in having this protection for a limited period, say, the first three or five years of the period of the lease. Hopefully, by the end of that period, any significant defects which would involve the tenant in major cost will have been identified.

Rent review

The provisions for the review of the rent in the lease will also need to track the works that have been carried out at the building. The landlord will want to receive rent based on the space as completed by it. The tenant will want to ensure that any works it has paid for will not enhance the rent.

Reinstatement

Finally, the reinstatement obligations – meaning the obligations that the tenant assumes to put the space back in its original state and condition at the end of the lease – also need to track the initial (as well as subsequent) fit out works. Clearly, the tenant should not assume liability for reinstatement for works carried out by the landlord. Reinstatement is a concept relatively unique to UK leases. Tenants in other jurisdictions are not usually required to assume such a significant burden. The landlord's argument is that if a tenant wants the ability to change its space, that is the tenant's choice and the landlord should be entitled to have the space back as originally given. The tenant's argument is that it is paying for the use of the space for the period of the lease and the rent reflects the fact that the space will be used and worn out over the period of the lease. The very last thing a tenant wishes to address on relocating, is arranging a complete reinstatement of the old space. Consequently, reinstatement generally becomes a matter of negotiation of a price. Tenants are beginning to win this argument. Some leases absolve tenants from any liability for reinstatement. Some leases set out a fee or a formula for the calculation of a fee to be paid by a tenant in lieu of any reinstatement obligations.

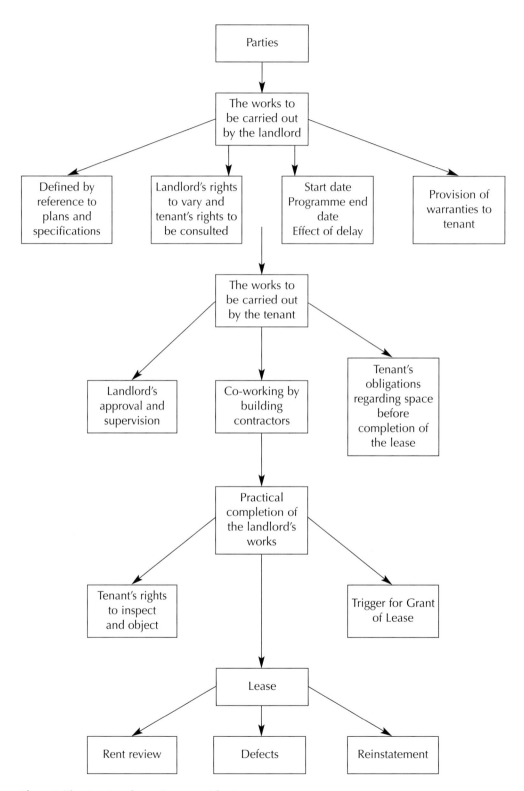

Figure 1: The structure for an Agreement for Lease

Construction

The occupier (whether as tenant or owner of the building) has now either acquired the land on which the new office will be built or the landlord or developer has handed over the keys to what may be just the shell of the new space. What happens next?

The first and fairly obvious point is that given most commercial space requirements are time driven, the occupier should be thinking ahead and co-ordinating fitting out intentions in good time before actually being in a position to start work. Others have written in this book of the many architectural, engineering and other considerations that need to be borne in mind during this preparatory period. This section of the book is to discuss the contractual ways in which these intentions can be turned into a reality, and the factors that an occupier must have in mind as to the different ways in which the construction team working on the new building or fitting out works can be structured, and the steps which need to be taken to protect the occupier, just in case it all goes wrong. Everyone starts a project with a rosy perspective and no intention of allowing disputes to arise; the design team and contractors are confident there will be no problem with the completed building, so why worry about legal documents? The thing about legal documents in this context, whether they are building contracts, appointments or any other ancillary documents, is that the best approach is to achieve documents that set out what both parties expect, and then to put them in a desk drawer with every hope that the parties will never need to rely upon them in a dispute context. The aim is to show clearly what services the client expects to receive, and how much and when he will be paying for such services. Clarity is in everyone's interests.

Base building/fit out interface

Aside of the many technical issues that must be taken into account in ensuring the proper interface of the base building works and the fit out, there may be issues of day-to-day working. If the timetable is tight, the occupier may wish to allow parallel working by the base building contractor and the fit out contractor. Although this has the potential to reduce the programme, there are many co-ordination issues involved in having two contractors working on site at the same time, and a clear working plan is needed to deal with access arrangements, delivery times, use of hoists, etc. A sensible working relationship between the two contractors is required, to avoid each claiming that its works are being disrupted by the other.

Procurement methods

Construction works can be procured in a variety of ways, of which the most common examples in the present market are 'design and build', 'construction management' or a more traditional route. The initial difference between these lies in the number of parties with whom the client has a direct contractual relationship. The best way to describe the alternative structures is diagrammatically, with the lines indicating contracts or appointments. From this it can be seen that the client has the most direct contractual relationship under construction management, and the fewest under design and build.

Under the traditional route (Figure 2), the design consultants are responsible for preparation of the design, and the contractor for its construction. The construction management route (Figure 4) is similar save that a series of contractors are responsible for different elements of construction. The key difference with design and build

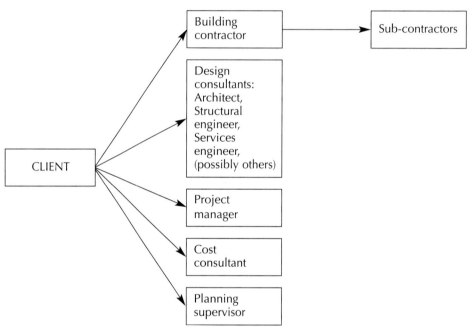

Figure 2: Traditional procurement method

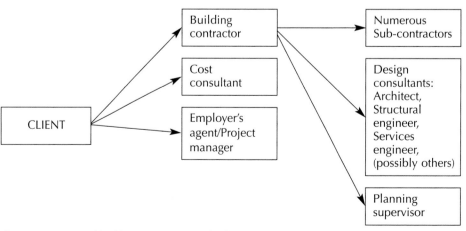

Figure 3: Design and build procurement method

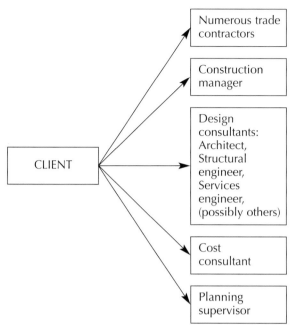

Figure 4: Construction management procurement method

contracts (Figure 3) is that where the contractor is responsible for both the design of the works and their construction, i.e. creating, in principle, a 'one stop shop' for responsibility for defects. There is also a hybrid approach where the contractor takes on design and construction liability for specified elements of the building.

Glossary

Design consultants — Refers to the architect, structural engineer, services engineer and any other consultant providing specialist design advice.

Planning supervisor — The consultant appointed under the Construction (Design and Management) Regulations 1992 with responsibility for ensuring the building is designed to be capable of safe operation and use once completed, and with responsibility for safety aspects during construction.

Project manager — This role may be handled in-house by the client, it may be combined with the cost consultant's duties or it may be a stand alone appointment.

Sub-contractors — Most contractors will pass down packages of the work to be carried out by sub-contractors, possibly due to the specialist nature of the package of works or simply due to the building contractor not having the in-house labour force to deal with the package.

Employer's agent	Under a design and build contract, the role of administering the building contract falls to the so-called employer's agent. The role is often combined with that of the cost consultant.
Construction manager	A contractor appointed to co-ordinate the trade contractors carrying out the works and to procure overall site facilities, e.g. security, scaffolding, site services, etc. but without any responsibility for constructing as part of the works.
Trade contractors	Contractors appointed by the client, each to carry out a defined aspect of the works, and likely to be fairly numerous. Many of these will, in practice, be the same companies as those acting as sub-contractors.

How to choose between procurement methods

Each of the three structures shown above have different advantages. The traditional structure gives a client close control over the works being undertaken, as the design development during the construction is carried out by the client's directly appointed consultants. The drawback to this is the need to complete design development before an accurate building cost can be obtained and a contractor appointed. A design and build contract enables the client to step back during the construction period, and gives the client single point responsibility (more or less) if there is a default in the works following completion, as the building contractor is responsible for both the design and the carrying out of the works. However, this gives the client less direct control over design development. Construction management enables a client to appoint trade contractors to carry out initial packages of work at a time when design of later packages of work has not been completed, or even commenced, i.e. to start work sooner, and hence presumably finish sooner. The real drawback of construction management is if things go wrong, either in terms of late completion of the works or a defect following completion, the client does not have a clear line of responsibility to a single contractor, but must identify the trade contractor who caused the delay or the defect, with the risk that each trade contractor will argue he was disrupted by another trade contractor or that the problem was, in fact, caused by another trade contractor.

The building contract

A building contract is, at heart, a fairly simple agreement setting out what the client wants built, by what date, and for what price. The complications come in trying to cover the 'what if' situations. What if the client wants to change the works he has asked for? What if there is a fire, a blizzard or a strike? What if one of the parties fails to honour its obligations or becomes insolvent? The 'what if' situations are about risk allocation, and it is in all parties' interests for terms to be agreed and clearly set out at the outset. If a building contractor knows he is being asked to take on a particular risk, he can assess and price it. The arguments tend to arise where something unexpected occurs.

Fixed price – guaranteed maximum price

Most building contracts are so called 'fixed price' contracts, that set out a price to be paid for a defined set of works. Sometimes a client requires the building contractor to use a specific sub-contractor or supplier for a particular package of works. If a price has not been obtained from the sub-contractor or supplier prior to agreeing the building contract, this element will have to be a carve-out from the fixed price. There are, however, a number of other things which could change the fixed price agreed for the defined works – if, for example, the client instructs some extra or different work that would affect the price. Also, most contracts will provide that if certain things happen to delay completion, for example the client giving late instructions, then the building contractor should be compensated for having to be on site for a longer period, which will have prolonged and so increased his site set up costs.

Some clients seek to achieve greater certainty of costing by providing for a guaranteed maximum price for the works. Even then it can only give total certainty if the client can commit to not instructing variations to the works, and if the client ensures it complies with all its own obligations promptly. A guaranteed maximum price arrangement will often be combined with passing certain risks to the building contractor, such as the risk of bad weather, delays of statutory or local authorities, strikes, etc. though each particular contract requires a negotiation about who is taking which risk, so the building contractor can assess and price each risk. Guaranteed maximum price agreements are also sometimes expressed in terms of the sharing of cost saving if the works can, in fact, be carried out for a lower figure.

Professional appointments

Each of the various consultants involved on the project will need appointment documents which, at heart, as with the building contract, are fairly simple documents defining services and fees, but again which need to cover a number of 'what if' situations. With a series of consultants involved in a project it is important for the client (and the consultants) to know who is doing what, and for the co-ordination and liaison responsibilities to be clear.

Standard forms

Many standard form building contracts and appointment documents exist, produced by bodies like the Joint Contracts Tribunal and various other professional bodies. Standard forms by their nature are not tailored for individual projects and should always be reviewed and adjusted as required for a particular set of circumstances. Also standard documents tend to reflect, to a certain extent, the interests of the drafting body and should be reviewed in such context.

Deeds of collateral warranty

Where the client is not the party appointing a particular company or firm, either because the company or firm is a sub-contractor, or because the appointing party is the original developer of the shell and core of the building, then broadly speaking the client will have no right to pursue a claim for breach of contract against such company or firm if there is a defect in the works. The client's rights will be limited to a claim in tort, which restricts their recovery, in general terms, to physical damage caused, without any consequential loss (e.g. loss of rent, trading losses, disruption) being recoverable. To enable the client to pursue claims for breach of contract, entitling it (subject to the terms of the relevant contract) to recover a broader range of losses arising from the defect, the client should seek deeds of collateral warranty from the parties with whom it does not have a direct contract or appointment. If the client is obtaining outside finance for the carrying out of the works it should anticipate the funder requiring similar protection, though since the funder will not be a party to any of the construction contracts and appointments, the list of collateral warranties required will be greater. Where extensive fitting out works are being carried out to a newly completed shell and core building, the landlord may also require deeds of collateral warranty from those of the fit out team whose design or works could adversely affect the structure, namely the building contractor and most of the design team. Taking a traditional contractual arrangement (see Figure 5), this means firstly seeking deeds of collateral warranty in favour of the client from the sub-contractors in column D and secondly seeking deeds of collateral warranty in favour of the relevant parties in column A from the parties in columns C and possibly D:

A	B	C	D
Landlord		Design consultants	
Bank	Client	Cost consultant	
Purchaser		Planning supervisor	
Tenant		Building contractor	Sub-contractors

Figure 5: Matrix of parties

A key point to remember in relation to deeds of collateral warranty is that they are intended as a confirmation of obligations set out in the underlying building contract or appointment, and therefore the recipient, i.e. the client for sub-contractor warranties and otherwise the landlord, bank, purchaser or tenant may require approval rights for, and certainly will want a copy of, such underlying document, so they know what rights they are getting via the deed of collateral warranty.

However, due diligence should also include seeking evidence of current professional indemnity insurance cover.

Decennial insurance

Decennial insurance, otherwise known as latent defects insurance, represents an alternative means of protecting the client's position in case of post-completion defects in the works. It is a single premium insurance policy, agreed prior to the commencement of works, with a deposit payable, and then formally put in place following payment of the balance of the premium on completion of the works. The insurance company will review the initial design proposals prior to commencement of the works, and appoint a monitoring surveyor to keep an eye on the works during construction, and to verify that they are fully complete before the policy is actually put in place. The policy will generally provide cover for ten years following completion of the works, though often with lesser periods of cover for certain areas of the building, e.g. flat roofs. Cover is for a specified level, which may be index linked, or may be capable of later increase to reflect increased costs by payment of a top up premium. The typical decennial insurance policy only covers the structure of the building, though additional cover may be available for mechanical and electrical plant and machinery. In today's market, cover is not usually available for fit out works, save as a bolt-on to an existing policy for the base building, and if such is the intention, the insurance company needs to be informed as early as possible in the base building period.

Decennial insurance is a damage based insurance, therefore physical damage is required before a claim can be made. The fact that a wall is not straight may be a breach of contract but it is not physical damage, and hence would not give rise to a claim. The insurance generally provides cover for repair costs only, i.e. not for any consequential losses caused by the defect. It does, however, have the advantage that it is triggered by a one off premium payable on completion, unlike professional indemnity insurance which requires continuing payment of annual premiums.

What if the works are finished late?

In the same way as if the landlord or developer is building the base building for the occupier and agrees to pay money to the occupier by way of damages for late completion, a similar position will apply as between client and building contractor on a contract either for construction of the whole building or for fitting out works. The client will, generally, in agreeing the terms of the building contract with the building contractor agree a figure, the sum of which will be payable on a daily or weekly basis in the event of late completion of the works. Such a figure must be a genuine pre-estimate by the client of the loss it may suffer if the works are finished late. It cannot be a penal figure; penalty clauses in this context are not enforceable. The contract should provide a mechanism for adjusting the completion date to reflect delays for which the contractor is not responsible, such as those caused by the client.

In the absence of such a mechanism, time will be treated as 'at large' and if a client-triggered event occurs, the contract completion date ceases to be relevant and the contractor is entitled to a reasonable period for completion. This is likely to be at least as long as the contract period originally envisaged, but leaves a lack of certainty as to when completion is required.

What about defects?

Two different situations arise here. Most building contracts provide for a so called 'defects liability period' during which the building contractor is contractually obliged to return to site and rectify the defect notified. This obligation is generally reinforced by the client holding a retention of a small percentage of the total amount payable under the building contract. This retention is released at the end of the defects liability period specified in the contract.

The other period of responsibility is that specified by statute and is the period within which a party may claim damages for breach of contract. If the contract has been executed by hand, i.e. simply signed by the parties, then a claim for breach of the terms of that contract may be brought at any time up to six years after the relevant breach of contract occurs. A different period applies if the contract has been executed as a deed, namely by attaching the common seal of the parties, by execution by two directors or by all the partners in a partnership (or those authorised to do so for the partnership) with such signatures being witnessed. In this case the period within which such claims can be brought is 12 years from the breach of contract. A rule of thumb on which a breach occurs is, generally speaking, to count from practical completion based on the team having a general duty until practical completion to rectify any problems, so it is only on handover that a breach of contract exists.

Defects checklist
If a defect does appear there are various questions to be asked and initial action to be taken. Points to be considered include:

- Does it arise from poor design or bad workmanship, or has it been either caused or exacerbated by maintenance or the lack of maintenance?
- Is the default one arising from design or workmanship?
- Who carried out the defective design or workmanship?
- Does the client have a contract/appointment or a deed of collateral warranty from such party?
- Prompt action may be required to avoid aggravating the problem, but it would be desirable to take photos, and invite the relevant parties the client believes to be responsible to inspect the defect.
- Even if urgent remedial works are required, the client must act reasonably. Try and get more than one price quote for carrying out the remedial works. If the defect is believed to be the responsibility of the contractor, the client may or may not wish

to invite the contractor believed to be responsible for the defect to rectify it. If the contractor agrees, this avoids the client paying another contractor and then having to seek recovery of the amount paid, and may protect the benefit of warranties in respect of other areas of the building by avoiding arguments as to which contractor carried out which works.

- Keep all documentation relating to investigations, repair and other costs incurred or losses suffered, and preserve samples, etc if appropriate. This documentation, along with the original construction contracts, appointments, drawings and all other site records are potential evidence which may be needed in seeking recovery of any losses.

- The pursuit of any claim for a defect is likely to be structured on the basis of failure to exercise the reasonable skill and care of a competent contractor, architect or other professional consultant and, to this end, it will be necessary to get evidence that a competent contractor, architect, etc would not have carried out the work or prepared design in that way. Early advice from an expert of the appropriate discipline as to what a competent contractor, architect, etc should have done is vital to establishing whether any claim exists.

Funding the fitting out of premises

The Agreement for Lease will either contain provisions giving the landlord's consent (by reference to plans and specifications) to a tenant's proposed fitting out or will set out a procedure for the tenant to subsequently apply for the landlord's consent, and the circumstances in which the landlord may withhold its consent to all or part of the tenant's proposals. The tenant will have employed architects, engineers and possibly also a quantity surveyor to produce plans and specifications for its fitting out works and to give an estimate of their likely cost. The next stage is to employ a contractor to carry these out.

Fitting out contract

As you will have read earlier most fitting out contracts will provide for the contractor to be paid monthly. Each month a certificate will be prepared by a contract administrator certifying the value of the works carried out during the last month. On practical completion of the works, a final account is prepared and the tenant makes the final payment for the works.

Paying for tenant's fitting out works

Before discussing the options available to a tenant, it is worth pausing for a moment and considering what – if anything – is to be paid in respect of the premises during the period in which a tenant is undertaking the fitting out works.

The Agreement for Lease will usually provide that the tenant is allowed to undertake it's fitting out works before the lease is completed. It will provide that even though the lease has not been completed, a tenant is to pay the landlord the cost of any services consumed at the premises such as electricity, water, etc. It is also not unusual to see provisions in agreements for leases providing that a tenant pays a full service charge in respect of this period, as if the lease had been completed and even though the tenant is not 'using' the full range of services. This is a situation that tenants' should try to avoid.

It is traditional for tenants to be given rent free periods to fit out the premises during which they do not pay any principal rent. The Agreement for Lease will provide that principal rent is to commence on a particular date in the future and not on the date on which the tenant commences the fitting out of the premises or completes the lease. The length of a rent free period in respect of a tenant's fitting out will vary according to the nature and cost of the works the tenant is to carry out, the rent the tenant is going to pay, the type and size of the premises. As a rule of thumb, a tenancy can usually expect a three- or six-month rent free period dependent on the state of the letting market at the time that the transaction is agreed. A tenant should ensure that it is allowed to use the premises for the use permitted by the lease as soon as its fitting out works have been completed. This way the tenant benefits if it completes its fitting out works earlier than anticipated.

Inducements

Tenants are often given inducements by landlords to agree to enter into a lease of premises because, for example, the letting market is weak, the landlord wants to achieve a particular rental level or in light of the cost of carrying out the tenant's works. This can take a variety of forms:

- **Rent free or concessionary rent period.** In addition to a rent free period purely for fitting out the premises, a tenant is often given an additional rent free period as an inducement to enter into the lease, or the landlord agrees to the tenant paying a reduced rent for a period.
- **Landlord's contribution.** Landlords will often agree to pay towards the cost of the tenant's fitting out works, particularly where the premises are not being constructed/fitted out by the landlord to Category A standard in return for the tenant taking the premises and agreeing a particular rent. In some circumstances, a landlord will even pay the majority, if not all of the costs of fitting out the premises. It is more usual, however, for the landlord to pay for specific items or elements.

A word of caution

A tenant should think about how any inducement is treated at rent review under the lease, whether the inducement is by way of a rent free period, concessionary rent period or a payment by the landlord. UK leases usually disregard the effect on rent of any rent free period granted for fitting out and of any works carried out by the tenant at their own cost. They do not commonly disregard works which are paid for by the landlord or rent free periods or concessionary rent periods which are offered as inducements. It is not uncommon for inducements of these types to increase the rent which a tenant will pay at rent review as the landlord will argue that a hypothetical tenant would pay more rent for the premises if it were receiving the inducement that the landlord gave the tenant careful drafting of the lease is required to avoid this.

Bank finance

If the landlord is not paying for the tenant's works, then the tenant will obviously have to do so. It may be in the fortunate position of having sufficient cash assets to pay the contractor's certificates as and when they fall due for payment. However, it is more likely that the tenant will pay for the fitting out works through an existing or new bank facility.

A tenant will have an overdraft or working capital facility from a bank. This will provide that he or she may borrow money from the bank for the purposes of their business within certain limits and subject to certain criteria. Before signing an Agreement for Lease, the tenant should ensure that any existing facility allows for monies to be borrowed to pay for the fitting out of the premises and that there are sufficient funds available under that facility to make the payment to the contractor as they fall due under the certificates.

If the existing facility is not sufficient or monies cannot be used to pay for fitting out works, the tenant will need to arrange a new facility. A credit or loan agreement will be entered into with a bank which will provide that the tenant may borrow monies up to a maximum amount and will set out the procedure by which the tenant may call for these monies to be paid to it (usually on three or seven days' prior written notice). In return, the bank will require a legal mortgage or fixed charge over the Agreement for Lease and lease, often with a floating charge over the assets and undertaking of the tenant. The legal mortgage/fixed charge will provide that the bank can sell or take over the lease if the tenant fails to repay the monies borrowed in the prescribed manner (usually monthly instalments, taking into account an agreed rate of interest to be paid to the bank on the money which has been borrowed) if the tenant becomes insolvent or if any of the other creditors of the tenant take any action to enforce any security that they may have for monies owed to them.

The legal mortgage/fixed charge will also provide that the bank may sell the lease to recover monies owed to it, or appoint a receiver to do so. The bank will also take a floating charge over all of the assets and undertaking of the company. Any assets or undertakings which are covered by a floating charge can be dealt with by the tenant in its ordinary course of business for so long as the tenant does not default on the terms of the facility from the bank. As soon as it does, these floating charges 'crystallise' into fixed charges, and the tenant is then unable to deal with any of the assets or undertakings concerned without the bank's consent.

Whenever taking out a new facility, a tenant should carefully check the terms of its existing facilities. These are likely to contain what are called negative pledges, agreements by the tenant not to give any security over any premises, assets or undertakings without that lender's consent. This is one of the ways that banks attempt to control the amount of borrowings or debt which a company has from time to time.

Conclusion

Many tenants do not fully understand the complex process of taking offices – especially in new buildings – nor the responsibilities they will assume in the lease. A detailed briefing at the beginning, and a properly drawn up timetable of events, often overcomes those uncertainties.

Author profiles

Ann Wright, Partner (property department)
Nabarro Nathanson

As well as heading the Offices Initiatives, a forum which develops and publishes cutting edge ideas and advice on offices, Ann Wright leads a team of 12 lawyers within the Property Department. Ann has over ten years worth of experience acting for a portfolio of high profile corporate occupiers, advising them on mergers, lettings, purchases and acquisitions, relocations and restructurings. Ann is also part of the team which is spearheading knowledge management and property streamlining corporate-wide.

Penny Moore, Partner (construction department)
Nabarro Nathanson

Penny Moore is part of the Projects Group, and acts for clients from the full range of the UK construction and development industries, funders, owners occupiers, developers, contractors, professionals and sub-contractors. Penny deals with projects ranging from shopping centres and offices, to universities, housing estates and infrastructure works. Her major clients include a range of major property companies and corporate occupiers and various local authority and other pension funds

James Madden, Partner (commercial property department)
Nabarro Nathanson

James Madden is a leading partner within the offices initiative. He undertakes investment and development work for UK and international commercial property investors, developers and lenders. He has acted on a number of high value investment portfolio sales, purchases and fundings, often for co-investors involving complex structuring and tax issues and the use of nominee companies and limited partnerships.

Nabarro Nathonson has one of the UK's largest and most active commercial property departments, handling some of the most complex and technically demanding commercial and legal challenges in the industry. During 2001, Nabarro Nathanson completed on a variety of deals worth in the regain on £10 billion.

6 Masterplanning

Guy Battle and Jane Mulcahey, Battle McCarthy
Phil Kirby and Myra Barnes, SecondSite Property Holdings Ltd

Introduction

It is a truism to say that masterplans are rarely built but without them development cannot happen. It is also true that the more detail that a masterplan contains, the more likely it is that permission will be granted, and yet, the more detail that the team commits to, the less flexibility there is to meet future changes and the less likely it is that the masterplan will be built as it was presented! This is the fine line that the developer and masterplanning team have to tread and why it remains crucially important to take time to consider all the options in the process. There are few short cuts and planning history is littered with rejected plans and developers left holding white elephants.

This chapter explains the issues that must be covered and the components that make a successful masterplan. Success is measured in the ability to deliver sustainable, long-term and economic solutions that contain sufficient flexibility to meet the changing needs of the communities that live and work in the affected area, as well as reflecting changes in occupational demands over time.

Importantly, the concept of new and emerging sustainable development is introduced and information is provided on the range of government policies that must be considered in the production of a masterplan, to ensure a holistic approach to the development, covering social, economic and environmental factors.

In addition, the role of the Environmental Impact Assessment in the masterplan process is outlined and the need for it to be an integrated part of the process from the beginning is stressed. Information on some of the risks that may need to be taken into account is also provided.

To highlight the flexibility and good design that a masterplan can provide, a case study of the Greenwich Peninsula has been included to show how the development of a masterplan can evolve and how lessons can be learnt for the future.

Figure 1: Greenwich Peninsula masterplan visualisation

What is a masterplan?

A masterplan is a grand scale overview of all the different influences, constraints and aspirations for a site, presented as a comprehensive, viable, achievable, and phased plan.

Masterplans are needed for the development of all sites, ranging from an individual building to groups of buildings, regardless of the size of the site area. In the case of a single building, attention will need to be given to factors such as the position of the building on the site, the links to the adjacent infrastructure and how the neighbouring properties will be affected. The more conventional view of a masterplan, however, is a plan produced for multiple buildings on a site that is to be developed to a phased programme (see Figure 1 and the case study at the end of the chapter).

There is always more than one solution for a site. Each individual masterplan is a view of one solution for a site at that particular time, given the circumstances that prevail at the time of its production. Alongside testing the site for its development potential and capacity under the different constraints, the purpose of the masterplan is to set out parameters, within which the development is to take place. For example, if the client wishes the site to be designed with a sustainable urban drainage system, this should be stated at the beginning of the process as such a system will have a profound effect on the design of the scheme.

The value attached to a masterplan for the development of a site and its neighbourhood is often not appreciated for its worth. Done well, the masterplan should result in the enhanced value of the site and the surrounding area. Done badly, and the area can be blighted for a considerable period. In order for a masterplan to be successful, an integrated design-led approach should be followed that embraces sustainable development criteria.

Sustainable development

Sustainable development is development which seeks to balance social, economic and environmental issues, defined in the Brundtland Report (1987)[1] as 'development that meets the needs of today without compromising the ability of future generations to meet their own needs'.

At a masterplan level, sustainable development means developing a design that maximises the inherent benefits of a site, whilst minimising any adverse impacts at all levels – social, economic and environmental (see Figure 2). In this respect,

---

1 World Commission on Environment and Development (1987), *Our common future*, Oxford, Oxford University Press.

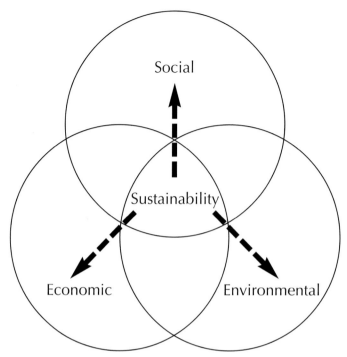

Figure 2: Integrated approach to sustainable design

sustainability should not be viewed as an 'add-on', but as an integral part of the process and to ensure that sustainable development principles are incorporated from the start, a holistic approach should be taken to ensure a good masterplan is achieved.

A metabolic process

Most of the urban environments that we inhabit today have grown organically to meet market demands. This has been a linear organic process (*see* Figure 3) and, indeed, most of the engineering systems that serve our towns are simple linear processes: input–process–output and waste. Seldom is there any real crossover between systems, the sharing of resources or utilisation of waste. For example, in a sustainable development a city's power plant would be placed near the sewage plant and the methane that is produced as a by-product of sewage processing, would be used directly to generate power and heat (where needed) for the community.

An alternative and sustainable model is one which breaks the development into a series of metabolic processes which may be integrated and linked, sharing wastes and resources to maximise efficiencies and minimise waste production (and costs). In this way the masterplan becomes a single holistic system, rather than a series of disparate parts (*see* Figure 4).

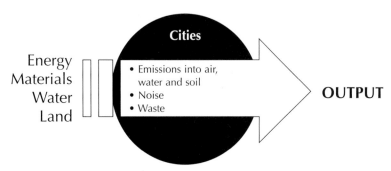

Figure 3: Linear model: inefficient and expensive to operate

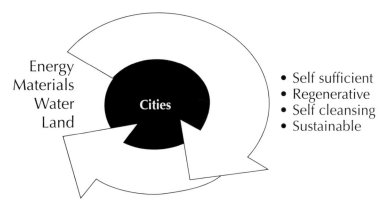

Figure 4: Circular model: better use of resources with lower running costs

A sustainable masterplan should endeavour to achieve the following:

- Produce more energy than is needed, by being climate responsive and integrating the use of renewable energy harvesting.
- Be Carbon neutral.
- Conserve, collect and store water for reuse on site.
- Should not increase the pressure on existing infrastructure.
- Promote a healthy, sustainable environment, which makes it a more attractive place to live and work.
- Enhance the natural environment and wildlife habitats and protect them from the adverse effects of development.
- Conserve and enhance those areas and features of the urban environment which contribute to the heritage, identity, sense of place and overall appearance of a city.
- Ensure that all new development is designed in such a way as to enhance the overall appearance and quality of the environment and maintain the amenities of existing residents.

- Reduce crime and the fear of crime by ensuring that all new development is designed to minimise the opportunities for criminal and anti-social activity.
- Promote the recycling of waste materials and ensure that all new development includes appropriate measures to deal with problems caused by its own waste generation and previous waste disposal activities.

Design process

But sustainable development is not easy. It often demands more time in development and it certainly demands a greater interaction between all disciplines, from the ecologist and meteorologist to the urban planner and the economist.

The Urban Task Force in their document *Rethinking Construction*[2] laid out the complexity of the process, viewing the urban planner as the conductor operating at the vortex of the design effort orchestrating individual efforts and bringing them together in an integrated and coherent manner.

Another way of describing the process was first proposed inadvertently by McHarg who described the need to create a series of layers of analysis and opportunities[3]. Each layer is optimised individually, and then placed together to form an integrated solution, with the optimum being the solution that satisfies the whole rather than a single objective.

Why you need a masterplan

A masterplan is used for a number of different purposes:

- **A tool to obtain outline planning permission for a major site.** A masterplan prepared to accompany an outline planning application needs to be sufficiently flexible to withstand a long development programme. The masterplan will provide a framework to create some certainty for the mix of uses, quantum of floor space and general design principles. It is usually best to determine maximum floor space and key aspects of the scheme, such as means of access.
- **A tool for marketing the site.** A masterplan prepared for marketing purposes will tend to follow along a similar line to that submitted for outline planning but with more visual material to indicate a vision for the site. Creating a vision is important in order to attract inward investment, generate commercial interest and help raise the profile of the site. The masterplan can also be used as a catalyst for the wider regeneration of the area.
- **Supplementary Planning Guidance by local authorities for major sites in their area.** A masterplan prepared for Supplementary Planning Guidance (SPG) is generally prepared by the council and, unfortunately, often tends to be too

---

2 Available at www.m4i.org.uk
3 McHarg, I (1995). *Design with Nature*, UK, John Wiley Europe.

prescriptive, providing unnecessary detail leading to unrealistic expectations by third parties. To be capable of implementation the SPG needs to be commercially viable and flexible so that it will withstand the fluctuations of the market over a number of years. SPGs can be very helpful where the development plan is out of date and is unlikely to be reviewed for a while. It is then possible for the local authority (LA) to adopt the SPG, which will then provide the ability to update the development plan proposals for the site in a reasonable timescale. The guidance must also be based on a scheme, which is economically viable – otherwise it is unlikely to be implemented.

Government directives

In order to ensure that developers take a responsible attitude to development, the Government has issued a number of policy documents setting out their objectives, which include:

- **Agenda 21, 1992**. An action plan for the 21st century that commits governments to work towards sustainable development, in partnership with local authorities, businesses, the voluntary sector and local communities.

- **A Better Quality of Life – a Strategy for Sustainable Development in the UK, 1999.** The strategy sets out the Government's four key objectives for sustainable development:
  – social progress which recognises the needs of everyone;
  – effective protection of the environment;
  – prudent use of natural resources;
  – and maintenance of high and stable levels of economic growth and employment.

- **A New Deal for Transport: Better for Everyone, 1998.** Sets out the Government's integrated policy for the UK and explains the need to extend choice and secure mobility in a way that supports sustainable development.

- **Building a Better Quality of Life – a Strategy for More Sustainable Construction, 2000.** The aim of the strategy is to provide a catalyst for change in construction across the UK and sets out how the Government expects the construction industry to contribute to sustainable development.

- **Climate Change the UK Programme, 2000.** The Government's strategy to address climate change and the UK's CO_2 emissions, in response to the Kyoto Protocol of 1997, the agreement that committed industrialised countries to reduce their overall emissions of greenhouse gases.

- **National Air Quality Strategy, 2000.** The strategy sets objectives for eight main air pollutants to protect health, vegetation and ecosystems and is reinforced by the air quality regulations.

- **Planning Policy.** Sustainable development principles are embodied in many of the Government Planning Policy Guidance Notes. In particular, PPG 1 General Policy and Principles, PPG 3 Housing, PPG 13 Transport, and PPG 23 Pollution and Planning Control.

- **Waste Strategy, 2000**. Sets new and challenging targets for local authorities to meet in order to reduce waste and increase recycling and reuse.
- **UK Biodiversity Action Plan, 1994**. Commits the Government to conserve and, where possible, enhance biodiversity within the UK.

Useful guidance can also be found in *Towards an Urban Renaissance*[4] – Final Report of the Urban Task Force. The report states: 'The diversity of urban neighbourhoods, means that different places will respond to pressure for change in different ways. This means that there is no blueprint for success.' However, the report goes on to say that success will be dependant upon five central principles:

- achieving design excellence;
- creating economic strength;
- taking environmental responsibility;
- investing in urban government;
- and prioritising social well-being.

The report also provides guidance on the role of the development brief, which it states should 'set out the vision for a development and ground it firmly into the physical realities of the site and its economic, social, environmental and planning context.'

Whilst much of this policy is guidance only, local authorities are asking for specific responses to the issues raised as part of their requirements for an Environmental Impact Assessment (EIA) and in determining planning applications.

The masterplan process

Introduction

In this chapter we will concentrate on the process of preparing a masterplan to obtain outline planning consent for a site, although many of the same principles will apply in developing the other options.

Stage 1: Identification of site and data collection

Identify site
Identify the area that the masterplan will cover. The site need not necessarily be confined to land ownership but should extend over the area that is to be redeveloped. It is important to ensure integration between the masterplan area and the existing urban fabric.

---

4 For further information visit www.rethinkingconstruction.org.uk

The lifespan of a masterplan continues until the landscape or development is complete or until a superseding masterplan is drawn up

project duration

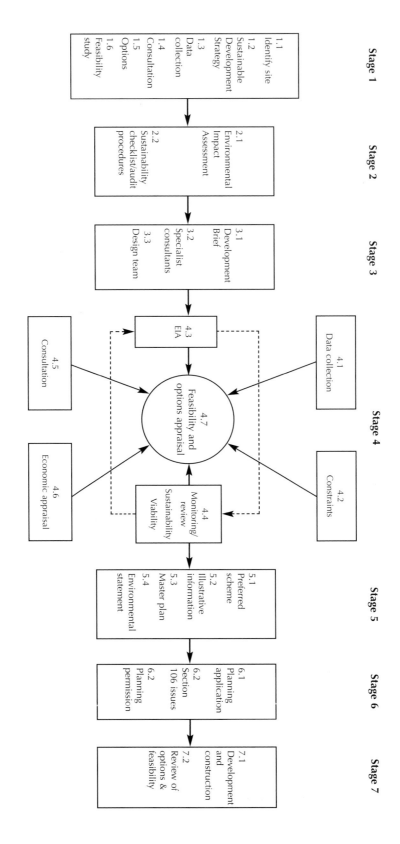

Figure 5: The Masterplan Process

Sustainable Development Strategy
In order for sustainable development to be treated as an integral part of the process, it is crucial that a Sustainable Development Strategy is produced at the beginning of the process. By putting a strategy in place, it enables the development team to focus on the key issues that need to be addressed as well as providing a useful checklist throughout the design process.

In broad terms, the strategy should cover, amongst others, the following issues:

Table 1 Sustainable Development Strategy issues

Environmental	Social	Economic
Land use	Community consultation	Employment
Transport	Community participation	Productivity
Water resources	Health and safety	Profitability
Energy	Equity	Investment
Pollution – air, land, water	Access	Risk assessment
Climate change	Amenities	Cost v. value
Ecology/biodiversity	Training	Whole life costing
Landscape	Security	Procurement
Waste management	Working conditions	Carbon trading
Materials	Education	

Data collection
Basic information needs to be assembled for an initial view on the potential uses on the site. This will need to include a consideration of title, restrictive covenants, potential disputes, planning policy: national, regional and the local development plan, together with a market appraisal to establish potential demand for different uses. Other issues to be kept in mind are future trends and changes in legislation, evidenced at any one time by the number of government green papers, consultation papers, etc. in circulation.

It is necessary to prepare a plan incorporating the positive as well as the physical constraints of the site and its surroundings, as well as future proposals for the area (tram, train lines, etc.). This will often reinforce views of the preferred uses for the site. Depending upon in-house skills available, it may be necessary to employ a planning consultant, an agent with appropriate development skills and an architect, in order to estimate the likely uses and quantum of those uses for the site. Depending on the site circumstances, you may be in a situation where a first stab at costs could be made and therefore the employment of a cost consultant may be required.

Following a risk analysis of the options, a broad brush financial appraisal should be carried out to guide on issues such as types of use, density, etc. It is important that full consideration of the financial effects of changes are undertaken before the site is discussed with the local authority, in order to react appropriately to their demands. It is in nobody's interests to produce a wonderful but unviable masterplan.

Care should be taken with regard to the terms on which you appoint external advisors as there may not be a next stage or, alternatively, it may not be considered beneficial to continue to use them, even if there is a will to proceed with the project. The agreements should, therefore, allow you to break at the end of each stage in the process and to have rights to use the work produced so far.

Consultation
(a) Local authority (LA)
An early meeting with the local authority planners is imperative, generally with both the development plan and development control departments. Such a meeting should give an idea of the policies for the site, whether there is likely to be support for the preferred uses, as well as the types of issues which are of particular concern. It is possible that even at this early stage the LA will give an indication of its 'wish list' for a Section 106 Agreement (Section 75 in Scotland), planning obligations which the LA will require as part of any planning permission.

Working with the LA is the best way to produce a masterplan, following an iterative process, usually over a period of months. Liaison will be needed with the different departments of the LA, e.g. transportation, environmental health, planning (both policy and development control), housing and education. Different LAs deal with consultation within the authority in different ways – it is therefore necessary to adopt a flexible approach to the process in order to respond to their requirements. A good relationship with the LA is invaluable; it may well save time in the long run even though it may be questioned at the time, since it may appear to be delaying the whole process. However, as long as you are working in tandem with the LA then you are likely to save time after submission of a planning application if you have managed to agree many of the points of principle prior to submission of a planning application.

(b) Community organisations
On larger and/or high profile sites in particular, it is often useful at the start of the consultation process to obtain a political audit. As a result, there is at least awareness of the kind of issues that are likely to arise during the course of the masterplan preparation. The audit should include an audit of political control within the LA, identification of key councillors, composition of committees and key concerns. The most important community and business groups in the vicinity should also be identified for consultation.

It is beneficial to obtain advice from the LA on the best means of approaching the local groups and, of those, which ones are the most influential. Direct discussion is generally the best way to proceed and is often led by the client/developer, rather than by the various consultants. The consultation process is often time consuming but is generally both informative and instructive. It should be remembered that the community groups invariably know more about the area/neighbourhood than the developer or the consultants. A good relationship with the local community will also be beneficial in the long term. This relationship needs to continue throughout the development process and can be maintained by the use of regular newsletters.

Options for site
There may be a number of options for developing the site: for single use (e.g. office park) or different mixes and proportions of uses on the site. The different options need to be set out so that they can be evaluated for both the likelihood of getting planning permission and also their financial viability. Inevitably, if there is a choice, then the most valuable mix of uses should be pursued unless there are good planning or financial reasons for not pursuing this option.

Feasibility study
At this stage in the process there will need to be some in-depth work carried out on the financial viability of the proposal, to establish whether it is worth spending the time, effort and cost of progressing further towards a masterplan and planning application. If not appointed previously, a cost consultant may need to be brought in at this stage. The time and cost for large development proposals should not be underestimated and, therefore, risk assessments covering all aspects, from political issues around the site through title issues, to an order of cost document should be undertaken. It can take from one to six years to achieve a planning permission, let alone start on site.

In assessing whether to progress, it will be necessary to have some idea whether or not the development is likely to fall within the criteria where an Environmental Impact Assessment (EIA) is required (*see* Stage 2 below). If an EIA is required, the amount of time and cost for the project (in order to achieve planning permission) will be increased significantly, especially if an EIA has not been considered from the beginning. Carrying out some preliminary costings at this early stage could prevent time and money being wasted, especially if an EIA has not been considered previously. Otherwise, discussions with the LA and community may progress along a route towards unviable aspirations, which cannot be delivered.

Stage 2: Environmental Impact Assessment

Is an Environmental Impact Assessment (EIA) required?
The importance of Environmental Impact Assessments as part of the planning process has increased considerably since 1999. EIAs are designed to describe the overall impact of a development on a site and its surrounding area from all aspects – social, economic and environmental. The EIA should be an integral part of the process. The earlier the EIA is incorporated into the process the better, so any identified issues can be assessed and provision made for them – for example, if an endangered species is located on the site.

The Town and Country Planning (Environmental Impact Assessment) (England and Wales) Regulations 1999 set out when an EIA is required. The Regulations provide a systematic method of assessing the environmental implications of developments that are likely to have significant effects.

The types of development that will need an EIA are listed in two schedules. Schedule 1 developments will always require an EIA and includes developments such as power stations and major infrastructure projects. Schedule 2 projects are developments that are likely to have significant environmental effects because of factors such as their size, nature or location; for example, an urban development project that exceeds 0.5 hectares.

In order to establish whether an EIA is required, the developer may request a 'screening opinion' from the local planning authority, before submitting a planning application. In view of the potential for a third party challenge to the planning decision, it is advised that legal advice is obtained. If there is any doubt over whether an EIA is required then it is advisable to carry out an assessment and avoid potential future cost and delay.

Having established the need to carry out an EIA, the developer may then request the local authority for a formal 'scoping opinion' to verify the information that should be included in the report of the assessment, the Environmental Statement (ES). The scoping opinion should be drawn up in consultation between the developer and the local authority, to ensure that all parties are in agreement with regard to the level of detail required. Environmental Statements can be copious and often run to several volumes.

Although the local authority may identify selective issues to be included in the EIA, generally most impacts of the development will need to be appraised, even if it is only to demonstrate that there is no impact and, therefore, dismiss the issue. It must be remembered that even if the scope of the EIA is agreed with the LA, other parties can always challenge the content. By ensuring all issues are covered, the potential for a third party challenge is minimised. It should also be noted that if there is an aggrieved party, the Human Rights Act could also be used to challenge and delay the process.

The Environmental Statement should include:

- A description of the development including site, design, and size of development.
- A description of measures to avoid, reduce and if possible compensate for or remedy significant adverse effects.
- Data required to identify and assess the main effects on the environment.
- An outline of main alternatives, studies and indications for choice.
- A non-technical summary.

The ES should be submitted with the planning application; failure to do so could result in the planning application not being registered which could, thereby, cause further delay and increased costs.

Points to note with EIA
- **The Rochdale cases**[5]. As a result of a third party challenge by the local community, a judicial review was undertaken for an outline planning permission for a proposed business park. The result of these cases has had specific implications for the EIA process:

    (a) The level of detail that should be provided in the Environmental Statement and planning application.
    (b) The possibility of a third party challenge to a planning decision has increased.

    The challenge was based on the assertion that the information provided with the outline application was inadequate to enable the application to be properly assessed. This challenge was upheld, which raised many questions over the ability to environmentally assess an outline application. Additional information was submitted to address the judge's criticisms and the application reconsidered. The revised application was also challenged and the challenge was quashed on the basis that as long as the specific proposals have conditions or obligations attached which tie down the proposals, and that any options have been specifically assessed, then outline permission can be granted.

    In summary, further information cannot be requested by way of a condition on a particular topic if this topic has been assessed as part of the ES, as it would imply that there was inadequate information to enable the proper assessment of a proposal.

    As a minimum, information on the floor space, location of uses, proposed massing, density and means of access need to be provided. Often, it will also be appropriate to provide siting of buildings. If options of buildings are provided, all of them need to be assessed.

- **Cumulative impacts.** Another requirement of the EIA process is to assess the cumulative impacts of the development. In some situations it can be very difficult to assess the cumulative impacts, for example, if there are other developments planned for an area but without any formal planning applications. It is important to ensure that careful discussions are undertaken with the local authority on the level of information that is required and that can actually be provided. It is worth referring to Paragraph 2 (1) of the 1999 regulations, which states in the definition of 'environmental statement' that it should include information 'as is reasonably required to assess the environmental effects of the development and which the

---

5 *R v Rochdale Metropolitan Borough Council ex parte (1) Tew (2) Milne (3) Garner* [2000] JPL, 54-82.

applicant can, having regard in particular to current knowledge and methods of assessment, reasonably be required to compile.'

Monitoring and review procedures
In order to ensure that sustainable development is being addressed throughout the masterplan process, monitoring and review mechanisms need to be put in place, such as a sustainability checklist or audit procedures. The checklist should be used after every revision of the masterplan (*see* Figure 6). It should be remembered that sustainability checklists and audit procedures will be used to assess the detailed design of the buildings and due regard to these should therefore be taken throughout the design process. Recognised audit procedures for use in the design development include:

- **BREEAM** – the Building Research Establishment Environmental Assessment Method, a comprehensive tool for analysing and improving the environmental performance of buildings from design through to management.
- **Ecohomes** – a flexible and independently verified environmental assessment method for residential buildings. It considers broad environmental concerns of climate change, resource use and impact on wildlife and the balance of these against the need for a high quality of life, and a safe and healthy environment.
- **Envest** – an interactive assessment tool that permits a comprehensive life cycle environment assessment. It permits tradeoffs to be made between materials performance and operational performance of the building over the full life cycle.

Further information on the above schemes can be found on the BRE web site at www.bre.co.uk

Table 2 Environmental Impact Assessment Process

Screening opinion*	To determine if EIA required (to be issued by local authority within 3 weeks of request)
Scoping opinion	To provide information on contents of ES (to be issued by local authority within 5 weeks of request)
Consultation	Statutory consultees to be consulted before scoping opinion adopted
Baseline surveys	To assess existing conditions/constraints
Environmental statement	To be submitted with planning application
Planning decision	To be made by the local authority within 16 weeks (not the usual 8)

* It is not necessary to go through this process if you have already decided to prepare an ES.

Sustainability Checklist

	Positive		Negative		Score
	major	minor	major	minor	
Resources efficient use of resources – energy and water conservation, waste minimisation, recycle materials/land/buildings					
Pollution minimise pollution of air, water, land, ecosystems					
Transport minimise the impact of the motor vehicle - encourage walking, cycling and public transport					
Land and built environment attractive and distinctive buildings and open spaces with a mix of uses for all the community					
Biodiversity protect and enhance species richness					
Employment opportunities and training for the provision of satisfying work					
Life time learning access to skills, knowledge, facilities and information needed to play a full part in society					
Enterprise provision of opportunities for local enterprise, new and existing					
Community safety reduce fear of crime for all					
Social exclusion access to facilities and services for all, address the inequalities in wealth, health, ethnicity, employment and education					
Leisure provide opportunities and facilities for all to be involved in leisure and culture activities					
Participation enable all sections of the community to be actively involved in decision making, meet local needs					

Figure 6: Sustainability checklist

Stage 3: Development brief

Produce the development brief
Production of the development brief broadly falls into two stages: information gathering and using that information to lay down the parameters for the development of the masterplan.

Initially, a plan needs to be prepared which incorporates all the physical constraints on the site and identifies the opportunities and problems presented. Armed with this, and the information already produced on title, political influences and local authority guidelines and aspirations for the site, it should be possible to establish the topics for further investigation. A checklist of the most common issues, which will influence the form of the masterplan, is as follows:

- location of utilities;
- traffic;
- access points – for vehicles, cycles and pedestrians;
- availability of public transport;
- existing site features of merit;
- existing landscape/ecology;
- adjoining uses which may cause problems, e.g. noise, dust, emissions caused by the proximity of other businesses;
- important view corridors;
- conservation areas;
- listed buildings;
- sensitive adjoining uses;
- linkages with the existing community;
- geotechnical/contamination and previous uses;
- archaeological issues;
- other planning permissions/development plan land allocations.

Identify specialist consultants
Having determined the aspects relevant to the development it will be possible to produce a development brief. It can also be decided which specialist consultants may need to be involved in the preparation of the masterplan.

It is essential that a very clear brief is given to each of the consultants and that this is set down with written terms of reference. The development brief and consequent works are likely to alter through the masterplan process. By providing clear terms of reference, the likelihood of any misunderstanding between the client and the consultant, as well as the opportunity for unnecessary work being carried out, is reduced, thus providing a more cost effective service.

Appoint design team
It is important to ensure that the brief is comprehensive when putting together the consultant team and that the range of skills and expertise required has been correctly

identified, to ensure contributions are integrated as early in the process as possible. A masterplan develops over time with each member of the team and, indeed, other stakeholders adding to the framework, improving it at each stage of the process. The broader the ownership of the masterplan, the less opportunity there will be for conflict and the greater the chance for a successful scheme.

There are two main ways of appointing the consultant team[6]:

(a) Appoint one overall consultant who will coordinate the other specialist consultants.
(b) Appoint the specialist consultants directly. If you have the skills in-house to manage a diverse team this is the preferred route, as it will provide the opportunity to choose directly the consultants considered most suited to the particular challenges of the project.

In this chapter we do not discuss the procurement process but it is important to make sure that the terms and conditions of contract cover the future circumstances of the process[7]. For example, if the site is to be sold on, it should be ensured that the appointments are assignable and that warranties are available for a purchaser. Of particular importance are issues such as timescale, insurance, payment terms, termination, copyright, scope and variations.

Timescale	Consultants need to be aware of the overall period resources are to be available, often because of other factors – full time working is not possible and for example, four weeks' work may be spread over six months.
Insurance	Depending on the discipline, professional indemnity insurance may be a factor in future sales and care needs to be exercised in setting the PI required to the level of risk, and not driving up the fee costs by setting an unrealistically high level.
Payment terms	Be clear at what stages, milestones and calendar dates payments will be made and if retention is held, how much and when they will be released.
Termination	For many reasons during the masterplanning process, progress may stop or change course. Therefore the ability to terminate (and at what cost) is an important flexibility to be included in the appointments.
Copyright	The age old problem, but it must be addressed. If you cannot achieve copyright, exclusive and free use of the designs you have paid for is the minimum you should achieve.

---

6 *see* Figure 7 Masterplan Design Team.
7 For further information on legal/contract issues in relation to Procurement *see* Chapter 4.

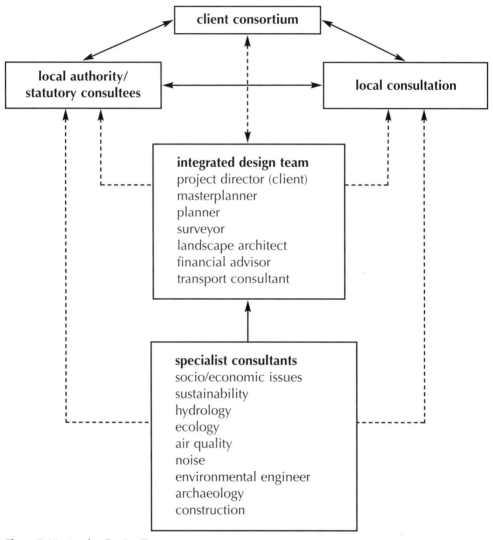

Figure 7: Masterplan Design Team

Scope	Clarity in the scoping document leads to a more efficient and consequently less costly fee bill. This needs to be extended to make sure that consultants employed do not duplicate work and responsibility for the different aspects of the masterplan and that each aspect is clearly defined.
Variations	For similar reasons to the termination point above, you have to have clarity on the issue. The plans will develop and vary as each influence and stakeholder inputs to the process. Furthermore, the market may change or a windfall opportunity may arise. How you achieve these and pay for them is best sorted out up front.

Stage 4: Feasibility options and appraisals

Detailed data collection
As the first stage of the assessment, it is important to ensure that comprehensive baseline surveys are carried out on the site to establish the existing conditions and constraints for the development. Generally, it will be necessary to undertake the following surveys, which will be required both for the ES and for the production of a quality masterplan:

- topography;
- traffic and transportation;
- noise;
- air quality;
- ecology;
- site constraints;
- ground conditions;
- archaeology.

Armed with this data it is possible to test whether the uses proposed for the site are likely to be acceptable. This data will also inform the drawing up of options.

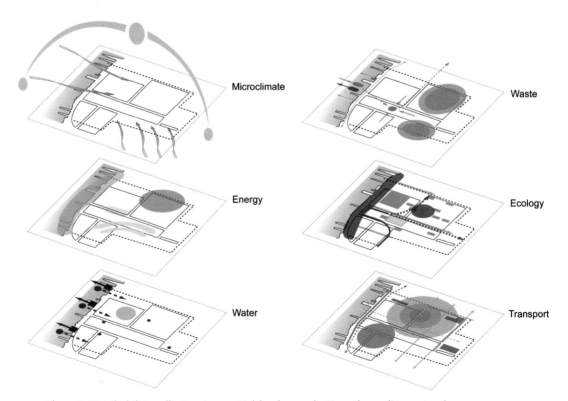

Figure 8: Detailed data collection is essential for the production of a quality masterplan

Assessment of constraints
A review of the baseline surveys will provide a full picture of the constraints of the site, which need to be taken into account when producing a masterplan. A constraints plan should be produced which will be the starting point for the masterplanner, used alongside the client's brief, in producing options for uses and density on the site.

Environmental Impact Assessment (EIA)
Having been through the process in Stage 2, it is important that the assessment of the impacts of the development is an integrated part of the design process. If the results of the assessment identify significant negative impacts, there can be far reaching impacts on the design of the scheme. It is, therefore, essential that the EIA is instigated at the earliest opportunity and continues to inform the design throughout the process.

By ensuring the necessary consultants are involved early on in the design process it enables the EIA to become a 'live' and proactive element of the design rather than a mere reporting tool. The risk of having to assess amended designs is also reduced, saving time and money.

Monitoring and review
A cycle of monitoring and review, by the client and design team leaders, must be continued throughout the design process to ensure that all the key issues and information from the consultation process are being considered appropriately.

Detailed consultation
At this stage it is advisable to carry out further consultation. There are various ways this can be done:

(a) Planning for real
    'Planning for real' exercises generally involve workshops over a weekend to allow people to voice their opinions on what should be developed on the site. This is a route that is advocated by many LAs, however, there are a number of pitfalls. The process often starts with a 'blank sheet of paper', which ends up in raising aspirations that cannot be delivered. If this route is followed, it needs to be very carefully managed.

(b) Public exhibition
    A public exhibition can be held either before submitting a planning application or after the submission. It is usually better to await submission and then hold an exhibition over about three days. It is best to ensure that there are people manning the exhibition that can answer both the general and technical questions. This approach is generally the most productive and informative form of public consultation and enables most members of the community to have their say.

(c) Public meeting
Care should be taken to try and ensure that attendees at any public meeting are representative of the local community. It is possible for a minority group to take over a meeting and provide a biased view on the proceedings. Such meetings also need to be carefully managed to allay any fears in the community and again ensure that aspirations have not been raised unrealistically.

Economic appraisal
The masterplan designers need to prepare a number of different options for the masterplanning of the site. Each may have a different emphasis and, of course, a different financial viability, e.g. a different balance of uses of different landscape structure. Choices will need to be made on whether to incorporate constraints within the masterplan or to pay for them to be removed as they either increase the net developable area or add value to the scheme in some other manner.

Initial options for masterplans rely heavily on a vision for the site created by a strong landscape structure to link the spaces between buildings. The different possibilities for the site also need to take into account location of utilities, which may be expensive to relocate, as well as the adequacy of utilities to serve the proposed development – again a potentially significant cost.

If the site is contaminated, any particular constraints need to be factored into the different alternatives for the site. Initial development appraisals will need to be carried out to ensure that any options produced are commercially viable.

At this stage a funding appraisal needs to be carried out and this can take many forms depending on the particular developer's circumstances.

Stage 5: Development of masterplan

Preferred scheme
Following an iterative process of consultation and review of the viability and design of the masterplan, a preferred masterplan will be produced which should be used as the basis of the planning application. This should be discussed with the planning authority prior to progressing the application so that as far as possible they are supportive of the masterplan design.

Illustrative information
When preparing a masterplan, more information will be prepared than is necessary to support a planning application. Information which the developer does not wish to be bound by in the future development but which is likely to assist in obtaining planning permission, should be submitted as illustrative information.

Masterplan
If the masterplan submitted for approval is for an outline application, which is most likely, it should maintain as much flexibility as possible. One way of achieving

flexibility is to submit a block plan for approval that indicates one or more uses per block, within a strong landscape framework, and to provide the remaining information as illustrative information.

Environmental statement (ES)
It is worth asking the LA for a formal scoping opinion, as explained earlier, but it is often the case that the team will end up assessing virtually all the relevant issues in the ES if only to show that there are no significant impacts. If all issues are not covered then the possibilities of being challenged are increased. In addition, even if the LA indicates that only a limited number of issues need to be assessed, it does not remove the threat of a third party challenge.

Section 106 issues
Any large scheme which warrants a masterplan is likely to involve a Section 106 (s.106) Agreement. Discussion on the 'shopping list' from the local authority tends to start early in the consultation stage. The 'shopping list' must be treated with a health warning. LAs will usually identify everything that they would like to be addressed in that area and not necessarily those aspects which are reasonably required as a result of the development. It is always preferable to have s.106 uses for the benefits of the site as well as the community served, e.g. local infrastructure or leisure/social facilities (gym/pool/crèche/landscape), which benefit the community and the site.

The negotiation of the s.106 Agreement is extremely important in achieving both a well-balanced and viable development. Some developers have been accused of 'buying' planning permission by agreeing to unreasonable s.106 Agreements. In many cases, this is due to the unwary landowners entering into sale contracts conditional on planning permission and s.106 obligations. The developer loses nothing by agreeing to unreasonable planning gain in order to achieve a favourable planning consent – as the cost of the agreement is deducted from the land value, the developer's profit is left undiminished. The development of brownfield sites, which is encouraged by government policy, involves large amounts of capital expenditure. Unrealistic s.106 Agreements are, therefore, not an option if the development of brownfield sites is to be realised.

Issues that regularly come up in discussion on the LAs 'shopping list' include:

- affordable housing;
- green transport plans;
- offsite infrastructure including public transport;
- and education provision.

One of the most difficult areas at the present time in relation to s.106 Agreements is the issue of education, with the requests for funding for educational needs varying tremendously around the country.

In general, LAs are often seeking contributions to make up the shortfall in public expenditure in aspects such as transportation and other matters. As a result, it will often be necessary to engage specialist advice prior to an agreement being made.

Stage 6: Planning application

Form of planning application
The planning application will consist of a number of different documents, notably:

- **A planning statement** – which should set out the key principles underlying the development proposals and policy background together with summarising the rationale for the development. It is suggested that this document should provide the LA with a comprehensive statement summarising the development proposals, which will provide the planning officer with the information needed to write the committee report.

- **The planning application forms** – including the mix of uses. In order to achieve a value for the site it is often a good idea to include 'up to' floor space figures to ensure that the development potential of the site is maximised. It may also be necessary, in order to maintain flexibility, to include some and/or uses to provide alternatives.

- **A transportation assessment.**

- **The plans which are to be approved** – these need to include at the minimum a location plan, a red line plan of the site and, if an environmental statement is required, a layout plan which may be a block plan of uses or footprints of the proposed buildings. If the masterplan submitted for approval is for an outline application, which is most likely, it should maintain as much flexibility as possible. One way of achieving flexibility is to submit a block plan for approval that indicates one or more uses per block, within a strong landscape framework, and provide the remaining information as illustrative information.

- **Illustrative information** – which should include a design statement attached to the masterplan, together with any information relating to the landscape design. Information which the developer does not wish to be bound by in the future development but which is likely to assist in obtaining planning permission, should be submitted as illustrative information.

- **An indication of the offer of any s.106 obligations** – this can be included in the planning application although it may be better to be fairly general at this stage, unless there has been extensive discussion with the LA prior to planning application submission. For example, it could be stated that an element of affordable housing will be provided without specifying the percentage and, similarly, with offsite infrastructure, it may be indicated that a contribution will be made to public transport without specifying how much until there have been further discussions on the requirements as a result of the development.

- **Environmental Statement (ES)** – if required is to be submitted with an application then it is worth asking the LA for a formal scoping opinion, as explained earlier.

It is also worth meeting the main consultees prior to preparing an ES – e.g. English Nature, where there are ecological issues of importance – so that most of the main points of concern can be covered at the outset, rather than awaiting responses to the ES. This is all in the nature of trying to ensure that the process runs as smoothly as possible and to save time. It is likely that virtually all the relevant issues will be assessed in the ES, if only to show that there are no significant impacts. If all issues are not covered then the possibilities of being challenged are increased. In addition, even if the LA indicates that only a limited number of issues need to be assessed, it does not remove the threat of a third party challenge. It must always be remembered that the trigger point for the preparation of an ES is only 0.5 hectares so if there is any question of doubt over whether an ES is required or not then it is advised that one is prepared.

Submit planning application
After submission there can be a seemingly endless series of meetings with the LA and other interested parties. As a result of these, there may be a necessity to amend the masterplan to accommodate some parties' needs. There may also be a need to provide an 'addendum' to the ES if points covered do not appear. If this additional information can be provided by way of clarification of the ES rather than as an addendum, this will prevent the clock starting again.

If it has been decided to carry out the public consultation exercise after submitting the application, then it is usually best to ensure that all parties have been consulted by the LA, prior to holding a public exhibition. In that way it will be ensured that the majority of people will have had a chance to review the application and a more informed response is likely. It is suggested that a leaflet is sent out about a week before the exhibition, setting out the key points relating to the development. The masterplan is very important at the exhibition as it will either sell or kill the scheme in the eyes of the local community. The form of the illustrative information is also critical to getting a positive response.

Where a planning application is supported by a masterplan, in order to establish a mix of uses and thus achieve a value for the site, then it is often a good idea to include 'up to' floor space figures to ensure that the development potential of the site is maximised.

Obtaining planning permission
It may be necessary to compromise on the ultimate mix or density of uses in order to gain the approval of the masterplan development. Any compromise must be carefully considered and the advantages/disadvantages assessed to establish whether the cost of such a compromise outweighs the cost and time involved in going through a planning inquiry, where the outcome is uncertain. However, there is no point in compromising to such an extent that the whole development is unviable or the integrity of the masterplan is threatened. It has to be a balance and the LA has to accept this too.

It must always be remembered that the ultimate aim must be to gain a planning permission of the optimum value within the quickest period of time. The maxim 'time is money' holds true for planning consents and ultimately a balance needs to be drawn between flexibility and deliverability.

Stage 7: Development and construction

Development and construction
Depending on the size of the site, the development and construction of the site can be a long process; in some areas taking ten years or more. The masterplan will come under considerable pressure during that period, not least from changing market demand but also from changes in political and economic circumstances. The masterplan process must, therefore, include a continuous process of reassessment and review in order to respond to these changes.

Example masterplan: Greenwich Peninsula

Developing the masterplan

In 1989 the first masterplan was prepared for a mixed-use development on one of Europe's largest former gas works sites, a 121 hectare (300 acre) site, in the London Borough of Greenwich. The masterplan was produced by Terry Farrell on behalf of BUD and proposed residential, retail and leisure, business, public open space and relocated business uses around a central landscaped area.

In 1990, the 80s boom period came to an abrupt end. As a consequence, the Terry Farrell masterplan (*see* Figure 9) went through a series of alterations, changing the focus from residential and retail, to employment generation. The revised masterplan produced by Llewelyn Davies, with British Gas as client, resulted in the submission of an outline planning application in 1992. In 1995/6 there were further revisions to the masterplan, and Llewellyn Davis and British Gas Properties were granted an outline planning consent on the scheme. Other key changes were the inclusion of a new tube station and the allocation of an area for education and community use. The plan still retained some essence of a central landscaped area, albeit in a different format from the previous one.

In 1992, the Rio Earth Summit resulted in nearly 180 nations signing up to Agenda 21 in order to enable a move towards more sustainable development. This in turn led to a change in planning policy and legislation and the production of the UK's first Sustainable Development Strategy in 1994: 'Sustainable development: the UK Strategy'.

In 1995/6 there were further revisions to the masterplan. The main changes involved the concentration of the landscaped spaces along the riverside in order to incorporate a proposal for a larger leisure/employment use (as a result of a proposed end user) in the central part of the site.

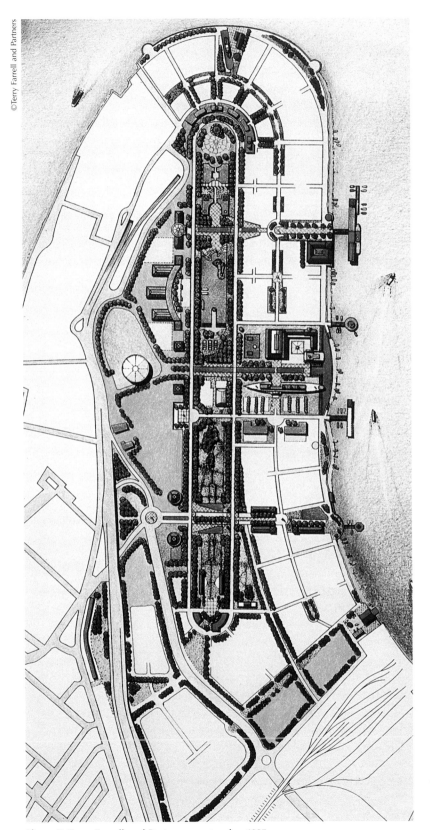

Figure 9: Terry Farrell and Partners masterplan 1995

133

In 1997, following the purchase of the former gas works and in order to facilitate the plans for the National Millennium celebrations, English Partnerships (the Government's Regeneration Agency) submitted a revised masterplan for the northern part of the Peninsula prepared by Richard Rogers. This year also saw Labour win the general election, after 18 years of Conservative control, and an announcement of their intention to produce a new Sustainable Development Strategy.

The Greenwich Peninsula Vision

The vision for the Greenwich Peninsula was to establish a new urban quarter which responded to the new planning policies and legislation. A sustainable mixed use development was proposed, consisting of a residential and commercial area, with leisure, shopping and recreational facilities all linked by a central park and extensive pedestrian, cycle, road and public transport routes to all areas of the site. The plan had the following urban regeneration, environmental and development objectives:

- to promote the regeneration of former industrial and derelict urban sites;
- to establish a clear and flexible infrastructure and public open space system for the site;
- to facilitate the planned Millennium Exhibition and maximise the long-term value of the public investment for the regeneration of the Peninsula;
- to maximise the potential of the new Jubilee Line underground extension;
- and to establish an environmentally sustainable urban environment.

The key elements of the masterplan were:

- **Land use framework.** A sustainable mixed use residential quarter with ancillary retail and community facilities, a new central business district, and larger scale commercial and employment uses in the southern portion of the site.
- **Open space.** A public open space system, including two urban parks with links to the river corridor, providing a co-ordinated sequence of complementary spaces.
- **Comprehensive Movement Strategy.** Excellent public transport links including:
  - a priority pedestrian and cycleway framework that is fully integrated into the public open space system;
  - the new North Greenwich Jubilee Line station, part of the Jubilee Line extension linking the site to central London and the London Underground system;
  - a transit link linking the site to neighbouring centres in Greenwich;
  - the London Transport interchange linking the site to the borough and south east London via an extensive bus system;
  - local buses providing access within the site;
  - and an on-site road system designed to minimise through traffic in residential areas but provide easy access to the planned commercial centres.

The masterplan, based on the Millennium Dome, for the northern part of the Peninsula was implemented. The southern part of the Peninsula has been developed largely in accordance with the design principles in the Llewelyn Davies masterplan of 1995/6.

The Greenwich Peninsula masterplan illustrates the changes that can occur over a long time in response to both political and economic changes, and the resulting changes to policy and legislation which need to be addressed. A well produced masterplan ensures that issues are considered from the outset, whilst retaining flexibility for development options.

The Greenwich masterplan is now being revised further with the continuing development of the northern Peninsula, for up-to-date information on the sites progress visit www.greenwichpeninsula.co.uk.

©English Partnerships

Figure 10: English Partnerships Greenwich Peninsula masterplan

Author profiles

Guy Battle, Director and Founding Partner, Battle McCarthy

Guy Battle is an environmental and building services engineer who specialises in the integrated design of low energy, environmentally responsive buildings. He has worked on a wide range of projects throughout the world including the GSW Headquarters in Berlin by Sauerbruch and Hutton and the World Trade Centre in Amsterdam by Kohn Pedersen Fox.

Jane Mulcahey, Associate, Environmental Planner, Battle McCarthy

Jane Mulcahey has nine years experience in planning and environmental policy in private practice and local authority. Her experience includes the formulation and implementation of sustainable development policy and projects, Masterplans, Local Agenda 21/ Community Strategies and Environmental Impact Assessments.

Battle McCarthy Limited is a multi-disciplinary consultancy with over 60 employees. The emphasis of the company is to provide an enhanced inter-disciplinary understanding for the creation of low energy, high environmental quality buildings and ecologically responsive landscapes.

Phillip Kirby OBE, General Manager, SecondSite Property Holdings Ltd

Phil trained as a civil and structural engineer and is a Charted Engineer. His early career involved work on a variety of schemes from sewage works, hotels to projects such as the Thames Barrier and Stockley Park Much of his work in heavy Civil Engineering as a Contractor was in marine, road, bridge and railway construction. As a client developer, projects include Broadgate, Staines, Chiswick Park, Loughborough and Leeds City Office Park.

Myra Barnes BA (Hons) Dip TP MRTPI, Partner, Salisbury Jones Planning

Myra was then appointed Head of Planning at British Gas Properties in 1993 where she managed all the planning workload covering the whole of the country. Specifically, she worked on projects such as Greenwich Peninsula, Beckton, Richmond, Kingston, Cambridge and many others. Myra left SecondSite at the end on 2001 and is now working as a Partner of a small planning consultancy, Salisbury Jones Planning.

SecondSite Property provides expert strategic advice on, and effective management of, property issues on behalf of the National Grid Transco Group, one of the four successor companies to what was formerly British Gas plc. It places particular emphasis on managing SecondSite's surplus contaminated land portfolio (comprising some 750 sites), and now the National Grid surplus sites (some 180) as well as providing services to National Grid Transco's occupied estate. Its aim is to add value, minimise risk and contribute to land regeneration.

7 Integrated landscapes

David Blackwood Murray
Derek Lovejoy Partnership

Introduction: what does the landscape architect do?[1]

The history of gardening is so strong in this country that, asked the question, most laymen would probably assume that the landscape architect worked in some branch of garden design. This does not paint a true picture today. The training and specialisation available to landscape architects means that they may face challenges ranging from major urban regeneration schemes, the siting of transport interchanges, the creation of parklands – often involving land reclamation, urban ecology and biodiversity, foreshore ecology, the protection of sand dunes, environmental assessments, planning inquiries and, indeed, private gardens.

Many land planners propose that land planning should come first to create the necessary guidelines for the architects. The most successful solutions, as we shall see from the case studies at the end of this chapter, come from a seamless understanding and co-operation between architect and landscape architect, each handling effectively the complexities of their responsibilities for the project from inception to completion as members of an appropriately skilled multi-disciplinary team. For urban projects in particular this team should have a broad understanding that also includes economics, social science and psychology!

A brief history of landscape

Eighteenth century landowners enjoyed the rustic and natural looking scenery of Lancelot 'Capability' Brown (1716–1783) and Humphrey Repton (1752–1818). Capability Brown planned for the future and we are the beneficiaries of his mature landscapes!

---

1 In their 1858 competition entry for Central Park in New York, Frederick Law Olmstead and Calvert Vaux described themselves as 'landscape architects'. Later Olmstead wrote: 'I am all the time bothered with the miserable nomenclature of "landscape architect". Landscape is not a good word, architecture is not, the combination is not – gardener is worse!' Quoted in Ian. H. Thompson (2000), *Ecology, Community and Delight: Sources of Values in Landscape Architecture,* London & New York, E & FN Spon. Ian Thompson then discusses the definition of 'landscape architecture' and the recent debates that have taken place (pp. 2-4). The title 'landscape architect' has stuck and is used in this chapter, although some practitioners prefer to describe themselves as 'land planners and designers' to indicate the wide range of work undertaken.

Today the planting of mature and semi-mature shrubs and trees to create an 'instant environment' is a requirement for many successful commercial projects.

Public space in cities evolved. In the medieval city there was relatively little public space beyond the market places and, perhaps, a civic square.[2] After the Great Fire of London in 1666 the inhabitants rejected plans by Christopher Wren or John Evelyn in favour of keeping the original narrow street patterns and land ownership.

King's Square (now Soho Square) was the first London Square to have an enclosed garden for the exclusive use of residents. By the mid 18th century most of the London Squares, created in developments outside the City itself, had enclosed private gardens. The Royal Parks, which were beginning to be surrounded by the growing city, were opened in part to the public, but it was not until the 19th century that concern for the 'health, enjoyment and moral improvement of the inhabitants' led to the incorporation of large public open spaces in city development and rebuilding plans. Public realm spaces are considered to be an integral part of good urban design today.

Traditional links between architects and landscape architects

What is interesting about much of this work are the close links between 'architecture' and 'landscape architecture'. Capability Brown, with a background as head gardener at Stowe, was himself a designer of buildings as well as working in close collaboration with his son-in-law, the architect Henry Holland (1745–1806).

Joseph Paxton (1801–1865) combined the skills of the gardener, as head gardener to the Duke of Devonshire at Chatsworth; the architect, as designer of the village of Edensor on the Chatsworth estate and the engineer, when he beat 233 other competitors to win the competition to build the great hall for the 1851 Exhibition and later to supervise its demolition and re-erection at Sydenham as the 'Crystal Palace'.[3]

Sylvia Crowe (1901–1997) as landscape architect[4] collaborated with Frederick Gibberd (1908–1984) as architect at Harlow New Town. Here the landscape design brief demanded the retention and enhancement of many existing features – trees, hedges and green areas – acknowledging the value of biodiversity and urban ecology which is recognised as vital today.

---

2 Pawley, Martin (1998), *Terminal Architecture,* London, Reaktion p.155.
3 I am grateful to Ron Sidell for this observation.
4 Collens, Geoffrey and Powell, Wendy (eds): Crowe, Sylvia (1999), *Landscape Design Trust,* London.

Developing the profession

The Americans formalised the status of the 'landscape architect' with the founding of the American Society of Landscape Architects (ASLA) in 1899. This was followed by the establishment of an academic course in landscape architecture at Harvard in 1900 and later at other universities such as Pennsylvania.

The 'Institute' in Britain, first called the 'Institute of Garden Design' was founded in 1929. Initially membership was by invitation. However, architect members with strong leanings towards garden design, such as Geoffrey Jellicoe (1900-96)[5], exerted their influence and the name was soon changed to the 'British Institute of Landscape Architecture' (now the Landscape Institute).

International influences

The International Federation of Landscape Architects was established in 1948. International conferences, most notably in Scandinavia, Switzerland and Germany, brought new ideas to the profession in Britain. Sylvia Crowe (1901–1997) described a 1958 conference in the USA as showing what the British Institute could achieve 'when it had attained the numbers and seniority of the American Society of Landscape Architects.'[6]

Town and Country Planning Legislation

The Scott report of 1942 laid the foundations of a national landscape policy and led directly to the Town and Country Planning Act of 1947, which required that 'professional advice should be sought for all new works likely to affect the countryside, since without landscape competence there would be no planning approval.'[7]

Collaboration and multi-disciplinary practice

We talked earlier of the close collaboration between architects and landscape architects. At Harvard during the 1950s Hideo Sasaki ran collaborative courses with the students of architecture, planning and landscape architecture. Sasaki believed in the 'integrated team' and his own practice (from 1957) of Sasaki Walker became one of the many multi-disciplinary teams to develop in the USA in the 1950s and 1960s in what Peter Walker has described as the 'first wave of corporate offices.'[8] Other American offices which combined architects, landscape architects, engineers and planners included Hellmuth, Obata and Kassabaum (HOK) and RTKL.

---

5 Harvey, Shelia (ed), Jellicoe, Geoffrey (1998), Landscape Design Trust, London.
6 Crowe, Sylvia, 'International Scene', Landscape Design, February 1979.
7 Jellicoe, Geoffrey, 'War and Peace', Landscape Design, February 1979, p.10
8 Walker, Peter and Simo, Melanie (1994), Invisible Gardens, Cambridge Massachusetts, The MIT Press.

Historic influences on landscape design for offices

We should bear in mind that the separation of workplace and home began in the 19th century when work began to take place in factories, rather than in workshops attached to the home, and owners, managers, professional men and financiers began to travel to separate offices. The unpleasant proximity of factories meant that the middle classes moved to the suburbs leaving the city centres to businesses and slums. Interestingly, we are now going full circle and returning to the concept of 'live-work' in many mixed-use developments and Lovejoy's certainly emphasise the importance of the interrelationship between 'live-work-play' in urban projects.

The 1950s, 60s and 70s
The Seagram Building by Mies van der Rohe and Philip Johnson, erected in New York (1958) became a 'defining image for the prestige office building',[9] of which a very significant element was the provision of a public plaza in front of the building. A plaza that led the City to rewrite much of its office district zoning in 1961 to encourage similar open public spaces in new projects. Now the provision of public space has become an established 'principal' in major urban projects today. In the hands of an enlightened developer these are positive and well-used additions to our public realm.

Internally, office buildings continued to provide cellular offices with open plan rooms for typists and clerks until the development from Germany of the concept of 'Burolandschaft'– open-planned offices which sometimes included some interior planting such as the ubiquitous rubber plant. However interior planting was not an essential element of Burolandschaft design. Sherban Cantacuzino describes it thus: 'Burolandschaft is not "office landscape". Office landscape is often applied rather loosely in this country to any random arrangement of furniture with screens and potted plants. The arrangement in true Burolandschaft is based on a thorough analysis of communications which determines the relationship of functional groups on the open floor as well as the relationship between individuals within each group.'[10]

So the driving forces behind 'Burolandschaft' were communications and paper flow.

The 1980s and 90s
During this period several influential American practices set up British and European offices and their work can be seen in projects such as Canary Wharf in London and in many corporate campus buildings – the new country estates – as well as in the establishment of business parks.

---

9 Curtis, William, J.R. *Modern Architecture since 1900*, London, 3rd edition, Phaidon (revised 1996).
10 People in Offices, 'Sherban Cantacuzino', *Architectural Review*, October 1970.

Features of office buildings at this time included 'atria', such as Coutts Bank in the Strand (1980)[11] possibly inspired by the Ford Foundation in New York (1963-8).[12] The atria concept was then extended to form 'internal streets'.[13]

Sustainability

Overview

The issue of the sustainability of the planet has been an emerging crisis that has gathered momentum over the last half century. It is now fully in the public domain and is increasingly being embodied in legislation. To quote Jonathan Dimbleby's Inaugural Lecture given at the Royal Institute of British Architects in April 2002:

> More and more people now recognise that economic development that is not environmentally sustainable is self-destructive . . . if we are to achieve sustainable communities in our own backyard, let alone across the globe, then far more is required individually and collectively of politicians and planners, developers and financiers, engineers and builders as well as by architects (to which we would add 'the end users') . . . all of them face together the task of really placing sustainable development at the heart of the future.

Sites for offices

Greenfield sites are now developed as a last resort. Great responsibility is required to ensure that as many existing features of the landscape as possible are retained and incorporated in the new design, and every effort must be made to enhance the existing environment.

Out of town developments should be at key transport nodes with workable green travel plans in place and enforceable.

Successful urban regeneration in the 21st century must learn from the failure of many earlier schemes, particularly those of the 1950s and 60s. To succeed, schemes need to have real content ensuring that the connections are right – connections of both transport and community.[14]

Brownfield sites provide an opportunity to create a quality environment in previously built up and often contaminated industrial areas in or around towns and cities.

---

11 Frederick Gibberd & Partners, RIBA Journal, Vol. 90, No. 8, 1983, p. 55.

12 Kevin Roche, John Dinkeloo & Associates were the architects and Dan Kiley was the landscape architect, *Architectural Record,* Vol. 183, No. 4, April 1995, p. 15.

13 Examples of internal streets include BA Waterside by Niels Torp Architects (completed 1998) and GSK House, Brentford by Hillier Group/RHWL and Swanke Hayden Connell Architects (2002).

14 My thanks to Ron Sidell for emphasising this point.

Urban sites are often the most challenging. Buildings and landscapes must be flexible and able to accommodate change. For existing buildings and infrastructure an independent analysis is required before any demolition should be considered. In the case of an established and mature, or maturing landscape, removal would be hard to justify.[15]

Healthy cities and urban green spaces

Ian McHarg advised us to understand the components for the healthy environment, 'for there the environment is fit, the adaptations are creative.'[16]

It is recognised that the sustainable solution is for people to live in urban environments in, probably compact, but certainly healthy cities. Part of the creation of the healthy city is the provision of open green spaces.

Urban green spaces are the subject of research by organisations such as English Nature. Ancient writings describe 'vegetation as the key to making cities pleasant'.[17] There are now proposals as part of the Biodiversity Action Plan (1994) and Local Agenda 21 to provide linear green spaces accessible to all by foot, bicycle or appropriate public transport.[18]

At the same time it is recognised that the provision of urban green spaces also involves issues relating to the 'public realm' including social and cultural restraints such as the fear of crime.[19]

The changing workplace

Current thinking and future trends

Practices such as 'hot-desking' and changes in IT leading to virtually 'paperless offices' where individual workspaces become irrelevant are changing the office culture. Recent office developments, such as BA Waterside, mean that individuals gain a sense of belonging by relating to other aspects of the working environment such as the landscaped spaces or the 'internal street'. In this way the building and landscape design are being used to facilitate this cultural change.

With the globalisation of business many offices are already operating on a 24-hour/seven-day week basis and this will probably become more widespread. If

---

15 See Broadgate case study: proposals for Finsbury Avenue Square and removal of trees.
16 McHarg, Ian (1969), *Design with Nature*, New York, Doubleday/Natural History Press.
17 Botkin, D.B. and Beveridge, C.E. 'Cities as Environments', *Urban Ecosystems*, 1, 1997.
18 Barker, George (1997), *A framework for the future: green networks with multiple uses in and around towns and cities*, English Nature Research Reports No. 256.
19 Harrison, Burgess, Millward and Dawe (1995), *Accessible natural green space in towns and cities: A review of appropriate size and distance criteria*, English Nature Research Report No. 153.

people spend more time outside the traditional working day in the workplace then it must provide a range of facilities that allow them to work, rest and play in safety: eating and meeting places, active sports and exercise facilities and quiet, relaxing break-out spaces. Landscaped gardens, terraces, courtyard, roof gardens, atria/internal streets and winter gardens can be designed to provide some of these facilities and so contribute to the success of the workplace.

Branding and corporate value

The offices of the future will be 'iconic brand centres . . . modern day versions of the gentleman's club, except here brand allegiance is the key rather than the requisite political allegiance of the past.'[20]

The quality, location and style of a headquarters' building reflects a company's identity and tells us much about its values and attitude to issues such as staff well-being and contentment, the wider community and the environment. The majority of companies want to be perceived as caring, inclusive and environmentally sensitive, and need to ensure that they express these values in all their activities.

The case studies will show that investment in high-quality buildings and landscape design can be an important factor in attracting and retaining staff and making them proud to work for an organisation.

Interior landscapes/sky gardens

A great deal of research has been undertaken in recent years into the value, both psychological and physical, of using plants in buildings such as offices, schools and hospitals. Plants have been shown to provide a sense of psychological well being for occupiers and research also suggests that vegetation may contribute to improving internal air quality.[21]

There appears to be an enthusiasm and desire for interior landscapes – this does not mean plants in pots in places, but lush greenery and living gardens.

However, conditions for interior landscaping are precise and must be satisfied at the earliest concept stages of a building. Experience to date suggests that glazed roof areas such as atria or internal streets and winter gardens can be planted and maintained successfully. One difficulty seems to come when top day lighting is not available and the plants and trees may be drawn sideways towards the light.[22] The garden in these circumstances may thrive better with smaller plants. This was the

---

20 Evans, Tim, Sheppard Robson Architects quoted in 'An Office Odyssey', *Office Trends,* May 2002.
21 www.plants-for-people.org . This website keeps up-to-date lists of research projects on the subject.
22 This appears to be a difficulty at Commerzbank in Frankfurt.

approach taken by Foster and Partners for the ARAG headquarters in Dusseldorf.[23] There are four 'sky gardens' on the eastern facade and the concept was to make workspaces within the gardens, rather than gardens within workspaces. A watertight and drained container for plants was provided over an entire section of floor plate and usable islands were then created within the planting for people. The lower gardens have lush, leafy green ground covering plants, while the upper gardens are more arid with boulder fields.[24] The choice of plants was critical for the scheme to succeed because a common problem is that, in many cases, the conditions in which plants thrive and humans feel comfortable are not entirely compatible – too dry, too hot, too humid.

Christoph Ingenhoven's second-placed entry for Commerzbank in Frankfurt appears to have a perimeter double wall in which he created a 'wintergarten' to act as a buffer between the interior temperatures and those of the outside, 'allowing carefully controlled amounts of fresh air to permeate the building at every level and giving the occupants the cheering influences of the sight and oxygenation of plants in many different ways.'[25]

However, there are also issues to resolve relating to latitude – tropical or temperate; the height of buildings and the effects of wind speed on plants outside the building envelope; the selection of appropriate species; installation, drainage and maintenance, and so on.[26] For temperate zones it may be that, within tall buildings, areas for carefully selected plants could be designed at various levels to be viewed from, but not integrated with, offices or break out spaces – unless people choose to enter them and join the plants' environment.

Urban roof gardens

A newspaper article tells us that 'Ken Livingstone, as Mayor of London, plans to force developers to put grass and trees on the roofs of all new office developments, blocks of flats and public buildings in London.'[27] The Mayor argues, according to this report, that plants on top of buildings would help to soak up carbon dioxide, contributing to making London's environment cleaner and encourage wildlife back into the city.[28]

---

23 Architecture Today, No. 58, pp. 12–13.

24 I am grateful to Robin Partington, Project Director, for this information.

25 *Architectural Review,* May 1992 .

26 Yeang, Ken (1999), The Green Skyscraper: A Primer for Designing Ecologically Sustainable Large Buildings, Munich & New York, Prestel; Yeang, Ken and Richards, Ivor (2001), Groundscrapers and Subscrapers, Chichester, Wylie-Academy. See also Ken Yeang's Menara Mesiniaga (IBM Tower) Kuala Lumpur, Architectural Review, February 1993.

27 Jonathon Carr-Brown, 'Red Ken plans a green-top London. The Sunday Times, June 9 2002

28 *New Scientist,* 11 May 2002, p. 11. Research from the Geological Survey of Canada in Quebec suggests that pollutants such as sulphur dioxide could greatly reduce the amount of carbon dioxide trees consume. However, there are many reasons to encourage trees and also many reasons to reduce carbon dioxide emissions!

Figure 1: Canary Riverside, London

Some successful 20th-century roof gardens include Derry & Toms[29] in London created in 1938 (now the Roof Gardens Night Club); Oakland Museum in California designed by landscape architect Dan Kiley in the late 1950s; Constitution Plaza,[30] Frankfurt by Albrecht Jourdan Müller and Berghof Landes Rang completed in 1988; and RMC at Thorpe in 1989 by the Derek Lovejoy Partnership and Edward Cullinan Architects.

Roof gardens present opportunities to add value to city centre developments. High-level roof gardens offer a private oasis away from the roar of the city traffic and the intensity of the working environment. Transformed at night with spectacular lighting, they can become magical places for corporate events and special occasions.

If the technical requirements are integrated at the outset of the design process, there are few constraints on the possibilities for activities and external garden spaces that can be successfully accommodated on roof deck areas. These could include:

- corporate entertainment and performance space;
- cafes and outdoor dining terraces;
- water features and swimming pools;

---

29 Architects Journal, 15 October 1980, pp.759-66.
30 Walker, Peter and Simo, Melanie (1994), *Invisible Landscapes*, Cambridge, Massachusetts, The MIT Press, p. 239.

- gardens featuring semi-mature trees, pergolas and other shelter structures, art and sculpture in traditional or contemporary designs;
- active gym and exercise facilities.

The Derek Lovejoy Partnership has undertaken several roof gardens, most notably at Canary Wharf where the Riverside scheme illustrates what can be achieved. One of the particular successes of the design is that it creates the illusion that it has been built on mother earth, although most of the landscape is in fact a roof deck (*see* Figure 1).

Public art

Public art is now an established element in development budgets. Over the last ten to fifteen years, with the media's encouragement, the public has become more knowledgeable about art and more critical in its assessment of the art placed in the public realm. This creates a challenge because 'however selected for the task, the artist faces the same difficulty as the public space designer in discovering and expressing ideas that are meaningful to a diverse and changing audience of users.'[31]

A 'new' approach is in the collaboration between artists, architects and landscape architects at the initial stages:

This idea is founded in the hope that artists may be in touch with deeper well springs of creativity that their counterparts in the applied arts, and that the design professionals will help the artist become aware of the practical and technical considerations involved in the design of public space.[32]

This process was adopted at Brindleyplace in Birmingham, where the developer (Argent) was very interested in art and wished to support young British sculptors. Argent consulted the Royal Society of British Sculptors which provided a short list of young artists to enter competitions for the various sites that had been identified early on at the planning stage of the scheme. The chosen artists then worked closely with the landscape architects.

There are several procurement agencies for public art. CBAT is one. It was formed as the Cardiff Bay Art's Trust with the responsibility of procuring hundreds of works of art for the Cardiff Bay Development Corporation. Canary Wharf[33] and Broadgate are among other developments which have taken public art seriously.

---

31 Carr, Francis, Rivlin and Stone, *Public Space,* p. 270.
32 *ibid.* p. 273.
33 Art Map: Public Art at Canary Wharf, available from the Canary Wharf Group, 1 Canada Square, London E14 5AB

Cost of landscape

As a general rule of thumb landscape design in the public realm accounts for approximately seven to ten per cent of the global construction budget – a roof garden would be nearer ten per cent.

The cost of the landscaping will be affected by the degree of maturity required immediately. Hedges, trees and shrubs of virtually any size can be obtained and, in our fast track urban world, semi-mature trees and shrubs are often a necessity – not only because we demand semi-mature landscapes from day one, but also because bigger trees and shrubs are more robust and can better withstand vandalism.

Another cost factor on urban sites is the cost of properly preparing the ground. It is not sustainable to import large quantities of topsoil, and so current thinking is to investigate methods of soil remediation. Sometimes the depth to be planted has to be separated with a physical barrier from the sub-soil beneath which may be contaminated.

When considering the overall life cycle costs of a landscape scheme it should be understood that greater capital investment at the implementation stage – doing it right first time – can help with aftercare and maintenance.

Adding value through landscape

The commitment to provide a high-quality landscape design is often a key to obtaining planning permission – so clearly an essential and valuable part of the process.

There have been no studies to date quantifying the added value that landscape offers to a development.[34] However, it is becoming increasingly clear that good landscape design does enhance the value of a development from the point of view of many of the parties involved. Francis Duffy[35] has pointed out that while there is not an equation to show that £x invested in landscape will produce £y in added value, the benefit and value gained will depend on other factors such as using the landscape design to improve the culture of an organisation or on the individual client understanding how to use the resources created by the design to gain the benefit it could bring. For example, staff satisfaction could be quantified before and after the scheme is implemented.

Lifespan and maintenance

A scheme may have been brilliantly designed and well executed, but both hard and soft landscaping will need care and maintenance. Plants do not all have the same

---

34 The Value of Urban Design, CABE/DETR, 2002.
35 I am grateful to Frank Duffy for taking time to discuss this issue.

lifespan and over time a certain proportion will have to be replaced. Gardens need old-fashioned gardeners!

Increasingly, forward-looking developers and financiers are taking up the challenge of investing for the longer term and recognising their responsibilities for lifespan maintenance. They are encouraged in this by the financial benefits gained from providing successful workplaces which have increased rental values and fewer untenanted periods.

Better design does not necessarily cost more to deliver and, taking into account the likely higher returns on investment, the cost of management and aftercare is really quite a small element. For example the service charge on a development such as Stockley Park is approximately £6/sq m/annum to provide services such as security and landscape maintenance.

However, it is important to understand at the outset both the available budget and the management system that will govern and maintain the space. The involvement of managers in the design process can ensure that the limitations and potentials of the management and maintenance system are understood. This will allow the designer, where appropriate, to 'resist the temptation to design with an over high standard of maintenance and management in mind.'[36]

The public realm

In the urban environment much of the space outside offices is public – the surrounding streets and squares – and this is where the challenge lies to reconcile conflicting interests, encourage social inclusion and create well-designed, safe, cared for and well-maintained environments that are open to all.

To move beyond exciting visions and paper dreams there does need to be a consistent political will and commitment to really invest in the community – in education, transport, health and leisure as well as in the public realm itself. Financial support may be provided in partnership with private enterprise, but not necessarily led by it.

Place making

The public realm provides the urban stage, meeting place and theatre for social intercourse. Visionary clients like the developers of Broadgate in London and Brindleyplace in Birmingham all understood how investing in the public realm could add value to their developments.

The Urban Task Force, CABE and other important stakeholders in today's city have encouraged, if not pushed, developers to create great places in which to work, rest

---

36 Carr, Francis, Rivlin, Stone, *Public Space,* p. 273.

and play, often related to a wider and more inclusive range of lifestyle facilities, including theatres, cinemas, entertainment, sports, schools and retail destinations.

The renaissance of our towns and cities has begun with wide-ranging visions and masterplans for change at local and regional level. In Bristol, Birmingham, Cardiff, Leeds, Manchester and Sheffield planning authorities have started to evaluate their prime asset – the town centre – to investigate how they can implement environmental improvements which will enhance their existing urban framework and provide an impetus for forward investment – designing places in which people can take pride.

Projects not planning – visionary tinkering

At a city level, the strategy followed by Oriol Bohigas (MBM Arquitectes) as Director of Planning in Barcelona was to focus on renewing and creating new public spaces and services by developing projects rather than concentrating on a masterplan.[37] The success of this approach was reiterated by his architectural partner David Mackay at the recent Architectural Review conference, 'Revitalising the European City'. The problem is that masterplans take time to develop and nurture and, as a result, are rarely implemented. So,

> . . . what the 'masterplanner needs to do is to start with the small issues which can be dealt with immediately . . . when enough of these have been completed you put them together as a strategic plan for a zone or the city' . . . by the time someone has developed the masterplan, it has, if you have been following Mackay, already been implemented.[38]

The Greater London Authority has initiated a 'public space plan' and ten pilot projects have been identified for public realm improvement schemes. It is hoped that the necessary financial backing will be forthcoming to support these.[39]

Making it work: design

Understand your user
Most people go to public spaces for specific reasons:[40]

- Comfort – food, drink, shelter, rest, shade.
- Relaxation – this offers greater release than comfort alone, a mixture of psychological comfort and recreation.
- Passive engagement – watching the world go by.

---

37 Buchanan, Peter, 'Regenerating Barcelona with Parks and Plazas', Architectural Review, June 1984, pp. 33-35.
38 Reported by Sutherland Lyall in Architectural Review, May 2002, p. 26.
39 *Making Spaces for Londoners,* GLA, July 2002.
40 Carr, Francis, Rivlin, Stone, Public Space, p. 87.

- Active engagement – exercise, watching an entertainer, looking at a fine piece of sculpture. These activities provide linkages between people and can prompt strangers to talk to one another.
- A sense of discovery, stimulation, exploration.

Good design

Good urban design is essential if we are to produce attractive, high-quality, sustainable places in which people want to live, work and relax....to achieve this we need to effect a culture change.[41]

The problem with designing public spaces, as Sir Stuart Lipton has pointed out, is that it is an art, not a science. There is no certain formula which, when applied, will result in a successful public space. There are, however, some considerations that appear to work and can give direction to the scheme.[42] At the same time it should be noted that urban design does not have to be overly costly to be well designed and well executed. The most expensive materials do not have to be used and, conversely, the use of the most expensive materials does not guarantee good design!

History and context
It is important to know and respect the history and tradition of the area. What is unique about this particular place?

Boundaries, connections and movement
Identify the boundary of the space and see how the space connects to the surrounding area:

Designing space means designing movement . . . the relationship between spatial layout, movement and co-presence is the key to the varied life of the city . . . the key to making a place feel human. A great deal of how a place or space works over time depends on getting this right.[43]

The character and identity of a place – creating an emotional connection
Create spaces with a recognisable and local identity so that you know where you are, a place in which you feel comfortable and secure but also a place that encourages an emotional response so that the space feels part of you, your place. Something wonderful might happen there and so there is a positive reason to go there.

---

41 Forward by Stuart Lipton, Chairman of CABE and Nick Raynsford, Minister of Housing, By Design: Design in the Planning System: Towards better practice, DLTR/CABE, Thomas Telford, 2001.
42 I am grateful to Stuart Lipton, CEO of Stanhope plc and Chairman of CABE, Michael Lowe of Arup Associates and Bill Hillier of Space Syntax for discussions and information on this subject.
43 Bill Hillier, Space Syntax laboratory, University College London.

People appear to respond to places where they have good memories, and events and activities are a way of creating memories, individual or shared, so that people feel connected to the place; a place for 'emotional dwell time' whether at a pleasant cafe or perhaps ice skating as at Broadgate. Encourage children to use the space, the shared memories can then spread to their families, schools and the wider community.

Roger Madelin, CEO of Argent, reflecting recently on lessons learned from Brindleyplace in Birmingham, said that when people go to Brindleyplace they remember activities such as the café, sitting outside on a nice day, visiting the Sealife Centre or the art gallery, and being by the canal much more than they remember or can recall any of the buildings.[44]

'Housekeeping' – maintenance, security and control
The space must work 24 hours a day – a good 'day' space must not be an intimidating 'night space'.

Public realm spaces must be inclusive and accommodate all users.

The use of any space must appear to be spontaneous but in large urban spaces there needs to be a degree of organised programming – managed 'events' of varying degrees.

Security can be undertaken with cameras and also by the presence of security guards – uniformed guards tend to give the wrong message about the space. A more positive approach is to link 'security' and 'maintenance'. The presence of gardeners and cleaners getting on with their daily jobs creates a corporate sense of caring for the space.

Key design elements to consider include:

- a focal point;
- hard and soft landscaping;
- art and sculpture;
- water.

Making it work: management

There are various initiatives on management strategies for the public realm such as the Central London Partnerships that promote specific management schemes for 'Business Improvement Districts' (BID), an American concept, established with the Rockefeller Centre in New York, and based on private investment and management. Broadgate in London is managed in this way.[45]

---

44 Lecture at the Prince's Foundation for course on 'Design Skills for the New Urban Agenda', 2002.
45 See case study.

©Ian Clook

Figure 2: Broadgate Arena, Summer, London

©Peter Mackiven

Figure 3: Broadgate Arena, Ice Rink, London

However, there must be longer-term perspectives in investment decisions and responsibility for aftercare, maintenance and space management must be established at the outset. The public sector is generally failing in its maintenance and care of the public realm in our cities. Apart from creating adequate budgets for public sector service, the public sector can also ensure contributions by developers by imposing aftercare requirements through the planning system.[46]

Making it work: citizenship

To quote Richard Rogers,[47]

> The public domain is the theatre of an urban culture. It is where citizenship is enacted, it is the glue that can bind an urban society . . . cities can only reflect the values, commitment and resolve of the societies which they contain . . . teaching children about their everyday urban environment equips them to participate . . . in the process of respecting and improving the city.

Summary

As we have seen, many of the issues are complex and detailed discussion on them is beyond the scope of this chapter. However some points to note include:

- **Delivery.** 'Cities . . . civilis . . . "to benefit the citizen" . . . to be healthy, inclusive and beautiful...in this country there is not a vision gap, but a delivery gap.'[48]
- **Sustainable development.** 'The obstacle is not lack of research or even clear targets but rather how to use limited public powers to redirect market forces and promote urban living.'[49]
- **Development of publicly owned 'public space'** has been lacking in Britain since the provision of urban parks in the 19th century. There is a government 'Urban Green Spaces Task Force' which published an Interim Report, *Green Spaces, Better Places* in 2002, calling for the provision of parks as part of the urban renaissance.[50] The Heritage Lottery fund has invested £190 million in parks since 1995 but the problem seems to be not so much one of funding the new facilities

46 Matthew Carmona of the Bartlett School of Architecture is currently researching the 'Managing of Urban Space' for the DLTR (now the Department of Transport and the Office of the Deputy Prime Minister). Due to be published in 2003.
47 Richard Rogers + Philip Gumuchdjian, *Cities for a Small Planet,* London, Faber & Faber, 1997
48 Edwin Knighton, 'City Spaces – Desolation or Sophistication?' Lecture at Leeds Metropolitan University on 13 March 2002, reviewed by Mark Burgess.
49 Nicholas Falk, 'Securing Sustainable Development', *Urban Design Quarterly*, Summer 2000, Issue 83, p. 10.
50 See Eleanor Young, 'No Walk in the Park', RIBA Journal, February 2002, pp. 258-60.

but of paying for upkeep unless the park can generate income through the provision of commercial facilities.[51]

- **Land ownership.** Of course there are excellent examples of responsible and imaginative private sector schemes of high design quality, which have been well-executed and are well-managed and maintained. However we must remember that in privately owned 'public realm spaces' there is ultimate control on who can use them. The public sector cannot be excused its responsibilities in this matter. In Barcelona, for example, there is a 'quality committee' by which the city architect and other relevant parties set standards for proposed schemes. The schemes are subsidised by the public purse and so the infrastructure and the streets are public while most of the buildings are private. This means that the public authority controls the public realm. In Holland, which is so much admired these days, the cities own the land and so set the standards for the public realm. However, in London, for example, most of the land is in private ownership – the GLA and the local authorities have relatively small land holdings. However, there must be significant public investment alongside private investment and the public authority must set the standards that are to be achieved and maintained.[52]

- **Traffic.** In a forthcoming report, *Reclaiming the Public Realm*, which is intended to diagnose the existing ills that adversely affect Britain's streetscape, a distinction is made between 'roads' which are for vehicles and 'streets' which are shared spaces.[53] We must not forget that our streets and squares are for living in!

The land planning and design process

Overview

Land planning is increasingly recognised as the logical first step in undertaking any development project. The most creative outcomes are achieved when land planners are retained by clients from the start of conceptual thinking – exploring the first ideas, widening the debate and influencing the siting and layout of proposals to ensure the provision of wider landscape and public realm benefits for people to enjoy.

---

51 For example, the London Docklands Development Corporations' 'Barrier Park' becomes the responsibility of the London Borough of Newham in 2002 without any long-term financial provision for its management – 'Public asset becomes public liability', Robert Holden in the Architects Journal, 1 April 1999, p. 37. On the other hand, Mile End Park, Tower Hamlets, has been described as a 'model urban green space' with ancillary commercial enterprises (see RIBA Journal, February 2002). The Urban Parks Forum is actively promoting the provision of new public parks as well as the restoration and care of existing parks. See www.urbanparksforum.co.uk

52 I am grateful to Ricky Burdett, Director of the Cities Programme at the LSE for discussing this point.

53 Forthcoming report by Robert Thorne and David Orr from Alan Baxter Associates for CABE and the (former) DETR . See also discussion on 'winning back public space' in Jan Gehl and Lars Gemzøe, *New City Spaces*, Copenhagen, Danish Architectural Press (2000).

Widening the debate/teamwork

Context. Firstly, designing is undertaken within a social and commercial context that may impose certain restraints. Land planning and design as a process starts with a thorough appreciation of the real world forces that will shape or at least influence a project and its ability to be delivered.

Secondly, designs, particularly in an urban context, require a thorough understanding of movement and the co-existing elements in and around a particular site and location.[54]

Listening, by both consultants and client, will foster a relationship in which all the issues can be explored, analysed, questioned, researched, summarised and synthesised to achieve a successful design solution.

Scrutiny. The design process by the land planner must be entirely auditable. Land planners appear routinely as expert witnesses at Public Inquiries, where their designs and plans are carefully scrutinised; they are regularly called upon to present and explain projects to Local Authorities, CABE and other public bodies and the landscape planners designs are nearly always subject to the statutory process of Environmental Impact Assessment.

Alternative solutions. Land planners are called upon to demonstrative alternative ways to deal with a site and sometimes, for instance in the green belt, it is even necessary to show evidence of having explored alternative sites.

The design process described: Paddington Central

This scheme illustrates the process of the land planner's work.

Members of the Paddington Regeneration Partnership are working together to create a new urban quarter. Eighty acres of 'blighted' land is being developed in stages to provide offices, houses, retail, health and leisure facilities. Each development is individual but linked to the others by a common approach to the public realm that will unite the separate schemes and mesh with the existing urban fabric.[55]

The catalysts for the development were improvements at Paddington station that have established it as a major transport interchange – the proposed Cross Rail and the opening of the Heathrow Express – making Paddington an international gateway to London.

---

54 Space Syntax Laboratory at University College London undertakes spatial analysis and design in this field.
55 Paddington Regeneration Partnership, 'Paddington Waterside: Creating a Place'.

The design of high-quality public realm spaces is vital to provide a sense of identity and place for this part of Paddington as a recognisable district within the wider character and context of Westminster.

The western end of the site, Paddington Central, was generally regarded as an impossible 'island' isolated by the confines of the railway, Westway and the canal. However Julian Barwick of Development Securities realised that the site had potential; there are hidden gems such as the canal and towpath, a major asset linking Paddington to Little Venice. If other connections could be established, the inaccessible 'island' could become the centrepiece of the new quarter. Julian Barwick's grit and determination paid off and he gained the support of Westminster City Council's Planning Department who accepted the high densities required to make the development viable. The ground had been laid for this approach by Richard Rogers and the Urban Task Force.

Development Securities appointed Ron Sidell of Sidell Gibson Architects to carry out the initial masterplan. As Ron Sidell explains:

This had to accommodate a complex range of requirements including:

- A framework of sites for an urban group of buildings on independent plots, built over a series of phases . . . separate but with a self-contained environment for each phase.
- The plots and areas for development had to allow for future adaptability to connect sites for larger buildings (as at Brindleyplace) in response to changing commercial needs.
- Connectivity – an urban network of spaces and routes to connect the surrounding neighbourhood with pedestrian and cycle routes through a previously blighted and private site.
- Risk analysis of the site's constraints and opportunities to provide facilities for Cross Rail, London transportation, Paddington station and a new bridge across the canal.
- Create a subterranean infrastructure to support future developments.
- Create zones of activities and use within appropriate areas of the masterplan – for example, putting residential buildings by the canal.
- Uniting the scheme to create an identifiable and unique urban quarter with a series of urban spaces . . . streets, squares and public spaces with public facilities that could be available in a 24-hour environment.

The process of listening, discussing, brainstorming and holding workshops brought about some changes in the landscape/public realm proposals. For example, the original concept for the square had been for a tranquil and traditional 'London square' with lawns and trees. However, the landscape architects saw the space as a focus for

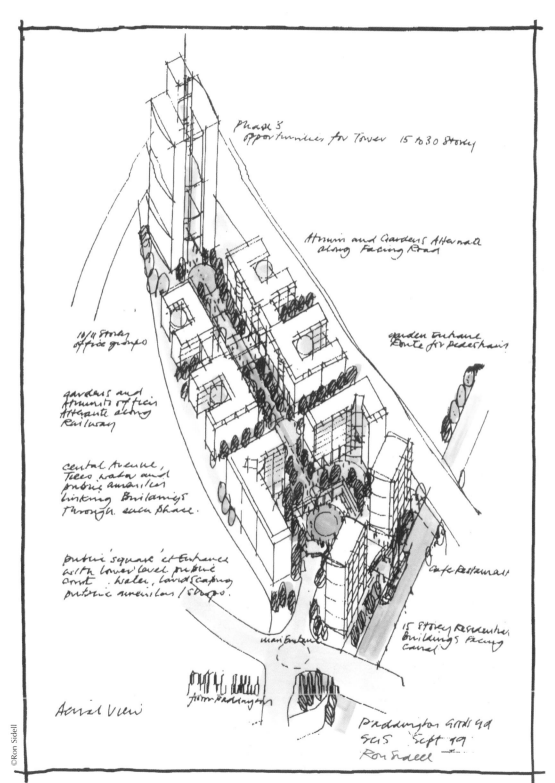

Figure 4: Aerial sketch master plan of Paddington by Ron Sidell

the site, the point of meeting and departing, to the residential area by the canal or to the offices on the central avenue and so the square became a curved arena, an active social hub with retail and leisure facilities and opportunities for organised events such as street theatre.

Phase One is due to open in spring 2003 and planning applications for Phase Two have been made. Two major office buildings, by Kohn Pedersen Fox and Sheppard Robson, will line the 'boulevard' – a central avenue with trees and reflective pools like shards of glass. The original landscape masterplan was reappraised during the design of these buildings and some features incorporated in the revised landscape design are echoed in the buildings. Kohn Pedersen Fox recognised that the landscape for the boulevard was part of a larger masterplan and that the overall landscape for the entire development must be coherent and so this was a case where the landscape tended to lead the way. All four designers involved – Sidell Gibson as masterplanners, Derek Lovejoy Partnership as land planners and Kohn Pedersen Fox and Sheppard Robson as architects of the boulevard buildings had to brain-storm all aspects of the scheme with each other and with the client.[56]

The boulevard will culminate in the Phase Three tower at the western end of the site. The tower will be designed by Foster & Partners with landscape design by the Derek Lovejoy Partnership.

The opportunities created, and the results achieved so far, illustrate the vital importance of team collaboration: the central role of Julian Barwick and Development Securities as the developer with commitment and vision; the support of Graham King, Planning Officer at Westminster; Ron Sidell and his team at Sidell Gibson for the initial masterplanning and subsequent understanding and close collaboration with David Blackwood Murray and his team at the Derek Lovejoy Partnership.

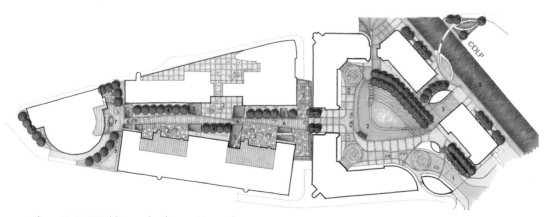

Figure 5: DLP Paddington landscape Masterplan

56 I am grateful to Lee Polizano and Ian Milne of KPF for their comments.

Case studies

In 'Invisible Gardens'[57] four main criteria were set out for the success of a shaped urban space:

- Is it loved?
- Is it maintained?
- Has its essence been preserved over time?
- If major change is contemplated, has the original designer been invited back to participate in the process of change?

Reviewing this chapter the key guidelines to success revolve around 'people':

- Successful place-making for people to appreciate and enjoy.
- A sense of place, familiarity, belonging, exploring and feeling safe.
- A place that encourages citizenship, social interaction, and respect for each other and for the place itself.

In addition there must be good design 'done right first time'.

Workplace roof garden

RMC Group International Headquarters, Thorpe, Surrey

Architects: Edward Cullinan Architects

Landscape Architects: Derek Lovejoy Partnership

Background
The project required a sensitive approach because it was located within the green belt. There were three existing houses on the site including a 17th-century classical house with its stable block, a 19th-century Arts & Crafts villa, two garden walls and many mature trees, all listed.

The new office accommodation was arranged as a series of single-storey wings enclosing interconnecting courtyards at ground level with hedged gardens created over the whole of the 4500 sq m area of roof covering the new buildings. The scheme returned the whole site to its landscaped appearance within the original garden boundaries. The first discussions for the project took place in 1985-86 and it was completed in 1990.

---

57 Peter Walker and Melanie Simo (1994), *Invisible Gardens,* Cambridge, Massachusetts, The MIT Press, p. 167.

©Michael Murray

Figure 6: RMC Headquarters, Thorpe Park, Surrey (Roof garden with original house in background)

The overall design objective was to integrate the architecture with the landscape. Hence, the landscape architects and architects worked closely together and with the client during the whole design and construction period.

The scheme has won many awards including the 1990 Civic Trust Streetley Special Award as Overall Winner, a 1993 Landscape Institute Award for the Derek Lovejoy Partnership and a 1990 RIBA National Award for Edward Cullinan Architects.

User and changing requirements:

- Twelve years on, changes to the building's requirements, brought about by the growth of the RMC Group and consolidation of local office accommodation, have necessitated a reconfiguration of the interior office space – 260 people now work in the building compared to the original 120 – and, additionally a reconsideration of the use of some of the enclosed courtyard areas. For example, the relocation within the complex of the headquarters' restaurant has incorporated a new external patio/terrace for al fresco dining.
- The anticipated, and hoped-for, use of the internal courtyards and paths across the roof gardens, as a means of access between the wings (weather dependent) has been a notable success. The nature of the architecture of the headquarters, particularly its single storey office accommodation, and the visual and physical accessibility to the gardens and landscape, has made an enormous contribution to the changed culture of the company, and to the employees who work here.

• RMC House continues to provide an attractive and unique environment in which to work; its construction represents an excellent showcase for many of the materials manufactured and supplied by the operating companies within the Group.

Summary 2002
Europe's largest roof garden is probably the most impressive integration of landscape and architecture in the UK today. Despite significant remodelling of the HQ interior to provide more flexible working accommodation for the increased staff numbers, the original vision for the landscaped gardens, pavilions, follies and reflective pools remains completely intact and continues to be appreciated by staff and visitors alike all year round.

Corporate Parkland

Sun Life (Axa) Headquarters, Bristol (1994–96)

Architects:	Robert Turner (now retired)
	Skidmore, Owings and Merrill, London.
Landscape Architects:	David Blackwood Murray,
	Derek Lovejoy Partnership, London

Background
The Derek Lovejoy Partnership worked closely with SOM's London office on an international competition winning masterplan to create this headquarters campus in parkland. The scheme had to provide for the accommodation of over 2,000 Sunlife employees under one roof and one of the key requirements was the provision of inspiring outdoor spaces for the staff to use and enjoy in good weather.[58]

Design
The qualities which created the winning design were the finger design of the buildings, which can be increased in future by 50 per cent, stretching out into the parkland which provides the visual anchor for the design. The extensive artificial lake creates an interplay with the buildings reflected in the water.

The parkland provides the main view when arriving by train at Bristol Parkway or travelling on the motorway. The orientation also captures a view of the near-by church tower. The decision was made to place all the parking at surface level rather than in parking buildings to avoid obscuring the view towards the buildings. The car-parking areas are subdivided by bands of evergreen shrubs and deciduous trees. All the parking is on one side of the buildings with the parkland on the other establishing

---

58 *Architects Journal,* 23 January 1997, pp. 42-45.

©DLP

Figure 7: Sun Life Headquarters, Bristol

an hierarchy of spaces from reaching the car park, arriving at the building, entering the internal street and finally emerging into the parkland beyond – the corporate campus as a 'country house'!

In more detail the landscape design required a masterplan for the 14-hectare site. The one hectare lake contains a central island and has attracted bird life including a pair of swans.

Changes in level are accommodated by grassed terraces faced with reconstituted stone and the surrounding parkland features more than 1,000 trees, planted as semi-mature specimens in a design that will enhance the parkland over the coming years. These include magnolias, Persian ironwoods, tulip trees, red oaks, dogwoods and pollarded willows to create a natural waterside environment at the edge of the lake.

The main entrance has gates specially commissioned for the project from the artist Giuseppe Lund.

Proximity to Bristol Parkway station means that a 'green travel plan' could be a workable option.

John Ireland, Project Manager for Sun Life, explains:

> It was of great importance to us that we provide an external environment that staff could appreciate and enjoy, and this is exactly what has been achieved . . . and is an example of what can be achieved by the landscape architect and the client developing a close working relationship.

Summary 2002
A recent survey of staff working at this flagship HQ has revealed the importance of the parkland and lakeside setting in providing a direct link with nature to enrich the working day. As the landscape matures, the illusion that the building was fitted into an existing park becomes a reality.

New City Park

Jubilee Park Canary Wharf (2002)

Landscape Architects: Jacques and Peter Wirtz

Background
Jubilee Park is about the size of Trafalgar Square and sits above Foster and Partners' Canary Wharf station and also, in part, over a new retail mall to which it is directly connected. Large office headquarters buildings look over the park on the north and south sides.

Peter Buchanan highlighted the poetics of landscape:

> For in the best landscape and gardens the magic is experienced not just because they contain plants, but because they are conceived as realms for the free play of the imagination, as triggers for contemplation, dreams and even the wildest lights of the imagination. And instead of diluting urban life, such poetics deepen its meanings.[59]

With this kind of expectation in mind Canary Wharf,

> retained the world renowned father and son landscape architects Jacques and Peter Wirtz[60], to design a park that contrasted with the height and formality of the adjacent buildings and offered a place of joy and contemplation.[61]

---

59 *Architectural Review,* June 1984, pp. 21-22.
60 Key projects by the Belgian landscape architects Jacques and Peter Wirtz include the 'Carousel' at the Tuilleries in Paris, the Jardin de Bierges and gardens at Alnwick Castle, and many private gardens.
61 I am grateful to Maurice Peakin of Canary Wharf for his comments and information on Jubilee Park.

©Folio Photography

Figure 8: Jubilee Park, Canary Wharf

The scheme
The park is, of course, to be experienced from within, but is also beautiful when viewed from the windows of the surrounding offices. A large number of trees were carefully selected to give colour and interest in all seasons of the year. The trees, semi-mature and the largest available in Europe, are placed to offer vistas and to create a variety of informal spaces.

Willowy, grass-topped dry stone walls and gravel paths meander through the park amongst the green swards and low growing shrubs. A series of linking raised pools cascade across the site creating sparkling fountains and the gentle background sound of flowing water.

Summary 2002

Canary Wharf began as a 'showpiece of international (American) corporate urbanism'.[62] But now, apart from the increasing numbers of office staff, it has also become a destination for Londoners – a regional shopping centre and meeting place.

Canary Wharf has already achieved several successful public realm spaces and Jubilee Park is a welcome addition. Canary Wharf is a private and well-managed estate, but perhaps Jubilee Park can be an inspiration for some other well-supported public funded urban spaces.

Connectivity

110 Bishopsgate, London

Architects:	Kohn Pedersen Fox Associates.
Landscape:	Kohn Pedersen Fox with Charles Funke

This case study considers the public realm implications of the proposed building.

The main objective of the architects and landscape architect was to 'create accessible welcoming spaces that forge links between the building and its context.'

Understanding the context begins with the site's historical significance as an important gate to the City of London from Roman times until the 18th century. Acknowledgement is also made of St Botolph without Bishopsgate[63] and St Botolph Aldgate[64]. The architects describe the main public realm issues:[65]

- The key to the proposals involves reconfiguring the existing traffic layout to reconnect the site to the surrounding city fabric. The tower is set back from the southern boundary to permit an additional lane of traffic on Camomile Street which therefore allows the closure of the section of Houndsditch to the north of the site and the creation of a new landscaped plaza.
- This space is treated in a simple robust manner with two lines of deciduous trees framing views to St Botolph without Bishopsgate and opening up again the reciprocal view to its sister church of St Botolph Aldgate.
- The landscaped space is conceived as an extension to the existing church gardens across Bishopsgate. Together they form part of a wider chain of green spaces linking Finsbury Circus with Devonshire Square.

62 Christopher Grafe, 'Unnatural Acts', Building Design, 26 July 2002, p. 32.
63 First mentioned in 1212. Escaped damage in the Great Fire of 1666 but was demolished in 1724 and rebuilt in 1725-8 by George Dance the Elder.
64 The church of St Botolph Aldgate was first built in the 10/11th century and the present building of 1744 is by George Dance the Elder.
65 I am grateful to Fred Pilbrow of KPF for this information.

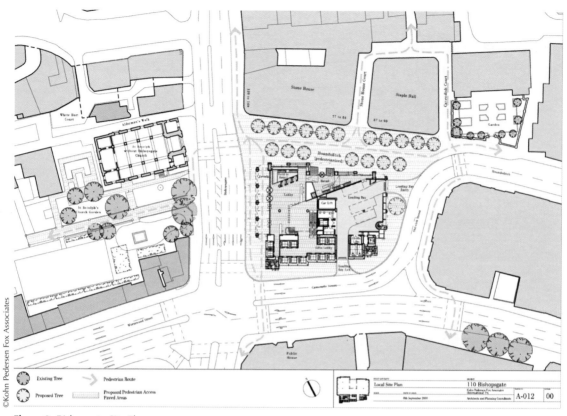

©Kohn Pedersen Fox Associates

Figure 9: Bishopgate Site Plan

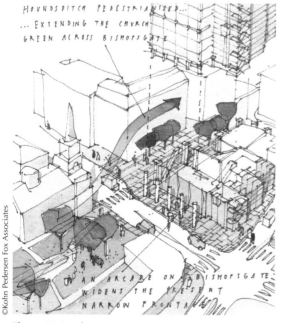

©Kohn Pedersen Fox Associates

Figure 10: Landscape context

©Kohn Pedersen Fox Associates

Figure 11: Perspective looking towards St Botolph and Bishopsgate

166

- Natural stone paving extends from the space to the public lobbies at the base of the building.
- There is public access to both the base and the top of the building. Cafés and shops will animate the space at the base. At high level there will be a sky restaurant.

Summary
Compared to the post-war buildings currently on the site the proposal for 110 Bishopsgate illustrates the much greater emphasis that is now placed on linking new buildings to the totality of their context.

New urban spaces revisited

Broadgate (1985-2002)

Developer:	Rosehaugh Stanhope
Architects:	Peter Foggo, Arup Associates (Phase 1, 1984-88)
	Skidmore Owings & Merrill (Phase 2, 1988–91)
Landscape:	Phase 1: Arups with Charles Funke
	Phase 2: SOM
Present Owners:	The British Land Company undertaking Public Space enhancement Programme.
Architects:	SOM
Landscape:	SOM with Townshend Landscape Architects

Background
'One Finsbury Avenue brought to London something that has seemed impossible – a speculative office building of real quality – and it started Broadgate on its way.'[66]

Phase 1 (1984-88) Buildings 1-4
Stuart Lipton of Stanhope Securities, Geoffrey Bradman of Rosehaugh and Peter Foggo of Arups worked together to win the bid to redevelop the redundant Broad Street Station on ten acres of land on the west side of Liverpool Street Station.[67]

---

66 John Winter reviewing the exhibition, 'Peter Foggo, Architect at the RIBA', Architects Journal, 8 September 1994.

67 Writings on the history and development of Broadgate include:
Building Design, 4 March 1988, pp. 14–16; *Architects Journal,* 24 October 1990, pp. 28-31; *Broadgate.* Photographs by John Davies and Brian Griffin, Text by Les Hutton. London, Davenport, 1991; Ricky Burdett (ed), *City Changes: Architecture in the City of London 1985–1995,* London, Architecture Foundation, 1992; *Building,* 6 February 1998, pp. 40-45' *Landscape Design,* May 1994, pp 9-43 (issue on Urban Landscape Design).

The new offices, following One Finsbury Avenue, had large floor plates with atria in response to the space requirements of 'Information Technology'[68] and changes in banking practice.[69]

What made Broadgate so different from other office developments in London was the creation, within the scheme, of major public open spaces onto which the 'front doors' of the office buildings opened. These spaces offered more than promenades or summer lunch spots for office workers. The central space and focal point was the circular arena with its winter open-air ice skating rink (especially attractive to children and schools) and its summer entertainment programme (see Figures 2 and 3).

Finsbury Avenue Square was designated as a quieter green space and the Octagon offered the point of entry from Eldon Street. The Arena and the Octagon also had bars, restaurants and some retail facilities.

Phase Two (1988–91)
Skidmore Owings & Merrill were appointed as architects for the development of Phase Two and the site was extended to cover 29 acres. Rosehaugh Stanhope worked alongside British Rail which was redeveloping Liverpool Street Station at that time.

In Phase Two the third, and largest, public open space was created at Exchange Square dominated by Exchange House. As Roger G. Kallman of SOM writes:

> In many ways Exchange Square is the most complex and interesting of all these outdoor spaces. It is unusual in part because of the number of levels created in the space but it is also interesting because this typography was governed by a number of engineering considerations, not least the need to ensure sufficient clearance for the active railway lines below. In addition to these issues, others were raised by heritage organisations concerned with preserving the vista at the 'country end' of the station's train shed building. This meant that the plaza had to be at its lowest elevation where it joined the train shed facade rising to its highest level on the opposite side of the square in order to preserve the views from within the station. The north-south fall across the square was achieved through a series of gradual steps which also serve as seating for crowds attending concerts, having lunch or engaging in recreation. Extended to the east, these steps become the cascade of the fountain which terminates in a 'rockery' pool. Overlooking the fountain at a higher lever of the plaza sits the Botero bronze sculpture, 'Broadgate Venus'. Also at the upper level along the northern side of the plaza is a group of chestnut trees which provides a pleasant alternative setting for users of this space. On the west side of the plaza are a set of sandstone walls which frame a generous ramp connecting the upper and lower levels and further define functional zones within Exchange Square. Near the centre of the plaza at the lowest elevation is a large expanse of grass used for

---

68 ORBIT study, 1983.
69 Rosehaugh Stanhope commissioned a report from DEGW on this.

©Miller Hare

Figure 12: Exchange Square showing new building at No. 10 (Hamilton House)

additional seating and at times for croquet and other sports as well as performance art. A stage provided on the southwest corner is covered with a tensile structure, which, owing to its sculptural form further animates the space. The final elements, which complete the plaza, are a series of wooden pavilions offering a range of catering facilities. These have been located on 'preferred' pedestrian routes as studied by the Space Syntax group.

Movement through, and use of spaces
All the public spaces in Broadgate are linked to one another and to the streets surrounding the whole development. The public spaces are a fundamental part of the scheme and a report by Professor Bill Hillier[70] carried out between October 1988 and

---

70 Space Syntax Laboratory, University College.

January 1990 showed that Broadgate was the 'best used public open space in and around the City of London.' The spaces were used by people both from the offices on site and also from outside – there was no 'ghetto effect'.

Public art
Another key element in the public spaces is the impressive range of carefully chosen and commissioned artworks, especially sculptures.

Public space enhancements 2002
Broadgate is now owned by The British Land Company plc.

Since Broadgate was first conceived and built there have been significant improvements in the surrounding areas. This means that Broadgate has become much busier with a heavier footfall which has accelerated the need to enhance and update the existing fabric and facilities.

The intention is to renew elements of the original scheme without compromising the integrity of the overall urban design or landscape masterplan. Space Syntax prepared an exhaustive study of the current pedestrian activity and the findings help to design the proposals for improvement which include:

- comprehensive lighting improvements;
- more retail and restaurant spaces;
- improvements to the hard and soft landscape throughout the estate;
- more open spaces for events and entertainment;
- Improved connections/'gateways' to some of the surrounding areas.

Some specific schemes to achieve this include:

- Upgrading and glazing the bar at the Arena and tidying the hanging greenery.
- Completely re-landscaping Finsbury Avenue Square involving the removal of the existing trees to be replaced with more suitable semi-mature trees; raising the level of the square so that pedestrians can follow their preferred routes across it; providing a restaurant at both plaza and lower levels as a focus at the centre of the space to help enliven the square.
- Interestingly, SOM originally proposed a water feature and lighting in the centre of the square designed in two sections and integrated with the paving. When the water feature was turned on it would be seen to have a diagonal path between the two areas that represented the line – the 'ghost' of Finsbury Avenue, a reminder of an earlier layer of history.[71] Apparently the decision was finally made to have a grid of lighting only.

---

71 I am grateful to Larry K. Oltmanns of SOM for this description.

Figure 13: The Octagon (before)

Figure 14: The Octagon (after)

- Among improvements at the Octagon will be the greater definition of entrances to the Arena and Liverpool Street Station and redesigned steps to create more space around the base of the Fulcrum (sculpture by Richard Serra) and improve views through to the Arena.

10 Exchange Square (Hamilton House)
At the same time Hamilton House, one of the original buildings on the site, is to be redeveloped. It sits at the northwest corner of Exchange Square on a small piazza connecting the square to Appold Street – the 'gateway to Hackney'. Developments in the surrounding area have significantly increased movement through this passage. The proposal is as follows:

More than just a new office building, 10 Exchange Square seeks to fulfil an urban mission of clarifying and enhancing pedestrian connections between the City and Broadgate. The redevelopment of the site allowed for a new gateway to be created on the western edge of the Estate. A series of textured glass walls define the space and visually conduct pedestrians through the new urban space. A generous cascading stair mitigates the change in levels from the street to Exchange Square. The entrance stair extends into the lobby space to provide alternative indoor and outdoor routes; while also allowing the external space to appear more expansive. At night, light will be cast on the base of the walls, providing a subtle glow that frames the space and lends further ambiguity to the definition between inside and outside. Along with the addition of a new public space, 10 Exchange Square resolved many contextual issues around the site. This was done in close design consultation with the Corporation of London to define the future scale to the north-western edge of the City. A gracious curving south facade opens the Estate to pedestrians allowing for a wide public space that gradually narrows as it gently ascends towards Exchange Square. Here a single storey glass pavilion with a bar and high-quality restaurant acts as an extension to Exchange Square, already a highly successful urban space. Additional flexible retail space on Appold Street provides for a variety of uses that will also fulfil the need for an active street front.[72]

Maintenance and security
The public spaces are well-maintained and clear of litter and vandalism. Broadgate is a private development and the whole area is closed to the general public for one day each year, usually on Christmas Day. British Land's management company, Broadgate Estates, ensures a high level of security and maintenance throughout the development.

Summary 2002
The current public realm improvements projects at Broadgate are partly the result of the scheme's overall success – it now has to accommodate greater numbers of people and activities. They also reflect changes in tenant and public requirements and the need to maintain the present and future status of the development.

However, looking at just two areas for enhancement, one wonders if the original concepts were at fault or if expectations have simply changed. For example, Finsbury Avenue Square.

Finsbury Avenue Square
The 1990 Space Syntax report showed that Finsbury Avenue Square was less busy than Broadgate Square (the Arena) but it was still popular and it was offered in the masterplan as a quiet square and, as the 'quiet space', it provided no organised activity, unlike the Arena and Exchange Square. Perhaps this kind of contemplative space in which to settle quietly is not currently desirable and a demand for more facilities such as another restaurant and an additional events venue has been identified.

There is generally a reluctance to cut down mature trees in an urban area. Unfortunately it would appear that the trees, in full leaf, shade the surrounding

---

72 I am grateful to Larry K. Oltmanns of SOM for these comments.

buildings and the square itself too much. Other elements such as the granite textured sett paving and sunken levels were also off-putting for pedestrian movement across the square. So, perhaps the elements of potential failure were there from the start.

The Arena

The public's requirements and expectations have become more sophisticated in the last 15 years and the changes to the Arena bar reflect this, as do the requirement to tidy up the ivy at high level and introduce clipped box at the lower planting levels.

Author profile

David Blackwood Murray, Chairman
Derek Lovejoy Partnership

David Blackwood Murray trained as a Landscape Architect from 1974-79. He was made a partner in Derek Lovejoy's London office in 1988 and in 2000 he became Chairman of the Group, which currently employs 100 staff.

Over 21 years in practice with the Derek Lovejoy Partnership has widened David's experience to include a detailed understanding of the interdisciplinary process of creative teamwork, working within the UK, Europe and more recently in Asia and the Middle East. Some of his landmark projects have been as diverse as the Magic Kingdom at Disneyland Paris, the roof garden at the RMC headquarters in Thorpe Park Surrey and the Ritz Carlton Hotel and beach resort in Dubai.

Relevant experience for offices includes:

- RMC Headquarters, Thorpe
- Sun Life Headquarters Bristol
- Scottish Equitable headquarters Edinburgh
- Arlington Business Parks in Oxford and Manchester
- Paddington Central
- Esso Glen Victoria
- Swiss Re Headquarters London
- Canary Riverside
- Regents Quarter Kings Cross
- Park Place Croydon
- Greenwich University

David's particular area of interest and concern is for urban regeneration and the public realm. He considers that this is a key issue to be tackled to achieve an 'urban renaissance' which is seen as being both desirable and necessary.

At Lovejoy each director continues to work in a studio environment with their team. The team is responsible for carrying out the project from inception to completion. This provides continuity and ensures that clients have a direct and personal link to their design team. Projects must be undertaken with real commitment and enthusiasm and it is the director's role to ensure that this happens.

8 Architecture

Robert Dalziel
Reid Architecture

The financial capitals of northern Europe are poised to receive a fresh crop of very tall office buildings, and at the same time debate rages as to whether city-centre offices are needed at all, given the advent of mobile time-flexible working practices made possible by new technology. These are positions at the extremes of architectural expression. But what is in no doubt is that office buildings, large and small, will continue to proliferate in the middle ground, and will continue both to symbolise and to support our contemporary working life.

What do we expect of great office architecture: that it delight the senses and the mind, that it raise our spirits and feed our imagination? Yes, of course. What also matters is the success of offices as places of work. Are there universal guidelines to assist designers in their search for the best performing solutions?

Modern architecture has reached a level of technological maturity where the aesthetic aspirations of early 20th century architect-pioneers can be realised consistently and reliably, and there is now a large and ever-increasing roll-call of notable modern office buildings of stunning appearance across Europe. Among these one could mention Henning Larsen's Nordea Bank complex in Copenhagen, Richard Rogers' headquarters for Lloyd's Register of Shipping in London, and Norman Foster's home for Electronic Arts in Surrey, Helmut Jahn's Deutsche Bahn building at the Sony Center in Berlin, Funf Hoffe by Herzog and de Meuron in Munich, and Renzo Piano's Banca Popolare in Lodi.[1] This selection of new and notable office buildings though limited, nevertheless covers a range of polarities including city centre and out-of-town, stand-alone and urban-integrated, and northern European to southern European. A chapter on the architecture of office buildings could merely catalogue these and other splendid projects.

But architecture is an all-embracing art, concerned with the construction, function and performance of buildings as well as their visual presence. This comment is not intended as an exhortation to architects that they should extend their vision of architecture beyond the purely visual. Those involved in building design cannot escape their responsibility for performance; it will be an inevitable consequence of their decisions, whether consciously anticipated or not. And this responsibility extends beyond building form to the impact of building projects on civic space and civic life, and the relationships between old buildings and new ones.

---

1 These buildings are featured as case studies on the following pages. On the drawings (W=) is plan width to window wall and (H=) is the floor to floor dimension in metres.

Nordea Bank, Copenhagen, Henning Larsen

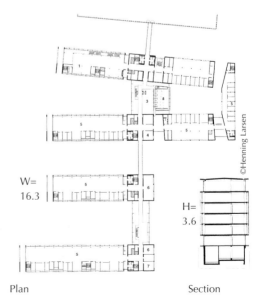

W=
16.3

H=
3.6

©Henning Larsen

Plan

Section

So any chapter on the architecture of office design should consider the influences that guide decision-making in achieving successful office and public environments, as well as drawing attention to the most striking examples of current architectural practice.

How is building form related to performance?

In the UK, where most office space is constructed by developers rather than owner-occupiers, design is somewhat rule-driven, and there are often uncritical responses to questions of, for instance, appropriate plan depth and engineering systems. The UK's British Council for Offices publishes a guide to specification, which in its most recent revision[2] stresses that the starting point in design should be a statement of specific user values such as identity and the ability to accommodate a particular workstyle. Target capital, operating and energy costs should also be recorded. The resulting brief (of anticipated performance) should then inform the various design choices and decisions that will shape the project.

The premise is that there is no single design solution that is right for all circumstances, so the emphasis has moved away from defining immutable standards, to offering guidance on an approach to formulating an appropriate specification tailored to the requirements of a unique development project. Consider the characteristics of two award-winning business units: the Canon Headquarters Building at Reigate designed by David Richmond Architects and the BA Combined Operations Centre at Heathrow airport designed by Nicholas Grimshaw and Partners.

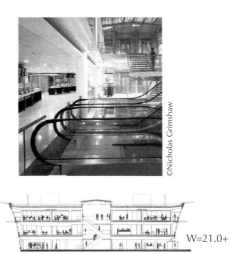

Figure 1: Canon HQ, Reigate

Figure 2: BA Combined Operations, Heathrow

Both are three-storey atrium-based administrative buildings for multinational service companies located in southeast England. And yet one is naturally ventilated with a

---

2 British Council for Offices (BCO) (2000), *BCO Guide 2000: Best Practice in the Specification of Offices*, London, BCO.

Lloyd's Register of Shipping, London, Richard Rogers

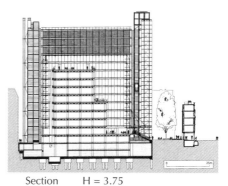

Section   H = 3.75

Plan   W= 9.0 + 9.0 + 9.0

©Katsuhisa Kida

©RRP

plan depth of 13.5 metres while the other is fully air conditioned and has plan depths in excess of 21 metres. Neither can be regarded as more correct, as they both respond well to their particular circumstances of site and client brief. What distinguishes them is the balance of value attached to recurring as opposed to capital cost, and the impact of local site conditions.

What then are the principal influences that shape good office design? The *BCO Guide,* and other standard references such as Raymond and Cunliffe's *Tomorrow's Office 2000*[3] consider, for instance, the relationship between plate width and a variety of performance features such as workstyle, comfort, energy consumption and capital cost. They take into account the effects of plan depth on the ability to sub-divide space and use it flexibly, and also consider the implications on the design of mechanical and ventilation systems. This analysis is summarised in the figure below taken from the *BCO Guide 2000,* which suggests a dichotomy between the European and US models for office building design.

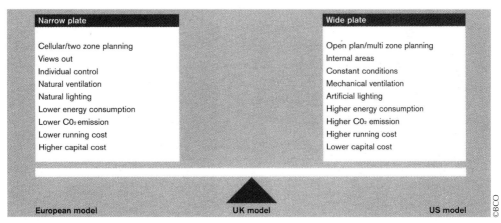

Figure 3: Building plan depth

Narrow-plates (13.5 metres or less) are characterised by cellular planning, greater individual control over natural lighting and ventilation, lower energy costs and high capital cost. Wider plates (21 metres or more), it is suggested, afford greater flexibility in planning a variety of internal layouts incorporating open plan and sub-divided space, and rely on mechanical air conditioning systems and artificial lighting to maintain constant working conditions, resulting in higher energy costs but lower capital costs.

The Probe studies undertaken by Adrian Leaman and Bill Bordass (of Building Use Studies) suggest that the narrow-plate model is a more comfortable one from the point of view of the user, and it is further observed that there is a direct relationship between user comfort and work productivity. The link between business productivity and building design is notoriously hard to quantify because building populations are

---

3 Raymond, S and Cunliffe, R (2000), *Tomorrow's Office, Creating Effective and Humane Interiors*, London, E & FN Spon.

Electronic Arts Building, Surrey, Norman Foster

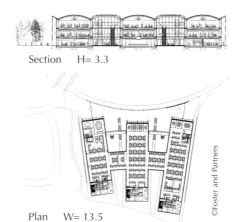

Section   H= 3.3

Plan   W= 13.5

©Foster and Partners

very different from each other, and it becomes difficult in any process of comparison to isolate the unique effects of different physical environments. However, two principal influences on productivity have been identified: the subjective well-being of the individual occupant (which is directly affected by the perceived control of natural light, temperature and ventilation), and the effectiveness of communication between members of working groups (which progressively deteriorates when groups exceed about five people). The general conclusions advanced in the best text on the subject[4], are that overall satisfaction and productivity tend to decrease the deeper buildings get.

If the narrow-plate naturally ventilated model is associated with greater productivity, then why is it not more widely employed in the UK (particularly with increasing emphasis on the need to reduce energy costs and achieve sustainability)? There may be instances when hostile conditions appear to dictate a sealed building solution (such as the BA Combined Operations centre located at Heathrow airport). City centre locations are also typically assumed to require sealed buildings, but some recent projects demonstrate that effective naturally ventilated solutions can be devised for relatively hostile environments. The Helicon Building in London designed by Sheppard Robson is a good example (see below).

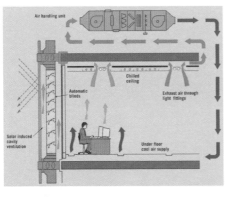

W= 16.5

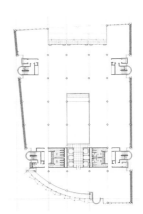

Plan

H= 3.75

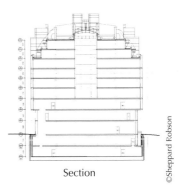

Section

©Sheppard Robson

Figure 4: Helicon Building, London

4 Clements-Croome, D (2000), *Creating the Productive Workplace,* London, E & FN Spon.

Deutsche Bahn, Sony Center, Berlin, Helmut Jahn

W=
7.0 + 7.0

Plan

H=
3.55

Elevation

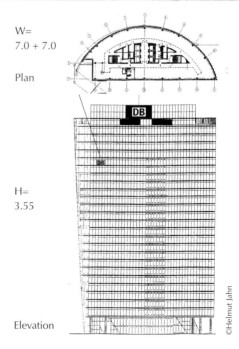

On a more modest scale, the new London office of Reid Architecture demonstrates that a naturally ventilated, comfort-cooled system can successfully be retro-fit into a reconstructed 1950s city-centre office building. And yet there is still predominance in the UK and America of relatively deep-plan office developments provided with full air conditioning.

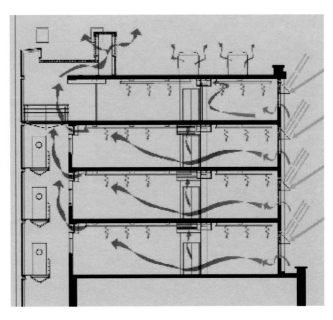

Figure 5: Reid Architecture Offices, London

Is building form a scientific or a cultural outcome?

To understand the differences in approach between the European and the UK/US model it is necessary to look beyond the objective or scientific criteria that might be presumed to lie behind design choices, and consider the cultural context in which these choices have been made. In *The European Office*[5], Juriaan van Meel makes the point that 'office design is not just the translation of functional needs or technological possibilities, but also a reflection of the society in which it is created.' Here he is referring principally to national context rather than company culture, and he has identified a number of important drivers affecting building height, floor-plate design and work-setting environment that result in different office development practices across Europe.

Consider, for instance, the drivers behind the different floor-plate models mentioned above: narrow/naturally ventilated versus wide/air conditioned. In his book van Meel observes that in northern Europe, most office space is created by end-users for their own purposes. They have relative freedom in deciding how to dispose of and arrange their space. An additional factor is the strength of employee representation that is

5 van Meel, J (2000), *The European Office,* Rotterdam, 010 Publishers

Funf Hoffe, Munich, Herzog and de Meuron

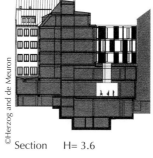

©Herzog and de Meuron

Section   H= 3.6

Plan   W= 9.5 (new) +
6.5 (existing)

characteristic of Europe, not only in terms of real union influence but also because of general cultural support for the principle of democratic participation in the workplace. The typical result is a narrow-floor plate in which all employees sit within 6.5 metres of a window, enjoy relatively high levels of natural light, and are afforded some control over their environment through access to openable windows. In many cases, a large proportion of employees are also provided with their own cellular offices.

In the UK, where most new office space is supplied by developers, there is an emphasis on construction and layout efficiency focussed on achieving developer/shareholder profit. In *The New Office*[6], Francis Duffy makes reference to a study by Carol Willis entitled 'Form follows Finance', which aptly summarises the relationship. The typical UK/US office plate will be relatively wide (15-21 metres) and will rely on air conditioning systems generally beyond the control of tenants or employees. Although the wide plate model is advertised as supporting the greater layout flexibility needed for today's dynamic team-based workstyles, there is no objective study that supports the belief that wide-plate space is better in this context than narrow-plate space. In *New Environments for Working*[7], the suggestion is made that narrow-plate buildings are not appropriate for a hive-type or secretarial pool workstyle, but it is not clear why, and no hard evidence is given. Further, although air conditioning is often sold as being associated with superior quality, there is evidence that a lack of research has led to gross over-capacity in heating, cooling and ventilation plant[8], all adding to the tenants' running costs. Therefore van Meel contends that the wide-plate model is a direct consequence of its cultural/procurement context and resulting commercial pressures.

He supports this view with a variety of examples, the most striking of which is a comparison between the SAS headquarters building in Sweden, and the BA Waterside building at Heathrow airport, both designed by Norwegian architect Niels Torp (*see* overleaf).

These two buildings are so alike in many ways, and not surprisingly, since the SAS building was clearly the inspiration for BA Waterside. Both evidently address the same business need i.e. airline administrative offices, and both are 'groundscrapers' which celebrate the vitality of a street-based layout providing real and useful amenities such as restaurants, shops and meeting spaces.

6 Duffy, F (1999), The New Office, London, Conran Octopus Limited.
7 Laing, A Duffy, F Jaunzens, D and Willis S (1998), *New Environments for Working*, London, Construction research Communications Limited.
8 Parsloe, CJ, *BSRIA Technical Report* TR21/95, Bracknell.

Banco Populare, Lodi, Renzo Piano

H=
4.0

Section

W=
8.0 + 11.0

Plan

©Renzo Piano

And yet, examination of the office plans reveals a radically different approach to the design and fit-out of the floor-plates, which can only have been driven by the cultural context.

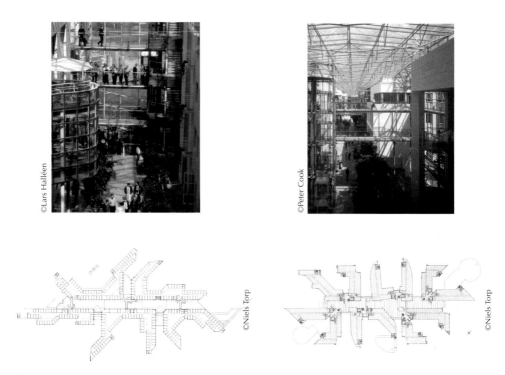

Figure 6: SAS Headquarters, Sweden   **Figure 7:** BA Waterside, London

A second example is a comparison of the offices of a single multi-national company ABN AMRO Bank, in Amsterdam and London (*see* below).

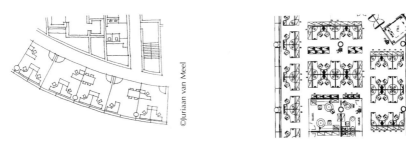

Figure 8: ABN Ambro, Amsterdam   **Figure 9:** ABN Ambro, London

Notwithstanding the evidently identical business processes, the workstyle, layout and plate characteristics are markedly different. This example seems to puncture the belief that a universal, or at least international, style of office design based on objective design principles is actually practiced.

Should designs respond to specific or generic needs?

In the IOD publication entitled *Buildings that Work for Your Business*[9], John Worthington argues that 'successful building is the result of a responsive briefing process and an attentive client.' The suggestion is that when a clear brief has been developed which sets out user values, the outcome will be a unique physical result embodying a specific need. Is this a realistic proposition in view of the above influences, which drive hard towards one solution in the UK/US and another in Europe? Whatever their relative merits, these patterns appear to be adhered to with equal rigidity.

Conversely, is it actually desirable that every individual building expresses the style of its initial occupant as if shrink-wrapped around a particular contemporary business process? When we look at the best historic city centres in Europe, the evidence is of a relatively static fabric of buildings of human scale creating pleasant civic spaces, used and adapted by countless occupants, each with their own differing needs. In Italy, where historic centres are revered and have been preserved, much modern office space has been successfully inserted into the existing fabric by conversion, renewal and adaptation (*see* below).

Figure 10: Solicitors' office in Bologna showing modern office which does not effect the existing fabric

9 IoD and Davis Langdon & Everest (2001), *Buildings that Work for your Business*, London, Director Publications Limited.

The result, as van Meel points out, is that contemporary Italian examples of famous office buildings are rare in literature on office design. The real challenges of incorporating sophisticated data and environmental systems into historic structures cannot be overlooked. But the significant point is that buildings can last a long time, particularly buildings of quality, and there is a strong argument therefore that designers can and should consider the likelihood of multiple tenancies and changing needs when fixing the essential features of new construction.

The counter-argument to this looser-fit approach would be that additional construction costs would be incurred. But in view of the fast pace of change in business processes and the general need for flexibility, is it not likely that considerable turbulence will have to be accommodated even during the first tenancy? Should not developers consider the likely workstyle requirements of their initial tenant at least? As tenants become better informed and more demanding, it will presumably be necessary for developers to become more responsive, but the habit of giving slight attention to performance in use is well ingrained. In *The New Office*, Duffy highlights the divorce which took place in the early development of the US model between the developer/landlords and their architects on the one hand, and the tenants and their interior designers on the other: the one group preoccupied with plate/construction efficiency and the other coping with an environment which compromised their operations and comfort by its constraints. In his words, 'the worlds of real estate and of building use had completely diverged.'

What do occupants want?

What then, more specifically, are the things affecting building design that occupants actually prefer? In *Buildings that Work for Your Business*[10], Adrian Leaman summarises the following 'virtuous' features, based on his extensive post-occupancy studies:

- Shallower plan forms (less than 15 metres) – allowing direct access to natural light.
- Cellularisation – defined and partitioned areas for particular functions such as meeting rooms.
- Thermal mass – creating stable, comfortable and predictable conditions, summer and winter.
- Controlled background ventilation without unwanted air infiltration.
- Openable windows and views out.
- High-quality toilets.
- Usable controls (for heating, blinds, ventilation).
- Usable interfaces to adjust air conditioning and lighting systems.

The importance of the usability of controls for building services is paramount. Buildings which rely on sophisticated and complex systems which are subsequently

---

10 Ibid n9

badly managed and maintained, and which consequently perform poorly, are doubly irritating to occupants, firstly because of the resulting discomfort and secondly because control over environmental conditions has been taken away from them. So Leaman advises that most occupants prefer natural ventilation for most of the year, whilst wanting the option of comfort cooling during short periods of hot weather during the summer.

Leaman's focus is on comfort, but there are other important considerations when evaluating office space from the occupant's perspective. Accenture uses a tool called the Building Rating Method (BRM) that allows the occupants to evaluate the strengths and weaknesses of potential locations and lettings worldwide. Buildings are rated against a range of factors illustrated on the radar graph (see below).

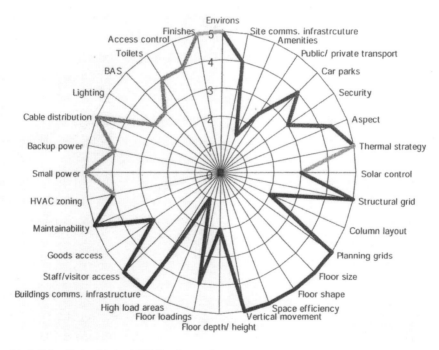

Figure 11: Building Rating Method (BRM) radar graph

Features are awarded points based on graded answers to a multitude of questions for each factor. Interestingly, the instructions for use state that 'questions are not concerned with how the building is currently being used or how you intend to use the building if you occupy it, as it assumes that the way the space is used will always change over time.'

The BRM looks separately at Section A: the location of the building (its accessibility and branding); Section B: the building shell (in terms of adaptability); and Section C: the building facilities and technologies installed within it.

Under Section A: Location, questions are concerned with how easy it is to get to the site from public and private transport, how the area around the building affects the working environment, how easy and safe is it to get into and out of the building, and how well the building reflects the company image.

Under Section B: Building Shell, questions very relevant to building design are posed. For each of the indicative factors given below, highest scores are awarded for the feature described (in quotations):

- **Thermal strategy** – 'Good building shape and orientation; walls, roof, windows and building mass integrated to optimise heat gains and losses thought the year; natural ventilation where possible.'

- **Solar control strategy** – 'Provides excellent protection from glare and overheating for west and east facing openings; allows user control of shading.'

- **Structural grid** – 'Multiple of planning grid; 9 m clear span to core.'

- **Column layout** – 'No internal or perimeter columns.'

- **Planning grid** – '1.5 m standard providing 3 m width offices and many options for sub-division.'

- **Floor-plate size** – '2,000 – 2,500 sq m in segments of no less than 500 sq m.'

- **Floor-plate configuration** – 'Four sides, 90 ° angles.'

- **Tenant floor-plate efficiency** – (net internal area over net usable area where NUA excludes primary circulation) – '89 per cent.'

- **Floor-plate depth** – *see* Table 1 overleaf.

In Section C: Facilities and Technologies, a further range of factors is considered including lighting, cable distribution, backup power, small power, and HVAC zoning. Under the latter heading, for instance, a maximum score is given to the following provision:

Fully zoned with individual control of temperature and ventilation throughout the building. User-friendly controls. Provision for out-of-hours use by individual or small group provided on each floor. Separate metering possible for potential sub-tenancies.

To summarise from an occupant's point of view, the optimum space is that which offers ease of access to public transport and amenities, is comfortable (i.e. provides access to natural light and ventilation), adaptable, maintainable and provides zoned and usable services systems. These preferences appear to be universal, notwithstanding national and cultural conditioning.

Table 1: Floor-plate depth to clear height ratio (rated 1–5)

		Glass to glass floor depth				
		<12m	12m – <13.5m	13.5m – 18m	18m – 25m	>25m
	Options for services location	Perimeter servicing satisfactory Natural ventilation possible	May be problems with perimeter servicing	Requires some form of cable distribution system through ceiling or floor. Mechanical ventilation required for deeper spaces, major ducting for AC may result >18 m		
Slab to slab height						
>4.5m	Perimeter/Raised floor/ Ceiling	4	4	4	4	3
4.0m– 4.5m	Perimeter/Raised floor/ Ceiling	5	5	4	3	3
3.8m – 4m	Perimeter/Raised floor/ Ceiling	5	5	3	2	2
3.6m – <3.8m	Perimeter/Raised floor/ Ceiling	5	5	3	2	2
3.4m – <3.6m	Perimeter only	3	3	2	2	2
3.2m – <3.4m	Perimeter only	3	3	2	2	2
<3.2m	Perimeter only	2	2	1	1	1

		Glass to core floor depth				
		<6m	6m – <9m	9m – 12m	12m – 15m	>15m
	Options for services location	Perimeter servicing satisfactory Natural ventilation possible	May be problems with perimeter servicing	Requires some form of cable distribution system through ceiling or floor. Mechanical ventilation required for deeper spaces, major ducting for AC may result >18 m		
Slab to slab height						
>4.5m	Perimeter/Raised floor/ Ceiling	3	4	4	3	3
4.0m– 4.5m	Perimeter/Raised floor/ Ceiling	4	5	5	3	3
3.8m – 4m	Perimeter/Raised floor/ Ceiling	4	5	4	2	2
3.6m – <3.8m	Perimeter/Raised floor/ Ceiling	4	5	3	2	2
3.4m – <3.6m	Perimeter only	3	3	2	2	2
3.2m – <3.4m	Perimeter only	3	3	2	2	2
<3.2m	Perimeter only	2	2	1	1	1

What is flexibility?

In *The New Office*, Duffy forecasts that:

> offices will become more saturated by information technology, more obviously
> places for meeting and interaction, less hierarchical, more diverse in style and
> structure and able to be changed more rapidly; they will tend to become smaller
> and be in less centralized, less predictable and more dispersed locations; above all,
> they will come under the increasing control of, and be more responsive to, ever-
> changing teams of intelligent and demanding end-users.

How are these evident requirements for flexibility to be translated into tangible
offerings by those who develop and design office space?

In the BCO publication, *The Service Challenge*[11], one of the headline concerns
expressed by occupiers was the changing head count as businesses expand and
contract, requiring companies to be able to turn space on and off quickly. UK
property directors are quoted as saying 'flexibility to me means the ability to
increase/decrease location or property type at a time that suits us' and 'the UK
industry is good at throwing up speculative office space, but as for flexibility of terms,
it doesn't understand modern business and doesn't feel the need to respond.' So there
is clear frustration with the inflexible lease arrangements typical of the UK, which
inhibit rapid and variable reactions to a volatile and changing business environment.

Responding to the need for flexible occupancy, Accenture is shrinking its downtown
space and supporting a more dispersed portfolio of properties, conceiving its total
workspace as a virtual network which embraces homeworking, satellite offices and
city-centre bases. The shock of the catastrophic destruction of New York's commercial
heart on 11 September 2001 has led Accenture to the significant realisation that it
cannot and, indeed, need not rely on centralised offices.

But what of the influence of the need for flexibility on the design of physical space?
Clearly the provision of a diversity of property types and sizes combined with more
flexible lease structures will give greater choice to occupiers, but what are the
implications of changing workstyles on the internal office environment? The ease of
sub-division of floor-plates into separate, conveniently serviced tenancies of variable
size, is essential. Techniques for achieving this kind of flexibility are generally covered
in the *BCO Guide 2000*. At Dawleywood, the latest phase of Stockley Park, cores
have been placed asymmetrically, yielding a variety of letting sizes and shapes for
each building level. Space with depths of 13.5 metres, 18 metres and 27 metres
separated by atria, is available from a common core.

---

11 Lipsey Morgan, K (2002), *The Service Challenge,* London, British Council for Offices.

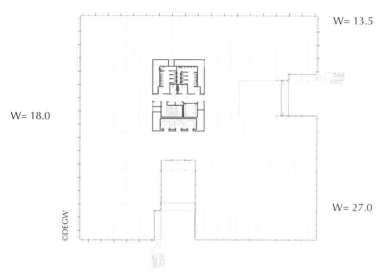

W= 13.5

W= 18.0

W= 27.0

©DEGW

Figure 12: Dawleywood, Stockley Park, KPF/DEGW

This arrangement not only offers greater choice to the potential tenant but also makes sub-letting easier in a difficult market.

Internally, tenants increasingly require a wider range of work settings in response to the new timings and ways in which work is carried out, including flexible short-term ownership of space. Office layouts need to be capable of being changed rapidly and completely both in terms of work setting arrangements, also in terms of the elements that are currently regarded as longer-lasting, particularly partitions, finishes and IT equipment.

There are implications here not only for the detailing of components and adaptability of data networks, but also for the nature of space, which should offer variety of shape both in plan and in section, including top-lit and large-volume space. Consider the variety and colour expressed by the winners of the Gestetner Digital Office Collection for 2001 which included Gissings' offices in Finsbury Circus, Ove Arup's offices in the West Midlands and Sheppard Robson's Toyota building in Surrey (*see* Figures 13 – 15).

Manhattan Loft Corporation has also attempted to capture this sense of flexibility and innovation in Bankside Central, its recently completed office building for occupiers from the media and advertising in Southwark (*see* Figure 16).

In *New Workspace, New Culture*[12], attention is drawn to a concept suggested by Philip Ross known as 'Unitel'. This combines the shared learning environment of the university with the temporary and personal accommodation of the hotel, and points

---

12 Turner, G and Myerson, J (1998), *New Workspace, New Culture*, Aldershot, Gower Publishing Limited

W= 5.5

Figure 13: Gissings, London

©FBM Architects

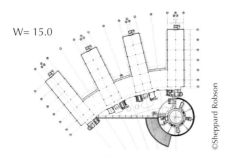

©Arup

W= 9.0 + 4.5 + 9.0

Figure 14: Ove Arup, West Midlands

W= 15.0

©Sheppard Robson

Figure 15: Toyota Headquarters, Surrey

©MLC

W= 15.0

Figure 16: Bankside Central, London

towards a new way of working in which 'one person has several places and one place has several people'. This, I suppose, is the essence of the imagined new flexible workspace.

In *Flexibility and Adaptability in Buildings*[13], two characteristics are distinguished. It suggests that flexibility has more to do with allowing quick changes of low magnitude, such as alteration of furniture layout, whilst adaptability is the measure of a building shell to accept major changes in occupancy, services and/or usage. Clearly both characteristics are desirable in a turbulent business environment, both for occupiers and developers, but the paper makes clear that it is possible to achieve one feature without the other. For instance, the tendency to produce very specialised (but flexible) buildings for specific end-users may nevertheless mitigate against long-term adaptability.

Transcendent or contingent?

Is the preferred office model that emerges from these influences, standards and points of view a universal one, transcending the specifics of client brief, cultural/economic context and local circumstance, or is it predominantly contingent upon all of these factors? In fact, the feedback gleaned from exhaustive post-occupancy reviews significantly aligns with many of the preferences embodied in Accenture's BRM. These, in turn, tend to support the principal characteristics of the European model which is largely user-driven, rather than the UK/US one, which is developer- and fund-driven. Could a generic office brief be conceived taking the best and most essential features favoured by occupants? If this were combined with the requirements imposed by speculative developers for economy and repeatability then perhaps a more viable and more appropriate office form could be created that would not only serve occupants' immediate and changing needs but also contribute to a more stable, adaptable and refined built environment.

Reinventing the wheel?

To the extent that generic requirements can be described for most office developments, is there a place for generic approaches to the construction of office buildings that could yield high quality at low cost? There is a movement for reform in the UK building industry that is concerned with increasing construction efficiency both by introducing more collaborative design and construction processes, but also by suggesting a more product-based approach to building design. This envisages standard rather than bespoke solutions and a reliance on design for manufacture and assembly rather than conventional construction. The essence of the approach is that the tedious and wasteful process of re-examining every possible planning and technical solution

---

13 Leaman, A Bordass, B and Cassels, S (1998), 'Flexibility and Adaptability in Buildings', in *Building Use Studies* by William Bordass Assocuates, RAN Cosultants Limited, London.

to each unique development requirement can be avoided, and instead that pre-existing optimised arrangements and solutions should be used and/or adapted for specific circumstances.

In the late 1990s, BAA and its chairman Sir John Egan, spearheaded this initiative, now the Movement for Innovation M4i, and it's bible, *Rethinking Construction*[14] strongly influenced the development of BAA's own Office Product. Three virtually identical examples now stand north of the runway at Heathrow Airport, designed by Rab Bennetts.

W= 19.5

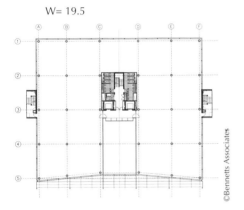

©Bennetts Associates

©Bennetts Associates

Figure 17: World Business Centre, Heathrow

The typical floor-plate is an almost literal translation of the diagram of an idealised floor-plate given in the *BCO Guide 2000* and its predecessor.

Whilst the product-based approach is clearly visible in the outline of these buildings and their regular and repeated planning, the use of standardised components and off-site manufacture is, as yet, minimal. Stephen Fox[15] outlines some of the difficulties:

> Materials are as essential to building construction as discrete components. Fundamental differences between consumer products and buildings make construction without the use of materials impractical, but the use of materials results in technological barriers to the transfer of consumer product manufacturing approaches. Leading manufacturers do not 'translate' a generic product when they receive an order. They generate order-specific manufacturing information to perform standard configurations of standard component data.

The critical difference between consumer products and buildings in this context is that the forms and finishes of buildings are not fixed. As Fox explains, 'it is neither feasible

14 Egan, J (1998), *Rethinking Construction*, London, Department of Environment, Transport and Regions
15 Fox, S and Cockerham, G (13 Jan 2000), *Facing up to Interfaces*, Architect's Journal, EMAP Construct and Fox, S (Apr 2001), Manufacturing Engineer, IEEE

nor viable for manufacturers to develop discrete components that can cater for all dimensional and aesthetic irregularities that are inevitable in the construction of buildings that do not have fixed form and finishes.'

Ironically, the BAA Office Product was a fixed, or largely fixed, commodity which would have been susceptible to manufacturing techniques had there been a sufficient and sustained future demand such as to justify the necessary pre-manufacturing development work by the supply chain. A very similar 'product' has been created at Stanhope's Chiswick Park (although atria have been omitted, creating substantial floor space more than 15 metres distant from daylight).

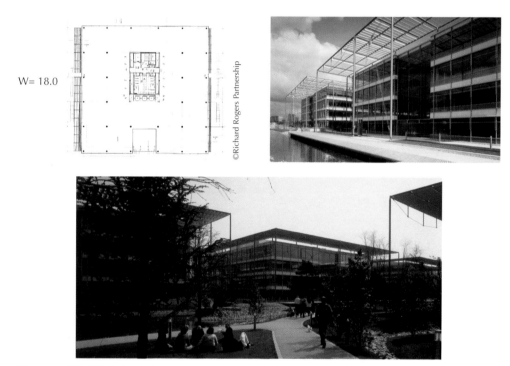

Figure 18: Chiswick Park, London

In this case, the building shells are relatively restrained and rely on somewhat extravagant out-rigging for solar shading and escape stair shelter to create aesthetic impact. They have at least the look of 'systems-built' construction. But the visual success of the scheme relies heavily on the arrangement of the buildings around civic space and on associated landscaping, and it is difficult to imagine how such a limited component set could be successfully reconfigured in other settings demanding radically different plan forms, building heights and/or surface treatments.

A further venture into the realm of the standard office product construction has been initiated by the Steelcase subsidiary, WorkStage, which having had limited success in the US, is now marketing in Europe.

Figure 19: Steelcase 'Workstage'

Generic product or generic component?

In his articles (above) Stephen Fox categorises standardisation under the following headings:

- Bespoke – uncertain forms and finishes.
- Hybrid – variable forms and finishes.
- Custom – certain known forms and finishes.
- Standard –- fixed forms and finishes.

He introduces the idea of modular product architectures in which each physical component group implements a certain set of functions. As he points out, 'this allows for more variety, lower cost and better quality; for example, Swatch produces many watch models at relatively low cost by assembling different combinations of standard sub-assemblies' (*see* Figure 20).

This suggests that building construction could be at least Hybrid, and perhaps even Custom, and still retain considerable latitude for variety of form and appearance without losing all of the cost and efficiency benefits associated with a standard product. In other words, if offices could be constructed of generic pre-engineered components or sub-assemblies (rather than conceived as full product buildings), then requirements for variety, versatility and aesthetic diversity might be achieved, as well as some of economies associated with manufacturing.

An attempt to follow this route is being made by the UK construction company Laing/O'Rourke. They have been working for over a year with an integrated supply chain including architects Reid Architecture and engineers Buro Happold to design a rich component set which can be assembled in limitless plan configurations and

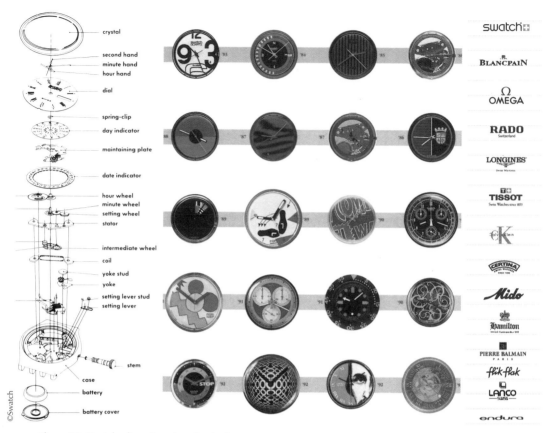

©Swatch

Figure 20: Swatch: diversity using standard components

variable heights, which affords choice in cladding (from glass curtain walling to stone-facing), and which accommodates four different servicing strategies from full air conditioning to full natural ventilation. The first building using this system, their Customised Office Solution, was constructed in 2002 as the headquarters building for the parent company of this enterprising construction firm (*see* Figure 21).

Writing in the June 2001 edition of DETAIL, a special issue focusing on modular construction, Richard Horden, the British designer of City Arcade (*see* Figure 22) comments:

> Whatever European kitchen manufacturer you take, their units all have identical dimensions. It is the variety of surface finishes, door handles, tops, etc. that make each model individual. This reflects exactly our approach to the concept of the European house, which would look different in Rosenheim or Epsom or Bari. The outward appearance of the houses would differ – like the cooker or the fridge in the example of the kitchen. One might express this in an exaggerated form by saying that the shirt of a Bayern Munich soccer player would also fit a Newcastle United player, but the emotional attachment – the sense of 'home' – and the reaction of the spectators would be quite different.

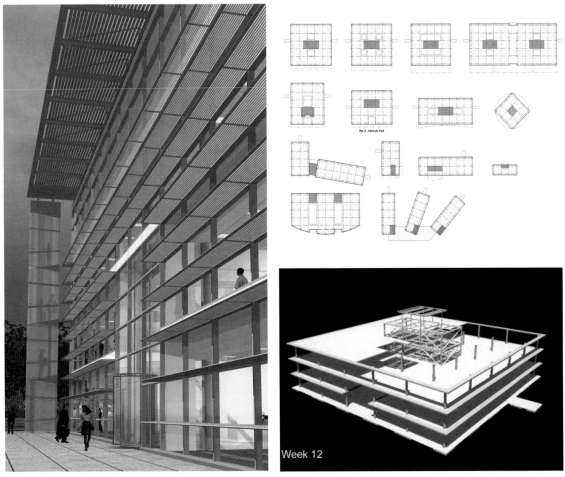

Figure 21: Laing/O'Rourke Office solution, Reid Architecture

Clearly, the same thinking could be applied to office construction. When asked about the future, Horden replied:

> The architecture of the future will use the techniques of flight assembly. In other words the components will be built in a factory by people or robots. They will be transported to the site and assembled. The future of architecture therefore has to do with the fitting together of all these parts. The way in which the sections of a building are joined together will be the determining factor, and it is this factor that will change.

Urban context?

In focusing on the nature and performance of the office object, designers cannot be allowed to overlook the important way in which whole buildings address each other and 'fit together' to create significant public space. We need a stable, supportive and

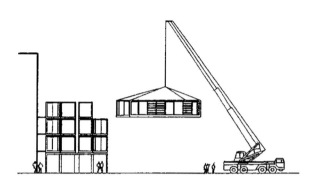
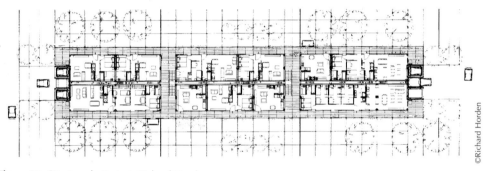

©Richard Horden

Figure 22: City Arcade Project, Richard Horden

visually nourishing physical environment to provide constancy in our complicated and increasingly virtual lives. In his address to the Royal Incorporation of Architects in Scotland in May 2001, Herman Hertzberger, the Dutch architect renowned for his mould-breaking office building Central Beheer, berated architects for 'always thinking of their buildings as objects to be published, like pieces of sculpture'. He pointed out that, at best, this might lead to a world full of beautiful objects, but with nothing significant in between them. These are the spaces, he said, that have the potency to provide social life. In *Space and the Architect*[16], Hertzberger develops the theme further and argues:

> When we attach the concepts of competence and performance to architecture, then we are distinguishing between what is relatively speaking fixed and so enduring (the long time-cycle) and what is constantly subject to change (the short time-cycle). There are so many examples of buildings which, after having lost their original use form, could be recycled because their competence proved not only

16 Herzberger, H (2000), *Space and the Architect,* Rotterdam, 010 Publishers.

suitable for quite another infill, but even went on to provoke it in some way. Here it holds that the less emphasis in the original scheme on the architectural expression of their function, the more accommodating this proves to be for new functions or applications.

So we conclude that, in the language of aphorisms, neither 'Form follows Function', nor 'Form follows Finance' are optimum, but that ironically, 'Function follows Form' may be the healthiest paradigm for the long term, and may foster the most balanced and attractive human environment.

A universal template?

On the face of it, the observations in this chapter may appear to be pulling in a variety of directions. The UK/US model is expensive to run and relatively unresponsive to occupiers' requirements. The European model is expensive to build, and is primarily responsive to solitary rather than team-based working (the new business paradigm). There is logic behind exhaustive brief-writing for end-user buildings, but this may lead to unnecessary specialisation inhibiting the ability to respond to short-term and especially long-term change. The evolution of generic standards and generic building types promises increased longevity and clarity of product, and also increased construction quality at lower cost, but brings with it the spectre of spatial and aesthetic monotony. And excessive focus on the design of individual monuments to organisations and individuals works against the creation of an integrated and humane built environment.

Nevertheless, it is possible to compile a list of desirable characteristics that are reasonably universal and also reasonably non-contradictory. Office buildings could be:

- **Accessible** – encouraging use of public transport, reducing environmental cost, increasing convenience.
- **Comfortable** – providing healthy conditions, including easy access to natural light and ventilation.
- **Practical** – offered in units of convenient size and constructed in appropriate modules which integrate dimensionally.
- **Flexible** – supporting rapid short-term changes in work-setting arrangement.
- **Adaptable** – generic, supporting large-scale and long-term changes in use and function.
- **Usable** – providing effective servicing systems that are easy to operate and maintain.
- **Economic** – employing principles of design-for-manufacture, including supply chain integration, to achieve optimum performance in terms of capital and running costs.
- **Urbane** – contributing to an integrated but diverse environment in which the space between buildings has meaning and vitality.

All of this can be said without becoming ensnared in discussions of aesthetics which are, nevertheless of great importance.

I leave the reader to apply these tests to the signature buildings featured at the beginning of the chapter. My personal favourite is the Funf Hoffe by Herzog and de Meuron in Munich, which combines all of the desirable characteristics of flexibility/adaptability of space and narrow-plate low-tech environmental design with a very sophisticated and beautiful application of modern materials all set, highly accessibly, in an historic city centre, integrated with a very comfy restaurant, an art gallery and convenient shopping.

Kathryn Bell, Director of Global Workplace for Accenture, eloquently expresses a sophisticated occupier's view on the question of universal form:

> What must be found is a model that balances the creation and governance of a global template with the way in which that template can be flexed to reflect national culture. The world is (sadly) becoming more homogeneous in its whole, but there are still national/cultural nuances. In organisations that have human knowledge as their principal asset, the recognition of these nuances is what creates great places to work and retains excellent people. The global 'cookie cutter' approach does not work, but we cannot have anarchy either.

Author profile

Robert Dalziel, Director
Reid Architecture

Robert Dalziel is a British architect and has been a Director of Reid Architecture since 1990. He specialises in the design of offices, airport facilities and long-span distribution buildings and has led teams responsible for a wide variety of commercial and industrial buildings since 1985, most recently including the competition-winning air traffic tower, hangars and office terminal for Farnborough airport.

Robert studied architecture first in Canada at the University of Toronto, and then at the Bartlett School, University College London. He sits on the Technical Committee of the British Council for Offices, and chaired the panel that contributed the architectural content of the BCO Guide 2000. He is also on the Board of the innovative group known as TeamWork, that demonstrates and promotes the use of advanced object-oriented collaborative computing techniques for the building industry.

The author would like to thank his colleagues at Reid Architecture for their support and particularly Paul Warner for his thoughts on design-for-manufacture.

Reid Architecture was established in 1979 and has been among the top ten architectural practices (by number) in the UK and Europe for the past five years. In addition to its airport and commercial work, the Practice is currently involved in a number of large-scale urban centre projects including sites in Cardiff, Enfield, Loughborough and Feltham in the UK, and Madrid, Alicante and Malaga in Spain.

9 Sustainability

Rab Bennetts
Bennetts Associates

Introduction

Sustainability now occupies centre stage in the worldwide debate about our future but, for many, it remains a vague and impenetrable subject. There is little doubt, though, that property in general and commercial offices in particular have a substantial impact, not only in specific environmental terms but also through their ability to enhance or hinder the economic and social development of our society.

Indeed, it is the interdependence of social, economic and environmental issues that makes sustainability so hard to define. This is a subject that is still in its infancy, dogged by over-complex analyses on the one hand and a surprising absence of hard facts on the other. One hard fact that is undeniable, however, is the global rise in temperatures – currently believed to be around 0.2°C per decade and increasing. The implications for climate change and the design of buildings are simply enormous; although the United States is still in denial, even the insurers have begun to realise that the traditional 50-year storm is now happening every couple of seasons and that the design of buildings must change accordingly.

There are a few more statistics from the environmental agenda that underline the scale of the problem and the need to make substantial progress within a short period of time. First, more than 50 per cent of the UK's carbon emissions come from the construction and operation of buildings, of which a significant proportion is offices. Second, as part of the UK's commitments arising from the Kyoto Summit, the Government has targeted a 20 per cent reduction in greenhouse gases – principally CO_2 – by 2010. Clearly, the time has come to get serious about the performance of our building stock.

At a strategic level, a pattern of legislation is already evident in the form of tougher building regulations, planning restrictions on buildings that depend on car usage, encouragement of mixed-use developments, landfill taxes and so on. Further indications of a consensus towards greater levels of sustainability include voluntary schemes such as BREEAM (the Building Research Establishment Environmental Assessment Method), which has now been used on several hundred office developments, not simply to improve performance but as a way of gaining a competitive edge over their competitors. The Government itself, which represents

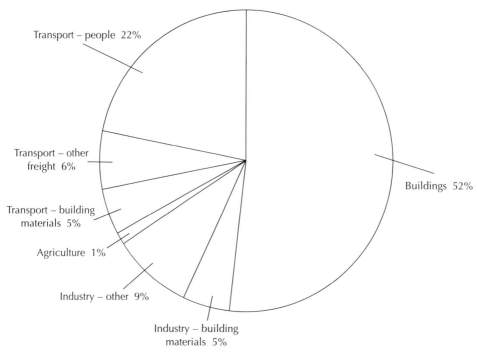

Figure 1: Pie Chart showing UK national energy comsumption (1995)

around 40 per cent of British construction spend, has announced procurement policies aimed at achieving a high level of results within three years, in its publication, *Sustainability – A Better Quality of Life*[1].

There is, therefore, a widespread acceptance in society as a whole that things must change, but the deep-rooted conservatism of the commercial property market suggests that voluntary measures will not be enough. Perhaps the most symbolic obstacle to change is the UK property market's increasing appetite for air conditioning – arguably the most energy-intensive characteristic of a modern commercial office. Behind the reasons for this lie some of the possible solutions:

- Unlike much of Europe, air conditioning in the UK is seen as a way of emulating the North American market, whether or not it is technically necessary to do so. In contrast, greater sustainability through energy efficiency is more likely to be found in local responses to climate than in a global standard.

- Conservatism among property advisers tends to reinforce previous stereotypes and discourage innovation. Whether change is enforced by legislation or by voluntary means, future sustainability obliges all parties to question past assumptions and to be open to new ideas if even modest improvements are to be achieved.

- A lack of real information about sustainability in general, and energy-efficiency in particular, is impeding the understanding of building performance. A traditional

1 For further information visit www.sustainable-development.gov.uk

reluctance to carry out post-occupancy audits, combined with professional reticence, is failing to identify clearly those innovative buildings that work and those that do not. The quest for greater sustainability needs hard data from which to determine a common understanding of the most viable solutions.

Although air conditioning is only one small part of the sustainability debate, it encapsulates the problem for the UK property sector – a reluctance to change. If voluntary change is unlikely, changes to the Building Regulations (Part L) and a European Directive called the *Energy Performance of Buildings* signal the way for mandatory improvements that will affect the future value of commercial property. The European scheme, in particular, which involves energy tagging on items like household appliances, is likely to affect the sale price of existing buildings as well as the longer-term value of new developments.

With this and the overwhelming concern with global warming in mind, the following section lists many of the tried and tested ways of improving environmental performance, so that developers and others can be less apprehensive about their application. Later sections in this chapter touch upon the broader questions of economic and social sustainability.

Environmental sustainability

To make the environmental issues simpler and more accessible, this section considers commercial offices after the decision has been made to develop. Although the purists may argue against oversimplification, there is a strong case for leaving strategic planning issues to others, as legislation already exists and is constantly being changed through the planning framework to reflect national or international concerns. By examining offices in this way, much of the social and economic agenda is circumvented, leaving the environment as the focus. Once again, the specialists could claim that this places sustainability out of context but, equally, it could be argued that the ability to make progress at project level does not compromise the bigger picture – indeed, it may make higher levels of sustainability more likely by virtue of a simpler perception of actual results.

Unlike some other aspects of sustainability, environmental issues are capable of objective measurement and there are already several sophisticated schemes that can be used to assess the impact of a development. The most notable of these is BREEAM, introduced a decade or so ago and revised with greater rigour in 1998. Most of these schemes, including Arup's 'Spear' programme[2], take sustainability in its holistic sense, with economic and social indicators ranked alongside those for the environment to give an overall rating.

Whilst these schemes encourage an integrated view of sustainability, there are many projects that may not require this level of sophistication, provided they consider as a

2 Visit www.arup.com/environmental

minimum a key group of measurable categories that are at the core of environmental sustainability. This is broadly the same approach that has been adopted by *Rethinking Construction* – the government-backed movement inspired by Sir John Egan to reform the UK construction industry from the grass roots upwards[3]. Taking each one in turn, these are as follows.

Operational CO_2

For most offices, by far the most significant environmental issue is the year-on-year energy used in the operation of the building and the carbon dioxide (CO_2) that is added – principally by electricity-generating power stations – to the world's atmosphere as a result. Until recently, the 'green' credentials of a building were measured according to its energy consumption but, by focusing on the CO_2 emission instead, an automatic allowance is made for 'renewable' energy sources that do not generate CO_2 at all. Nevertheless, energy efficiency is still the basic requirement and the following strategies illustrate how substantial reductions in carbon emissions can be achieved. They also point the way to business competitiveness through lower running costs. Not long ago, service charges for commercial offices were so small as to be insignificant when considered alongside the rent and location. Now, however, with the advent of the 'climate levy' and other forms of taxation, service charges could tip the balance between one property and another. It takes little imagination to foresee that an energy-inefficient building may be difficult to let in, say, 15 years' time.

Renewable energy
Much of the carbon dioxide produced from buildings emanates from the gas or coal-fired power stations that supply electricity to the National Grid. Reducing the demand from these sources of power inevitably leads to a two-pronged strategy of reducing consumption on the one hand and using 'renewable' energy on the other. As the term suggests, renewable energy is unlike fossil fuels in that it is replaceable – i.e. solar power, wind power and wave power – and all of them avoid emission of greenhouse gases like CO_2. It is fair to say that the last of these, wave power, is still in the pioneering phase, but solar power can already be applied locally to all types of buildings and wind power is steadily increasing its share of the National Grid.

Those office occupiers who want to make use of renewable energy can do several things. First, for a modest premium, they can elect to have a percentage of their electrical power from wind farms through a specific arrangement with their power supplier. Second, they can incorporate solar panels or photovoltaic cells into the design of their building. At the Wessex Water project in Bath, five per cent of electricity comes through the Grid from wind farms and most of the building's hot water comes from solar panels mounted on the roof above the toilet cores. Both of these items were achieved at modest cost. Unlike solar panels, photovoltaic cells generate electricity from the sun's radiation and have a longer payback period,

---

3 For further information on *Rethinking Construction* visit www.rethinkingconstruction.org.uk

although the cost is dropping as the market increases. Third, in many parts of the country, boreholes can allow cool groundwater to be used as a 'free' cooling medium for water-based air conditioning. There are few installations at present, but the indications are that it can be successfully used, albeit at the cost of a borehole and reasonable predictions as to the temperature of the water supply. In London, for example, the groundwater is slightly warmer and, therefore, less effective than elsewhere. It is also possible to use nearby lakes or rivers for cooling in certain circumstances.

Any debate about alternative, 'clean' fuel sources cannot avoid mentioning nuclear power but, until the central issue of nuclear waste disposal is resolved, it is likely to remain politically unacceptable.

©M Reynolds

Figure 2: Solar panels on roof top

Thermal stability, possibly with night cooling
The idea of using the thermal mass of a building to stabilise internal temperatures is hardly new, but seems to have been forgotten by the creators of today's lightweight, short-life building stock. Entering the cool interior of a medieval cathedral on a hot summer's day illustrates the point, but modern offices in the UK need only a modest amount of thermal mass to reduce the energy required both for heating and, more significantly, for cooling. Provided the structure is exposed to the internal airstream and can be allowed to cool down out of hours, a conventional office with moderate internal heat gains can be 'air conditioned' by using the structure passively, rather than by, for example, a conventional fan-coil system. Mechanical services engineers now routinely attribute 20–30w/sq m of cooling capacity to the structure, if there is sufficient mass and surface area.

For this to be most effective, the profile of the exposed structure needs to avoid warm air pockets and the working pattern of the occupants needs to accommodate out-of-hours cooling. A 24-hour office would therefore gain the benefits of thermal stability but not 'free' cooling from the structure.

Flat slabs are slightly less effective than ribbed or vaulted structures, as the surface area acts on the same principle as radiator fins. It is often suggested that the visual appearance and acoustic performance of the more interesting, exposed structures contribute to a more rewarding workplace.

Good daylighting

Artificial lighting accounts for a substantial proportion of the electricity consumed by commercial offices, so any attempt to turn the lights off will, by definition, result in a reduction of operational energy. Lighting controls, people sensors and sophisticated

Figure 3: Thermal mass illustrated by vaulted concrete structure at PowerGen Headquarters, Coventry

©Bennetts Associates/Peter Cook

Figure 4: Interior Wessex Water showing working areas close to natural daylight

switching arrangements are already in widespread use, albeit with varying degrees of cost and reliability. The big gains, however, are likely to be achieved by increasing daylighting levels and ensuring that its distribution is relatively even from the window to the office interior. Only by avoiding dark patches – for example, by using light 'shelves' in combination with solar shading – will occupiers feel comfortable with the lights turned off. As a result, the services engineer's heat gain calculations can safely assume that a high proportion of the lights are switched off during the peak summer's day.

It goes without saying that the daylit office is a far more pleasurable experience than the deep-plan space that relies on artificial lighting. Current research linking the sense of well-being in the workplace with higher productivity strongly suggests that the human qualities such as daylight will be key to the office of the future.

Minimising internal heat gains
The connection between internal heat gains and the need (or otherwise) to expend energy on mechanical cooling is self-evident.

Internal heat gains within office buildings can vary greatly, sometimes as low as 30w/sq m but occasionally exceeding 100w/sq m. Achieving appropriate comfort conditions in commercial offices therefore depends on a rigorous assessment of the heat gains coming from each source, including people, lights, solar radiation, computers and so on. Indeed, it is often argued that historic over-estimates of internal heat gains is one of the key factors in the excessive use of air conditioning systems. By questioning some of the traditional assumptions, however, a number of completed buildings have demonstrated that heat gains in a temperate climate like the UK can be substantially reduced to the point where conventional air conditioning can be avoided. Heat gains from the sun can be greatly reduced by external sunshading and consistent levels of daylight can reduce heat gains from artificial lighting to an average of less than 10w/sq m. The impact of computers, too, is often over-estimated, with recent studies suggesting that heat gains in a normal office are less than 15w/sq m. Surveys of BT's densely occupied 'Workstyle' offices suggest that heat gains are around 17w/sq m, as opposed to the 25–30w/sq m that was initially predicted.

Common sense can also play a part in reducing cumulative heat gains, for example, by resisting the temptation to locate the most heat-intensive activity such as a main conference room on the facade that suffers most from solar gain. Even if air conditioning cannot be avoided completely, value-engineering the heat gains in this way can reduce the need for mechanical cooling to only the hottest weeks in the year.

Reducing solar gain
Modern architecture's love-affair with transparency can no longer be reconciled with the energy demands of large expanses of unshaded glazing. Quite simply, heat gains from the sun dwarf those from computers, making air conditioning unavoidable for office buildings that do not have adequate solar protection.

Keeping the sun off the glass – and for that matter, internal elements such as desks that would otherwise become heat-emitting radiators – requires careful analysis of sun-angles, as the orientation of each facade will require a slightly different response. The easiest condition is the south-facing facade, where a simple, horizontal projection will shade the largest area when the hottest summer sun is at its highest point. East and west facades are much more difficult, on account of the low sun angles. Even north-facing facades in the south of England get some low-angle sunshine late on a summer's day and, in Scotland, the problem can be quite severe, although temperatures are generally lower. Clearly, the orientation of the building can influence the effectiveness of solar control and, where there is a choice, the optimum condition is a building that has its longest facades facing south or north, with short elevations to east and west.

Alternatives to external sun-shading include high performance or reflective glass but, setting aside questions about their appearance, they are unlikely to exclude solar radiation as effectively as a physical barrier. Double wall constructions, where the shading devices are contained within a ventilated glass cavity up to a metre wide, offer a visual alternative to external louvres, but results have been inconsistent and there is some evidence that high temperatures within the cavity have resulted in excessive heat-transfer into certain buildings.

Solar gain is not the same as glare, however, and some form of internal operable blind is almost always necessary. Placing micro-blinds within the cavity of double glazing units is moderately effective for both solar and glare control, if external shading is impractical. Most curtain-wall manufacturers offer in-cavity blinds as a standard product.

Figure 5: Reducing solar gain, Wessex Water south facade

High levels of insulation
In common with all building types, today's commercial office should be well insulated, not only from heat loss but also from heat gain. The Building Regulations are constantly being upgraded, but the UK still falls well behind the standards of most European countries. Increasing the amount of insulation is one of the quickest ways of achieving a pay-back on investment, with consequential savings in both capital plant and operational running costs.

Airtightness
A new requirement of the Building Regulations is that a standard of airtightness should be achieved through the external envelope. A number of studies carried out in recent years, such as 'Probe', demonstrated that large amounts of energy were being wasted through poor detailing or workmanship in the facade, rendering many energy-saving devices obsolete. Pressure-testing completed buildings, something that is normally greeted with derision by contractors, is now mandatory for major office buildings. Time and money needs to be allocated at an early stage in the design and construction process to this demanding task.

Local controls
There is considerable evidence to suggest that office occupiers are prepared to accept a wider range of internal conditions if they have local control over their environment. In a centralised, air conditioned office, occupiers tend to complain when temperatures drift beyond a fairly narrow band whereas, in an office with

natural ventilation, people will accept a wider range of conditions on the basis that they can always shut or open the window. Local control of this kind enables designers to adopt a more loose-fit philosophy, with consequential reductions in energy consumption.

Local controls can also mean simple devices such as thermostats on radiators and other operating devices that are perceived to be easy to use and effective in a short time-span. Computerised building management systems (BMS) can achieve many of the same objectives but there is clearly a link between their perceived simplicity in operation and their ability to provide user-satisfaction and, hence, to fulfil the full potential for lower energy consumption.

Mixed-mode or natural ventilation
Sustainability is often equated with natural ventilation, but there are some real difficulties with its use in commercial offices. Arguably the critical issue is flexibility, as ventilation across the floorplate requires a minimum of obstructions, such as partitions. Where the end-user is known and can accept the limitations imposed by this discipline, natural ventilation is often viable but, for the market as a whole, this is normally too restrictive. There are also questions to be answered about a possible reduction in air quality, if too few people open the windows, and comfort, if occupiers experience draughts. All of these drawbacks are solvable by good design, but it seems that, on balance, 'mixed-mode' ventilation represents a better all-round solution, especially for the commercial market. Emerging research by Building Use Studies has shown that mixed-mode buildings tend to record the highest levels of user satisfaction in terms of comfort. Once again, the implications for productivity in the workplace are significant.

With mixed-mode, the primary ventilation system is mechanical – possibly through the raised floor – and opening windows are available as a fall-back. For much of the year, opening windows may be sufficient but, in summer, air supply and some cooling can be made available. In winter, instead of losing warm air to the outside through opening windows, excess heat can be reclaimed by mechanically recirculating air to the plantroom. Therefore, the loss of energy efficiency through the use of ventilation fans in summer is more-or-less balanced by the increased efficiency through heat reclamation in winter, with the spring and autumn seasons seeing the optimum use of natural ventilation.

Mixed-mode has several further advantages. A fan-assisted air supply allows flexibility in partition layouts in the normal way and mechanical cooling can be added if heat gains indicate that there is a real need. In these conditions, chilled beams or panels represent an efficient alternative to cooling the airstream itself.

In urban locations that suffer from traffic noise and pollution, there is no necessity to open the windows when conditions are unfavourable. It also guarantees a predictable level of fresh air supply, whereas purely natural ventilation sometimes results in poor

©Peter Cook

Figure 6: General office space at John Menzies headquarters showing displacement ventilation grilles in the raised floor

internal air quality when insufficient people open the windows. Nevertheless, the obligation to use passive engineering techniques to reduce energy consumption, such as thermal mass and solar shading, applies equally to mixed-mode ventilation as to any other system.

Heat reclamation

As noted above, the opportunity to reclaim heat in mixed-mode buildings is significant but, with nearly all office buildings, the opportunity to reclaim heat exists all year round. As much as 80 per cent of an office building's heating requirements can be met by reclamation from internal gains.

Combined heat and power

For some years, larger projects have found it possible to generate their own power by installing combined heat and power (CHP) plants. It seems likely that smaller projects will follow suit as the hardware becomes more readily available. In some areas, such as the City of London, localised power generation is available to groups of buildings or districts on a similar basis, as it is generally cheaper and more energy-efficient to produce electrical power, hot water and, possibly, chilled water locally.

The fact that the take-up is far from universal reflects the age-old conflict of interest between developers, who look to the least capital cost, and tenants whose interests are best served by lower long-term costs. The inevitable requirement for some form of back-up supply is also sometimes used as a reason for avoiding the capital investment in CHP plant, but tax allowances have been introduced by the Government to encourage its use. The pay-back period for CHP appears to be as little as three to five years, which compares favourably with almost all other energy-efficiency measures. In some cases, it may be possible to export excess power to the National Grid.

Reductions in VAT are available to the local authority sector for CHP systems, suggesting an approach to taxation policy that could in time be extended to the office sector.

Seasonal fluctuations in internal temperatures

For those who are accustomed to natural ventilation, going into an air conditioned office in summer can be an uncomfortable experience, sometimes resulting in catching a cold. The rigid adherence by many office developers to 22°C +/– 2° seems absurd, when definitions of comfort fluctuate so wildly. By contrast, the energy-efficient office aims to achieve an internal summer temperature that feels lower than the outside by several degrees, but the actual temperature is allowed to drift in response to external conditions. For example, on rare days when it is 30° outside, surveys suggest that 26° is widely felt to be acceptable inside. It is when internal temperatures exceed 27° that higher numbers of complaints are received by facilities managers. By allowing some slack in the control of internal summer temperatures at the briefing stage, the cooling load can be reduced significantly. It is also worth noting that office occupiers in hotter countries have a more realistic dress code than the more conformist UK, allowing for cooler clothing in summer when internal temperatures are slightly higher.

Use of computers

Not surprisingly, post-occupancy research on buildings such as Wessex Water's Operations Centre indicates that computers have a huge bearing on the amount of energy consumed by an office. What is surprising, however, is the amount of power consumed when computers and other office equipment are on stand-by overnight and at weekends. When establishing the levels of energy-efficiency, most design benchmarks assume that computers will be operational for 11 hours per weekday on average, whereas initial survey results now suggest that, as with the TV at home, more energy may be consumed by computers on stand-by than in the hours of operation.

In view of the high levels of obsolescence in the IT industry, it seems questionable for IT departments to advise leaving computers on stand-by in the interests of longer equipment life. Clearly, a great deal of energy could be saved if computers, photocopiers, printers, etc were turned off when not in use.

Peak-lopping

Rather than condition the air supply on a constant basis, mechanical cooling can be limited to peak periods only, to ensure that temperatures do not stray beyond certain upper limits. Using energy sparingly in this way, for instance on hot afternoons during the summer months, allows the building to use natural systems for much of the year, whilst retaining reasonable control over internal comfort conditions.

Biomass

In a perfect world, any increase in carbon dioxide emissions should be compensated for by new planting that can absorb the additional pollutants. The amount of carbon that can be absorbed varies according to forestry (hardwood, softwood, species) and climate, and whether it is new or established forest. The Edinburgh Centre for Carbon Management (ECCM) estimates that a hectare of sustainably managed oak woodland can absorb around 236 tonnes of carbon, (equivalent to 865 tonnes of Carbon Dioxide) over a 100 year lifetime. So a 10,000 sq m building that emits, say, 30 kg of carbon dioxide per square metre per year needs around 35 hectares of woodland to have nil carbon impact on the planet over a 100 year life. In a small, congested country like the UK, this is clearly a tall order, but extreme measures such as this may be necessary in the long term if the increase in global temperatures cannot be slowed down by other means.

Carbon footprinting, as it is known, can be carried out by organisations such as ECCM, with new tree planting arranged through the Carbon Neutral Network and Future Forests.

Carbon trading

As a way of sharpening the focus on Green House Gas (GHG) emissions, the UK Government is backing a voluntary scheme for commercially trading the benefits of energy efficiency. In principle, companies set targets for GHG reductions in return for climate-levy tax breaks and those who exceed the target can sell their excess to those who fall short. Current participants include Shell, Tesco and Land Securities. It may not be long before the scheme is mandatory and there could be trading between individual projects as well as companies. The commercial advantages of being energy-efficient may no longer be the province of the occupier alone.

©Peter Cook

Figure 7: Typical office space at Wessex Water

The cumulative effect of these energy-saving devices is hard to overstate. Whereas a typical, fully air conditioned office building might consume in the order of 300-400kwh for every square metre per year, the most energy-efficient examples such as Wessex Water's Operations Centre and the BRE's new offices are consuming around one-third of that amount, without any significant compromise in working conditions. The amount of carbon dioxide emission is reduced accordingly, unless of course the project has invested in renewable energy sources as well, in which case the reduction will be even greater.

Although new buildings are best able to adopt most if not all of these ideas, many are clearly applicable to refurbishments as well. Some of the 60s' slab blocks now being demolished because there is believed to be insufficient room for air conditioning, would be capable of refurbishment, provided the external envelope was properly engineered with solar shading, good levels of daylight and thermal performance. Adequate comfort conditions could therefore be achieved in most cases with minimal services, allowing total demolition – hardly the most sustainable policy – to be avoided.

Post-occupancy monitoring
Performance improvements do not end with design and construction. Although the property industry is notoriously reluctant to share performance data, especially when it is none too favourable, there is a great deal of evidence to suggest that initial energy consumption is often poor compared to the design intent and that at least a year's fine-tuning is necessary for a new building to reach optimum energy performance.

Monitoring is not costly, but it needs to be thought through from an early stage in the design process, with the specification including items such as separate metering for different areas of the building, the hours of occupation and for different types of use. Armed with the data from an annual cycle of temperature variations and usage patterns, building managers, designers and contractors can start to distinguish between, for example, fabric heat losses or excessive use of artificial lighting, and make adjustments accordingly. Doing this properly needs time and a cool nerve, as the first results may be discouraging, but the benefits are significant. Such is the complexity of building procurement and operation, that improvements of 20–30 per cent appear to be a reasonable expectation as a result of post-occupancy refinements.

Using data from post-occupancy monitoring, benchmarking office buildings for their performance is an essential step towards pan-industry improvement. Companies like Land Securities are now prepared to publish the results of their buildings' performance and the BRE is accumulating a data bank with which to establish best practice, not to mention the standards for future regulations.

Embodied CO$_2$

Whereas operational CO$_2$ represents the carbon dioxide emissions from the year-on-year consumption of non-renewable energy, embodied CO$_2$ derives from the actual energy used in constructing the building. Efficient use of materials, transport of construction products, waste recycling and prefabrication all have an impact on the environment and, as with operational energy, measuring the CO$_2$ emission highlights the issue of greatest concern.

It is often argued, however, that the energy used in construction is vastly outweighed by the energy consumed in a building's lifetime and, in consequence, it is less important. Whilst this has been true in the past for conventional buildings that use a lot of energy, recent studies have shown that the embodied CO$_2$ can sometimes exceed the total operational CO$_2$ if basic assumptions about life span and energy efficiency are questioned. This means that the efficiency of the building process is rapidly becoming as important as energy efficiency itself. By way of illustration, an energy-efficient building that is unduly complex in its construction may be self-defeating, as the energy saved over its life span may be outweighed by the energy used to build it.

The list of possible improvements to the construction process is endless, but there are several key concepts or ideas that can make a significant difference as described below. Taken together, their real significance is that they represent a change of attitude towards design and construction that could fundamentally affect the perception of new buildings in their environment.

Lean construction
'Lean thinking' is a technique imported from the car industry by Sir John Egan, with a view to eliminating over-specification and other forms of inefficiency that bedevil the design and construction process. Although Egan's initial mission was to improve production performance, its relevance to sustainability is obvious, in that the sparing use of resources and the reduction of waste will inevitable reduce carbon dioxide emissions and pollution. The concept of lean construction, which was already practised by developers such as Stanhope before Egan's arrival, is as much about attitude as any other factor; simplicity, repetition, ease of construction and 'just sufficient engineering' require collaboration between design professionals, contractors and their supply chain in a way that is all too rare at present.

Choice and evaluation of materials
Any project that is concerned with the emissions and resource depletion arising from construction must consider the huge variations between the different materials that are available for each part of a project. Whilst this may sound complex, it is now possible to appraise a product's sustainability credentials with the help of programmes such as 'Envest', available from the BRE, or specialist consultants. The BRE's database includes information on over 3,000 materials sufficient to identify, for example, the lifetime impacts in terms of embodied carbon dioxide or the likelihood of third world labour being exploited in its production.

©Bennetts Associates

Figure 8: Aluminium extrusions – an energy intensive component

©Bennetts Associates

Figure 9: Use of pre-fabricated components at Wessex Water

The practical application of this information is crucial, as it allows designers to assess the impact of, say, aluminium, steel or timber-framed window assemblies before the design becomes too advanced. Similarly, it is possible to see the dramatic differences between PVC-based floor finishes such as nylon carpets (oil-based products such as PVC are Greenpeace's current enemy number one), and those based on much lower emissions like wool or even linoleum. By making objective decisions supported by hard information of this kind, it is possible to reduce embodied carbon dioxide emissions by as much as one-third.

All the major sectors of the materials supply chain are reconsidering their sustainability strategies and there is no doubt that the next few years will see intense competition to secure the 'green' market. Steel and its historic rivalry with concrete is the obvious example, but the aluminium curtain walling market is another that will be obliged to address its energy-intensive manufacturing process, probably with the aid of hydro-powered smelters (i.e. with a renewable energy source) in Scandinavia. Specifiers such as architects are already insisting that suppliers submit details of their sustainability policy along with their tenders.

Off-site prefabrication
By virtue of their repetitive nature, commercial offices should lend themselves to construction methods that make full use of larger-scale assemblies that are manufactured in controlled, dry and safe conditions. Quite apart from the social aspects of treating construction workers with more respect than a wet building site can offer, prefabrication can reduce waste and increase quality.

Waste avoidance and recycling
Reducing the CO_2 emissions from waste is described in the next section.

Construction transport off-site, on-site
A large proportion of the emissions generated by the construction process is attributable to transport — during manufacture, transportation to the site and the

construction process itself. Both intellectually and commercially, this is arguably the area that could see the greatest change to the design and construction of buildings other than operational energy itself.

Cutting down on transport emissions by using materials that are close at hand would entail nothing less than reversing the worldwide-supermarket approach that dominates the office market at present. Curtain walling from Europe, stone cladding that is quarried in India and fabricated in Italy, steel from Japan . . . the list of unsustainable practices is well entrenched. Moreover, the lack of products availability in the UK resulting from many years of under-performance clearly cannot be reversed quickly.

The wider cultural implications of using local sources are discussed below, but attempts have already been made at a new approach, with varying degrees of success. Buildings that are made from local materials are not necessarily the province of enthusiasts for low-scale, timber-framed construction. With the exception of curtain walling, the Wessex Water project in Bath found that most major components could be obtained within the region from suppliers whose prices recognised the potential for a shift in the market.

On the construction site itself, there is still much that can be done to reduce emissions. Requirements for properly maintained plant and machinery, a 'green' travel

©Peter Cook

©Peter Cook

Figure 10: Granite from India and curtain walling from Italy on a City of London Project

Figure 11: Local materials, as used at Wessex Water

plan for site workers (e.g. car-sharing or public transport), and the elimination of wasted journeys through a 'right-first-time' approach can be incorporated into the contract documents prior to tender and monitored through the construction period. In terms of transport movements, safety is, of course, a primary consideration that impinges on social sustainability.

Cut and fill

Excavation normally produces substantial transport emissions off-site and, whilst this is rarely avoidable on urban locations, the less densely developed sites may allow the excavated material to be placed nearby or incorporated into the landscaping. Ideally, the cut and fill should balance, leading to greater economy and lower CO_2 production.

Recycling generally

Recycling construction waste is dealt with in the next section, but there are also opportunities to select materials that have a high capacity for recycling at the end of their intended use. British manufactured steel includes around 30–40 per cent of recycled steel; aluminium can be 100 per cent recycled, although the market for new aluminium is outstripping the recycled market many times over. Some manufacturers, such as Interface Carpets, are offering new products that are made from 80 per cent recycled material. The BRE database of embodied energy referred to above takes account of the potential for recycling.

Because of the enormous range of variables within the construction process and the limited number of detailed studies carried out to date, it is hard to state with accuracy how much CO_2 can be avoided with these measures but, from data collected by the Building Research Establishment, it does appear that reductions of between a third and a half can be achieved.

Whilst this is still highly significant, there are arguably larger gains to be made by making buildings more readily adaptable, so that they do not need to be thrown away when their first intended use has expired.

Calculating the carbon implications of development is the scientific manifestation of environmental sustainability, but the cultural implications of 'green' policies are profound. From the extensive lists of design and construction issues above, it should be clear that local climate and sources of materials are critically important considerations for optimising both operational and embodied energy. The pursuit of sustainability is likely to mean that the relationship of buildings to their immediate environment is bound to find expression in their appearance, both internally and externally, in the form of solar control, the choice of materials, the pattern of ventilation and even the choice of structure. An office building in, say, Singapore could not – and should not – look the same as one in northern Europe. Closer to home, there are numerous reasons why an office in the West Country, for example, should have different characteristics to the equivalent building in Scotland.

> In theory, re-establishing a link between local climate, materials sources and the form of buildings seems an obvious mechanism for greater sustainability in its broadest sense. Whether or not the world of commercial offices, with its customary adherence to universal standards, has the will to accommodate such variations is open to question.

Waste

Whereas global warming is a relatively recent phenomenon, good husbandry of resources has always been recognised for its long-term significance and, even though the UK is presently one of the worst performers in the developed world, the issues of waste and recycling have been in the public consciousness for some years. Most local authorities only have bottle banks or paper collections whereas, in parts of Europe and the United States, there are fines for failing to recycle, for example, aluminium cans. However, the introduction of the landfill tax in 1996 has kick-started a process that should ultimately lead to dumping being the last resort. At that time, it was estimated that some 70m tonnes of construction, demolition materials and soil ended up as landfill – some 17 per cent of the nation's total. Some parts of the country, such as Kent, have virtually run out of landfill sites, so it is becoming a social and economic problem as well as an environmental one.

The overlap between reducing waste and reducing embodied CO_2 is self-evident, but there are several areas where designers and contractors can make a significant difference.

Lean construction, off-site prefabrication
Recycling should be a last-resort strategy, as reduction of waste begins with avoidance. Many of the subjects described in the previous section, such as lean construction and off-site prefabrication would result in reduced waste, through the pursuit of low embodied carbon dioxide emissions.

Mock-ups, complete design, right-first-time
Whether or not a building is prefabricated, the use of mock-ups or trial assemblies is proven to reduce the amount of waste from mistakes. Similarly, the completeness of design or fabrication information normally has a direct bearing on the amount of wasted effort and materials at later stages. Early investment in design time always pays back.

Cut and fill
Quite apart from the reduction in transport emissions from the policy of balancing the cut and fill on a site as described above, the cost of exporting surplus material to landfill sites is becoming increasingly expensive as the Government introduces new taxes. Together with the climate levy, the landfill tax is one of the clearest indications that attitudes will be changed by enforcement if voluntary means is not successful. As a result of this tax, a market in recycling construction waste is emerging.

Once again, the value of early design time is evident in the substantial savings that can be achieved from careful cut and fill calculations. Recent projects from the 'Rethinking Construction' demonstration programme indicated savings of 30 per cent.

Recycling
With the advent of the landfill tax, it is now becoming viable to separate different types of construction waste and recycle them. The construction manager MACE used the Wessex Water scheme as a pilot, demonstrating that, even in a fledgling market, there was a net financial benefit to the project. As waste recycling companies exploit the potential that has been highlighted by the new tax, recycling site waste is likely to become a fixture on most projects. Once again, the requirement for waste recycling can be incorporated into the contract documents prior to tender.

The Government has set a specific target for increased use of waste and recycled materials as aggregates in England from about 30m tonnes per annum to 55m tonnes by 2006.

One further, intangible benefit of recycling seems to be that building sites tend to be cleaner and more disciplined. The 'Rethinking Construction' programme of demonstration projects has shown that the better run construction sites result in higher levels of quality, profitability, safety and customer satisfaction than industry norms.

Pollution
It hardly needs saying that pollution at site level is a form of waste that must be avoided. Statutory regulations and inspections exist to control this aspect, although even reputable contractors have track records that could greatly improve.

Figure 12: Skips for recycling waste

Waste, like safety, is an attitude. High quality site facilities, with canteens, good toilets and changing facilities are synonymous with high levels of site discipline, quality and reduced waste. For contractors to resist the temptation to economise on these items, a clear list of requirements should be included in the contract documents by the quantity surveyor or contract administrator. Although a high level of site facilities implies a higher initial cost at tender stage, experience has shown that the end product is likely to be more reliable in terms of quality, cost and the time taken for delivery.

At a social level, the property market should be concerned at the increasing skills shortage in the construction sector and the clear evidence that poor site conditions are partly responsible.

Protection from damage
The elimination of waste is a continuous process from the design stage, through production, construction to completion. Adequate protection from damage after handover is the last part of this process.

As with the other key issues, there is a need to quantify waste to ensure that real progress is being made. The obvious unit of measurement is the cost of landfill, but it is also possible to measure the volume of materials that end up in the disposal skip. Consistency in the unit of measurement will be difficult until a much wider sample of projects can be surveyed, but the 'Rethinking Construction' indicators suggest using cubic metres per 100 square metres of construction.

Water

Hosepipe bans alternating with local flood warnings suggest that all is not well with our climate. Greenpeace and others have pointed out that, in the early 1960s, there were around 60 natural disasters per year throughout the world whereas, by the end of the 1990s, the number had increased to about 200. The climatic changes are generally attributed to the phenomenal increase in greenhouse gas emissions and it is increasingly clear that instability is here for the foreseeable future. Careful use of resources, such as fresh water, has become a key concern even in the UK, not only on account of its possible scarcity but also because of the energy needed in its production.

Water conservation falls into two broad categories: first, reduction of water drawn from the mains by collection of rainwater for general recycling in buildings together with the use of high efficiency fittings and, second, careful design of ground level surfaces to avoid depletion of the water table. The most effective policies to bring these about are as follows:

- high efficiency fittings, such as spray taps, showers without power pumps, etc.;

- leak detection;
- 'greywater' recycling, from roofs and elsewhere, for w.c. cisterns, garden irrigation;
- drainage through reed-beds;
- porous surface finishes in car parks, with filter layers.

As an indication of the gains that can be made, water consumption at the Wessex Water headquarters remained more-or-less constant when they moved from their previous buildings, with total consumption of around 35 litres per person per day, despite the addition of a larger restaurant, showers and so on. More significantly, whereas their older buildings had no greywater recycling, the amount of fresh water from the mains in the new building was reduced to just 16 litres per person per day – a 55 per cent reduction – through the use of three large, underground tanks. (Despite their size, these tanks were completely emptied during the dry winter period of 2001–02.) The use of porous paviors in the parking areas allowed surface water to drain directly into the ground without having to go through a petrol interceptor, helping to maintain the water table and avoiding construction of a new sewer from the site into the local drainage system some distance away.

Biodiversity

As yet, there is no obvious consensus about the way of measuring the biodiversity or ecology of a project, but there is no doubt over the strategic objective. Whether the site is urban, brownfield or out-of-town, the intention must be to ensure that, at the very least, a development does not result in the depletion of its natural habitat. Positive enhancement is, of course, preferable.

The species index is perhaps the best method of appraising sites, whereby the number of different species per hectare is surveyed prior to development, so that a policy of enhancement can be devised for planning approval and subsequent monitoring.

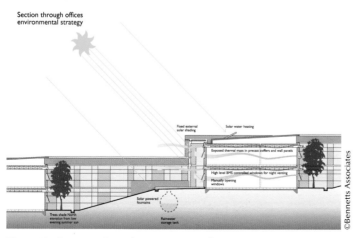

Section through offices environmental strategy

Figure 13: Cross sectiion of Wessex Water showing water storage tanks below embankment

©Grant Associates

Figure 14: New planting at Wessex Water

Enhancing biodiversity is not merely a statistical exercise, however, and the necessary changes in attitude to the design of external spaces will see landscapes that have less to do with marketing and image and more relevance to longer-term values. The ubiquitous landscape and water 'features' will give way to sensitive use of plant species that can sustain appropriate fauna, together with natural swales and methods of drainage that support water conservation. Where appropriate, protection of existing trees or the addition of planted roofs can enhance sites or buildings where the opportunities for new landscape are limited.

As with the new forms demanded of buildings for improved energy consumption, so too the changes in landscape design for enhanced biodiversity tend to produce developments that are more interesting and subtle than a more conventional approach, with regional variations providing one possible answer to criticisms of stereotyped uniformity.

Transport

The transport implications of commercial offices are immense, touching on aspects of construction, planning policy, location, personnel management, pollution and, of course, global warming. Gone are the days, it would seem, when out-of-town developments could obtain planning permission with one car space for every 20 square metres of floor area. The absence of a convincing public transport network only serves to reinforce the contradiction between the public's desire for personal mobility and the need to curtail the emissions and congestion resulting from car usage. There is no question, though, that national planning policy has largely turned against developments that generate what is perceived as excessive car usage in favour of urban or brownfield developments, particularly those that relate closely to transport interchanges.

The impact of transport on office developments is such that it can outweigh the energy consumption of the building itself. Research by the BRE indicates that, in terms of overall emissions, the out-of-town air conditioned office is the worst offender, followed by the out-of-town low-energy office. There is nothing more open to question than the 'green' building surrounded by acres of parking. Next in line is the urban air conditioned office, with the low-energy urban office being the all round best performer.

Clearly, if urban offices represent the future on account of their transport implications, there must be an optimum balance between energy efficiency and future flexibility in a workplace that cannot normally rely on opening windows.

For those commercial offices that do rely to some extent on the car, the 'Green Travel Plan' has become the inevitable requirement of planning authorities who need firm evidence of a reduction in car usage before they can grant consent. Some local authorities are also using Section 106 of the Town and Country Planning Act (1990, as amended 1991) to enforce post-occupancy monitoring to ensure that car usage is in accordance with the approved plan. As the contents of green travel plans are still developing, they can vary from one authority to another, but the emerging model suggests a combination of carrots and sticks on the following lines:

Carrots:
- encouragement of, and provision for, cycling and walking; secure cycle parking; showers; and possibly financial incentives;
- company shuttle bus from local station, or park and ride;
- financial contribution to improve local bus service;
- incentives for car sharing;
- facilities for on-site shopping (e.g. Internet).

Sticks:
- parking restricted to essential users;
- parking charges.

Developing a green transport plan invariably means surveying the existing situation with a recognised transport consultant, so that credible targets for traffic generation and mitigation can be agreed with the local authority.

Performance indicators for environmental sustainability

In recent years, performance measurement has become one of the mantras of modern industry and a trend that began in the motor manufacturing sector has become accepted practice elsewhere, even in the notoriously inconsistent construction industry. The co-ordinating body for measurement in the construction industry is the DTI-backed initiative, 'Rethinking Construction', which embraces the Construction Best Practice Programme (CBPP) and the Movement for innovation

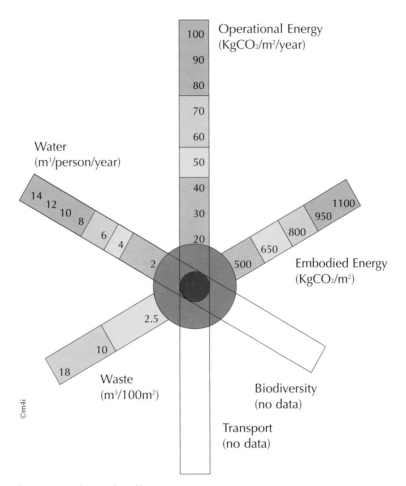

Figure 15: Performance indicator for offices

(M4i). A series of initial Key Performance Indicators, dealing with general subjects such as safety and delivery, is accompanied by Environmental Performance Indicators that are intended to provide substance in an area previously lacking in objective data. The indicators enable different building types to be measured on a common basis, with a restricted range of no more than six issues that relate to environmental sustainability only. The intention is that they are sufficiently simple to be adopted across as wide a spectrum of the industry as possible, unlike some of the more complex forms of assessment.

The Environmental Performance Indicator for offices is reproduced in Figure 15. The following notes should be read in conjunction:

• The data has been arranged like a 'wind-rose' diagram, with the greenest performance characteristics towards the centre. The orange and red areas indicate poor performance.

- Although enough data exists to put precise figures to four of the six subjects, two remain blank for lack of a sufficiently large sample. It is expected that this will be remedied as more and more projects measure their outputs.

- Transport in this context refers to the construction process only and not to the wider issue of vehicle movements relating to the finished building.

- There is only one scale of measurement for each subject. Whilst there are different industry standards in the Building Regulations for energy consumption depending on whether or not it is an air conditioned building, for example, the performance indicator obliges performance to be measured against the most efficient, which is likely to be partially or wholly naturally ventilated.

- Ideally, a design should be tested against the indicators at Outline or Scheme Design stage, so that adjustments can be made in light of the results before construction commences. The same indicators can be used to monitor actual post-occupancy performance.

The full text accompanying the Environmental Performance Indicators can be downloaded from www.m4i.org.uk, together with a survey form designed to build up the BRE's data bank.

Social and economic sustainability

The emphasis of this chapter of *The Commercial Offices Handbook* is on environmental sustainability, largely because it is better researched and understood than economic and social sustainability, and has already been accepted by office occupiers as central to our future well-being.

But, however impressive a building's 'green' credentials may be, there is little point in pursuing environmental improvements if the building does not work for its users or is disliked by the community at large. Equally, an office development that is economically successful but harms its environment is flawed as a long-term solution. Sustainability can sometimes imply a trade-off between conflicting ideologies, but experience suggests that optimised environmental, social and economic solutions can be found together, given the right attitudes.

Economic sustainability – the functional workplace

It should not be surprising that the pursuit of environmental sustainability in the commercial office coincides in many respects with a more productive and pleasant workplace. Instead of uninspiring flat ceilings and draughts from air conditioning grilles, there is the prospect of a more tolerant ventilation system combined with an appropriately designed, exposed structure that has greater visual stimulus. The option of opening windows enhances local control for the occupants, whilst high levels of natural daylight combined with control over solar gain at the perimeter imply a much more benign workspace. Provided the workplace is comfortable, the evidence from

Figure 16: The functional workplace – Wessex Water

surveys suggests that air conditioning is not so important to occupiers as some letting agents suggest. A 1991 survey by property consultants Richard Ellis identified that human qualities were the most important, such as outside awareness, the ability to open a window and visual interest, and that 89 per cent of office occupiers would prefer not to have air conditioning if there was a choice.

Although the features of a 'green' office are often attractive in themselves, the need for greater care and integration in the design and construction process could be contributing to a better crop of buildings. Whatever the reason, research projects are establishing a clear link between the quality of the workplace and productivity. Statistically, the most obvious issue is absenteeism, but many organisations have reported lower staff turnover and that most elusive quality of all – higher productivity. As the 'people' costs of an office building dwarf those of construction and operation, any kind of gain in this area is of the utmost significance.

Economic sustainability also requires buildings to be capable of adaptation as business needs change and this, too, corresponds with an environmental need to avoid rapid obsolescence in our building stock. Fewer columns, straightforward floorplate shapes, adequate floor-to-floor heights and the ability to convert to other uses all contribute to sustainability. The ability to accommodate substantial changes in servicing demands is particularly critical in avoiding premature redundancy: a low energy or naturally ventilated office building should always be capable of being retrofitted for an occupier with higher heat loads or a greater proportion of cellular space than the initial owner or tenant. It is also possible to argue that the environmentally benign office is more resilient to change, as its operating systems and physical characteristics are less fragile than the closely controlled interior – a quality described by the theorist and researcher Bill Bordass as 'reasonable robustness'.

©Miller Hare

Figure 17: Broadgate development showing mixed-use site

Social sustainability – the responsible office

Office parks or urban developments have often been described as 'ghettos' that are devoid of life after working hours and at weekends, but there is an increasing realisation among investors as well as occupiers that a more balanced community has commercial value because of society's preference for increased vibrancy and diversity[4].

The need for sustainable urban regeneration, with a mixture of high-density uses, has been well documented in strategic papers such as those of Lord Rogers' Urban Task Force and is increasingly being reflected in some aspects of Government planning policy. Mixed uses are now a requirement of most local authorities' Unitary Development Plans – the statutory documents used to guide most conventional planning decisions – and office buildings are now more likely to be accompanied by retail or residential accommodation as a result. Planning consents are also likely to be conditioned by an obligation to improve the public realm in some way, such as street paving, landscaping or a contribution to a public building.

If the social aspects of planning policy are relatively easy to identify, there are less obvious manifestations of social sustainability that an office project should not neglect.

---

4 See Figures 13 and 14 and 'Broadgate Revisited' case study in Chapter 7.

Working conditions in much of the construction industry continue to act as a deterrent not only to quality but also to job security, self-esteem, safety and the social stability that goes with a well-trained and resourced workforce. Developers and consultants can help to change the industry's failings by championing best practice and by insisting that contractors negotiate or tender on the basis of properly defined site facilities, training and safety policies. Quite apart from the social benefits that this would bring, there are clear economic benefits at stake if the decline in the industry's skill base is to be reversed. As fewer young people are attracted to the construction industry and the average age of the workforce rises, so too do building costs in times of high demand. If routine development or refurbishment projects are to be affordable in future, a sustained improvement to construction's reputation may be the key.

Within the office building itself, user consultation, social interaction and the provision of amenities within the workplace can foster longer-term sustainability through a sense of well-being and lower staff turnover. This is dealt with elsewhere in *The Commercial Offices Handbook*.

The optimum solution

What, then, is the specification of the environmentally sustainable commercial office? The following is a suggested list of basic requirements:

- narrow or medium width floorplates with good daylight;
- exposed structural soffits, or perforated ceilings to allow passive cooling;
- main services in a deep raised floor;
- the ability of the base building to accommodate fresh air ventilation through the floor with heat reclaimed from the return air;
- the ability of the base building to accommodate additional mechanical cooling for exceptional requirements;
- opening windows to supplement mechanical ventilation;
- high levels of insulation, including glazed areas;
- high levels of airtightness;
- solar control and glare control at every opportunity.

Summary

In one form or another, sustainability touches upon all aspects of the commercial office and, as such, it is not a marketing feature that can be added later. Nevertheless, for Europe if not for the United States, its commercial value will increase as the market becomes more conscious of public demand for better, more responsible buildings and taxes of various kinds place a premium on the profligate office development.

A number of aspects of the development process stand out as being particularly critical. First, design must be at the forefront, with true integration between the work of architects, structural engineers and services engineers being especially important in achieving a building form that has the least impact on the environment. Second, the most appropriate solutions are likely to be based at least in part on local conditions, including climate, materials and transport. This in turn should lead to buildings that are more at ease with their locality. Third, office buildings should be robust, so that they can withstand frequent change with minimal waste. It should not be necessary to throw away most of a building after only 25 or 30 years. Fourth, the performance of office buildings should be measured, not only in the design phase but also after completion, with the information being shared by the industry to ensure that it continuously improves.

There is one further aspect, however, that may ultimately dictate the course of events. Far from being stilted by so-called 'green' design, those office buildings that have already embraced the sustainability agenda have been liberated to the extent that they appear to be preferred by their occupants over the conventional alternative. Emerging research suggests that higher levels of productivity combined with lower absenteeism will be far more significant to commercial occupiers in the long term than any marginal savings on, say, fuel consumption or waste recycling. This, surely, is true sustainability, where action to reduce the environmental impact converges with the needs of social and economic fulfilment.

Information sources

The following websites provide helpful additional advice:

www.energy-efficiency.gov.uk
The Energy Efficiency Best Practice Programme (EEBPP) is the UK Government's principal energy efficiency information, advice and research programme. It maintains the biggest library of independent information on energy efficiency in the UK. It promotes best practice through free publications and events, and encourages action with advice and support at every stage from planning to design, implementation and management.

www.designadvice.co.uk/da_advice.html
Introduction to the Design Advice Service, which offers a one day general consultancy on a chosen building project, paid for by a cashback scheme.

www.bre.co.uk
Building Research Establishment website.

cig.bre.co.uk/connet/mie/
An exchange that allows the construction industry to buy and sell used and second-hand construction materials over the internet.

www.usablebuildings.co.uk/Probe/ProbeIndex.html
Useful part of the usable buildings site with the Probe (*Post-Occupancy Review of Buildings and their Engineering*) Studies online (which are published in the *Building Services Journal*). The studies have some very good information on the actual performance of buildings and on user satisfaction.

www.chpclub.com
The CHP Club enables users to access information, exchange experience, ask questions, and share good practice.

www.envirowise.gov.uk
Waste management site Envirowise has produced over 200 publications offering simple, practical advice to help UK companies reduce costs and improve environmental performance.

www.environgov.co.uk
Environmental Governance is an networking organisation aimed at property owners committed to increased sustainability.

www.cbpp.org.uk
The Construction Best Practice Programme – one of the key components of the Government's 'Rethinking Construction' agenda.

www.m4i.org.uk
The Movement for Innovation website – part of the 'Rethinking Construction' programme – and the source of the Environmental Performance Indicators referred to in this chapter. In addition, the website has guidance on good site practice that supports social sustainability.

www.construction.dtlr.gov.uk/research/index.htm
The umbrella website for the 'Rethinking Construction' programme.

www.sustainmagazine.com
A magazine devoted to sustainability, with invaluable information sources, including suppliers and consultants with sustainability specialisms.

www.foe-scotland.org.uk
The Green Office Action Plan, Friends of the Earth Scotland. This covers the management of the sustainable office, with information on, for example, paper recycling, ethical sources of office supplies, energy purchasing and so on.

http://www.bsjonline.co.uk/index.asp
Building Services Journal, Builder Group. The magazine that publishes the influential 'Probe' studies on building performance.

Author profile

Rab Bennetts, Director
Bennetts Associates

Rab Bennetts was born in Aberdeen, trained as an architect in Edinburgh and worked at the multi-disciplinary firm Arup Associates for ten years on projects such as the Finsbury Avenue, Broadgate and Stockley Park developments. Together with his wife Denise, he formed Bennetts Associates in 1987 and has since pioneered environmental sustainability through a succession of major office, educational and cultural buildings.

PowerGen's headquarters in Coventry began a sequence of award-winning projects that included offices for BT and John Menzies at Edinburgh Park and culminated in Wessex Water's Operations Centre in Bath, singled out by the BRE as the 'greenest' commercial building in the UK at that time. Subsequently, the lessons of these owner-occupied buildings have been applied to developments for BAA Lynton, Stanhope and New Edinburgh Ltd, as well as City University Business School, Brighton Central Library and Hampstead Theatre.

Bennetts Associates' 45-strong London office in Clerkenwell illustrates sustainable principles in an urban setting, with regeneration of two existing buildings combined with new, energy-efficient construction. The firm also has an office in Edinburgh.

Rab Bennetts is a frequent contributor to conferences and publications on sustainability, and chaired the Sustainability Working Group for the Movement for Innovation – the Government-backed think-tank that forms part of its Rethinking Construction programme.

Building engineering

Note from the Editor

Buildings consist of five principal elements: structure, services, cladding, finishes and the spaces between. None of these may be designed in isolation since they all, to some degree, interact. The building engineering elements that enable a building to function effectively traditionally lack the aesthetic appeal, or glamour, that is associated with other areas of architectural design input. The exception to this is the increasingly sophisticated level of engineering expertise that goes in to procuring the skin of a building, the facade.

But a failure to acknowledge the importance of the successful integration of the building engineering elements will result in the procurement of a building that miserably fails to achieve the objective of sound architectural design, Loose Fit, Long Life and Low Energy.

The following chapters – Structure, Facades, Building services, Vertical transportation and Architectural acoustics for offices – though presented separately, comprehensively present the elements of building engineering in manageable chunks, guiding the reader through the process from structure-type to the consideration of issues such as vertical transportation and office acoustics.

10 Structure

Richard Terry
Arup

Introduction

So, what is structure?

The Oxford English Dictionary defines a structure as 'a supporting framework or whole of the essential parts of something.'

The Institution of Structural Engineers defines structural engineering as 'the science and art of designing and making, with economy and elegance, buildings, bridges, frameworks and other similar structures so that they can safely resist the forces to which they may be subjected.'

What is particular about the structure of an office building? Clearly, it must allow the business of the occupants to function safely, efficiently and without interruption. It ought to do so invisibly and with low levels of maintenance.

A well-considered structure will have a number of important characteristics:

- **Form** – it will have a form entirely compatible with the function, characteristics and quality standards of a contemporary office building. It will also have a form compatible with the context and aesthetic of the building.
- **Strength** – it will have the strength to sustain gravity loads from the building itself and from occupants, furniture, equipment, partitions and associated storage. It will also have the strength to sustain horizontal loads from wind (and, in exceptional circumstances, from earthquake).
- **Stiffness** – it will have sufficient inherent (so-called) stiffness to avoid undue deflection of the building or parts of the building under load. It will also have sufficient stiffness to avoid undue vibration under load.
- **Value** – it will contribute to a best value solution for the total building (but will not necessarily provide the best value structure).

Increasingly, it is also important that the structural engineer has considered the broader issues of society, economy and the environment or 'sustainability'. In particular, he or she will have considered the impact of the structural design on our natural resources, both in construction and in operation

The choice of an appropriate structure for a particular office building can be complex and will be influenced by many things, including building location and type, site characteristics, client brief and design aspirations, considerations of programme, procurement, cost and value. That choice can rarely be taken without a full understanding of the architectural intent and of the building services solutions for the building. Increasingly, the structural system comprises one component of an integrated engineering solution to the building as a whole.

In this chapter, we will do several things.

- identify a range of building types;
- consider the building site and its possible influence on the design of the structure;
- gather the client brief and the other principal criteria for the design of the structure; and
- consider the range of solutions available to the structural engineer in the design of the structure for a particular office building.

Building types

Office buildings are quite varied in type. They tend to be sited either outside our towns and cities in business parks, such as Stockley Park near Heathrow, or in the centres of our towns and cities on individual sites, often within a central business district, such as in the City of London (see Figures 1 – 4).

The business parks provide open and straightforward sites with easy access. Projects are invariably new-build, simple and low-rise. Often, the design for one building informs the design and construction of several buildings on adjacent sites. Structural solutions are simple too. Repeat-, modular- and component-based designs can bring great benefit. Form and materials are increasingly influenced by the opportunity to adopt natural and mixed-mode ventilation systems and integrated engineering solutions.

By contrast, the town and city centre sites are confined, include significant constraints and are difficult to access. Projects are often new-build but can be refurbishments. Where existing buildings are listed or sited in a conservation area, projects may be new-build but, for example, behind a retained facade. Designs are set out to maximise area and buildings tend to be taller, either medium-rise or, in instances, high-rise. Designs respond to site shape and to other significant constraints and tend to be more complex. Structural solutions are more complex too. However, it remains important to find repeat-, modular- and component-based solutions, where at all possible. Form and materials are less regularly influenced by the environmental systems.

This Chapter concentrates on new-build projects.

Figure 1: Aerial view, Stockley Park

Figure 2: Aerial view, City of London

Figure 3: The Square, Stockley Park

Figure 4: 88 Wood Street, City of London

The site

Site hazards

Every new site offers opportunities – and potential hazards. A wise development team will seek to identify and keep careful track of the potential hazards and will work to ensure that each of them is mitigated. Some of them will be obvious, some less so. The obvious ones will tend to be above the ground surface whilst the less obvious ones will be buried below. Without a dedicated programme of site investigation, the buried hazards are likely to remain hidden until they are found as 'unforseens' during site construction.

The ground

The major hazards and constraints that need to be investigated include:

- ground conditions;
- groundwater regime;
- buried obstructions (including drainage and foundation systems of buildings to be demolished);
- buried services, including tunnel systems for utilities and transportation;
- boundary conditions, including adjoining and neighbouring properties (and their foundations);
- remnants of vegetation, such as the roots of trees or roots of noxious or invasive plants like Japanese knotweed;
- archaeology;
- mining works;
- and contamination of ground and groundwater.

Buried services are expensive to divert but are even more expensive to replace or repair after being hit by construction plant. Some, such as high-voltage cables or gas mains, are also exceptionally dangerous. Importantly, plans showing services are notoriously inaccurate.

Early investigation is recommended. At this stage, the project can normally be adapted so that the potential impact of any high cost risks are minimised. As the project progresses, the opportunity to adapt it and to mitigate the impact is reduced. Problems discovered after the start of construction are usually expensive and time-consuming to deal with.

Site investigation

A site investigation comprises two distinct phases: the desk study and the ground investigation.

Desk study
The first stage of a site investigation should be the desk study, allowing the scope and costs of the subsequent ground investigation to be optimised. The desk study should investigate at least the following areas:

- **Site history** – to warn of former industries in the vicinity of the site which could have contaminated the ground, or groundwater or other historical features such as back-filled ponds, brick pits or old structures which could affect foundations.
- **Topography** – to reveal risks such as incipient slope instability.

- **Geology** – to reveal risks such as major geological features, e.g. scour hollows or alluvium-filled former river courses.
- **Local stratigraphy and ground conditions** – to investigate the particular soils beneath the site and to warn of problems for their use in foundations, e.g. swelling clays, soils of very low strength and stiffness, or permeable gravels which could allow water to inundate excavations.
- **Buried services** – to detect buried services, including railway and other tunnels, which could be affected by the ground investigation or by the building foundations.

The desk study can also provide data of benefit to the development team by, say, warning of surviving archaeology which could affect the granting of planning permission or identifying a source of good quality soil which might be used as fill material.

A good desk study will:

- give background information on the site and allow an initial scheme design to be developed, including the need for ancillary structures such as retaining walls;
- identify the ground-related hazards that need to be investigated in greater detail during the ground investigation. Without a desk study, the ground investigation becomes a hit-and-miss affair. What are the chances of identifying, for example, a former pond ten metres across when your boreholes and trial pits are at 20-30 metre centres?
- provide a basis for foundation design, allowing more economical foundation types to be identified.

Ground investigation
There are a myriad of different techniques for investigating the ground. Choosing the particular techniques to use on a particular site are matters of judgement. *Without Site Investigation Ground is a Hazard*[1], a booklet by the Site Investigation Steering Group (SISG), gives outline guidance on why a ground investigation is required and examples of what could otherwise go wrong. *Planning, Procurement and Quality Management*[2], gives detailed advice on which professionals should be engaged, how the ground investigation and its interpretation should be incorporated into the design process, and how the ground investigation should be procured. These documents identify the following roles:

- The client's principal technical advisor (PTA), who will often be the architect. The PTA will be in charge of the design team and control the design process.

---

1 SISG (1993), *Part 1: Without Site Investigation Ground is a Hazard*, London, Thomas Telford.
2 SISG (1993), *Part 2: Planning, Procurement and Quality Management*, London, Thomas Telford.

The PTA together with the structural engineer, is the most important decision-maker regarding the quality of site investigation. They will normally recommend the appointment of a geotechnical advisor unless the structural design team already includes such a person.

- The geotechnical advisor (GA) will have sufficient experience to control the site investigation process.
- The geotechnical contractor is engaged to carry out the ground investigation.

Most ground investigations should use *Specification for Ground Investigation*[3], as this has been broadly adopted as the UK national specification and as those throughout the industry are familiar with its content.

After completion of the ground investigation, the data should be interpreted by someone with geotechnical experience. Some of the information is often contradictory. Over-reliance on statistical techniques can be misleading in solving geotechnical problems; often it is the apparently spurious data that turns out to be the most significant.

The ground investigation should determine the following factors as appropriate for the particular set of development proposals:

- Stratigraphy and its variation across the site. The depth of investigation should be appropriate for all likely foundation options and the spatial frequency of exploration points should ensure that likely variations in key layers are catered for.
- Those ground properties and parameters required for the design of the temporary and permanent works. Less testing usually means less certainty, which in turn leads to a more conservative foundation design.
- Groundwater conditions and their variation across the site, with depth and with time. The only reliable way to establish groundwater conditions is to measure water levels in standpipes and piezometers – all too frequently this is not undertaken, which explains why misunderstood water conditions are one of the main causes of problems on construction projects and also on the completed structures.
- The detection of any significant levels of contamination in the ground or groundwater. These are needed for the protection of construction workers and subsequently for building operatives, so that the structure and connecting services can be made sufficiently durable and that spoil disposal costs can be assessed at an early stage. The latter can be at least five times higher for contaminated spoil.
- Boundary conditions, including adjoining and neighbouring properties. A thorough knowledge of the form and level of the sub-structures (foundations, basements, etc) of adjacent, existing buildings will be necessary for the design of

---

3 SISG (1993), Part 3: Specification for Ground Investigation, London, Thomas Telford.

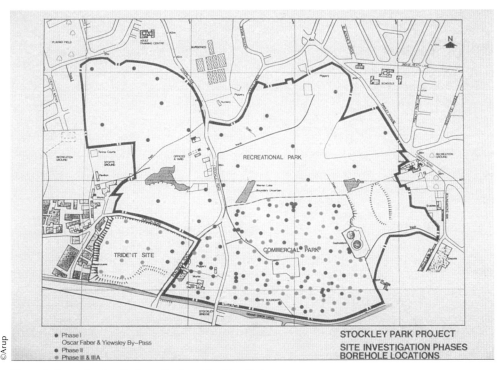

Figure 5: Example of a site investigation, Stockley Park

the sub-structure of the new building. It will also inform discussions with third parties and their representatives, including Party Wall surveyors, about the impact, if any, of the new building on the adjoining and neighbouring buildings.

Where the desk study has identified an archaeological potential beneath the site, the ground investigation may well be extended to include a specialist archaeological investigation, specified by archaeologists. Very often, such an investigation is a requirement of the planning authority.

A cautionary note
When there are site investigations, they are often inadequate. They are considered a commodity to be bought in at minimum cost, rather than an important element to be incorporated into the flow of the design process. This can lead to inappropriate site investigations where the total amount expended might have been sufficient, but the information obtained does not address the specific problems of the development on the site.

Inevitably, even properly planned site investigations sometimes fail to detect features in the ground that will lead to problems during construction. It is seldom practicable to sample more than 0.001 per cent of the ground beneath a site. However, problems which arise following an appropriate ground investigation are usually easier to resolve.

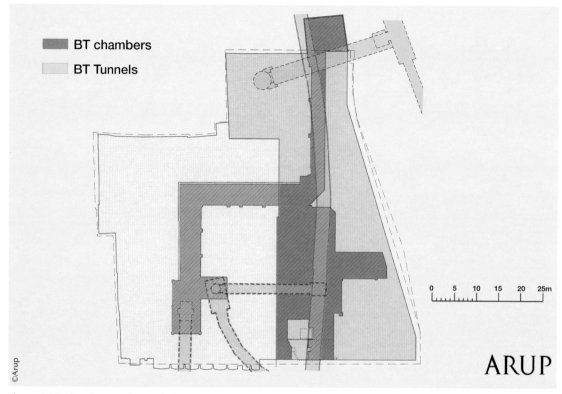

Figure 6: BT chambers and tunnels beneath 88 Wood Street

Tunnels

Office buildings in urban areas, especially London, frequently need to accommodate tunnels running either beneath them or immediately beside them. Deep tunnel networks in London include roads, National Rail, the tube, British Telecom, Mail Rail, electricity and water. Shallower tunnels exist but are normally buried under roads and pavements, thus presenting less of a constraint.

When a new commercial building is planned which could affect tunnels, the effects of the development on the tunnel normally have to be agreed with the tunnel owner and his consultants. Obviously, measures must be put in place to make sure that the tunnel cannot be directly hit by piles. However, measures are also required to make sure that the stress changes in the ground caused by excavation of the site or loading of the foundations do not unduly distort the tunnel so that its operations become impaired or its water resistance compromised.

In addition, it is usually a requirement that new buildings, conceived after a proposed tunnel route has been safeguarded, should be designed to accommodate the construction of the tunnel.

Structural requirements

The brief

A clear brief is an essential component of any successful office project. It provides a fundamental starting point and sets objectives against which designs can be measured and tested.

It is important that the client owns the brief. It is equally important that all team members contribute to the brief and are familiar with, and accept, its contents. The client and their team should, sensibly, test the key issues of the brief against site constraints, available budgets and target programmes at an early stage.

A complete brief will consider issues ranging from the client's broad aims for the project to the particular design criteria for it, across the disciplines. For the structural engineer, it is important that the particular structural requirements are identified, as set out below.

Design life
The design life of the primary structures of an office project can vary but is generally set at 60 years. For concrete structures, properly designed and detailed, little or no maintenance will be required during that period. For steel structures in damp environments, maintenance of their corrosion protection systems will be required and a 'life to first maintenance' of those systems should be set.

The actual life of a structure can be significantly enhanced through regular maintenance. However, it is worth noting that many buildings constructed in the 1960s have already been demolished and redeveloped!

Grids and spans
The planning grid sets the fundamental module for the structural grid and, therefore, the structural spans within the building. The *BCO Guide 2000*[4] recommends the following:

- **Planning grid** – 1.5 m.
- **Column grid** – 7.5-9.0 m, although requirements for longer spans are often to be considered.

---

4 BCO (2000), *British Council of Offices Guide 2000: Best Practice in the Specification for Offices,* available at www.bco-officefocus.com

Live load

The live load on an office floor represents the load (or weight) from people, furniture and loose equipment, as well as that from storage and lightweight demountable partitions on that floor. The *BCO Guide 2000*[5] recommends the following:

- **General area** – 2.5 kN/sq m over approximately 95 per cent of each potentially sub-lettable floor area. The figure is consistent with the loading threshold defined in British Standard 6399 – Part 1.
- **High loading area** – 7.5 kN/sq m over approximately five per cent of each potentially sub-lettable floor area, to allow for filing, mass paper and general office storage.
- **Partitions** – 1.0 kN/sq m generally, to allow for the self-weight of typical office partitions.

A client brief will often call for live loads in excess of 2.5 kN/sq m. Today, live loads of 3.0 kN/sq m and 3.5 kN/sq m are common. Historically, live loads of 4.0 kN/sq m and 5.0 kN/sq m have been specified.

However, a load of 2.5 kN/sq m represents some 250 kg/sq m or three large people on each square metre of the floor!

Figure 7: Office floor showing elements that form the 'live load', Merrill Lynch Financial Centre, City of London

5 with reference to the *Stanhope Position Paper: An Assessment of the Imposed Loading for Current Commercial Office Buildings in Great Britain*, August 1992.

Basement waterproofing requirements
Basement structures are always likely to be in contact with water, either temporarily when, for example, a water main bursts, or permanently, when sitting at levels within the permanent groundwater regime. In each instance, it is important to define the protection level from water within the basement. This is generally a function of basement usage.

Guidance on watertightness is given in BS 8102[6] and CIRIA Report 139[7]. A summary of that guidance is set out in Table 3 (*see* Appendix).

Flexibility for future alterations
Inevitably, as needs change over time, the original structure will undergo future alteration. The degree of inherent flexibility for that future alteration should be agreed in the brief (and may include consideration of future loadings and of particular requirements to infill atria, introduce new staircases, etc.).

Target cost and quality
The design options are regularly measured and tested against aspirations for cost and quality. Often those aspirations are in conflict. A target cost will, at least to a degree, dictate quality from the outset and should be clearly stated in the brief. It will often be expressed as a unit cost in £/sq m and benchmarked against other similar buildings.

Materials

The choice of materials for the structure of an office project may be influenced in several ways. The principal structural (and constructional) characteristics of common concrete and steel floor systems are presented in a later section, entitled 'Floor structure'.

However, the choice may also be influenced by the architecture or aesthetic of the building: a concrete element may be exposed or a steel frame expressed; the quality of material and finish gains much greater importance; durability is more of an issue; and for steelwork, fire protection is more complex.

The choice is also increasingly influenced by the opportunity to adopt natural and mixed-mode ventilation systems and integrated engineering solutions (especially in a business park environment). An exposed concrete soffit, for example, can enhance the thermal performance of the building and allow such systems to be both practicable and economic.

---

6 British Standards Institution (BSI) (1990), *BS 8102:1990: Code of Practice for Protection of Structures against Water from the Ground*, London, BSI.
7 Johnson, R A. (1995), *Water resisting basements - a guide. Safeguarding new and existing basements against water and dampness*, London, CIRIA.

Applied loadings

The loadings applied to any building structure constitute the most important set of design parameters for that structure. The total set are summarised in Table 1 (*see* Appendix).

Structural design

Foundations

The most heavily loaded parts of any structure are the foundations. They are also the parts which are virtually impossible to uncover and inspect after installation and which, arguably, are most prone to defects. It is vital that experienced professionals design and construct them and, in so doing, follow a coherent process.

Trends towards longer spans with fewer columns (and taller buildings) are increasing loads on individual columns and their foundations.

Foundations have two functions:

- To support the applied loads without significant risk of failure.
- To support the applied loads with sufficiently small movements so that no function of the building is impaired, i.e. no cracking, sticking of doors, cutting of service connections, etc.

Foundations can receive vertical loads, horizontal thrusts and applied moments and must resist them with an appropriate factor of safety and so that settlements are within acceptable limits.

Shallow foundations
Generally, shallow foundations will be most economical, especially if loads are relatively light and the water table is deep. Options include:

- trenchfill – for the lightest loads;
- pad footings;
- strip footings;
- rafts – for heavier loads.

If rock or granular soils are close to the surface, allowable bearing pressures will be higher (say 250kN/sq m, roughly equivalent to a six-storey building with a 7.5 metre square grid on three metre square pad footings).

If stiff clays (like London or Oxford Clays) are close to the surface, bearing pressures will typically be lower (say 150kN/sq m, roughly equivalent to a three-storey building with a 7.5 metre square grid on three metre square pad footings) and settlements may be considerably higher. Stiff clays when unloaded, for instance at the bottom of basement excavation, can result in large heave movements and these can complicate foundation design.

Great care is required for shallow foundations on clay-type soils near trees, especially if some trees need to be cut down close to the points at which the foundations will be cast. Trees extract water from the ground and the ground near cut down trees recovers water. These moisture content changes in the ground can therefore result in large movements of the ground that frequently lead to damage.

As shallow foundations will normally be most efficient, techniques of ground improvement have been developed to stiffen soil which would otherwise be too soft. These ground improvement techniques are most effective for very low-rise buildings on areas of fill, such as business parks reclaimed from former industrial usage. While ground improvement is reliable when appropriate controls are applied, it generally will not be as reliable as a piled solution. It should therefore only be used when it results in cost or programme savings over piles.

Piled foundations
For weaker ground or heavier loads, or where tighter control on foundation movements is required, piles are needed. Piles come in many varieties to deal with different circumstances. A summary of common pile types in the UK is shown below:

	Bored	**Driven**
Common types in the UK	• Large diameter auger • Underreams • Continuous flight auger (cfa) • Tripod • Minipiles	• Precast concrete • Steel circular and H-sections • Driven cast in-situ
Normal diameter range (m)	• 0.15-2.1 m for large diameter auger • 0.3-1.2 m for cfa	• 0.25 m square • 0.2-1.5 m tubes
Normal maximum depth	• 60 m for large diameter auger • 28 m for cfa	• 20 m+ for precast concrete

Bored piles are most versatile and can be used for high column loads. In favourable ground conditions such as the east of London, their capacity is limited by the crushing strength of the concrete, which corresponds to about 18MN load for a 1.5 metre diameter pile. In central London, a similar pile founded in London Clay would have a capacity of about 8MN.

Bored piles are often used instead of driven piles in urban centres because of concerns about the effects of noise and vibration.

Hand-dug piles have been used in situations where very high column loads are applied to a site where rig access is impossible. Virtually all instances of their use have been for air rights' developments over railway stations or tracks.

Driven precast concrete piles can be very economical for low-rise developments away from people who would be adversely affected by noise and vibration.

Steel piles tend only to be used to support structures built over docks, harbours or rivers. However, for pile positions within five metres of land, bored piles installed through a steel casing can offset the high mobilisation costs of marine working.

Reuse of piled foundations
Sites in the centre of big cities often undergo frequent redevelopment due to changing occupier demands. Since the 1950s, modern buildings have been constructed with wide column spacings, requiring the use of pile foundations. These often occupy the prime locations around the perimeter of a site presenting obstacles to future foundation construction. Old underreamed piles with expanded bases consume additional space. Other restrictions can arise from the presence of underground tunnels related to transport, communications and utilities, or the existence of valuable archaeological remains beneath the site.

Some sites in London are currently on their second or third set of foundations but the continued construction of more and more piles in the ground is not sustainable. The feasibility of redeveloping urban sites will reduce if the cost of installing fresh foundations becomes disproportionate and this will have an impact on land values. Existing retaining walls, strip foundations and raft foundations are often reused, but the reuse of pile foundations is less common due to the uncertainties over construction quality and concrete durability, and the concerns of the promoters, their funders and building insurers.

However, there are technically sound approaches to assessing the risks in reuse and these have been successfully undertaken at a number of sites. Increasingly, this will become the only viable, cost-effective solution for the redevelopment of many sites above congested ground.

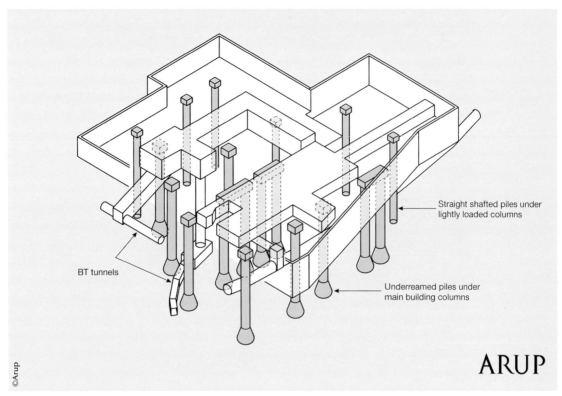

Figure 8: Piled foundations at 88 Wood Street

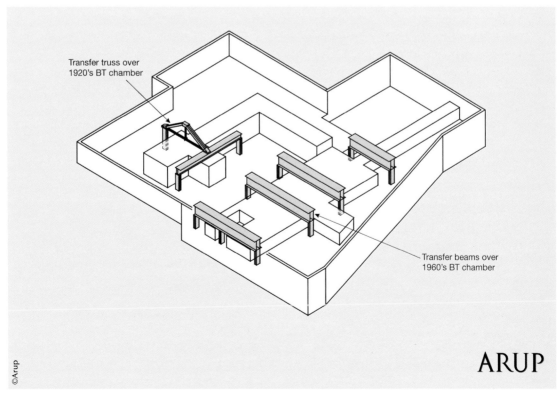

Figure 9: Steel transfer structures at 88 Wood Street

Sub-structure

Basements are becoming increasingly attractive in many UK urban centres because of planning constraints on building heights. They can be used for provision of delivery areas, car parking, storage, water tanks and plant space.

The following factors frequently dictate the choice of wall type and construction sequence:

- proximity to neighbouring buildings and their sensitivity;
- water table level;
- depth of basement;
- ability to use final floor plates for horizontal propping, dictated by the floor-to-floor heights and the number of holes in the slabs;
- vertical loading from the superstructure, whether it is helpful to carry loads on the perimeter wall and whether shallow or piled foundations will be most economical.

Normally it is most economic if the temporary and permanent works can be combined.

Two main types of construction sequence most commonly used are: 'bottom-up' and 'top-down'.

This section concentrates on walls that perform both the temporary and permanent requirements for support of the excavation sides with appropriate propping, etc. Table 2 (see Appendix) gives a general description of the advantages and disadvantages associated with different types of embedded retaining walls as appropriate to general UK sites.

In urban areas, a need to keep ground movements within acceptable bounds normally dominates the design. In greenfield areas, there is usually little need to control ground movements so economy and programme drive the choice.

No embedded retaining wall should be assumed to be completely watertight. Guidance on watertightness is given in BS 8102:1990 *Code of Practice for the Protection of Structures from the Ground* and CIRIA Report 139, *Water-resisting Basement Construction – a Guide*. These documents give guidance on the means by which particular grades of basement space can be achieved. The qualities and requirements for these grades are summarised in Table 3 (see Appendix).

Hard-hard secant pile walls or diaphragm walls alone may provide an acceptable level of water retention if a low grade of basement space is all that is required. For higher grades of space, structural facing walls designed to BS 8110 in front of contiguous or hard-soft secant pile retaining walls (for Grade 1 space) or the more onerous BS 8007 (for Grade 2 space) or drained cavities (for Grades 3 and 4 spaces) should also be provided.

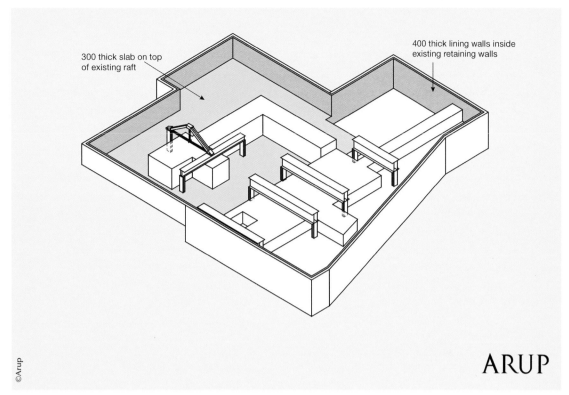

Figure 10: Basement slab and lining walls at 88 Wood Street

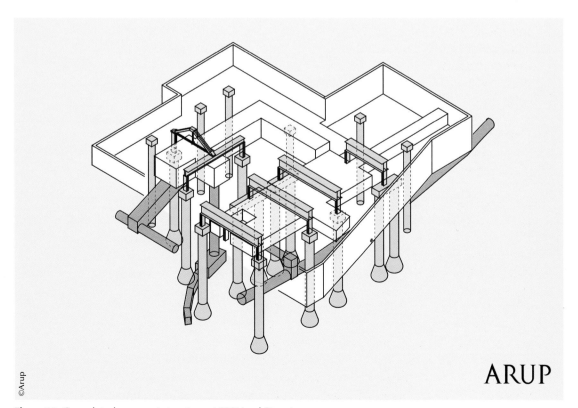

Figure 11: Complete basement structure at 88 Wood Street

Drained cavities are designed to be kept essentially free of water to prevent penetration of water vapour into the sub-structure. A means of removing any water which flows into the cavity is required, and ventilation may also be necessary for this purpose. Thames Water has concerns about allowing groundwater to be discharged into their sewers, and permission to do so is normally only given after assurance that the flows will be very low.

Problems of poor waterproofing are unfortunately common and are usually due to the following (avoidable) factors:

- failure to anticipate water levels over the design life of the building;
- failure to understand the building owner's requirements for the basement space, or to explain the possible consequences of the designed performance on the selected grade of use;
- poor design or detailing;
- bad workmanship.

A broader view on water
In addition to measuring water levels, it is important for the geotechnical design to take into account the factors which cause those water levels (hydrogeology) and possible long-term changes that could occur to them. For instance, in the Victoria area of London, water levels have been drawn down locally through dewatering by London Underground and the Royal Parks. Water levels are up to three metres lower than would otherwise be the case. While water measurements on a site would only indicate the current situation, this broader understanding suggests designing for higher water levels in the future since continued pumping by others cannot be relied upon.

In London and a number of other cities around the world, water levels are rising. This phenomenon is sometimes incorrectly linked to climate change or wrongly blamed for water leaks into basements. In London, rising water levels are explained by a fall-off in private water abstraction from the deep chalk aquifer. This leads to a recovery of water levels, in some areas rising by up to 70 metres. In most areas, the shallow sand and gravel layers (Thames Terrace Gravels) are insulated from the effects of this rise by the thick deposits of clay found as part of the London Clay and the Lambeth Group Clay (formerly known as the Woolwich and Reading Beds). Thus, only some critical structures in particular parts of London will be affected. Clearly, the broader view can be as important as current on-site conditions.

Floor structure

For commercial developments, the floors make up the bulk of the structural framework and the selection of the right system is always a key project decision. It is normal for many factors to influence the choice, and a number of options are generally considered and evaluated before the project team settles on a particular system.

The choice of floor structure can be influenced by factors such as:

- **The architecture of the building** – is the structure exposed to view and a major factor in the character of the building?
- **Column grids and floor spans** – what arrangement of columns best suits the occupier's needs?
- **Building services strategy** – how can the structure and services solutions work in harmony to occupy the least volume and to minimise cost?
- **Fire rating** – does the cost or practicality of achieving the required fire rating influence the choice of material(s)?
- **Cost** – what is the most economic solution for the building as a whole?
- **Programme** – how important is speed of erection? Are there significant programme differences between options?
- **Site constraints** – does the size or shape of the site mean that off-site prefabrication is advantageous? Are there site issues related to noise or construction traffic?
- **Planning constraints** – is the building height limited? Is floor depth critical?
- **Foundations** – are the foundations expensive or difficult, and is it helpful to minimise building weight or alter column grids?
- **Thermal mass** – how can the mass of the building reduce cooling requirements?

In addition, as environmental factors become increasingly important, issues such as embodied energy in relation to building life, and the potential for re-use and recycling of materials add further complexity to the decision-making process.

Floor systems
For most commercial developments, the floor structure will be constructed using only two basic materials: concrete and steel. One might imagine that this would leave the designer with a limited palette from which to work. However, there are a wide range of floor systems in common use, and this in itself is evidence that no one system or material is universally applicable to all circumstances.

There are two basic categories of floor structure:

- Concrete frames, which can be precast, but are more usually cast in-situ (or a combination of precast and cast in-situ).
- Steel frames with concrete floors, where the floor slabs are likely to be constructed using either composite metal decking, or precast concrete units.

The most common floor systems are listed in Figures 12 and 13 below, together with an indication of the span ranges for which they are likely to be cost effective.

Concrete frames that are cast in-situ will be constructed on falsework and formwork. For flat slabs, or arrangements where primary and secondary beams are of consistent depth, table forms are likely to be used. This modular system of formwork allows fast floor cycles, and construction times for concrete frames can compete with those for steel.

Steel-framed floors require no temporary falsework or formwork, and can generally be erected at speed. However, the floors will still require in-situ concrete to be placed on either metal decking or precast concrete panels, and the steelwork has to be fire-protected.

The *BCO Guide 2000* makes a comparison between steel and reinforced concrete systems, as follows:

Steel or reinforced concrete?

Steel	Reinforced concrete
Relatively lightweight	Relatively heavy
Greater depths. Minimum depth solutions inefficient	Shallower depths. For modest spans, flat slabs give minimum depths
Good for longer spans *but* depth requirements imply combined structure structure and services zone	For longer spans, post-tensioned slabs give minimum depths
More efficient on rectangular grids than on square grids	Can be efficient on rectangular and on square grids
Inherently good for holes and fixings (into soffit)	Holes and fixings can be accommodated but strategy must be considered early. Holes should avoid pre-stressing tendons. Concrete soffits give option of chilled beam cooling

Cost and speed of erection is always improved if there is substantial repetition between floors. This is usually possible through the careful planning of column grids. Transfer structures should be avoided where possible by adopting a grid that works at all levels, even wherever the usage is quite different.

Co-ordination issues
One of the early decisions for any building is to settle on a suitable floor-to-floor height. For inner city sites where planning constraints can be onerous, refining the floor heights to maximise the number of storeys can bring a crucial commercial benefit to a scheme.

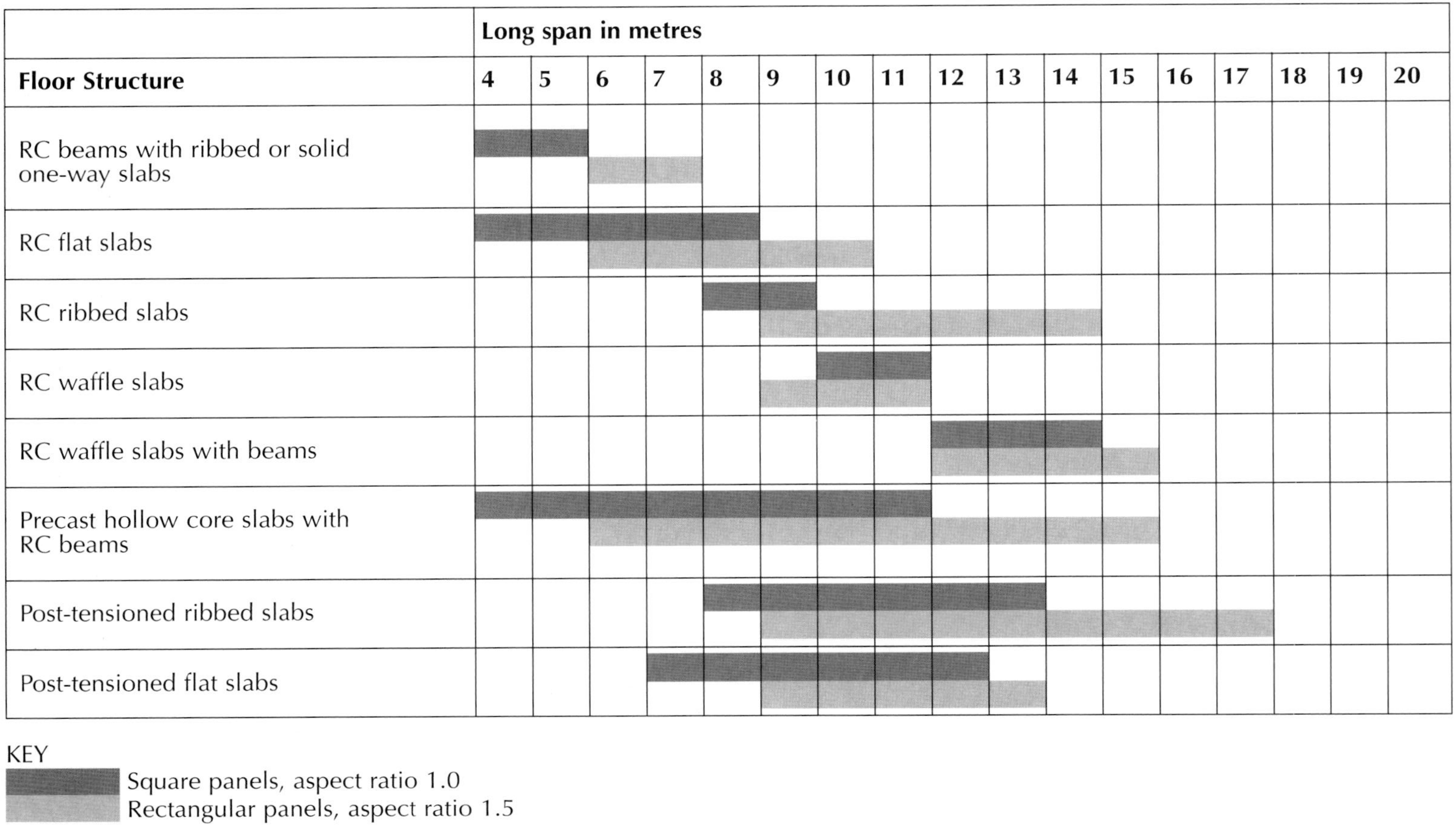

Long span in metres

Floor Structure	4	5	6	7	8	9	10	11	12	13	14	15	16	17	18	19	20
RC beams with ribbed or solid one-way slabs																	
RC flat slabs																	
RC ribbed slabs																	
RC waffle slabs																	
RC waffle slabs with beams																	
Precast hollow core slabs with RC beams																	
Post-tensioned ribbed slabs																	
Post-tensioned flat slabs																	

KEY

- Square panels, aspect ratio 1.0
- Rectangular panels, aspect ratio 1.5

Figure 12: Common floor systems – concrete frames

261

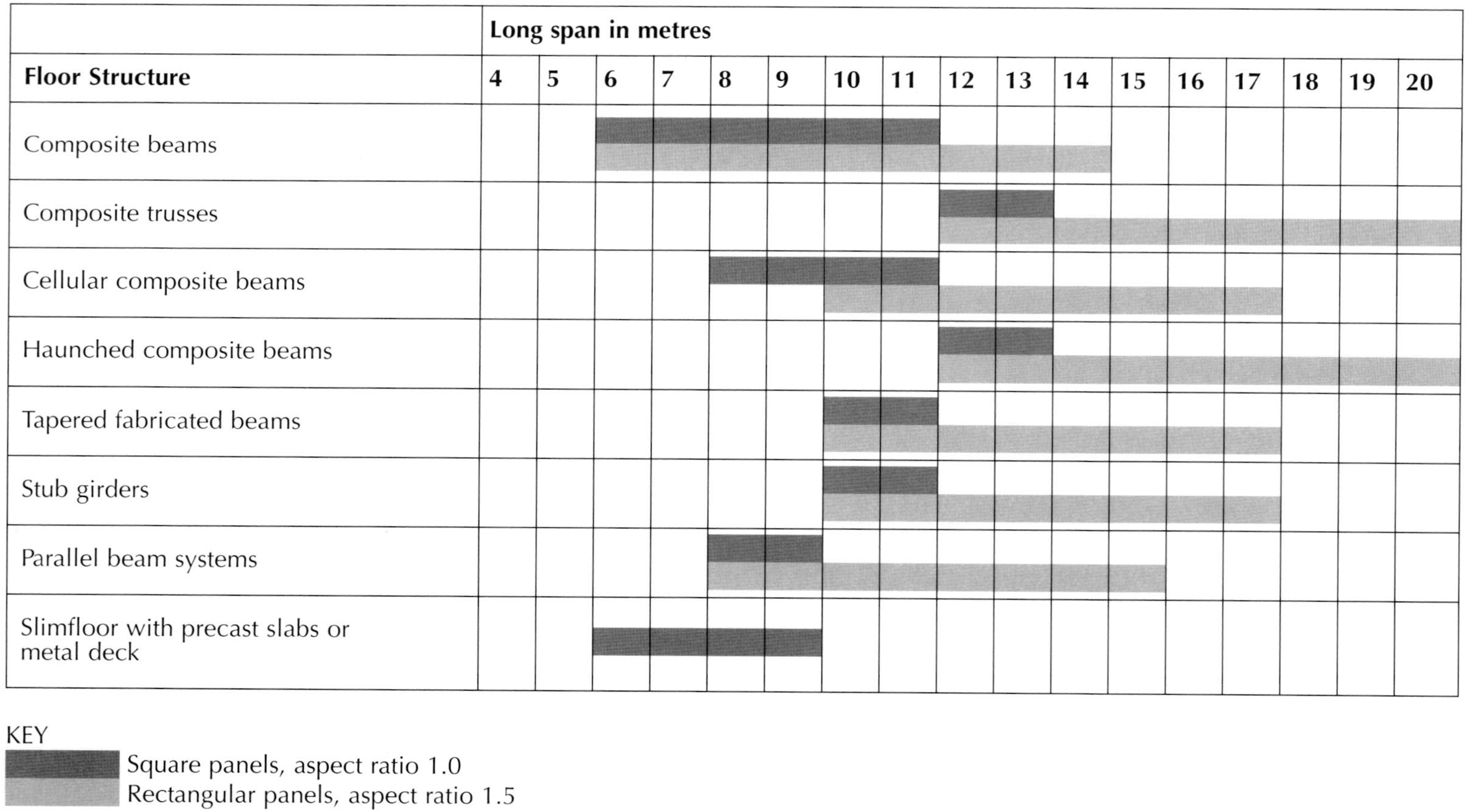

Long span in metres

Floor Structure	4	5	6	7	8	9	10	11	12	13	14	15	16	17	18	19	20
Composite beams																	
Composite trusses																	
Cellular composite beams																	
Haunched composite beams																	
Tapered fabricated beams																	
Stub girders																	
Parallel beam systems																	
Slimfloor with precast slabs or metal deck																	

KEY

Square panels, aspect ratio 1.0
Rectangular panels, aspect ratio 1.5

Figure 13: Common floor systems – steel frames

A typical floor build-up is as follows:

Raised floor zone	150 mm
Structure and services zone	600 – 1100 mm
Ceiling and lighting zone	100 – 150 mm
Clear height	2600 – 3000 mm
Total floor-to-floor height	**3450 – 4400 mm**

In the floor build-up, due account should be taken of construction tolerances, and floor deflections that happen prior to installation of the raised floors and false ceilings. It is normal for a movement and tolerance zone to be incorporated beneath the floor structure, but far less common for tolerances on slab levels to be explicitly covered. In such a case it should be noted that the clear raised floor height could be 20 mm less than expected if the slab tolerances are unfavourable.

Co-ordination of floor structure with services distribution is one of the key factors in minimising floor heights. Three approaches can be used, and are shown in the table below. The floor options from Figures 12 and 13 have been assigned to these three options:

Co-ordination approach	Floor options (from Figures 12 and 13)
Separate clear zones for structure and services	All concrete floor options Composite beams Slimfloor with precast slabs or metal deck
Overlapped zones for structure and services	Haunched composite beam. Tapered fabricated beam
Integrated zones for structure and services	Composite trusses Cellular composite beams Stub girder Parallel beam system

Heavily integrated structure and services solutions reduce planning flexibility, but do result in low-depth floors. They are generally only applicable to buildings with regular, and preferably orthogonal, grids.

Integrated solutions are most appropriate for long-span floors which, by virtue of their depth, can accommodate zones for services.

263

Serviceability issues

Adequate strength of a floorplate is an obvious design requirement, but not the only one. Movement of the floor under static and dynamic loads is also an important consideration.

Floor deflections are typically limited to:

Deflection under live load	Span/360
Total deflection	Span/200

Consideration should always be given to the consequences of floor deflections to ascertain appropriate limits. Around the perimeter of a building, lower deflection limits may be needed for cladding to perform reliably. Inside the building, the detailing of internal partition heads may also influence target deflection limits.

Where necessary, the total deflection of a floor can be partially offset by pre-cambering.

In addition to considering static deflections, the trend towards longer-spanning lightweight floor systems, with their tendency to lower natural frequencies and reduced natural damping, has caused engineers to be more aware of dynamic criteria for the serviceability limit state. In office buildings two sources of vibration excitation need to be considered: people walking across a floor with a pace frequency of between 1.4 and 3.0 Hz; and a sudden impulse, such as the effect of the fall of a heavy object.

Long-span steel floors are most susceptible to problems associated with floor vibration, but long-span pre-stressed concrete floors should also be checked. Reference should be made to the Steel Construction Institute publication *Design Guide on the Vibration of Floors* for design purposes.[8]

Traditionally, in conventional practice, a natural frequency limit of 4 Hz is placed on individual beam designs, which typically results in adequate floor performance. However, our understanding of the dynamic response of floors has increased greatly over recent years, and it is possible to accurately predict floor accelerations under given transient loadings, and to design the floor structure accordingly. Special care needs to be taken if floors are likely to be used for activities such as dancing, or where moving machinery is present.

In city centre sites it is also possible to have sources of structural vibration originating from objects outside the building, such as railway lines or underground tunnels. Vibrations from such sources can be designed out, at a cost, through the use of isolation bearings (for further details see Chapter 13).

---

8 Steel Construction Institute (SCI) (1989), *SPI-P-076 Design Guide on the Vibration on Floors*, London, SCI.

Where floor plates extend over a large footprint, thermal and shrinkage movements of the slabs can cause unacceptable cracking. Floors which are more than 100 metres long are likely to need movement joints along their length. Stiff walls and bracing lines should be located to avoid unduly constraining free movements of the slabs.

Stability

All buildings require a clearly defined stability system to resist horizontal loads from wind and, in exceptional circumstances from earthquake, and to prevent buckling of the load-bearing walls and columns. It will typically comprise one or more vertical walls or frames, which together possess adequate strength and stiffness to transmit horizontal loads from all directions to the foundations. The floors of the building are essential components of the system and act as 'diaphragms' to maintain the plan shape of the building and distribute the lateral loads from their point of application to the stability system.

It is common to limit the relative horizontal movements between adjacent floors to h/300, where h is the storey height, to prevent damage to cladding and internal finishes. For tall buildings, the dynamic interaction between wind and the building can produce horizontal accelerations that cause discomfort to the occupants.

The stability system in a low-rise building will normally have little impact on the architecture and planning of the building. Low-rise buildings will generally possess one or more cores housing lifts, stairs and service risers. If these are suitably located, they can be provided with walls that can provide adequate stability. These walls can be constructed from reinforced concrete or braced steel frames. To be effective, the cores should be reasonably symmetrically located and provide adequate resistance to both lateral and torsional loading. Buildings with large plan dimensions may incorporate movement joints to limit thermal and shrinkage movements, in which case a separate stability system will be required for each segment.

The stability system in a medium- and high-rise building will have greater impact on the architecture and planning of the building. In such cases, the stability system drives the architecture of the building.

In these buildings it is common to place offices around the perimeter of the floor to maximise their external views, and house lifts, stairs and services in a single central core. For buildings up to around 50 storeys this core can economically provide the required stiffness and strength. As with low-rise structures, the core can be constructed from reinforced concrete or steel system. If the building has a steel-floor system, a steel core will simplify construction as connections will be simpler, and problems associated with mixing trades will be avoided. A steel core designed for strength alone will often not have adequate inherent stiffness to limit lateral movements compared to concrete, which has a higher stiffness to strength ratio. Floor cycle for concrete walls can be comparable to steelwork if jump- or slip-form construction methods are used.

Figure 14: Central core, HSBC building, Canary Wharf, London

Figure 15: Perimeter frame, 30 St. Mary Axe, City of London

Figure 16: Outrigger system, North-East Tower, Hong Kong

©Arup/Central

©Arup

©Arup

For taller buildings, or those in areas with strong winds or earthquake, a central core will not be able to resist the lateral loads alone, and it will be necessary to assist it by mobilising the perimeter structure in some way.

A common approach is to provide the external frame with in-plane stiffness by connecting the columns with diagonal braces or beams, to form a closed 'perimeter tube' capable of resisting some or all of the lateral load. Braced systems provide a more direct path for lateral loads than moment frames, and therefore tend to be more efficient in their use of materials. Column spacing in a moment frame will be limited to around six metres, and the beams and columns will need increased depth in the plane of the facade. A perimeter tube can be designed to work in conjunction with a central core or alone, and can be moulded around almost any shape.

An alternative hybrid system, the 'outrigger' system, mobilises the central core and components of the perimeter structure.

Robustness

The partial collapse of a block of flats at Ronan Point, London in 1968 triggered a debate in the UK about the robustness – and potential for disproportionate collapse – of building structures.

That building was a 22-storey residential block, constructed of precast concrete wall and floor panels. A small gas explosion in a 16th floor kitchen blew out a storey-height, load-bearing wall panel. This event triggered the collapse of the floor above, followed by the walls and floors up to roof level. The falling debris from above caused the collapse of the floors and the walls below and so, the progressive collapse of the entire corner of the building.

The collapse was identified as being due to a lack of robustness in the joints between the precast walls and floor slabs and was disproportionate to the event causing it.

The Building Regulations were amended in 1970 to require that checks are made to ensure a degree of robustness and to negate the potential for disproportionate collapse of a building structure (in buildings of more than five storeys).

Put simply, the regulations require the provision of effective horizontal and vertical ties within the building structure. Where that is difficult to achieve, the regulations require a more rigorous analysis of the risks of disproportionate collapse.

For an office building framed in in-situ concrete or in steel with in-situ concrete floor slabs, these effective horizontal and vertical ties are easily (and often inherently) included. For a building framed in precast concrete (unusual in the UK) or including precast concrete floor elements, particular attention must be paid to the junctions and connections between units.

Beyond that, it is the designer who must identify possible and particular causes of accidental loading – and make provision for them in his design of the structure. Those causes may include, for example, vehicular impact and terrorist bombs.

Fire protection (of structure)

The Building Regulations require that 'a building shall be designed and constructed so that, in the event of a fire, its stability will be maintained for a reasonable period'. That reasonable period of fire resistance varies with the purpose group and associated fire load/fire severity, and the building height. Sprinklers play an important role in reducing fire severity.

For (the purpose group of) offices, the fire load is reasonably low (and the hazard medium) and the regulations define the period of fire resistance, in minutes, for a range of heights, as follows:

	Height < 5 m	Height < 18 m	Height < 30 m	Height over 30 m
No sprinklers	30 mins	60 mins	90 mins	Not permitted
Sprinklers	30 mins	30 mins	60 mins	120 mins

A reinforced concrete frame has inherent fire resistance. Provided the components of the frame are correctly designed and detailed, no additional fire protection is required.

A steel frame has little inherent fire resistance and additional fire protection is required. A range of systems can provide that additional protection. These systems can be applied either on-site or off-site and are listed in Tables 4 and 5 (see Appendix).

In addition, our improving knowledge of the behaviour of steel structures in real fires, gained through testing and research by BRE (Building Research Establishment) et al, and an increasingly analytical approach to the design of these systems of fire protection can lead to a rational reduction in the requirements for fire resistance of the structure – and consequent reductions in materials and costs! Further, the regulations state that 'a fire safety engineering approach that takes into account the total fire safety package can provide an alternative approach to fire safety.' Such an approach can also lead to rational reductions in the requirements for fire protection of the structure.

Integration and interfaces

Buildings consist of five principal elements: structure, services, cladding, finishes and the spaces in between. None of these may be designed in isolation since they all, to some degree, interact. The elements must be spatially co-ordinated (so that there are no physical clashes) and each must take due account of the performance requirements of the others. In the case of the structure it is, quite literally, the framework that supports everything else.

One of the earliest decisions in the design process is to agree the zoning strategy for the building. Does each of the principal elements occupy its own zone? Should any of the zones overlap or be combined? How much space should each occupy? Inevitably, the optimisation of any one zone is likely to have a detrimental effect elsewhere. For example, structural floor depths will be minimised by reducing their spans, but additional columns may compromise the space planning. The challenge for the design team is therefore to arrive at an holistic design which is the best fit to the client brief, architectural aspirations and site constraints. The implications of four typical zoning strategies are considered below:

(i) Loose fit
Here each zone is separate and does not overlap with its neighbour. Interaction between principal elements is therefore minimised, and the design of each element may be optimised to make best use of, for example, standard components. These designs tend to be spatially inefficient, however, and not suitable for dimensionally-constrained sites where, for example, storey heights may be restricted.

(ii) Tartan grid
Efficient grids tend to be orthogonal and multiples of the planning module (typically 1.5 m). Tartan grids alternate long and short spans. Whilst this constrains the space planning, it allows a reduction in floor depth by overlapping the structure and services zones (the primary services being located in the short-span zone where structural depth is reduced).

(iii) Integrated floor
Here services are distributed through holes in the structural beams. The overall beam depth is governed by the hole requirements for the services. This has the unusual effect that a deeper services zone will generate a deeper structural zone. It is an approach that is therefore appropriate for long-span (15 m and more) steel floors. The disadvantage is that flexibility in design of the services is reduced, since the services must distribute through the holes provided. It is not practical to alter these beams post-erection.

(iv) Integrated cladding
The structural zone may be integrated with the cladding zone in particular circumstances, such as an architectural requirement to see the structure expressed in the elevation. This is difficult to achieve successfully as the cladding must satisfy many performance criteria, which may be compromised by an inadequate consideration of structural integration (e.g. cold bridging leading to condensation).

The structure must be designed to accommodate the requirements of all that it supports. Frequently, these requirements become the governing criteria for the structural design. For example, the permissible sway (horizontal) deflection under wind loads will rarely be set to the limit for overall stability, but will instead be governed by user comfort (for tall buildings) or permissible cladding movement (it is difficult to design a cladding system that can accommodate large movements). Similarly, local beam deflection limits are determined by what they support. Edge beams tend to be stiff (cladding again), whilst internal beams may be more flexible as the floor and ceiling finishes are more tolerant of deflection (note, however, that internal beam design is often governed by user comfort criteria for floor dynamics).

Secondary structures (such as atrium lift towers) are very sensitive to interface requirements because the loads that they carry are small, and so strength-based designs tend to be very flexible. It is therefore particularly important that these designs take full account of the interface requirements of, for example, the lifts and building users.

The structural design should also be sufficiently flexible that it can accommodate inputs that arrive quite late in the process. These, typically, come from two sources: contractor input and tenant requirements. Contractor input to the structural design is generally limited to steelwork connection design, and occasionally to reinforcement detailing. These tend to be routine inputs that can be readily accommodated. Input from interfacing contractors tends to be more problematic. For example, if a precast frame is to support contractor designed cladding, then all the cast-in details will need to be designed before the cladding contractor is appointed. It is therefore essential that the design responsibilities at critical interfaces are agreed early in the design process.

Finally, the design should be sufficiently flexible to accommodate input from the tenant design team. Typically the fit-out design will be concurrent with the shell and core construction, and so the design should be able to adapt quickly to minor changes such as local abnormal loads (tenant plant/kitchens), additional risers, numerous small holes, and the need to be able to install (lightly loaded) fixings anywhere.

Construction issues

The structure must be designed in the certain knowledge that it can be built. A construction sequence must be developed such that, at each critical phase, the requirements for any temporary works, and the implications for the permanent works, are fully understood and can be accommodated. Ideally, the construction method and sequence will be considered in sufficient detail to optimise four key (but somewhat conflicting) requirements: cost, programme, quality and safety.

Urban sites tend to have been previously developed. The existing buildings will normally extend to the site perimeter and incorporate a single level basement. The existing retaining walls will either be masonry (with under pavement vaults) or concrete, and existing foundations will either be pads or strips. City centre sites may be further constrained by underlying tunnels, and may have significant archaeological potential. The new development will seek to maximise floor area. It will probably, therefore, occupy the full footprint of the site and be somewhat irregular in shape. It will have one or two basement levels (which will extend below groundwater level) and be founded on piles. The superstructure frame (either steel or concrete) will have ten or more stories, with floors that are largely repetitive, and be stabilised either by steel bracing, concrete walls, or framed connections.

So, how then will it be built?

The new perimeter retaining wall will have several functions:

- It will be installed from existing ground or basement level, through existing obstructions.
- It must retain earth and groundwater during construction and in the permanent condition. It must also provide a groundwater cut-off to prevent flow into the excavation.
- It will probably carry the foundation loads for the superstructure.
- It must not move excessively, or generate undue noise during construction.

These requirements are most easily satisfied by the use of a secant pile wall, although diaphragm walls may be considered. The basement is then constructed from the top down. The ground level slab, or part thereof, is usually cast prior to commencing excavation. This avoids the need for temporary props as excavation proceeds. Internal columns will have been installed by plunging steel columns into the foundation piles. Excavation then proceeds to formation level which requires large openings in the ground slab for plant access. Ideally, the perimeter walls will be able to span vertically in the temporary condition. If not, the intermediate slabs will be installed during excavation, although this will confine working space. Simultaneously with the basement construction, the superstructure frame is erected. Steel and concrete frames require similar erection times, provided the concrete frame is designed to facilitate speed of construction (by using table forms and prefabricated reinforcement).

Steel frames are designed to act compositely with their concrete slabs. They are therefore quite flexible in the temporary condition when supporting wet concrete. If props are to be avoided, the design should allow sufficient tolerance in it to accommodate the deflected shape of the floor.

Steel frames need to be fire protected (unlike concrete which has inherent fire resistance). Consideration should be given to the use of off-site intumescent paint (cost permitting) as this speeds up and simplifies site operations.

The structural frame remains on the critical path until cladding commences. The connections that receive the cladding should therefore be simple, robust and tolerant. This can be achieved with cast-in fixings in the slabs.

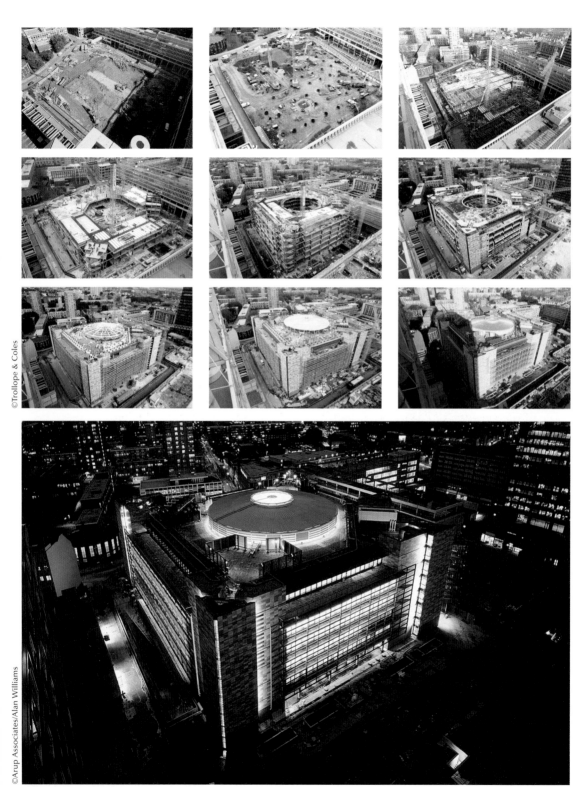

©Trollope & Coles

©Arup Associates/Alan Williams

Figure 17: Construction sequence, Triton Square, London.

The tolerance of the erected structure should be set to that which can be readily achieved on site, without the need for special measures. It is more economic to accommodate tolerance in the design (if provision is made early enough) than it is to try to build without it. Although current automated fabrication processes will accommodate very fine tolerance in steelwork fabrication, consideration must always be given to the tolerance required for erection (particularly in tall buildings where axial shortening of columns is significant).

Business park sites tend to be less constrained than urban sites. The footprint of the buildings can therefore be optimised to suit space planning. These buildings typically feature 9 x 9 m floor grids and are low-rise founded on pad footings with shallow (or no) basements that may be constructed in open cut. The aim is to produce a standard product that can be repeated. The design and construction processes are therefore closely integrated.

The principal feature of the structure is the frame. Square (9 x 9 m) grids are efficient in concrete. Post-tensioned flat slabs are economical, since the formwork is simple, and post-tensioning minimises depth whilst allowing large sized pours (as the stressing operation will control cracking). The columns will either be precast concrete or steel, whilst stability will be provided by steel bracing installed after the slabs are stressed. While this form of construction is very efficient, the challenge for the design team is to develop a strategy that will accommodate holes through the slabs without the disruptive effects of providing trimmer beams or large quantities of additional reinforcement.

Getting it right!

Getting it right and avoiding problems should not be difficult. Most problems tend to be due to a small number of factors which are easily countered. These include:

- **Using the wrong designer** – the organisation must be competent to undertake the work, and the right people from that organisation must be assigned to the project.
- **Confused responsibilities** – the design and procurement process must be coherent with clearly allocated responsibilities for every step of the way. Using a single design organisation is easiest but several can also prove very effective, provided interface responsibilities are clear.
- **Poor checking/reviewing** – the key to avoiding problems is to anticipate what might go wrong and then ensuring that the design can cater for that problem. This involves learning from the experience of designers who have previously been involved in similar projects.
- **Unclear procurement** – communicating the complete design intent to the construction team is of paramount importance, particularly on more complex projects. Specifications must be clear and the contractor's understanding of the design should be checked for compliance by careful review of his or her method

statements. The procurement route should ensure that sub-contractor interfaces are well managed in order to minimise subsequent claims.

- **Poor supervision** – particularly where work will be covered over or become inaccessible, there is only one opportunity for appropriate and knowledgeable checks to be made. If these are not made diligently, then the client team has no easy way of resolving discrepancies or resisting claims.

Appendix

Table 1: Summary of applied loadings

Loading type	Description	Code
Dead loads	Self-weights of all permanent structural elements, permanent walls and partitions, finishes, services systems, ceilings, etc.	BS 649 Schedule of Weights of Building Materials.
		BS 6399 – Part 1 Design Loading for Buildings – dead and imposed loading.
		BS 6399 – Part 3 Design Loading for Buildings – roof loading.
Live loads	These are non-permanent imposed loadings such as people, furniture, equipment, storage, plant, etc. They are a function of space usage.	BS 6399 – Part 1 Design Loading for Buildings – dead and imposed loading.
Partitions	Self weight of demountable, lightweight office partitions are also live loads.	BS 6399 – Part 3 Design Loading for Buildings – roof loading.
Wind	Wind loads are the result of wind pressures acting on all exposed surfaces of a building. Pressures act on facades elements and roofs.	BS 6399 – Part 2 Design Loading for Buildings – wind loading.

Table 1: Summary of applied loadings – *continued*

Loading type	Description	Code
Seismic	These are not generally relevant for offices in the UK but may have to be considered in special circumstances.	N/A
Thermal	Structures exposed to changes in temperature are subject to thermal expansions or contractions.	BS 5950 –Part 1 Structural Use of Steel.
	Thermal movements can be significant and should be taken into account in the design of buildings.	BS 8110 – Part 2 Structural Use of Concrete – special circumstances
	Alternatively a structure that restrains those movements needs to be designed to resist all forces arising from the thermal load case.	
Water pressures	Water in the ground produces pressures to be considered in the design of basement structures, such as retaining walls and slabs.	BS 8102 Protection Against Groundwater.
Soil pressures	Soil behind retaining walls produces pressures that need to be considered in the design of those elements.	BS 8110 – Part 1 Structural Use of Concrete.
Vehicle loads	Loading bays for heavy trucks are often included at the ground and basement levels of office developments. Structures need to resist the global and local effects of those loads.	BS 6399 – Part 1 Design Loading for Buildings – dead and imposed loading.
		More specific literature on self-weight of vehicles.

Table 1: Summary of applied loadings – *continued*

Loading type	Description	Code
Impact and accidental loads	Office developments are often bounded by roads or railways. They may also have designated car-parking areas. The effects of accidental impact loads should be considered in the design of key structural elements. Structures designed for special circumstances may need to resist the effects of more onerous accidental loads, such as bomb blasts or explosions in general.	BS 6399 – Part 1 Design Loading for Buildings – dead and imposed loading. More specific literature on impact loads.

Table 2: General considerations for choice of retaining wall

	Description	Cost	Water retention	Wall stiffness
Diaphragm	Formed from adjacent reinforced concrete panels, typically 1 m wide x 5 m long x say 20 m deep.	High +	Good, especially with water bar.	High ++
Hard-hard secant	Secant pile retaining walls are formed from overlapping piles installed next to each other. All piles in a hard-hard wall are made from reinforced concrete. The necessary equipment provides very good verticality.	High	Good	High +
Hard-firm secant	With a hard-firm pile wall, every second pile is formed with a low strength concrete section with no, or minimal, steel. This pile is assumed to provide permanent support to the retained soil and water but does not contribute to the wall's structural strength. The firm pile concrete mix does not normally contain enough cement to comply with BS 8110, implying that the wall might not fully comply with BS 8102. This is not likely to be a real engineering problem.	Medium	Good	High
Hard-soft secant	With a hard-soft pile, every female or primary pile is formed from a weaker, unreinforced cement-bentonite mix to ease installation male or secondary pile.	Medium	Temporary only. (Conventionally limited to 5 m head of water). Needs a permanent RC liner wall.	High

Table 2: General considerations for choice of retaining wall – *continued*

	Description	Cost	Water retention	Wall stiffness
Contiguous	A contiguous pile wall is formed from a row of piles installed next to each other. The piles are normally spaced so that there is a slight gap between adjacent piles. Soldier pile wall with lagging is an alternative.	Medium	No (unless used with mini-piles or grouting to block holes). Needs a permanent RC liner wall.	High
King-post walls	A king-post wall is formed from a row of piles spaced further apart than a contiguous wall, with beams sticking up above formation level. Timber or concrete lagging planks are inserted between the vertical beam flanges to retain the soil.	Low	None	Medium to low
Mini-pile walls	Small diameter piles with no overlap.	High	No (unless used with grouting).	Low
Sheet-pile	A sheet-pile wall is formed of interlocking steel piles providing a continuous wall. These walls are used in cantilever for small dig levels but are more commonly adopted with anchors or props for significant digs. The piles are commonly driven into the ground but can be pushed into the ground in certain ground conditions where there are tight limits on noise and vibration.	Medium to low	Low, can be increased with proprietary system. In the permanent case, clutches can be welded shut. May need a permanent RC liner wall.	Medium

Table 2: General considerations for choice of retaining wall – *continued*

	Description	Cost	Water retention	Wall stiffness
Soil nail walls	A row of steel dowels is placed into drilled holes on a cut soil face and is grouted into position. After each level of cut, more nails are added, until by the time formation level is reached, an array of grouted dowels covers the cut slope.	Low	None	Low
Open cut	As described with stable slopes and dewatering. Either the permanent structural walls made out of reinforced concrete or gravity walls can be used to support the backfill that is placed around the structure.	Low*	Pumping needed.	N/A

* Unless fill is contaminated, putting up the excavation cost.

Table 3: Grades of basement

Grade	Basement usage	Performance level	Form of construction
1 (basic utility)	Car parking, plant rooms (excluding electrical equipment workshops).	Some seepage and damp patches tolerable.	Normal reinforced concrete designed in accordance with BS 8110 – Part 1.
2 (better utility)	Workshops and plant rooms requiring drier environment, retail storage areas.	No water penetration but moisture vapour tolerable.	Tank protection. Reinforced concrete designed in accordance with BS 8007 to control crack widths.
3 (habitable)	Ventilated residential and working areas including offices, restaurants, etc, leisure centres.	Dry environment. Active measures to control internal humidity may be necessary.	Tank protection. Reinforced concrete designed in accordance with BS 8007 to control crack widths. Drained protection: drained cavity wall and floor construction with damp proof membrane preventing moisture ingress.

Table 3: Grades of basement – *continued*

Grade	Basement usage	Performance level	Form of construction
4 (special)	Archives and stores requiring controlled environment.	Totally dry environment. Active measures to control internal humidity probably essential.	Tank protection.
			Reinforced concrete designed in accordance with BS 8007 to control crack width.
			Drained protection: ventilated drained cavity wall with vapour barrier to inner skin and floor cavity construction with damp proof membrane preventing moisture ingress.

Table 4: Fire protection – systems and materials

Sprays	Vermiculite gypsum plaster	Mineral fibre with organic/inorganic binders	Vermiculite cement	Other cementitious materials	
Boards	Resin-bonded mineral fibre board, profile or box	Gypsum wall board (plaster board)	Calcium silicate board	Vermiculite/gypsum boards with mesh or fibre reinforcement	Preformed steel encasement incorporating vermiculite board
Intumescents	Thin film, solvent based	Thin film, water based	Epoxy resin based		
Encasement	Concrete	Blockwork	Brickwork	Expanded steel lath and plaster	

Table 5: Fire protection – system properties

System	Cost	Impact/ abrasion resistance	Steel surface preparation required?	Durability	Advantages	Limitations	Maximum fire resistance
Sprays	Low.	Varies with density of system.	Not usually.	Sprays available for internal and external applications.	Easy to apply. Fast to apply. Easy to cover complex details. Cementitious sprays inhibit corrosion. Can be applied directly to steel.	Wet trade. Over spray needs masking or shielding of application area on site. Primer can reduce adhesion. Affects other trades – on-site costs increase though the material is cheaper. Poor in winter conditions. Poor appearance.	4 hours.
Board	Mineral fibre: low. Plaster-board: medium Calcium silicate: medium – high.	Varies, medium to good	No.	Boards available for internal and external applications.	Factory manufactured – so guaranteed thickness. Clean, dry fixing by glue, stapling or screwing – so reduced interference with other trades on site. A good surface finish is possible (but impacts on price) – so suitable for visible members.	Slower than spray. Fitting required around complex details. Increased labour costs for fixing on site. Not good for external (although some systems available).	2 hours generally. 4 hours for calcium silicate

Table 5: Fire protection – system properties – *continued*

System	Cost	Impact/ abrasion resistance	Steel surface preparation required?	Durability	Advantages	Limitations	Maximum fire resistance
Intumescents	1 hour: low 2 hours; high Epoxy: very high	Low to. medium.	Yes. Blast cleaned surface and compatible primer.	Grades available for internal and external applications.	Thin. Good appearance, decorative finishes possible. Fast to apply on site. Complex details easily covered. Post-protection fixing simplified. Application possible off site.	Wet trade on site, precautions required against over-spray, suitable environmental conditions required. Must specify for appropriate durability.	Maximum 2 hours, more ususally 90 minutes.
Encasement	Very high	Excellent – robust against impact and abrasion.	No.	Varies with system but generally good.		Building weight increased. Time consuming on site.	Varies with system.

Author profile

Richard Terry, Director
Arup

Richard Terry is a structural engineer. He joined Arup as a graduate engineer in 1978 and has worked for them in offices – on a wide range of projects – in Europe, Africa and the Middle East. Today, he is a Director of Arup and leads a multi-disciplinary building engineering team in London.

His work in the commercial office sector began in the late 1980's on Embankment Place, the air-rights office building above Charing Cross Station in London. It continues today and his portfolio includes new build, facade retention and refurbishment projects, all in London. It also includes a growing number of 'tall buildings'. His original involvement on Embankment Place has engendered a particular interest in railway buildings, then airport buildings.

He consistently seeks to integrate the work of the structural engineer with the work of the architect and of the building services engineer. He is increasingly interested in the issues of environment and 'sustainability' – and in design solutions that respond to them. He looks forward to the regeneration of our cities and, in particular, of London!

Richard is also a Director of the British Council for Offices (BCO). He chairs the BCO Technical Affairs Committee and has co-authored the BCO Guide 2000.

Richard acknowledges the contribution of his colleagues Tim Chapman, Pietro Perelli-Rocco, Tim Roe, Paul Cross, Peter Bressington and Richard White in the preparation of these words on structure.

11 Facades

Andrew Hall, Arup
Ken Shuttleworth and Richard Hyams, Foster and Partners

The following chapter is set out in three sections. Ken Shuttleworth initially sets out the context of facade development from his architectural perspective at Foster and Partners. In the subsequent section Andrew Hall of Arup Facade Engineering defines the technical framework in which current commercial offices are designed. The chapter concludes with a case study on London's City Hall by Richard Hyams of Foster and Partners.

Introduction

Innovation and technological advances have both played their part in the evolution of the facade for our buildings. In the 30 years between the design of our first glass and gasket system for the Fred Olsen Amenity Centre (1968–70) and the complex, energy-efficient facade of the City Hall (home of the Greater London Authority) (1998–2002), the industry has made extraordinary advances. With the facade industry developing new materials and construction methods, and with architects pushing the industry ever further, designs have evolved with few boundaries and today anything seems possible.

Foster and Partners' philosophy is one of innovation and development. Much of our work is pushing the frontiers of professional knowledge. In its day, the hanging facade of the Willis Faber & Dumas Headquarters in Ipswich (1971–75) represented an unprecedented advance in glass technology on a large scale. Each of the glass panels was hung from the panel above using the inherent structural properties of the glass to support and retain the facade. The development of the gasket system can be seen on the Sainsbury Centre for Visual Arts in Norwich (1974–78), where a complete ladder-style vulcanised gasket system was used to seal the entire building skin.

Our first developments in solar shading can be seen on the Hongkong and Shanghai Bank in Hong Kong (1979–86), where an external glazing structure incorporated horizontal fins to shade the building's users from intense solar rays. Each of our facades has developed from project to project to produce intelligent, energy-efficient facades that not only work in tune with the building's ever-more sophisticated internal conditioning systems but also give definition and expression to the building's form.

The ITN Headquarters in London (1988–90) saw a move towards a more layered design. The two layers of glass are separated by a layer of air, housing blinds which provide shading and glare control. The heat generated from the sun has little impact on the comfort of the user inside. This was followed by the development of the triple-glazed facade – a trend which the introduction of the revised Part L regulations reinforces. The Citibank Headquarters in London's docklands (1996–2000) was internally vented whilst the hanging facade of the Business Promotion Centre in Duisburg (1990–93) was vented to the outside, bringing a new level of efficiency to the system.

Advances in computer technology have brought great benefits to the world of architecture. With sophisticated nesting and cutting software, the glass and facade industries can produce larger and more complex shapes, thus reducing waste and allowing the designers more freedom. This is perfectly illustrated by the roof of the Great Court at the British Museum (1994–2000), with its 3,312 panels all of unique dimensions.

The advances in computer technology, along with the knowledge and experience gained from 30 years of facade design, have produced complex building forms such as the Headquarters for Swiss Re (1997–2004) and City Hall. In these buildings, traditional concepts of vertical walls and rectilinear floorplates are abandoned in favour of more organic forms and angled walls. The computer models and digital information used in the design process can be passed directly to the fabricator for the production of building components. With more sophisticated design and construction tools being developed all the time, the future is looking ever more exciting.

Design issues

System selection

There are many aluminium glazing systems available which can be categorised by two factors: framing configuration and glazing restraint.

Framing configuration
Systems range generically from:

- site-assembled 'stick' systems (can be suitable for up to six storeys but rely heavily on quality of labour);
- cassette systems (partially pre-assembled in the factory with associated quality control enhancements);
- unitised or panelised systems, which are pre-assembled in the factory, deliver the benefit of reduced installation periods with greater quality control of the final product. Such systems, although generally more expensive, tend to be more appropriate for repetitive commercial facades with limited surface modelling. Interlocking pre-gasketed aluminium profiles reduce to a minimum the reliance on site labour to achieve a high performance enclosure.

Glass restraint

Glass, whether single or double glazed, can be restrained either mechanically or by adhesives. Full mechanical restraint for framed systems can be provided using pressure caps on either two or all four sides of each infill panel. In order to achieve a fully flush external appearance, desired by many architects, restraint to double-glazed panels can be provided by isolated clips fitting into the edge spacer of the double glazed units. The outermost pane therefore relies on the use of structural adhesive for restraint.

The use of aluminium carrier frames bonded using structural silicon to the inside of the glass on either two or all four edges is well established. The requirements for supplementary mechanical restraint depend on local authority requirements, glass configuration and building maintenance. Mechanical restraint for point-fixed glass systems is provided by a range of button or counter sunk bolt connections with the latest developments transferring under-reemed fixing technologies from the stone industries to enable 20 mm-diameter point fixings.

Standardisation/bespoke

There are many so-called 'standard' systems on the market. This term tends to refer to those systems consisting of standardised repetitive kits of parts which have been tried and tested on a range of projects. These are typically offered by systems suppliers through approved fabricators and installers. Great care needs to be taken in customising such systems as modifications beyond their design parameters have often led to design failures. These window stick and cassette systems have been refined into unitised or panelised systems defined by generic weathering principles and construction offered by those companies primarily involved in medium to high-rise constructions. A degree of project-specific modifications may be made to suit structural requirements, glass and spandrel configurations and overall geometry.

There are many taller buildings whose size, complexity, visual intent and/or performance requirements enable costs of further customisation to be ameliorated over a sufficient area so as to be economically viable. The point at which a truly bespoke 'one-off' solution becomes feasible and appropriate needs to be carefully considered. However, such bespoke facades are rare as the majority take well established principles of drainage, pressure equalisation and framing glass connections and re-configure them to meet project specific requirements. At the Museum of Latin American Art in Buenos Aires (AFT Architects), glazing configurations ranged from 'shingled' overlapping glass to fixed and opening glass panels. In order to create a integrated holistic solution with uniformity of appearance and structural interface, a truly bespoke and aluminium system was developed.

As well as all the generalised issues above, there are many intermediate and hybrid solutions which have been developed to meet the multiplicity of architectural and performance requirements.

Frame/envelope interfaces

Hard copy
   Best Practice: Deflections/tolerances/movements.

At the earliest opportunity, the designers of the structural frame and the designers of the building envelope need to seek consultation on the effects that building frame movements and tolerances will have on the jointing between building envelope elements and the connections between the building envelope and the structural frame.

Almost without exception, it is better to provide extra stiffness to structural framing members around building perimeters to limit movements in the building envelope elements, rather than to design frames to minimum code requirements and then have expensive retrofit stiffening done on site. The only exceptions are if building envelope systems can be designed to span structural column to structural column, or if ground-bearing, self-supporting building envelopes are being considered.

Generally, better overall envelope performance is achieved if the envelope passes outside the structural frame. If it does, a nominal gap of at least 50 mm should be allowed for between the inside face of the envelope and the outside edge of the structural frame. It is preferable, for health and safety considerations, for the bracketing connecting the envelope to the frame to be connected to the top surfaces for floor slabs. At least 150 mm clear zone above the target level of the floor slab should be allowed for these brackets.

Commentary
Practically every building site has its stories of delays caused by brackets not fitting because of over-ambitious tolerance expectations and structural frames having to be strengthened to meet deflection criteria demanded by the building envelope contractors.

Early on in the design process the structural engineer and building envelope designer need to carry out movement and tolerance studies and agree jointing principles for the envelope and corresponding stiffness criteria for the perimeter structure. As each building will be unique, a study should be carried out on every building.

The building owner needs to ensure that one of the various consultancy agreements he sets up allows for the carrying out of these studies.

Performance

Design life

Hard copy
   Best Practice: BS.7543: 1992, amendment 1998.

The following requirements are considered normal for offices:

Building design life: 60 years

Design life for envelope

a) Replaceable elements	Will last less than 60 years and replacement has to be considered at design stage. For example, double-glazed units (20–25 years), sealants (20–25 years).
b) Maintainable elements	Will last 60 years with periodic treatment. For example, opening window ironmongery, weathering gaskets on opening windows.
c) Lifelong	Will last 60 years without any maintenance. For example, bracketing attaching cladding to primary structural frame, cladding framing members.

Commentary
   a) ISO 15686 on the service life of buildings is being prepared and is expected to be adopted as a British Standard, at which point BS 7543 will be withdrawn.
   b) Inconsistency in the use of terms to describe durability can lead to misunderstandings and wrong specification. The following terms are used in BS 7543:

(i) Service life	Starts when the envelope is complete and has been handed over, and ends when the only way to deal with unacceptable loss of performance is by replacement or excessive expenditure on operation, maintenance or repair.
(ii) Required service life	Assessed by considering length of time, conditions in which the envelope will have to perform, a minimum level of performance below which the function becomes unacceptable, and conditions of use and maintenance.
	Note that funding of building construction often implies a required service life, at least as long as the period of the loan used to finance the building. Note also that letting/leasing arrangements may be such that a major

refurbishment, including a new envelope, may be required at the end of a lease and, therefore, the lease period might define the required service of life. The required service life is defined by the building owner.

(iii) Predicted service life Assessed by reference to previous experience, this involves the measurement of natural rates of deterioration and accelerated ageing tests. The British Board of Agreement Certification should be used wherever possible. The building owners, designers and manufacturers provide this information.

(iv) Design life The design life of a component should be no less than the required service life, and should be such that failure of parts of the construction will not cause failure of the whole construction, and should be related to a rational plan for use and renewal. The required design life is evolved in discussion between the building owner and the designer.

(v) Durability limit The point at which the only way to deal with unacceptable loss of performance is replacement or excessive expenditure on operation, maintenance or repair.

Areas where misunderstandings can arise and where consultation between building owners and designers is required include deterioration in appearance (e.g. external finishes); where major repair or partial replacement is needed to keep an item in service (e.g. facade maintenance equipment); the critical nature of failure to perform in a particular situation (e.g. failure of sealant joints) and where no or limited information is provided to manufacturers and suppliers on the intended use of their materials.

(vi) Effects of failure For a particular building envelope each effect (from 'danger to life' through 'costly repair' to 'no exceptional problem') can be given a ranking to highlight where a failure of durability would be most serious.

Watertightness

Hard copy
  Best Practice: Performance requirements are defined in the Centre for Window and
  Cladding Technology (CWCT) *Standard for Curtain Walling*. Testing to verify
  compliance is described in the CWCT Test Methods for Curtain Walling.

The following requirements are considered normal for offices.

Performance under test:

- No leakage through to the internal face of the curtain wall under a static test
  pressure differential of 600 Pascalls held for five minutes when tested in
  accordance with CWCT Test Methods section 5.
- No leakage through to the internal face of the curtain wall under a dynamic test
  pressure differential of 600 Pascalls held for 15 minutes when tested in
  accordance with CWCT Test Methods section 6.
- No leakage through to the internal face of the curtain wall under a hose test
  carried out in accordance with CWCT Test Methods section 7, when tested on a
  test specimen off-site and on the actual wall on-site.

Commentary
  a) If individual 'punched-through-the-wall' windows are incorporated into an
      envelope, the BS 6375 Part 1, *Performance of Windows* could be considered by
      the building owner/designer. Note, however, that the performance requirements
      are significantly less onerous than the CWCT requirements for curtain walls and
      should only be considered for smaller buildings in locations with a benign
      climate.
  b) There are draft European standards in circulation for assessing watertightness of
      curtain walls and testing them to verify compliance. The static test method is
      very similar to the CWCT Test Method. The dynamic test method is considered
      to be an improvement on the CWCT Test Method and is starting to be specified.
      The legal implications of continuing with the more stringent CWCT document in
      preference to the European Standards will need to be considered in due course.
  c) It is acknowledged that none of the tests accurately reflect real weather but
      generally it has been found that when a curtain wall test specimen successfully
      passes the tests noted, it will perform satisfactorily on the building, provided
      always that the design has been thoroughly reviewed and what is tested
      accurately reflects what is built.
  d) If test data is available for similar designs, then it is reasonable to accept such
      data and therefore save the considerable expense of carrying out specific tests for
      a particular project. The building owner and designer need to agree whether the
      new design is sufficiently similar to the design for which test data is available
      before accepting this approach.

Airtightness

Hard copy
   Best Practice: Performance requirements for curtain walls are defined in the Centre
   for Window and Cladding Technology (CWCT) *Standard for Curtain Walling*. Testing
   to verify compliance of curtain walls is described in the CWCT *Test Methods for
   Curtain Walling*.

Performance requirements and test procedures for the whole completed building
envelope are described in BSRIA Technical Memorandum TN10/90 Air Leakage of
Office Buildings (CIBSE TM23).

These requirements are now a mandatory requirement under the new Part L of
the Building Regulations.

The following requirements are considered normal for offices:

Performance under test:

   • The permissible air leakage rate through the curtain wall should not be more than
     1.5 cu m/hour/sq m of wall for fixed areas and not more than 2.0 cu
     m/hour/linear meter of joint for opening areas under a static test pressure
     differential of 600 Pascalls held for five minutes when tested in accordance with
     CWCT Test Methods section 4.
   • The permissible air leakage rates for fixed areas and opening areas for static test
     pressure differentials of between 50 Pascalls and 600 Pascalls should be not more
     than the values given in Figure 1 of the CWCT *Standard for Curtain Walling*.
   • The permissible air leakage rate for the whole completed envelope should not be
     more than 10.0 cu m/hr/sq m at 50 Pascalls test pressure differential, and with any
     air leakage paths evenly distributed about the envelope, tested to CIBSE TM23.

Commentary
   a) If individual 'punched-through-the-wall' windows are incorporated into a facade,
      then BS 6375 Part 1, *Performance of Windows* could be considered by the
      building owner/designer. Note that the performance requirements for opening
      areas are very much less stringent than the CWCT requirements for curtain walls
      and really should not be used for office buildings.
   b) There are draft European standards in circulation for assessing air permeability
      of curtain walls and testing them to verify compliance. The performance
      requirements are much less stringent than the CWCT requirements. The test
      method is very similar to the CWCT test method. In due course, the legal
      implications on continuing with the more stringent CWCT document in
      preference to the European standards will need to be considered.

c) If test data is available for similar designs of curtain walls, then it is reasonable to accept such data and therefore save the considerable expense of carrying out specific tests for a particular project. The building owner and designer need to agree whether the new design is sufficiently similar to the design for which the test data is available before accepting this approach. However, CIBSE test data is unique for each building tested and should not be accepted as proof of performance for a different building.

d) If the floor area is >1000 sq m then the air infiltration level must be tested unless alternative evidence can be provided that details are suitable.

Thermal performance

Hard copy
Requirement: Building Regulations Approved Document L1 and L2, *Conservation of Fuel and Power.*

Introduced as a direct response to the Kyoto Protocol agreements the new Part L Regulations provide a methodology for reducing the carbon emissions of new and refurbished buildings. Although not addressed in this section, replacement windows, walls and heating systems in existing buildings will also have to comply[1].

New build
The requirements have implications at three key stages of the building process:

Design stage

- Assessment of the energy efficiency benefits and holistic view of facades and building environmental strategy.
- Enhancement of building envelope thermal performance.
- Reduction of solar overheating.
- Continuity of thermal envelope.
- Air leakage performance.
- Improvement of services efficiency.
- Assessment of cold bridging.
- Preference for low carbon fuels (i.e. gas over electricity).

Construction stage

- Assessment of as-built air tightness performance (for buildings greater than 1000 m^2).
- Demonstration of insulation continuity.

1 For further information see *Energy Conservation* by Sarah Lupton, RIBA Enterprises, 2003.

Occupation stage

- More detailed commissioning procedures.
- Recording of energy performance.
- Closer monitoring of energy consumption.

Compliance methods

The regulation has three different compliance equations of which the design team must select which is the most suitable to be applied to each project. The more complex procedures often enable greater latitude and design freedom.

Elemental method

The revised elemental method restricts the allowable extent of trade-offs between elements.

The main issues are:

- Reduction in U-values (use of double and triple glazing, low emissivity coatings, argon filling, warm edge spacers).
- Limits of solar gain (leading to the refinement of external shading, high performance glass).
- Trade-offs between areas of facades and efficiency of services.
- The restriction of glazing under the solar overheating requirement to limit summer thermal discomfort.

There are three methods of complying with the solar overheating requirements:

(i) Restricted areas of glazing defined by orientation. (note these percentages are fairly restrictive).
(ii) Proof that solar gain <25 sq m.
(iii) Proof by detailed calculation that in the absence of cooling and ventilation, the space will not overheat if subjected to internal gain of 10W/sq m as CIBSE A5.

Whole Building Method

This method defines carbon emission standards for the whole building. The performance of the air conditioning, heating and lighting are all assessed.

Using this method, permissible glazing areas may well increase over the elemental method when energy efficiency methods such as heat exchanges, high efficiency boilers and lighting controls are adopted. This method currently applies only to offices, schools and hospitals.

Carbon Emissions Calculation Method

This approach is the most complex but flexible of the three methods. To comply, the annual carbon emissions of the designed building most be lower when compared with those of a notional building of the same size, whose facades and services pass the elemental method.

This method can include detailed hour-by-hour calculations of environmental conditions, user controls and a range of HVAC strategies. Typically extensive computer design input is required but due to its infancy, different packages give widely varying results for the same input data.

Sound insulation

The acoustic environment inside a building is dependent on a number of factors, including the following:

- Occupiers' use of the space, including equipment.
- External noise sources, such as traffic or aircraft noise, and the sound insulation of the building envelope.
- External vibration sources, such as road or rail traffic.
- Noise levels from building services serving the space and in adjacent plant locations.
- Internal sound insulation from walls, floors, ceilings, doors, etc.
- The type and geometry of the architectural finishes in the space.

There is also a requirement to control the emission of noise from the building to comply with the planning conditions of the local authority and to maintain the amenity of the surroundings.

The design of the acoustic environment should take all the relevant factors into account.

The appropriate standard of aural privacy between offices requires the sound insulation between the rooms and the minimum background noise levels to be controlled.

Usually the background noise level is produced by the operation of the building services, which should be controlled to meet the following criteria (NR = Noise Rating):

- Entrance halls and toilets   NR40
- Open-plan offices   NR38
- Cellular offices   NR35
- Conference rooms   NR25 – 35 (subject to size)

Providing there are no other contributing noise sources, the NR given above should be determined by measurements of L_{Aeq}.

The sound insulation of the building envelope should reduce the external noise to a level such that when combined with the building services, noise shall be within a defined range:

- Open-plan offices   45 – 50 dBL_{Aeq}
- Cellular offices   40 – 45 dBL_{Aeq}
- Conference rooms   35 – 45 dBL_{Aeq} (subject to size)

The specification of facade sound insulation performance often should include octave band sound reduction indices, particularly at low frequencies, to cater for the dominant character of external noise.

In the BREEAM (the Building Research Establishment Environmental Assessment Method) credit for indoor noise is sought, the low end of the L_{Aeq} range given above for open-plan and cellular offices must be met. In the case of naturally ventilated buildings it may be appropriate to accept higher values, if acceptable to the client.

The construction of the building envelope should also incorporate the necessary detailing to maintain the sound insulation at the junction with the floor slab and to maintain the sound insulation of internal partitions.

The mid-frequency reverberation time for offices should be between 0.4 seconds and 0.7 seconds, subject to volume.

Vibration levels in office areas within a building, as a result of internal and external sources, should be limited to Curve 4 of BS 6472. More sensitive areas may require a better standard.

Structure borne noise, i.e. noise generated in the building as a result of vibration resulting from adjacent road or rail traffic, etc. should be limited such that the maximum noise level regenerated by such events should not exceed the following criteria:

- Open-plan offices   50–55 $dBL_{Amax(slow)}$
- Cellular offices   45–50 $dBL_{Amax(slow)}$
- Conference rooms   40–50 $dBL_{Amax(slow)}$ (subject to size)

Security and safety

Facades may be enhanced to deal with a range of real or perceived risks and threats including:

- accidental damage;
- material failure (e.g. spontaneous failure due to Nickel Sulphide inclusion in glass)
- vandalism;
- or bomb blast.

Accidental damage
Designers must consider the different issues, roles and consequences of failure of both vertical and overhead glazing.

- Because glass can break in any situation designers must consider the risks and consequences.
- The Building Regulations Part N requires designers to consider the potential risks of glass failure, and the necessity and location of safety glass.
- BS 5516 covering overhead glazing require designers to consider safe breakage. The CWCT guideline for sloping/overhead glazing adds the consideration of glass restrains and containment of the broken glass panel.
- Beyond the design of the facade/glazing elements themselves designers must consider:
  - any person/object who may fall through it;
  - usage of the space and risk to the building occupants;
  - consequences of the failure beyond the mere cost of replacement;
  - influences of maintenance.
- The strategy for vertical glazing needs to consider similar issues to that for overhead glazing.
- This consideration must extend beyond external facades to balustrades, internal partitions and even punched windows.

Material failure
Glass failure can be caused by mechanisms throughout all stages of the project from fabrication, installation or during building occupancy.

Toughened glass

- Toughened glass has the inherent risk of spontaneous failure due to nickel sulphide inclusion. The risk of failure of installed glass can be reduced by heat soak testing the glass during fabrication. The consequences of failure can be further mitigated by laminating the toughened glass.

- When monolithic toughened glass is used without edge protection, e.g. frameless cantilevered glass balustrades, the vulnerability of the glass to edge damage caused during fabrication, handling, installation and subsequent maintenance must be considered alongside the consequences of failure.
- General stresses at the boundary conditions and edges of the glass must be considered, as spontaneous failure may occur due to thermal stress cracking and/or edge damage.

Vandalism
There are various design guides available when designing facades for which the risk of damage due to vandalism is considered high. These risks range from petty damage caused by opportunistic individuals, more serious damage inflicted to gain illicit access, to deliberate and sustained damage caused by activists.

The need and liability of any facade to withstand each level of risk needs to be judged against the deemed consequences e.g. financial, severity, replacement.

Bomb blast
Government guidelines for the enhancements of facades to withstand bomb blasts have three levels:

Enhancement level A – for use in existing buildings. Baseline measures consisting of the application of Anti Shatter Film and bomb blast curtains.

Enhancement level B – protective glazing in new buildings where the risk to the building is low. Requirements for Enhancement Level B can be summarised as follows:

- Laminated glass of minimum thickness 6.8 mm in single glazed windows.
- Toughened glass of minimum thickness 6 mm in the outer leaf plus laminated glass of minimum thickness 6.8 mm in the inner leaf in double-glazed windows.
- Alternatively laminated glass of minimum thickness 6.4 mm or + 6.4 mm in both leaves of double-glazed windows could be considered, although the combination of toughened and laminated glass described above is generally preferred.
- Frame elements should generally be designed and detailed in line with normal non-blast related good practice, although internal pressure plates and 'snap-on' glazing beads should be avoided.
- Enhancement of frame connections and fixings to the primary structure up to about double the design wind pressures, using a load factor of unity.
- Windows should be designed and detailed to facilitate inspection, removal and replacement of individual damaged units.
- Glass selection should take account of thermal safety issues as well as blast protection.

Enhancement level C – for new buildings or major refurbishments it is recommended that a higher degree of protection be provided where the risk to the building is significant and a further reduction in the hazard to the occupants is warranted. Requirements for Enhancement Level C can be summarised as follows:

- Strengthened frames and glazing systems purpose designed and detailed to resist specified blast loading.
- Laminated glass of at least 7.5 mm (having a 1.52 mm pvb interlayer) in single-glazed windows or as inner leaf of double-glazed units. Where it is required for a specific design threat level, a greater thickness of laminated glass can be provided.
- Glass to be structural-silicon sealant glazed into rebates of 25 mm minimum depth.
- Design blast pressures to be appropriate to selected glass and pane size.
- Frames and fixings to be designed, using a load factor of unity, to accommodate forces both perpendicular to, and in the plane of, the glass.
- Enhanced yield strengths for dynamic loading appropriate to the selected materials may be used in the design of frame members.
- Frame connections and fixings designed to remain elastic under 150 per cent of design load.
- Frames for opening windows to include hinges and multiple locking points capable of carrying the same loads as fixed windows. Tests show that these are critical for inward opening windows. Outward opening is preferable.
- Glass selection should take account of thermal, acoustic and handling issues, as well as blast protection.

Having minimised the initial likelihood of a blast occurring adjacent to the building, measures which maintain the integrity of the facade itself during and after a blast will offer the greatest benefit to occupant protection and those in the proximity of the building.

Both annealed and monolithic toughened glass fragment in a blast, can cause injury to the building's occupants due to both the entry of blast pressure into the building and fragments of glass travelling at high velocity through the space.

The most effective protection is offered by the use of laminated glass properly anchored in its glazing rebates and restrained to the frame.

Blast loads, both positive and negative, need to be transferred through the framing, and its bracketry to the building structure.

Case study: Facade design of City Hall – Home of the Greater London Authority

Site, orientation and form

Site

City Hall is located on the south bank of the River Thames adjacent to Tower Bridge and opposite the Tower of London – a world heritage site. The building is home to the Mayor of London, members of the London Assembly and the staff of the Greater London Authority. The commission to design the building was awarded to Foster and Partners and Arup following a competition in 1999, and was opened in July 2002.

City Hall was the first building to be completed within the More London Masterplan. Developed by CIT, the masterplan provides more than two million square feet of accommodation in ten mixed-use buildings. It sits alongside a large public space – similar in size to Leicester Square. The entire masterplan site will be pedestrianised; all vehicles entering the site will do so by means of an underground roadway with access to loading bays and parking for all buildings. The absence of traffic noise and pollution and the building's riverside position affords the opportunity to use natural ventilation in an inner city site.

The 'More London' development is located within five minutes walk from London Bridge Rail and Underground stations and Tower Hill Underground station, and is close to numerous bus routes. The site can be reached by public transport from most parts of London within one hour.

Figure 1: City Hall riverside view

Orientation and form

The siting and orientation of the building are a response to the surrounding context and contribute to the building's high level of energy efficiency. The building lies on a true north-south axis and has a form based on a sphere. The building leans towards the south, which allows more daylight to enter the northern side of the building and the riverwalk, and provides some passive shading to the south.

The facade design brief was based on an extensive computerised solar analysis of the building's form. The data also led to the development of a tailor-made shading strategy whereby the solar and glare control shading is located on the outside of the building envelope.

Energy efficiency

Energy efficiency is of primary importance in the design of City Hall. Having established a sound basis for low energy design, the design team applied passive energy-saving techniques to further reduce the building's energy usage.

The insulation performance of the facade was set at a level in excess of the current Part L Regulations, which are more stringent that those regulations in place at the time of construction. A double-skin cladding envelope encloses the building, integrating opaque, translucent and transparent panels with integral shading devices responding to the building's orientation. This layered cladding system is used for all the office facades. It abuts the assembly chamber facade to the north, which consists of a double-glazed triangulated single skin. The triangular form of the chamber facade describes the volume of the chamber within. Internally, a single-glazed acoustic skin encloses the chamber and ramps.

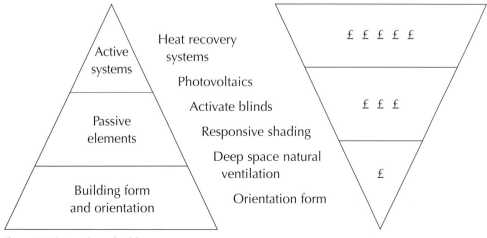

Figure 2: What makes a building green

The building's energy consumption is further reduced by the use of perimeter opening windows, a low-level air supply incorporating recuperation of internal energy, and passive chilled-beam cooling devices using borehole water pumped from deep below the earth's surface. Analysis indicates that, as a result of the combustion of these energy saving devices, the annual energy consumption for the building's mechanical systems will be approximately a quarter of that of a typical high-specification air conditioned office building.

Geometry

The design of this building used some of the most sophisticated 3D computer modelling and form analysis techniques available at the time of its design. Some of the techniques were actually new user-designed tools added to the existing computer programs, which were unable to provide the level of detail and function required. The 3D computer model built by the team generated all the information required, including plans and sections. All the elements of the building were modelled in three dimensions.

The final form of the building is not a conventional geometric shape. Instead, the form is generated from the constraints of the site, the sun angles and the required floor areas. The shape is formed by a series of non-concentric circles, the diameters of which are set by design curves which describe the section of the building.

Because the form was generated by circles, which are simple geometric shapes, it could be calculated and checked with simple mathematics. This ensured that the computer model used to define all the glass sizes and panel locations was absolutely correct.

The facade planes are twisted because the circle centres that define them are not concentric. An internal partition grid of 1.5 m generates the mullion positions. It was necessary to shift the mullions from the vertical in order to overcome the twist of the panels and to create a flat glass trapezoidal panel. Each of the building's glazing panels is unique. In order to ensure that each panel would fit perfectly when brought to site it was essential to record the panel positions on spreadsheets. These spreadsheets enabled the glass supplier to provide accurate tender prices rather than making inflated assumptions about the cost in relation to the assumed complexity of the prefabrication. The spreadsheets also provided the facade fabricators with a means to produce schedules and cutting lists. Furthermore, the spreadsheets also allowed the team to audit the design by comparing the output of a computer model with a mathematical calculation of the panel locations. The office facade manufacturer used the data from the spreadsheets for the computer-controlled fabrication of the mullions and transoms.

Figure 3: Exploded diagram of City Hall

Facade performance

The building skin forms the boundary between inside and outside. The skin tempers the internal environment by filtering the external environment.

The facade design takes into account the following factors:

- Heat loss (U-value).
- Heat gain (solar control).
- Glare.
- Natural ventilation.
- Air infiltration.

The performance of the facade for U-value and solar control is a key factor that has a considerable impact on the building's mechanical and electrical engineering strategy. Two major factors determine the design parameters: the amount of heat entering the building through the facade in the summer months, which will require mechanical cooling; and the amount of heat escaping through the facade during the winter months, which will require heating.

These two factors affect the mechanical plant in an air conditioned building, or the internal temperatures in a non air conditioned building. Natural ventilation can help to reduce the running costs of plant for an air conditioned office by decreasing the length of time in a year the plant needs to be operational. In a very simple way, opening a window is an immediate way of controlling one's environment.

The office cladding is a vented triple-glazed flush facade. The inner skin of the system is made up of insulated spandrel elements and a low emmisivity double-glazed unit 1200 mm in height set 900 mm off the finished floor level. The cavity between the two skins houses shading blinds, which provide both solar shading and glare control. Natural buoyancy effects drive air movement within the cavity which cools the blinds, thereby enhancing the efficiency of the system. The vented cavity also provides the air inlet for the natural ventilation. An automatic top opening vent allows the hot air to escape at high level when the lower vent is opened.

The Building Regulations Part L – *The Conservation of Fuel and Power* – sets out the maximum permissible heat loss for buildings. In order to comply with the regulations, the actual heat loss of the building cannot exceed the 'allowable' heat loss for a notional building with the same surface area. The office facade must not exceed a heat loss of 6.6W/K per linear metre in order to comply with the regulations.

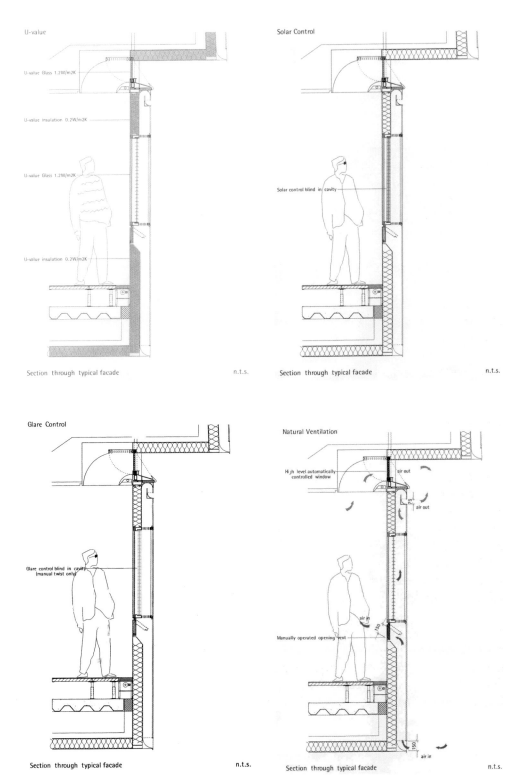

Figure 4: Facade design with reference to U-value, solar control, glare control and natural ventilation

Heat gain – solar control
Solar gain through the facade throughout the summer has a significant effect on the energy consumption of the building's cooling systems. The office facade system achieves an average peak internal heat gain of 120–156W, which gives the building a peak average of 135W per linear metre around the entire facade. The chilled beam layout in the ceiling is tuned to suit the heat gain through each facade panel.

Studies were carried out using the 3D model of the building. From this analysis the performance required of each cladding panel could be calculated.

Natural ventilation
Natural ventilation will lead to reduced energy consumption and running costs, and increased levels of fresh air.

Low-level vents in the facade allow air to enter the perimeter offices. Air is exhausted through an automatic high-level vent. The size of these vents was determined from a study to analyse the airflow through slots of different sizes. This was carried out using Arup's in-house Thermal Analysis program 'VENT'.

Glare control
Solar shading devices can often also solve a building's glare control requirements. The blinds in the outer cavity of the facade serve both functions.

The blinds are manually operated by turning a dial mounted on the vertical mullion. The colour and reflectance of the blinds were critical in meeting the glare-control criteria.

Construction

Setting out and tolerances
The complex geometry of the building dictates that a conventional 'line and level' setting-out regime would be inappropriate. A 3D survey and setting-out strategy was required whereby the designer's 3D model and trade contractor's 3D fabrication drawings were able to interact with sophisticated Electronic Distance Measuring Theodolites.

In this way project control points were positioned and as-built conditions were surveyed with great accuracy relative to the designed position of any point on the 3D model. This strategy required that the key structure and envelope trade contractors had to use the same level of sophistication in their own setting-out. An off site checking regime needed to be developed so that that elements such as the three-storey-high faceted tubular columns and cladding panels were surveyed and checked on 'virtual mock-ups'. A three-dimensional laser setting-out and measuring was used during construction to set out the building. Small holographic targets were positioned on all the elements that required a high level of positional accuracy. These

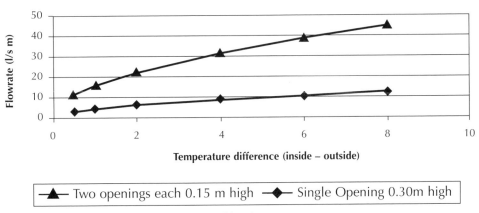

Figure 5: Natural ventilation flow rate per metre of facade

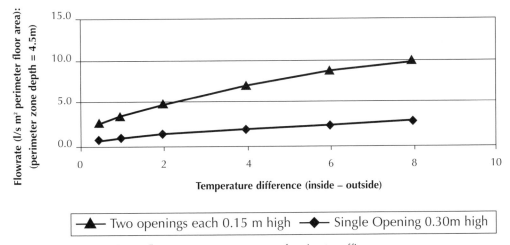

Figure 6: Natural ventilation flow rate per square metre of perimeter office

targets reflected the laser beam projected from the setting out machine, allowing the machine to generate read-outs in three dimensions. The final adjustments could then be made and the elements fixed in their final positions. The facade panels were temporarily erected in the factory to enable the manufacturer to survey the as-built panels before they arrived on site. This ensured any fabrication tolerances were eliminated before the panels arrived on site and the brackets could be placed in relation to the actual rather than the theoretical panels. Because the panels have unique positions in the facade, they were individually numbered and brought to the site on palettes. The elements were then lifted into position and fixed to the slab via the head and base brackets. The level of detailed design was such that each of the panels had a unique lifting position in order to ensure that the bottom edge of each of the trapezoidal units remained horizontal. Due to the high level of computer modelling and careful control and checking of all the off-site prefabrication units, every facade element of the building fitted first time.

Author profiles

Andrew Hall BA (Hons) Dip Arch RIBA, Director Facade Engineering
Arup

Andrew Hall joined Nicholas Grimshaw and Partners (NGP) in 1986, where he developed his interest in the design of the building envelope. His key projects included design and implementation of bespoke facades for the British Airways Combined Operations Centre (Heathrow, London), British Pavilion for the 1992 Expo (Seville, Spain) and Ludwig Erhard Haus, Stock Exchange (in Berlin, Germany)

After having joined the Facade Engineering team at Arup, in 1994, two years later Andrew became Director, responsible for overall leadership for the London team. A year later his role expanded to act as leader of the global facade business network with an international inter-disciplinary team of over 100 specialists based in Sydney, Melbourne, Hong Kong, Johannesburg and San Francisco.

Ken Shuttleworth Dip Arch (Dist) RIBA HonDDes, Partner
Foster and Partners

Ken Shuttleworth first worked at Foster Associates in 1974 as a team member on the Willis Faber & Dumas project. After an architectural study tour of the United States and Canada, he returned to the practice in 1977 to work on the IBM Technical Park at Greenford and the Hammersmith Centre.

In 1979 he began work on the Hongkong and Shanghai Bank, moving to Hong Kong and taking responsibility for all aspects of design from inception to completion. He was appointed a director of Foster and Partners in 1984 and became a partner in 1991.

Since his return from Hong Kong in 1986 he has worked on the design of many projects including Chek Lap Kok airport in Hong Kong, the Al Faisaliah Complex in Riyadh and Oxford University Social Studies Faculty and Library. London-based projects include the Millennium Bridge, Citibank Headquarters in Canary Wharf, and the More London Masterplan including the headquarters for the Greater London Authority.

Richard Hyams BA (Hons) Dip Arch (Dist), Project Director
Foster and Partners

Richard Hyams joined Foster and Partners in 1991 for his year out after completing an Honours degree at South Bank University. After graduating with distinction, he rejoined the practice in 1994 and worked on the Al Faisalliah Complex in Riyadh and the 32-storey World Port Centre in Rotterdam. Richard worked on City Hall from inception to completion, taking responsibility for the facade design and shape of the building and later designing the internal fit-out.

12 Building services

Mark Facer and Julian Olley
Arup

Introduction

The design of building services in the UK will never be the same again. Design has previously been dominated by issues of capital cost, space take, and short term marketability. Low energy designs have been the exception.

To cut the country's carbon emissions, the recently issued Part L of the Building Regulations (Part J in Scotland) sets new requirements for the building fabric and the performance of plant. It came into force on 1 April 2002. Building services and offices now need to be designed and operated to reduce their effect on global warming.

The new Part L requires that fenestration, lighting, building plan form, building slenderness, storey height and building services systems are considered together. These are mutually dependent and changes in any one may prevent compliance. Services designers will now have to be involved formally in submissions to Building Control. Previously the architect has been solely responsible. As with the superseded Part L there is a certain amount of flexibility in the rules to allow variety in design but limits are set for areas of glazing in relation to both heat loss and heat gain which vary for different orientations. There are three 'methods', broadly the same as those in the superseded Part L except that the emphasis is on the carbon emission of the building services rather than on straightforward energy use.

The new Part L is the start of a process which aims to reduce the UK's carbon emissions by 60 per cent over the next 50 years. In relation to whether that is essential, it is worth remembering that the earth's population has doubled in the last 50 years and increases in levels of carbon dioxide have, until now, correlated closely to increases in global population. Fortunately, designing buildings to reduce their energy consumption and, therefore their carbon dioxide emissions, will be beneficial in many other ways. Closer liaison within the design team will result in more detailed consideration of the effectiveness of the whole building. Buildings are likely to be more comfortable as they should be better at moderating extreme outside conditions. For the same reason, building services systems should be simpler to control and operate. Designers will have to apply flair and imagination to conceive and implement appropriate buildings in changing circumstances. The results should be all the more effective for having been formally submitted.

This section describes the principal building services options, highlights the issues that determine whether a building will use reduced levels of energy, identifies the issues which are important to occupiers, and describes the likely effects of the recently issued Part L and beyond.

Air conditioning systems

A surfeit of acronyms

Air conditioning and heating systems are frequently described by acronyms – VAV, VRV, LPHW, LTHW, fan assisted VAV, VVT and FCU are typical of the genre.

For most people the attempt to memorise the acronym is as far as they get. Essentially, the systems supply warm or cool air to match heating and cooling requirements respectively, whilst delivering at least a minimum quantity of fresh air. Sometimes the systems are designed to change the room surface temperatures as well. This is important as, surprisingly, people are slightly more sensitive to surface temperatures than air temperatures.

Sometimes air conditioning systems are also designed to control humidity levels. Even simple systems produce drier conditions inside than outside and this is usually beneficial. The exception is when it is very cold and the outside air is already relatively dry. Those who have taken a skiing holiday will know that the way to avoid a very dry and uncomfortable nose overnight is to place a damp towel on the radiator. As the UK's winters are short and relatively mild it is only occasionally that there is a need to add moisture to avoid discomfort and static electricity discharge problems. Humidity control in offices is often, in practice, not specified by designers, or turned off by operators, and is usually not noticed by occupants. Exceptions include spaces such as meeting rooms that are supplied with high quantities of fresh air but are unoccupied. These may get very dry in winter without humidity or other control. Similarly, the designers of low energy systems that rely on uncooled outside air in summer will need to consider whether the resulting relatively high internal humidity levels are acceptable.

Air conditioning systems would be very simple, and there would be very few acronyms, if the whole building could be heated or cooled as a single zone. In reality, different parts of the building require varying amounts of heating and cooling. Sometimes parts of the building require heating whilst other parts require cooling, particularly on sunny mid-season days. To control office temperatures the quantity of air can be varied by a variable air volume (VAV) system, or the air temperature can be varied as with a fan coil unit (FCU) system, or both can be varied by a variable volume and temperature (VVT) system.

An ideal design will provide the necessary control of temperature, fresh air and humidity with the least complication. The building services' designer will stand a better chance of achieving this nirvana if, first, the building fabric moderates the loads it imposes on the internal environment and buildings systems and, second, the building use is not over-specified for occupancy and office equipment use.

What is popular?

The increased use of heat generating office equipment, rising traffic noise levels and the popularity of deep plan and multi-storey offices has made air conditioning increasingly the norm. Occupiers are not always convinced that this is progress, regretting the demise of the openable window. Nevertheless, air conditioned offices are let at a premium.

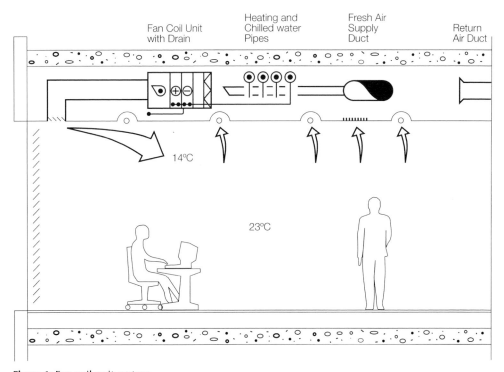

Figure 1: Fan coil unit system

Twenty years ago the two most common air conditioning systems for large offices were fan coil systems and variable air volume systems.

Fan coil systems consist of a multitude of ceiling mounted units each incorporating a small fan, a cooling coil and a heating coil. These units are supplied with a limited quantity of fresh air, heating water, chilled water and a drain. They provide good constant air movement and variable quantities of heating or cooling. Their performance can be uprated relatively easily, by increasing fan speed, adding additional units or substituting larger units for those initially installed.

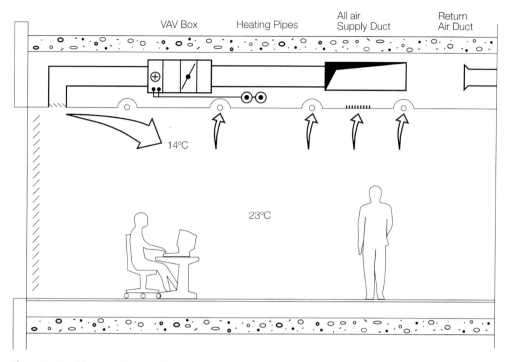

Figure 2: Variable air volume system

The variable volume system was considered to have a number of advantages for the end user and to be the system of choice. Its principal advantage was the reduced quantity of pipe work and the removal of any drainage from above the ceiling. Control of temperature was achieved by varying the air quantity with a temperature controlled damper. The air was supplied by a large central air handling plant in a remote location. Consequently, risks of water leaks and the need to carry out maintenance in the office ceiling were much reduced. The disadvantage, however, was the size of the associated air ducts, risers and the plantroom. These would typically account for about six per cent of the area served.

The cost of space and the restricted slab to slab heights but, principally, the office equipment revolution has changed views. The need to increase the output of air conditioning systems in existing buildings and to cope with greatly increased use of computers often resulted in the addition of fan coil units. The flexibility of the fan coil system became attractive to users and its limitations became acceptable, through familiarity.

Today the fan coil unit system is the most common air conditioning system for large offices in the UK. It has become the standard system against which others are measured.

Advantages and disadvantages of the main types of air conditioning systems

Most air conditioning systems are ceiling based. This is convenient, as false ceilings are almost universal, and to a large extent the arrangement separates the complications of air conditioning systems from the details of desk layouts. However, the popularity of raised floors in offices provides other opportunities. A system which introduces cool air at floor level and extracts warm air at ceiling level is enhanced by the fact that hot air rises, although the difficulties associated with supplying cool air close to sensitive legs and between changing desk layouts need to be considered.

The principal advantages of the ceiling based, fan coil unit system are its flexibility, space efficiency and relatively high output. Its maintenance requirements remain its principal disadvantage.

Newer developments include chilled ceiling systems and upflow/displacement systems. Both are associated with low energy buildings because they are essentially low capacity systems.

Chilled ceilings are more popular on the Continent (where they originated), than they are in the UK. In their purest forms, water at 16°C is piped through ceiling tiles to form a radiant chilled ceiling, or through a set of big finned elements in the ceiling to

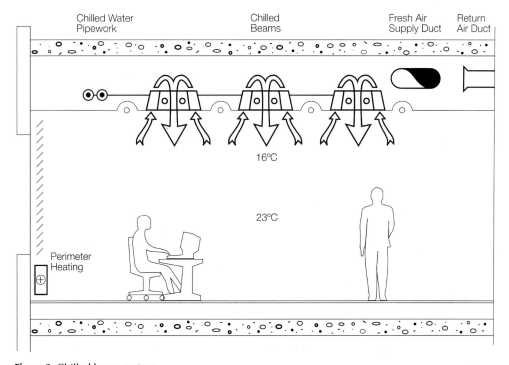

Figure 3: Chilled beam system

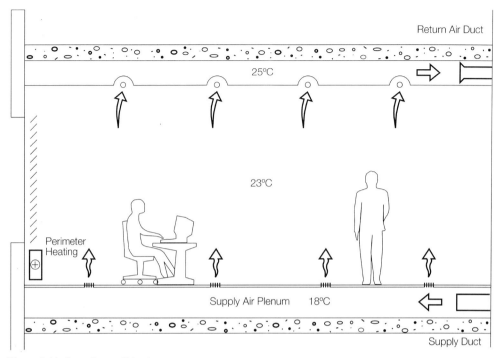

Figure 4: Upflow air conditioning system

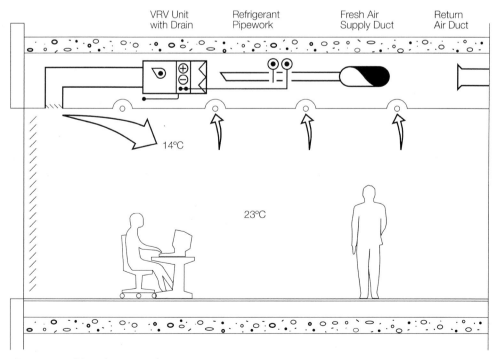

Figure 5: Variable refrigerant volume system

form passive chilled beams. Air is cooled as it passes over the ceiling or through the finned elements where upon it falls into the office. The radiant chilled ceiling also provides some radiant cooling, as its name suggests. The energy required to pump cooled water around the building is much less than that required to blow cooled air around, so these systems can be genuinely energy saving. However, their performance in their purest form is very limited and if a fan is added to form an active chilled beam and improve output they become less energy saving and not dissimilar to a fan coil unit. The size of the finned ceiling elements or cooled ceiling tiles and the extent and complication of the associated pipe work make them relatively expensive and difficult to integrate into many ceiling designs, though it does suit the typical Continental office layout of a central corridor with offices either side.

Upflow air conditioning systems are also of limited performance in typical office applications though their performance can be uprated by increasing air flow. They operate on the basis of providing mildly cooled air at 18°C or 19°C, at floor level and extracting the same, relatively large, volume of air through the ceiling. The heat gain from people or equipment tends to go straight up into the ceiling before it becomes a load on the space. The air supply temperature remains constant whilst the extract temperature varies with the load. The advantages of the system are its potential for low energy in use, its essential simplicity and its relatively good value. Its disadvantages are its limited performance at typical air change rates and the need to move floor grilles and re-cut carpet in the event of significant office layout changes. One design aim must be to ensure little, or no equipment in the floor void. This avoids the potential problem of maintenance under raised floors. To operate effectively, it is also essential to ensure that the raised floor is reasonably airtight with leaks through the tiles and perimeter and core walls kept to a minimum.

In recent years the manufacturers of small split-system office air conditioners have developed the technology to allow a single outside chiller unit to be linked with refrigerant lines to a number of indoor units. The technology involves changing the quantity of refrigerant to each indoor unit, on demand, hence the term 'variable refrigerant volume', or VRV. These units are largely self-contained and are particularly appropriate to small-scale office refurbishments, especially if they are selected as heat pump units. However, specifiers should be aware that costs per unit area for a large office may be relatively high and that the refrigerant lines need to be balanced and sized accurately. It is therefore not as easy to rearrange the indoor units as it is with a fan coil system. The reliance on refrigerant distributed throughout the occupied space is also seen as a disadvantage from an environmental viewpoint.

There is, of course, no single system that has all the advantages and all the performance. If there were, this would be a very short chapter. The principle characteristics of the different systems are shown overleaf.

What is common for all systems is their improved performance when the building itself is designed to moderate external loads and when internal gains from lights,

Function	System	Fan Coil Units (FCU)	Variable Air Volume (VAV)	Chilled/Activated Beams	Upflow Air Conditioning	Variable Refrigerant Volume (VRV)
Sense of comfort		✓	✓	✓	●	✓
Speed of construction		●	●	●	✓	●
Speed of commissioning		●	●	●	✓	●
Suitability for open-plan		✓	✓	✓	✓	✓
Suitability for cellurisation		✓	✓	●	✗	✓
Flexibility in design		✓	●	●	✓	✓
On-floor maintenance		✗	●	●	✓	✗
Typical floor heights		●	✗	●	✗	●
Level of open-plan control		✓	●	✓	✓	✓
Level of cellular control		✓	✓	●	✗	✓
Central plant space requirement		✓	✗	✓	✗	●
Riser space requirement		✓	✗	✓	✗	✓
Supplementary cooling capabilities		✓	✓	●	✗	✗
Perimeter heating requirement		✓	✗	✗	✗	●
Condensate requirements		✗	✓	✓	✓	✗

✓ Good Performance   ● Average Performance   ✗ Some Constraints

Figure 6: Ventilation and air conditioning strategies - system comparisons

office equipment and occupants are specified appropriately. All too often, especially in the UK, equipment heat gains are over-specified to impress potential tenants or through ignorance about actual use. The result can be air conditioning systems which are over-complicated, oversized, costly to buy, costly to run and costly to maintain.

Trends

The most popular air conditioning system for speculative offices remains the fan coil system. It is an institutionally acceptable system which is widely recognised by occupiers, agents and potential tenants and is therefore the best understood but by no means the universal choice. There are many exceptions and variations.

The air conditioning designs for the offices at Canary Wharf are based on an all electric system which combines features from both VAV and fan coil unit systems. It is a high-capacity fan assisted VAV system which avoids pipe work in office ceilings by incorporating electric heating and relatively large floor-by-floor recirculation air handling units in the office core. The fresh air system is sized at minimum rates to reduce riser sizes. It doubles as the smoke extract system in the event of a fire.

Chilled ceilings and chilled beams are evolving technologies with energy saving potential. The new Part L, which allows compliance on the basis of energy use, may trigger increased consideration and adoption of such systems because, without fans, they deliver cooling relatively efficiently. However, they are usually low to medium cooling capacity systems and they cannot, by themselves, reduce a building's cooling load. Further, the common assumption that these devices can be used with displacement systems should be viewed with caution. True displacement of the room air removes at least half of their cooling output, and chilled beams, in particular, will induce downdraughts that destroy the displacement principle.

Upflow air conditioning systems, where the air is supplied from the floor rather than the ceiling, have a small but growing percentage of the overall market. Users of such systems, mostly owner-occupiers, like their simplicity and compare churn costs favourably with those of other systems. Because the floor void is used to convey air and the outlets are the sole air handling devices in the occupied zone, ductwork and room terminal costs are much reduced compared to other systems. Typically, it is used in offices where cooling loads are relatively low but it has now been successfully used in a number of projects in the financial services sector where equipment gains are very high. At the Merrill Lynch Headquarters, a recently fitted out City building, it was considered to be the only system capable of providing comfort with the anticipated, very high, office equipment gains. It copes with the high equipment load because the dealer desks are designed to allow warm air from the equipment to rise directly towards the ceiling and not mix within the room. Growing experience with such projects suggests an increased acceptance by institutions of the system. One of the offices at Argent's Brindleyplace, Birmingham, has an upflow system and Stanhope is offering it in a speculative office development at Chiswick Park, West London.

VRV systems will continue to have a role in smaller developments and refurbishments where their relatively high cooling capacity and flexibility will ensure a significant market share.

Air conditioning loads

Some naturally ventilated office buildings remain comfortable for all but a few days per year. Others are uncomfortably hot. Our homes in the UK tend to be in the former category. What are the key issues involved?

Density of use is a key factor. Offices are typically occupied at about one person per ten square metres. A house will usually be much less densely occupied, especially during the day. Domestically, lights are generally switched off during the day and computer use is likely to be occasional rather than constant. In warm weather, dressing down would be the norm. Finally, windows in most residential buildings are a limited proportion of their elevations.

Heating, lighting and computer use can be quantified and the normal unit of measurement is watts per square metre of floor, W/sq m.

A watt is a unit of power or heat flow rate. A typical electric fan heater is rated at 2000 watts. So running it for an hour would result in an electricity consumption of 2 kWhr for which the charge would be about 12 pence, depending on tariffs. Electricity is metered in kilowatt hours, but gas is traditionally metered in cubic feet of gas. The latter can be easily converted to a kWhr equivalent. Air conditioning loads are conveniently stated in units of watts per floor area, W/sq m, as the resulting figures are easy to remember and compare.

The new Part L compares buildings and systems in relation to their discharge of carbon into the atmosphere through the burning of fossil fuels. Each fuel has a particular factor for converting energy delivered, in kilowatt hours (kWhr), to kilograms of carbon released, kgC. Some fuels are much more efficient than others. Production of electricity is carbon intensive because of the inefficiencies involved in generating and distributing it. Gas, on the other hand, can be combusted and changed to useful heat relatively efficiently.

Occupants

People themselves generate power which ends up as heat. The quantity depends on activity level, ambient temperature and size. A typical office worker personally produces about 150 watts continuously – two light bulbs' worth. Some of this power simply warms the surroundings and some is produced as water vapour.

In the office gym some characters will be producing as much as 400–500 watts, a substantial part as 'vapour'. Others will be taking it easier.

Those interested in calculating their own heat production should note that the Calories quoted on the typical sandwich are actually kilocalories, and 1 kilocalorie per hour x 1.163 = 1 watt. You generate the energy you eat, roughly.

Allowing 150 watts per person and a typical occupancy rate in offices of one person per 10 sq m, the total sensible and latent (vapour) heat gain from occupants is about 15W/sq m.

Office equipment

In pre-computer days the default office equipment design load was 5 W/sq m. The increasing use of computers, printers, copiers, faxes and similar equipment has seen allowances multiply. Early allowances were over generous. First, the rating plate on the equipment was assumed to define the heat output. In use, the running current, and hence heat output, turned out to be much less than the rated current. Second, speculative offices were marketed partly on the basis of equipment allowances. An office with an air conditioning system designed for 75 W/sq m seems, at first glance, better than one designed for 25 W/sq m. However, in practice the load in a typical office will in all likelihood be about 15 W/sq m. The apparently better, but in reality over-specified, office will have the cost and operational tendencies of a Ferrari running at 30 mph. Something to be avoided, I am told.

Arup organised a survey of the existing offices of a pre-let tenant who had specified an equipment gain requirement of 45 W/sq m for his new offices. The survey was carried out on the floor of the tenant's existing building where computer use was known to be highest. The results showed a gain of 25 W/sq m in a small computer testing room and an average of about 11 W/sq m on the floor where computer use was highest. The average in the whole building was not measured but would have been about 8 W/sq m. With this knowledge a new design figure of 25 W/sq m was agreed, coupled with an allowance for an extra 30 W/sq m over ten per cent of the building. This decision allowed a completely different type of low energy air conditioning system to be considered, and chosen, for both the new building and, indeed, the tenant's future buildings.

Whilst equipment gain in normal offices is primarily dependent on occupancy and computer use it also depends on holidays, sickness and meetings away from the office. The British Council for Offices (BCO)[1] recommendations are a good guide to current practice. Recent surveys have confirmed their appropriateness but have also highlighted the issue of equipment gain during unoccupied periods which, in even

1 BCO (2000), *The British Council for Offices Guide: Best Practice in the Specification of Offices*, London, BCO.

typical offices, have been measured to be 40 per cent or even 60 per cent of daytime use. It is interesting to note that this effect is as marked domestically as it is commercially. Fridges, freezers and PCs can account for a large fraction of annual consumption, particularly in households where all the occupants go out to work or school.

It should be noted that office equipment heat gain has to be paid for firstly through the use of electricity and secondly as an air conditioning load. It is worth switching off unused equipment and lighting when not required.

Dealer areas impose high office loads and need special consideration. The increased use of information technology equipment, with several screens on each desk and high occupancy densities have led to a rising trend in load allowances. However, in practice this is tempered by more efficient equipment and the removal of some computing power to separate rooms. Dealer room systems are often designed for between 90 and 130 W/sq m of equipment gain but some with extreme allowances of 250 W/m² have been installed. This allowance is equivalent to a single bar, 1kW, electric fire in every four square metres of floor space, i.e. at two metre centres. Such allowances lead to air conditioning designs which dominate the building form and space take. These loads are very unlikely ever to be realised in practice. Most dealer rooms will generate less than 50 W/m² when measured over the whole floor.

Typical equipment heat gains
A typical office with computers in use is 15–25 W/sq m.
A typical dealer room, office equipment gain is 50–130 W/sq m.
(For further information see *BCO Guide 2000.*)

Lighting

In the 1960s and early 70s it was believed that lighting levels would rise ever higher. This was based on laboratory experiments which suggested that people preferred brighter conditions up to a peak of about 2000 lux, beyond which increases are not easily discernable! A few buildings were designed with very bright lights and good insulation to avoid the need for heating. This was a good way of selling electricity.

The 1970s energy crisis caused a rethink and office lighting levels stabilised at around 500 lux.

The trend now is for lower lighting levels with increased control. This has been brought about by the increased use of computer screens. Where once occupants tended to consult their lawyers if lighting levels were lower than specified, now they are concerned if the levels are too high. Glare from office lighting and daylighting is also an issue that concerns occupants. It is interesting to look at highly glazed buildings and note how often blinds are fully lowered, even on cloudy days. In some buildings, the intensive use of computers results in users preferring to work with the lights off, even well away from the perimeter. In these circumstances the reduced glare from smaller windows is an advantage.

The new Part L requires lighting schemes to meet or exceed defined levels of efficiency and encourages the use of efficient fluorescent installations. This is described in more detail in the 'Electrical services' section of this chapter.

A typical office fluorescent lighting heat gain is 10–15 W/sq m.

Fresh air

Fresh air needs to be delivered to the typical office at a rate of about 8 lit/sec person or 1.3 lit/sm^2. The purpose of the fresh air is to remove contaminants and dilute odours. It is important therefore to have a sufficient amount. At the same time, heating fresh air in winter and cooling it in summer is a significant energy load so it is important to have only necessary minimal quantities, at design conditions.

Call centres are a relatively new but large office space user. The occupants sit at computers and telephones and are positioned close together for reasons of space efficiency. As normal office design fresh air rates are insufficient for higher occupancy levels and increasing the fresh air capacity of an existing system can be very costly, some developers allow a generous initial fresh air quantity to attract such tenants.

On the Continent it is not unusual to see systems with 100 per cent fresh air and no recirculation. This practice is combined with comprehensive heat reclaim devices which exchange useful heat between intake and discharge, a practice that could become more common in the UK. The downside of this arrangement is the potential increase in energy consumption resulting from the need to humidify 'excess' quantities of fresh air.

The cooling duty required to condition fresh summer outside air to room levels is about 15 W/sq m for normal offices and 30 W/sq m for a call centre

Infiltration

Most of the UK is blessed with a temperate climate. It does not often get very cold. It is therefore not surprising that our buildings are more leaky than they are in Scandinavia, for example.

Air leakage is not generally a significant design issue. Nevertheless, as building insulation improves, the proportion of heat loss due to infiltration increases and the new Part L sets standards for leakage rates and requires tests. Essentially, a big fan will be fitted to the front door to pressurise the building to a pressure of 50 Pa, equal to 0.2 in wg, the pressure exerted by 0.2 inches of water. The airflow through the fan, and therefore the leakage rate, is measured relative to the area of the facade and compared with a standard.

The new Part L requirements are not onerous compared to Scandinavian levels but building façades and details will need to be considered afresh, as site testing of façades in the UK has been very much the exception rather than the rule. Experience suggests that overall infiltration rates of 3–4 cu m/hr/sq m of exposed surface are not difficult to obtain with present day curtain walling. The new Part L allows 10 cu m/hr/sq m.

A typical infiltration heat gain is 5 W/sq m in a perimeter zone.

Solar

Have you ever sat on your car keys on a sunny day and, after a brief pronouncement, wondered why the keys were so hot? A piece of metal in the sun in summer can get too hot to touch comfortably. Coincidentally, a radiator on a well commissioned conventional heating system should also be too hot to touch comfortably.

This gives a clue to the power of solar radiation. The piece of metal is heated by the sun and cooled by heat loss to its surroundings, reaching equilibrium at 'radiator temperature' of about 75°C. The incoming solar intensity must therefore be similar to the output of a single panel radiator, up to 900W/sq m. Imagine each office window replaced, on the sunny side of a building, with a single panel radiator of the same size.

The solar gain in perimeter offices with large windows can therefore be disproportionate to other loads. The solar gain through a 2.5 m x 2.5 m clear glazed window with internal blinds could peak at about 2200 W, or 160 W/sq m for a 4.5 m x 3.0 m perimeter office. If the window faced north, or had external shading, or solar control glazing, the solar gain to the office would, of course, be very much less. The wide range and variability of solar gains is a notable characteristic when compared to other gains.

A typical solar gain in a perimeter office can be anything up to 160 W/sq m.

Typical load comparisons

Based on a typical office, the air conditioning cooling loads described in the preceding sections can be summarised diagrammatically as in Figure 7.

The design of the air conditioning system in the perimeter offices is therefore dominated by the size, type and orientation of the windows.

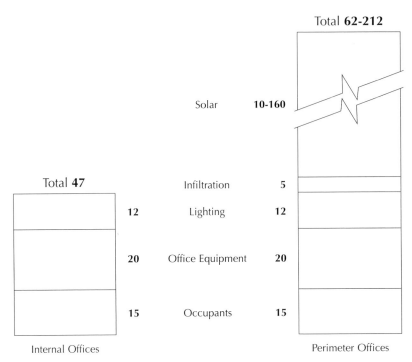

Figure 7: Typical internal and perimeter office cooling loads (W/m²)

It should be noted that the difference in cooling load between internal spaces and perimeter spaces with large areas of glazing, or between perimeter offices with and without solar gain, can easily be a factor of three. The air conditioning system has to control its cooling output to match such variation.

It is for this reason that the new Part L, for the first time, limits solar gains by defining maximum areas of glazing on different facades. The aim is to reduce solar gains to an average, over the day, of 25 W/sq m based on a 6 m deep perimeter office. It is obvious from the figures above that the office building industry will have to become familiar with smaller windows, external shading or efficient solar control glass, particularly for narrow plan buildings.

Electrical services

Introduction

For the majority of offices the electrical services will have a significant effect on the final design of the building, but are of less importance than the choice of mechanical services strategy at concept and scheme stages.

The reason for this difference is that the plant space and risers to accommodate the electrical services are considerably smaller than those for the mechanical services and they are normally easy to define for a given size of office.

It is important to know when this does not apply, and this is normally for office buildings that will be used for the financial services sector of the office market. In these buildings the requirement for very reliable electrical supplies, which can also be maintained without loss of power to the occupants, provides a considerable design challenge. In this type of building the total electrical plant space with multiple transformers, standby diesel generators, uninterruptible power supplies and the like can approach or even exceed the total space for mechanical plant.

The secondary or ancillary electrical systems such as lighting, fire alarms, security, small power and lightning protection will all have a significant effect on the final detail design or use of space, but very little at the earliest stages of a project.

Lighting

Office lighting has gone through a series of changes over the last 20 years, with appearance, energy efficiency and technical requirements alternating for precedence. The combination of wholesale use of IT equipment and the new limits imposed by part L is likely to start another round of redefinition of what the standard for office lighting should be.

For offices, Part L sets limits on the overall efficiency of the combination of the light source, the lamp, and the luminaire itself. The limit is set at an efficacy of not less than 40 luminaire lumens per circuit watt. In addition a very small allowance of 500 watts of feature lighting is allowed in the total building. Ten small, twinkly downlights could use the whole of this allowance in a building that may have 500,000 feet of useable office space.

The range of efficacy for lamps is large; ranging from 11 lamp lumens per watt for normal tungsten lamps typically used in domestic houses to a much more impressive 90 lamp lumens per watt for fluorescent tubes. There is a similar range for the luminaires themselves, ranging from, say, 20 per cent efficacy for an indirect uplight onto dark concrete to 80 per cent for a good quality modular linear fluorescent.

It is the result of multiplying lamp and luminaire efficacy that gives the figure for comparison with the Part L limit of not less than 40 luminare lumens per circuit watt. From the typical figures given above, it will be self evident that the majority of lighting in office spaces is likely to have to use fluorescent tubes for the source in order for the whole building to comply with Part L.

It seems likely that for all but the most simple of offices it will be necessary to carry out an analysis of the total building lighting and compare this with a theoretical scheme using the 40 luminaire lumens allowance.

The design of lighting is, of course, not only about the energy efficiency of the system, but also about the appearance of both the luminaires themselves and the overall appearance of the lit space. In the last few years there has been a realisation that a move away from the lighting of large open-plan office space by the most efficient method, to one that provides a better working environment, is a valid design option. In these schemes it is not only the light level that falls on the working plane – usually a desk – but also the illumination of vertical surfaces and the ceiling that are considered. A 2001 addendum to the CIBSE lighting design code[2] requires that the illumination of these surfaces is at least a minimum proportion of the illumination of the working plane. Some fittings which only light downwards, for maximum efficiency, for example Category 2 fittings, will now need to be matched with fittings that light other surfaces. Alternatively, luminaries which perform a multiple function, for example lighting partly up as well as down, can be selected. This approach tends to move the appearance away from the dark cave often seen in deep plan offices making extensive use of IT equipment to a more pleasant space with a brighter appearance.

The options for the control, switching and use of dimming for the lighting in office spaces has become ever more complex over the last ten years. Some systems vie with the buildings BMS system for title of the most complex and most difficult to commission.

The nature of the lighting control system (LCS) is often quite different in speculative and owner-occupied buildings. The speculative building will normally have either a relatively straightforward LCS or, indeed, none at all, just having provision for the addition of a system in the future as part of the tenants fitting out.

In larger speculative or owner-occupied buildings, the LCS can be very complicated, with each luminaire individually addressed and capable of being dimmed. The dimming systems available allow individual occupants to control the luminaires above them directly from their PCs or telephones – this approach has been used recently on a number of the very large dealing floors. The dimming system can also be automatically linked to daylight sensing, positions of blinds and occupancy sensors. All of these control strategies are designed to minimise the waste of energy while providing good quality lighting to the work surface when needed.

One of the major functions for a lighting control system in any substantial office is to allow the erection or removal of partitioned offices in open-plan space without the need to change any electrical wiring. All of the major systems can now achieve this as the connection between a luminaire and its controlling switch is no longer a physical one but is carried out in software. In most cases it is unlikely that a lighting control system can be shown to be economically viable purely on the basis of energy saved. It is a combination of the desire to reduce the use of energy and the ease of churn that makes the systems so popular.

2 CIBSE CLCD (2002), NEW code for lighting (CD-ROM), UK, CIBSE.

Information technology

On any major office project one of the few certainties is that the leading edge IT systems in use at the start of the concept design will be considered defunct by the completion of the fitting out and occupation. It is necessary then, in this area more than any other, not to design for today's fashion but to allow for tomorrow's necessities to be incorporated. The guiding principle for making this provision is to consider the three Rs: rooms, routes and risers.

Rooms must be provided for the telecoms providers to install their equipment and connect the cables installed externally in the road to those used internally. These rooms are not very large but they must have good, immediate duct connections into the streets outside. Often they will need ventilation or cooling as active telecommunications equipment is used to convert signals arriving on fibre cables to electrical signals on copper. In buildings to be used for financial services occupants where multiple rooms will be needed, they should be separated from each other as much as possible and have connections into different external streets for assured continuity of supply.

The routes from these rooms to the tenants of the buildings need to be as easily accessible as possible, as these cable tray or trunking routes are likely to have new cables added at regular intervals as tenants subscribe to new services. It is totally unacceptable to have these routes above sealed ceilings or to need scaffolding to access them.

The risers taking the telecoms services to the office floors must be accessible from common areas, so that new cables can be installed without having to access another tenant's premise. They should also be physically secure. Wherever possible, at least two risers should be provided and they should be in separate cores, in order to prevent a single accident cutting off all communications to all tenants.

Within the office space itself, provision should be made for the tenants to install local equipment rooms. These house both communications equipment and servers, and are in effect mini computer rooms and should be designed as such. Where a tenant occupies multiple floors they will normally require that the equipment rooms on each floor are stacked vertically above each other and connected by risers within the confines of the room.

Major central computer rooms have many special design requirements, and these are often specified by the end user's own IT staff. Typically, they will require the room to be protected from both physical and water damage, hence above ground level locations away from the facade are popular.

The servicing of these rooms is very intense, and should be designed to allow maintenance of all the equipment without having to enter the room. This will often require a corridor around the entire perimeter of the computer room. The huge amount of cables and use of underfloor cooling systems will often require a deep raised floor, a depth of 450 to 600 mm is not unusual. The normal problems of steps or ramps up to this level from the normal finished floor level can take a considerable amount of space, making the room larger.

Cabling for both telephones and data connections to the desks is now relatively straightforward, the days of each manufacturer having its own bespoke cabling system are thankfully long gone. Many building occupiers will now flood wire their buildings – this means cables which can be used for almost any IT purpose are run on a regular grid to all parts of the occupied space. This grid is not run to suit any specific furniture or room layout as it is certain the needs will change constantly in many organisations. This approach to wiring is clearly easiest in offices with raised access floors; it has however also been successfully installed in buildings with flush floor or perimeter trunking cable containment systems.

Standby generation

In many office buildings there will be a statutory requirement to provide an alternative source of electrical power to the normal mains supply. This will typically be required to supply power to fire fighting lifts, smoke extract fans and sprinkler pumps.

In Europe, the most common way of providing this alternative supply is to use a diesel or gas powered standby generator, of these the most common in the UK is the diesel generator. All diesel generators have one set of common defining features: they are noisy, smelly and require large amounts of air to cool them!

If the generator is only to be used in the event of fire, then the noise is unlikely to pose a major problem to the office occupants, although the generator will still be required to be tested from time to time and possible disturbance to neighbours should always be considered.

Some office occupants will require that they can continue their normal business function during a mains power failure. This can vary from just supplying power to the lights and minimal office equipment to supplies to the entire office and all of the mechanical heating and cooling systems. In this latter case the space for the generators, oil storage, ventilation and louvres can be very substantial. Also clearly in this latter case, the noise from the generators cannot be allowed to prevent normal office operation – this often requires specialist acoustic measures to be taken to isolate the generators from both the outside and other parts of the building.

Ancillary systems

Within the field of electrical services there are many miscellaneous systems such as fire alarms, security and CCTV systems, small power and lightning protection systems.

All of these systems will affect the detail design of the building and will need to be carefully co-ordinated with elements such as ceiling and floor systems.

It is important when detailing these elements that the most likely locations of future partitions are considered; in a well designed office it should be possible to erect or demount partitions with little if any modification to the electrical services. If complete flexibility to locate partitions at almost any location is really required, then designing to accommodate this may result in an unnecessarily expensive installation. In this latter case, it may be better to design the systems with minimal initial expenditure but ensure modifications can at least be carried out easily and without damaging ceiling or floor panels.

Passive building design

The principal issues

The aim of passive building design is to moderate external conditions using the building envelope, mass, form and fabric to result in relatively comfortable internal conditions with the minimum of active intervention in the way of heating or cooling. An office building which can be successfully naturally ventilated in summer and simply heated in winter would be a good initial template for a low energy passive design.

For a naturally ventilated office, the principle design aim must be to avoid summertime overheating and the need for air conditioning, largely by consideration of window sizes and shading. Natural ventilation is achieved through openable windows and trickle ventilation at night. Room heights are generous to allow warmer air to rise above the occupied zone and to encourage cross ventilation. The mass of the building is exposed to occupants, either directly or through the use of a perforate false ceiling, providing a heat sink which reduces internal summertime temperature peaks. In the UK this low energy passive design is relatively easy to achieve for shallow plan buildings in quiet locations.

The design gets more complicated if the site is noisy and natural ventilation through openable windows is not possible, but many of the principal design features will remain. Large ducts and silencers might replace openable windows though it should be noted that stack effect, using the buoyancy of warm air to generate movement, results in a very small driving force compared to wind pressure, or a fan. A naturally driven duct will need to be sized for an air velocity of about 1m/sec rather than the 5m/sec typical of a mechanically driven system.

The aim with passive design is first to achieve a maximum overall load on a perimeter office of no more than about 60 W/sq m through control of solar loads. Allowing typical values for occupancy and computer use, the windows must be designed to limit solar gain to about 20 W/sq m which is equivalent to clear glazing at about 16 per cent of the outside facade area. Shading or solar control glass will increase this percentage. As can be seen from the figures given in the section on electrical services, the key issue in passive building design is the control of solar loads.

Occupier issues

What do occupiers really want?

The feedback from occupiers to office designers is not as effective as it could be. For the speculative office the designer may be as much influenced by the developer, the agents and the potential tenant's agents, as by the likely occupiers. The situation with owner-occupied offices is not much better. The owner-occupier will often be unfamiliar with the process of building and will not be in a position to provide considered occupier input at the relevant, early, design stage.

Air conditioned offices currently generate a significantly higher rent than non-air conditioned offices, suggesting that occupiers like air conditioning. At the same time, some buildings appear to generate a contented workforce and others do not. The worst buildings get labelled as 'sick'. Studies of these show little in the way of common failings but dark brown interiors, noticeably tinted windows and working for an unsympathetic employer are best avoided.

The BRE carried out an interesting study of a number of offices in 1995 and asked occupiers for their views on the comfort of their respective offices. The results from *BRE Information Paper IP 3/95* appear at first surprising, but more logical on consideration.

Occupiers were relatively little concerned by actual temperature and humidity levels. On the other hand, they were very concerned about conditions that were not under their control. In the simpler buildings, openable windows were seen as important features. In the air conditioned buildings, simple controls or easy access to a good facilities manager were valued.

The very best satisfaction levels were achieved in a well designed, air conditioned building with a helpful building manager. However, naturally ventilated buildings did well in general and some air conditioned buildings rated very low. Within the results it is possible to detect a trend favouring simple buildings with simple systems, easily understood by both occupiers and maintenance staff. Buildings designed for low energy rated well in the study.

Above all else, the occupiers responded favourably to a feeling of control over their environments. Given some control, the actual internal environmental conditions could vary widely without dissatisfaction.

The paper notes that buildings designed for low energy can incorporate relatively simple heating and cooling systems. They are therefore easier to control and maintain.

If the mechanical systems do go out of commission, conditions in the offices will remain fairly stable.

With the new Part L emphasising the environmental desirability of smaller windows, there is a need for renewed debate with occupiers in relation to window related issues such as glare, comfort, daylight, views in, views out, outside awareness and solar control glazing.

Productivity and building design

I am not aware of productivity tests on identical workforces in different buildings. Any such test would probably grossly affect the office workers' productivity anyway. Arup helped with the design of a major headquarters building in the US, one aim of which was to help achieve a high level of productivity. Shortly after the building was completed the company introduced a new product line and nose dived. It is still recovering. How often does the building of a plush new headquarters signal a change in fortune?

Nevertheless, I find convincing a short paper published in the *Property Journal*[3] on the relationship between buildings and productivity. They simply asked occupiers whether they felt they were productive at work. The results showed a strong correlation with particular buildings. The occupiers of some buildings said they were productive and the occupiers of others said they were not. The paper does not attempt to quantify the effect but I am convinced that it demonstrates the link.

Office occupier preferences and their views on productivity are interesting when considered together. The 1995 BRE Study showed that occupiers liked buildings with the characteristics of those designed for low energy, where the fabric design allowed simple environmental systems through the moderation of external extremes. At the same time occupiers consider some buildings productive and others non-productive.

All building designers and developers should be interested in the link between low energy design, simple environmental systems, good user control, and high productivity.

Global warming, environmental and legislative changes

Lessons in the use of energy over the last 30 years – people adapt

My father joined Shell in 1937. He wondered whether he had made the right decision as the world's known oil reserves amounted to 13 years' production. He contemplated a relatively short career.

---

3 Raw, Roy and Leaman (August 1993), 'Sick Building Syndrome, Productivity Control', *Property Journal.*

I joined the building industry in 1972 during an energy crisis. OPEC had reduced oil production and dramatically increased prices. Big houses and big cars became difficult to sell. Lighting levels which had been expected to rise towards 2000 lux were questioned. Marks & Spencer took every second lamp from their fittings. The expectation was that the standard of living would drop. Until that time, Gross Domestic Product had been closely linked to energy use.

The only certainty in designing buildings was that energy costs would never fall.

Since 1937, new discoveries mean that known oil reserves, in relation to annual production, have continued to rise. It currently stands at about 40 years. Of course, increasingly the remaining oil is from smaller oil fields, from older oil fields, from deeper seas or from unusual sources such as oil sands.

Since 1972, energy costs have fallen and even now, relative to other costs, they are very low. Big houses and four-wheel drive vehicles for the school run are popular. After a brief downturn GDP has continued to rise but it is no longer related directly to energy use.

Lighting levels have continued to fall, encouraged perhaps more by the use of computers than a desire to save lighting costs.

The big lesson from the last 30 years is that people adapt quickly to new circumstances. When energy costs rose, people changed their habits and used less energy. This is recorded in statistics and matches personal experience. During the recent petrol strike did you drive more slowly to conserve fuel? Did you feel you had wasted ten precious minutes on your journey or did you feel quite good about how slowly the fuel gauge went down? Would you add insulation and draught proofing to your house if your annual heating bill was £3,000 rather than £1,000?

The world, and the developed world in particular, must reduce its carbon emissions. Whether it be through a sense of responsibility for the future, fashion, legislation or simply energy costs, a radical change in attitude is required. This does not at first seem an attractive proposition but the reality will surely be that people will relish the challenge once they understand it, quickly adapt to new circumstances and eventually shake their heads as they recall old habits and customs. As always, the successful will be those keeping ahead of the game.

Energy costs against other costs

A large proportion of the energy we consume in this country is used for heating and cooling buildings. To significantly reduce energy use and carbon emissions, the building and transport industries must lead the way. The paradox is that energy costs are relatively low compared to other costs in buildings and by themselves will do little to change habits, unless they rise by a factor of two or three, I suggest.

The proportion of the UK's energy used by buildings is shown in the diagram below.

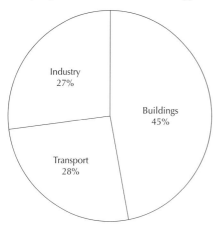

Figure 8: UK's energy use

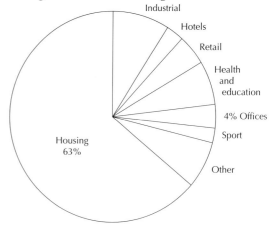

Figure 9: UK building's energy use

The energy use in offices is typically as follows:

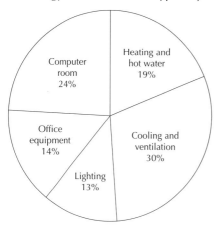

Figure 10: Energy use in a typical office

Energy costs are very dependent on use. It is relatively easy to design buildings which vary in their heating and cooling loads by a factor of three. An office with carefully controlled solar gain might have a cooling requirement in a perimeter office of 60 W/sq m. The same office might have the biggest possible unshaded windows and have a peak cooling load of 180 W/sq m. In practice, it is worse than this threefold increase would suggest. Real office energy costs actually vary by as much as a factor of ten, largely as a result of poor maintenance. This is, of course, more likely if the environmental systems are complicated, with heating systems fighting cooling systems to maintain comfort conditions against the odds.

However, typical energy costs remain relatively low when compared with rents, maintenance and other office costs (*see* Figure 11). It is evident why energy costs, by themselves, are rarely a top priority with building occupiers.

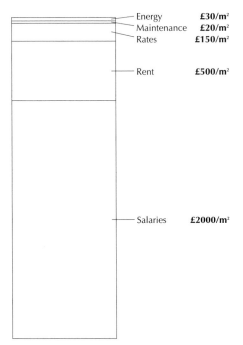

Energy	£30/m²
Maintenance	£20/m²
Rates	£150/m²
Rent	£500/m²
Salaries	£2000/m²

Figure 11: Typical running costs and other office costs

Nevertheless, the evidence in the section on passive building design suggests that designing a building with comfort and low energy as priorities results in offices which are both popular with their users and, in all probability, productive. Not only that but such designs will be well placed in the market if energy costs increase relative to other costs, as seems likely, if not inevitable.

All this makes the new Part L a good thing.

New Part L and beyond

Introduction to Part L

The new Part L requires that fenestration, lighting, building plan form, building slenderness, storey height and building services systems are considered together. These are mutually dependent and changes in any one may prevent compliance. Reasonable provision will need to be made for the conservation of fuel and power in buildings by:

- limiting heat losses and gains through the fabric;
- limiting heat loss from hot water pipes, hot water vessels, air ducts, etc;
- providing energy-efficient heating systems;
- limiting exposure to solar overheating;
- making provision so that air conditioning systems do not use more energy than is reasonable;

- limiting heat gains by chilled water and refrigerant vessels and pipes, air ducts, etc;
- providing energy-efficient lighting systems;
- providing sufficient information so that the building can be operated so as to use no more energy than is reasonable.

Services designers will have to be involved formally in submissions to Building Control. Previously, the architect had been solely responsible. The new rules will result in increased design time, certainly initially and probably even when designers are used to them. Considerably more cross discipline work will be involved, particularly if non-Part L standards are being considered. There are two documents with which the designers of offices will need to become familiar - the *Building Regulations, Approved Document L2, 2002* edition, and *Energy Consumption Guide 19*, (Econ 19). The latter schedules 'typical' and 'good practice' energy consumption figures for four office types, naturally ventilated cellular, naturally ventilated open-plan, air conditioned standard and air conditioned prestige. It is based on early 1990s surveys of a large number of occupied buildings. The aim of the new Part L is to result in buildings within the category defined as good practice.

As with the superseded Part L, there is a certain amount of flexibility in the rules to allow variety in design. There are three 'methods', broadly the same as those in the superseded Part L except that the emphasis is on the carbon emission of the building services rather than on energy.

Elemental Method
The first of the three methods of compliance is the Elemental Method, based on standard U-values of each element and standard percentage areas of windows, roof lights and doors. The values can be increased within maximum limits to allow trade offs between U-values of different elements and their areas. The main changes between the new and superseded document are as follows.

Main Changes L2 (commercial)

2002 edition:
- lower U-values;
- thermal bridging and airtightness requirements;
- avoid solar overheating;
- carbon intensity requirement for heating and air conditioning;
- metering;
- log book for occupants;
- lighting requirements;
- local authorities have right to test on site.

The principal issues for the designers of the building are related to U-values, areas of glazing and airtightness.

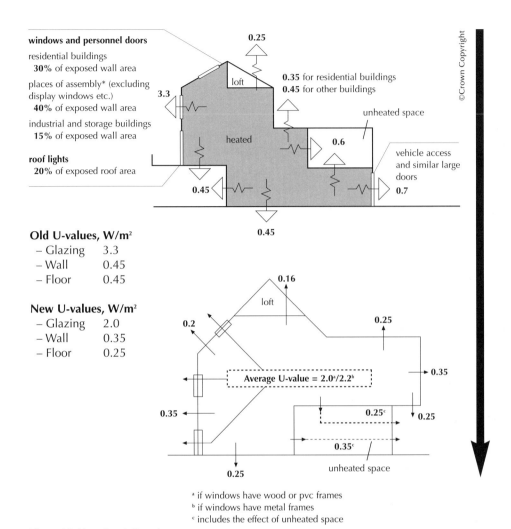

©Crown Copyright

windows and personnel doors

residential buildings
 30% of exposed wall area

places of assembly* (excluding display windows etc.)
 40% of exposed wall area

industrial and storage buildings
 15% of exposed wall area

roof lights
 20% of exposed roof area

0.25

0.35 for residential buildings
0.45 for other buildings

loft

3.3

unheated space

heated

0.6

vehicle access
and similar large
doors

0.45

0.7

0.45

Old U-values, W/m²
 – Glazing   3.3
 – Wall   0.45
 – Floor   0.45

New U-values, W/m²
 – Glazing   2.0
 – Wall   0.35
 – Floor   0.25

0.16

loft

0.2

0.25

0.35

Average U-value = 2.0ᵃ/2.2ᵇ

0.35

0.25ᶜ

0.25

0.35ᶜ

0.25

unheated space

ᵃ if windows have wood or pvc frames
ᵇ if windows have metal frames
ᶜ includes the effect of unheated space

Figure 12: New Part L Requirements

The maximum percentage areas of openings (windows) as a percentage of the exposed wall are 40 per cent for windows and 20 per cent for rooflights. Trade-off between construction elements to provide design flexibility is allowed, taking into account the heating system efficiency.

The required U values for a window is 2.2 W/sq m°C, if it is metal framed, and 2.0 W/sq m°C if UPVC framed. To meet the standard value may require the use of argon filled low-e double-glazed units. Designers may need to choose between more expensive argon filled units or slightly smaller windows.

Whole Building Method
The Whole Building Method requires that the Carbon Performance Rating (CPR), of the total services installation should not exceed tabulated benchmarks for this

method, again based on Econ 19. The Building Research Establishment has published a detailed methodology for the calculation. It allows greater flexibility than the trade-offs of the Elemental Method.

The detailed methodology, defined by the regulations, for the calculation of energy use and carbon emissions provides a firm framework for the analysis and approval of alternative building designs and systems.

The methodology appears to allow considerable scope for the adjustment of glazing areas and other design issues outside the norms defined by the Elemental Method, especially for deep plan buildings

Carbon Emissions Calculation Method
The Carbon Emissions Calculation Method requires the carbon emissions to be no greater than those from a 'reference building', designed exactly to the Elemental Method standard values, serviced in the same way, and analysed by the same method. It allows account to be taken of solar gains and internal gains, but in both the actual and reference buildings, the maximum U-values and air leakage again must not exceed those of the elemental method.

The regulations do not define the calculation methodology and this will add significantly to the risks associated with the approval of unusual designs by this method. Not only will the design team need to define the building and its services in more detail and at an earlier stage than is now generally the case; but Building Control will need to understand and agree the methodology, at least in principle.

Climate change levy

The climate change levy is a levy on energy costs related to the overall efficiency of the production and transmission of energy sources: elements, gas, oil, etc.

It is already adding about 15 per cent to energy costs and the levy has been set up so that future increases can be made relatively easily.

The future

The most obvious and immediate change in office design generated by the new Part L is likely to be a reduction in areas of glazing. Part L restricts the use of glazing to reduce both heat loss and heat gain. Multiple panes of glass and shading will allow areas of glazing to be increased accordingly but the cost of these may restrict their application.

Whether designers choose to work within the glazing area restrictions defined by the new Part L or whether they choose to prove compliance by the whole building or carbon emissions method, the areas of glazing in office building will be under intense scrutiny. As the most variable and biggest air conditioning load, it is the most significant in determining the thermal comfort, system size, system complexity and energy costs of many office buildings. It is also, of course, hugely significant in determining the visual interest for occupants and the image of the building inside and out.

Part L is a push in the direction of a more sustainable future. Whether office design responds to the push or reacts against it remains to be seen. After an initial reaction, I anticipate, and hope, for a positive response.

Author profiles

Mark Facer BA (Cantab) Engineering, IMechE, Chartered Engineer, Director
Arup

Mark Facer is a Director of Arup and is based in London where he leads a multidisciplinary design group. Since joining Arup, in 1972, he has been responsible for the mechanical services design of a wide variety of new and refurbishment projects in the UK and abroad.

Significant City of London office projects include Embankment Place and Moor House (currently on site) for Greycoat, and Governors House and Aldercastle, for Argent. He has been responsible for several of the offices at Brindleyplace in Birmingham, also for Argent.

Abroad, Mark had a key role in developing the design of the huge Eastgate speculative office project in Harare which successfully uses night time ventilation in lieu of air conditioning in the heart of Africa.

Julian Olley CEng MIEE BSc (Hons), Director
Arup

Julian Olley is a Director specialising in the multidisciplinary design of offices, commercial, and refurbishment projects requiring extensive building services installations. The projects he has led include base build, refurbishment and fit out of headquarters and financial services trading buildings.

Julian has spent the last ten years leading multidisciplinary teams and aims to bring to all projects the benefits that can be realised by close integration of the different design and construction disciplines.

His particular technical skills include all aspects of power distribution, standby and mains conditioning systems, vertical transportation, as well as site services such as high voltage generation and distribution.

Recent Projects include: Moor House – a speculative office development in the city of London, HSBC London HQ, West LB, and 120 Fleet Street.

13 Vertical transport

Peter Boardman
Dunbar & Boardman

Lifts and escalators

While architects have to balance aesthetic and urban considerations with the client's requirements prior to detail design, the lift and escalator consultants have a different set of priorities. As part of a team we are simultaneously dealing with a number of more basic building related issues. Our primary function is collectively making the building-investment economics stand up. With too few lifts and escalators, the circulation fails and the rental levels suffer; too many lifts and we take too much space and the rental income will drop as a result. It goes without saying that the core property investment is also effected.

Of course, equally important is the focus and management of the thousands of people and visitors to the building in question. Essentially, lifts and escalators form natural lines of communication, ensuring that the building ticks harmoniously through its existence. Once these fundamentals are set, the detail design can begin.

However, vertical transportation does give the architectural world the opportunity to make striking features, as in such cases as the glazed cars in the Lloyds building in London and the escalator/lift combination in the Hongkong Shanghai Banking Corporation building in Hong Kong.

Up to standard

The present British Standard for lifts is known as BSEN 81, with part 1 for traction equipment and part 2 for hydraulic equipment. The modernisation of lifts is still carried out under BS 5655 part 11 for traction lifts; however this standard is about to be superseded in 2003/4.

Requirements for fire-fighting lifts are encompassed in the British Standard BS 5588. The principle criteria for the provision of these lifts are: travel above ground floor (or fire access level) in excess of 18 m, travel to basements in excess of 9.5 m or a single area 900 m square at any level above ground. There should be a minimum of one eight-person 630 kg capacity with Class O finishes within a travel distance of 30 m – 40 m from each other depending on the route for hose reels.

Traffic guidance

Waiting time is a function of the 'system interval'. These terms are often confused. Interval times should not exceed 25 seconds to meet particular client requirements and 30 seconds as the general norm. The amount of passenger traffic transported is described as 'handling capacity' and measured as a percentage over five minutes.

British Standards advise that, for a multi-let property, a lift system should handle 12 per cent of the building population above the main floor in five minutes. Significantly, it also states that for a single-let property, the lifts should move 17 per cent of the population over the same period. However, the British Council for Offices (BCO) (www.bco.org.uk) does not make this differentiation and advises 15 per cent handling capacity whatever the nature of the tenancy. For clarity, the worst case scenario is a single let property with lunchtime traffic and staff restaurant situated at a high level.

It is easy to fall into the trap of considering a multi-let property as simply a building with more than one tenant. In fact, if a collection of the tenants occupy more than two floors which represents a significant critical mass, or potentially a 'head office' function for individual tenants, thus creating significant inter-floor traffic. Therefore, lift traffic, in turn, increases demands on the system and lightens service expectations. This then becomes a special case and should therefore be considered to be a 'single tenant' scenario.

For 'tall' buildings a slightly different methodology applies, as discussed below.

In summary, the entire subject of lift traffic hinges on the perceived density of occupation. Architects can often be wise before the event and opt for a lightly populated space. The BCO follows suit and considers up to 14 sq m per person as a base line whereas 10-12 sq m per person would be a wiser choice, thus introducing sufficient flexibility for the life of the building. Visit www.dunbarboardman.com for further information on the subject.

Beam me up Scottie!

Well, not quite but a step in that direction. *Destination Based Control Systems* have arrived.

It is normal for conventional lift installations to be 'called' by up and down buttons from each landing entrance. Assuming a given lift car has available capacity, the nearest lift will stop to a call, the passengers enter and a floor is selected. The journey is shared with a random number of people to a selected number of floors. This system of vertical transportation is how the industry has developed and, indeed, this has worked reasonably well thus far. However, with the advent of computerisation, it has been possible to develop a system that is hypothetically better than the system described above.

Instead of standing at a landing and advising the system which direction one intends to travel, the passenger informs the system of one's intended destination via a key pad/touch screen. The control system evaluates the known demand on the one hand and groups together individuals that require travel to the same destination, optimising the service accordingly.

When one places the destination on the landing key pad/screen, a particular lift will be displayed, say, A, B, C, D, E or F (for a group of six lifts) and the individuals will walk to that lift. When the car arrives to intercept the passengers they will enter the car and no further buttons are pressed. The car will simply take the passengers to their destination.

The up peak 'interval' for the whole building will not necessarily improve but the 'handling capacity' is significantly enhanced. Conversely, where the car capacity remains under-utilised or when deployed in existing buildings, the resultant improvement will be noticed in the 'system interval' and therefore 'waiting' times generally.

A perceived drawback of this service is not so much the system in itself as the confusion that may be created by the people who will use it. The concept is counter to anyone's normal experience of operating a lift and as such there may be a prejudice against the idea. However, the application of 'touch screens', now an everyday used technology, has broken down the barriers of concern. Another advantage is that the screens can be located away from the lift shaft walls (giving the system further advance knowledge of users), they are easy to use, attractive and can also display a company's logo or other information.

Keeping in step

Staircases can provide a useful function in the planning process for vertical transportation strategy. They should be accessible in their location and will divert traffic away from the lift cores. Attractive processional staircases can have a life of their own, in terms of design and function.

In short, the quality of staircases and their accessibility can draw high levels of traffic which can avert expenditure for the provision of additional lifts. Since lifts travel though the building, the use of staircases at lower levels increase the net lettable office space at higher floors. Podium floors and mixed use leisure areas are good examples of stair usage in conjunction with the provision of escalators, referred to below.

Standard lift equipment

Loved by quantity surveyors and tolerated by architects, standard lifts do have a purpose as they provide cost-effective solutions for most buildings. However, the designer must adhere to the sizes stated in the manufacturer's documentation.

Remember that the dimensions given are 'clear plumb' and tolerances should be added, usually 50-100 mm, depending on the type of construction method and height of the building.

As a general rule, lift companies often show the minimum size that they can work within, which often conflicts with their competitors. Choosing one particular design early on reduces the tendering options at a later stage.

Secondary lift systems, such as fire-fighting lifts, goods lifts and disabled access systems can all be dealt with quite adequately by standard solutions.

Standard glazed cars are available from some of the larger manufactures but inevitably will come with their design limitations.

Hydraulic lifts

Historically, hydraulic lifts provided an easy solution for the low-rise market and are a potential answer to planning issues on mid-rise developments. The general problem is that once hydraulic lifts are supplied in a busy office or hotel, or serves over six floors, then reliability problems will occur with greater frequency. Explore the other options as your first choice. The future will prove to be the expansion of the range of machine room-less lifts referred to below.

For special applications such as car lifts, hydraulic lifts will continue to be used. These will be provided by the smaller supplier companies as the larger multi-nationals concentrate on higher volume mass-produced equipment.

Hydraulic lifts cars are moved through the shaft by a ram located either beneath the car (direct acting) or a ram situated in the shaft (side acting). However, the direct-acting system is now frowned upon, because of the requirement for an annual corrosion/defect inspection.

Travelling speeds are limited to a maximum of 1 m/s with cooling, and flight times are slow, as there is a need to start the pump and wait for the increase in hydraulic pressure before the lift can move.

However, the hydraulic market may fight back for a limited time with series of new applications, but this may prove to be too little too late.

Eliminate the machine room

Skipping the machine room altogether is an architect's dream. We can now have lifts that fit into standard shafts with no need for the machine room, remote or otherwise. Kone developed the concept and hold the patent for the term 'machine room-less' lifts. Other companies, however, have developed similar products: Otis with its Gen2,

Schindler with the Mobile, and Thyssen with a similar range. Some of the independent companies can buy generic products that achieve the same result.

The concept is that the lift machine is housed at the shaft head and the controller is either located adjacent, in the shaft, or on the top-floor landing. All other elements of the lift design remain the same. The present application for the range is mainly up to ten floors at speeds of between 1 m/s and 1.6 m/s.

For modernisation applications, Kone is the only company at present to offer any solutions. Its 'Monospace' product, re-engineered as 'Fury' offers variable geometry to suit most shaft applications in the capacity ranges of four to 13 persons.

It should perhaps go without saying that this type of product will replace hydraulic lifts where the latter are presently under-performing in terms of speed or reliability.

The waiting game

Although lifts and escalators are designed to a given standard design, the actual manufacture is 'to order'. The engineering of a particular scheme is only relevant to non-standard solutions and hence the lift industry's requirement for extended contract lead times. Current demand in the European market means that lead times are 16 weeks for smaller high volume products, including escalators, 20 weeks for standard lifts and 26 weeks for bespoke equipment and solutions.

With the building industry responding faster to client requests, the lift industry is increasingly out of step. This increases the pressure on property professionals, so we all need to think ahead and deal with the lift and escalator planning in the early stages of the project.

Modular systems

For projects requiring fast installation, modular systems can provide the solution. The machine room, each floor and the pit section are built off-site. They are then delivered and installed on a timely basis and the equipment is either 'moth-balled' or commissioned depending on the building's state of completion. The advantage is that the lifts can be delivered within the shaft enclosure and the interface with the other trades is minimal. Also, the equipment is assembled in a factory environment and the final product is therefore improved.

The downside is that it can be seen to be more expensive. The key to the equation is the building's structure costs. If the building can be designed to be structurally sound without the lift shafts being an integral element then the modular system can be designed accordingly. Shaft cladding costs can also be duplicated.

A design team will either see the collective benefits to make the concept work or choose to see the complications and bury the idea.

Glazed expression

None of the manufacturers sells, as a standard, whole glazed front-wall enclosures but they are available from Selcom, Sematic and others. Look at Links www.wittur.com and www.sematic.com

Dunbar & Boardman have successfully used these designs in buildings with atrium spaces and shopping centres.

Picking the environs

Lift cars are the area that all architects can influence. Adding a bespoke stone floor can prove to be expensive as it may require upgrading the lift machine and safety gear systems. However, a stone design (usually a tile) chosen from the manufacturer's range can be accommodated within the base design. Establishing the requirements early on and not being constrained by other members of the team is the key to your design freedom.

Short lead times and highly specialised designs force the lift companies to use smaller fabricators with high levels of success. However, the architect or the consultant do need to take a great level of interest to ensure the product is as expected.

Finishing touches

With pushes and other operating fixtures, try to use the manufacturers standard if you want the contractors' costs to remain in the realms of normality. The contractors often sub-contract the work to which 'overhead' and profit is applied.

However, there are specialists that support the industry. CE Electronics, www.ceelectronics.com and Dewhurst, www.dewhurst.co.uk are examples of well known suppliers to the market, at reasonable cost.

There are a number of new developments in information systems that are now available for lift cars. The larger companies have formed links with technology and media groups to supply news and other sales platforms that can be tuned to the user's requirements. The idea is that the technology will generate an income for the client, possibly off-setting the costs of lift maintenance.

It is also possible to install flat-screen televisions complete with sound systems blasting MTV or worse. Bloomberg or other information channels are popular in the 'City' district of London.

Going up

High-rise towers

Some of us are privileged to have had the opportunities to be involved in high-rise towers, that is buildings of more than 50 storeys or 150 m high.

Other than in the central business district of cities, I believe that the only inner city high-rise buildings to gain planning permission will be mixed use and mainly residential at the top (serving a local need), with an office zone towards the middle and retail at the ground floor zone, with car parking beneath. This scenario represents one of the most diverse requirements for vertical transportation.

Up to 60 levels it is possible to 'elevate' buildings conventionally with a series of single-deck lifts, each bank serving elements of the building for the particular interest of residential, office and the like. Above this number of levels, one may consider double or triple-deck cars, depending on the office content of a given scheme with sky lobby stop-off points or some form of interchange at, say, every 25-30 floors. This will usually mesh with mechanical/plant zones.

The ultra high-rise 'tall' schemes (more than 150 levels) may require non-conventional systems that can transport more than one car per shaft and permit cars to travel horizontally, form one shaft to another. The technology for this is available we simply have to await the commercial opportunity to use it. The manufacturer, Otis have developed one concept, known as the Odyssey system but other companies are investigating the situation.

The escalators angle

They come in all sizes and two fundamental angles. They are available from 600 mm in width (which is too narrow), but a minimum width of 800 mm is recommended. Escalators 1000 mm wide are best suited to retail environment and 1200 mm wide escalators can be found in some airports, particularly in the flat passenger walkway version. These devices are best deployed where a high volume of passenger traffic management is required or low-level large floor plates are to be served.

To increase the levels of safety only specify 30-degree escalators, unless particular site conditions warrant otherwise. It is also possible to specify a balustrade height of 1100 mm to align with the building's balustrades. Further, the practise of off-setting one of the balustrades is a useful mechanism for crowd and congestion management.

Escalators that are to be located in exposed areas can be specified accordingly. Such features will include galvanised trusses, waterproof switches, heating, and lubrication systems.

There are a number of recent innovations that have been mainly architecturally driven, mainly in the form of more glass, mirrors and improved lighting.

An information system is about to be launched, with the duel purpose of communicating safety messages and create advertising opportunities for the owners. Architecturally, the practice is questionable, unless tastefully and sensitively co-ordinated.

Finally, check the after sales service and agree good response times.

Modern ethics

By the end of 2004, The Disabilities Discrimination Act will require all buildings to be made accessible to disabled people. Part M of the Building Regulations is the standard to be referred to.

Larger lift companies have subsidiary interests in this area. However, for specialised access solutions refer to www.uk-lift.co.uk and www.stannah.co.uk

Quality benchmarks

Ride quality is measured in a number of ways – not quite as shake-rattle-and-roll but quake, jerk and a general measurement of background noise. Kone and Otis are the leading Western manufacturers promoting these issues, but if you intend to pursue these issues then be prepared to pay for them and have access to the measurement tools to quantify the results.

The quality of lift system response times has been referred to above. Jerk rates (the rate of change of acceleration) and the acceleration can be pre-set. These issues generally affect performance and the qualitative aspects of ride quality. As these potentially compete with each other, a balance needs to be established to achieve sensible values.

Once the equipment is installed, reliability levels can be agreed and, if required, penalties can be written into the maintenance contract.

Commissioning and signing-off the project

Checking the product and putting the equipment through its paces before the project is handed over is the duty of the specifying consultant. The commissioning process is the important last check that all is well – or not – enabling the consultant Personal Indemnity Insurance to remain intact. Many safety devices are factory tested but can fail once installed on-site. Some tests can highlight borderline situations, which may just go unnoticed without the presence of a 'referee'.

It is also important to check that the machine room does not overheat and is adequately illuminated. With modern traction equipment the temperature issue is now less of a problem but the matter remains important for hydraulic installations. Lighting is an important health and safety item.

Maintenance thereafter

There is a legal duty to maintain equipment once it is installed and for this to be independently inspected twice a year.

Good reliability is a reflection of the quality of manufacture and installation process. It also ensures a happy end user, and potentially gains a future client or retains the one you had in the first instance. However, the best intentions of the building process can be unravelled by poor maintenance after the event, or shoddy administration of this process.

Therefore, after sales service should be a key part of the initial evaluation. There are many types of maintenance contracts, each of which can be modified to your requirements. Keep the records up to date.

An idea of costs

Standard lifts can be a cost-effective method of procurement for new construction projects. Modernised lifts are by their nature a bespoke or individually specified solution and can still be cost effective as the building work can be reduced to a minimum, e.g. retaining existing entrances.

Evaluate the options before committing to a given solution. Question your advisors to give you confidence of their knowledge of the subject matter. For larger projects, test the market!

To assist the evaluation of tenders the following table is intended as an aide-mémoire. Non-compliance with a given element may have an impact of cost. Compare like with like.

Table 1 Evaluation of tenders; listing elements for compliance

Contractor	A	B	C	D
Bid fully compliant with your requirements? Type, car size, speed, etc?				
Tender price build up Contract preliminaries Compliance with CDM Regulations Notified body approvals Lift design, manufacture, etc? Lift cars and finishes Maintenance during DLP Builders and electrical works Retention bond Provisional sum for contingencies				
Total (£)				
Optional costs (£) Additional per person costs for factory inspection				
Maintenance price (£) Comprehensive maintenance after expiry of DLP				
LEIA index at time of tender Contracts Maintenance				

Summary of websites

The 'major' lift and escalator companies within the market will be known to the reader. However, a few of the specialists referred to above are:

www.alimak.se
Rack and pinion lifts.

www.ceelectronics.com
Bespoke operating and information systems.

www.dewhurst.co.uk
Operating systems – pushes; etc.

www.dunbarboardman.com
Lift, escalator and mechanical handling consultants.

www.gartec.com
Disabled access systems.

www.sematic.com
Doors and entrance systems.

www.stannah.co.uk
Disabled access systems; goods, service and residential lifts.

www.uk-lift.co.uk
Specialist access solutions.

www.wittur.com
Control systems and entrances.

Author profile

Peter Boardman, Director
Dunbar & Boardman

Peter Boardman joined the lift industry from school in 1970. After completing a formal apprenticeship and gained a technician's qualification from Bolton Institute of Technology continued working for Express Lifts in various technical and management roles. After a short period in consultancy Peter formed his own consultants practice with Henry Dunbar in 1981. Dunbar & Boardman has grown progressively throughout the intervening period and now operates from eight location and is affiliated with consultants in the USA.

Dunbar & Boardman is now an accepted part of the property market and building design fraternity and is considered to be a leader in its field of expertise. Notably, Peter has worked on the Jumeria Beach / Burj al Arab developments in Dubai and China World Trade Centre in Beijing. In addition, he deals with the day-to-day business of a growing practice and undertakes expert witness duties, from time to time.

14 Architectural acoustics for offices

Malcolm Wright
Arup

Architectural acoustics

To provide an environment for people that is just 'pleasant', or to meet specific criteria for particular purposes, requires control over sound, or noise, and vibration. Whereas the terms 'sound' and 'noise' are often used as synonyms it is usual to think of noise as unwanted sound, rather like weeds are considered to be unwanted plants, although what is one person's sound may well be another's noise. Too little sound may be as much of a problem as too much noise, e.g. where steady, unobtrusive sound inside masks intrusive noise from outside.

Acousticians seek to control the aural environment to match the needs or expectations of the end users. This also entails the control of vibration, which may be disturbing itself and may also be manifested as noise.

Seeking acoustic advice early in the design process often avoids the juxtaposition of noise and vibration producing spaces and sensitive spaces, and the avoidance of difficult and costly solutions. For example, not locating a hotel loading-bay over the conference facilities can save the acoustician's fee several times over, as expensive floated structures and resiliently isolated constructions are avoided.

Alternatively, an acoustician can supply the advice necessary for the planning of several sensitive and sound producing facilities into a restricted site.

This chapter cannot be considered to be a replacement for an acoustician but it does seek to provide a comprehensive review of target acoustic design criteria for office buildings and the major factors that need consideration in achieving them.

In addition the following aspects are included:

- the external environment – building envelope sound insulation and noise emission;
- the office environment – cellular and open plan;
- plant rooms;
- base build and fit-outs;
- multi-tenanted buildings;

- the unconventional;
- and a quick acoustics check-list.

Introduction

The selection of an appropriate acoustic environment for different areas in an office development is guided by the use, or uses, of the space and the volume. Essentially, all the subsequent acoustic design can be traced back to achieving suitable criteria relating to these factors. The use of a space will determine a suitable range for the acoustic design criteria; the volume of the space will fix the criteria within that range.

Satisfying the selected criteria will be dependent on a number of related design issues, including:

- the activities within the space, including equipment;
- external noise sources, such as road and rail traffic or aircraft noise;
- external vibration sources, such as road and rail traffic;
- noise levels from building services serving the space and in adjacent plant locations;
- internal sound insulation from partitions, floors, ceilings, doors, etc.;
- the nature and geometry of architectural finishes.

The challenges in maintaining appropriate acoustic conditions in modern offices result from changing approaches to the concept of what an office should be, the trend to lighter weight structural solutions, the desire for more environmentally friendly building services and the higher densities of occupation and activities – both within the office building and outside.

Neighbouring environment

Office buildings are often exposed to high noise levels from road, rail and air traffic as well as to the increasing possibility of perceptible vibration and structure-borne noise. A close proximity to main transport routes or transport interchanges, etc. requires assessment of likely residual noise and vibration within the completed development and comparison with selected design criteria, followed by appropriate mitigation measures.

Airborne sound insulation

The airborne sound insulation requirements of the building envelope are derived from ambient noise data, measured around the site. A noise survey is also important, prior to demolition and construction, to demonstrate that the effects of new developments, or modifications to existing ones, do not justify noise nuisance claims. To provide sufficient data for building envelope design and to enable appropriate noise emission limits to be set, it may be necessary for the survey to cover a 24-hour period. If the environment of the site is to be significantly changed by the development it may also be necessary to modify the measured data to cater for significant changes in the mix and quantity of road traffic and other noise sources.

The residual external noise levels in internal spaces must be controlled by the sound insulation of the building envelope but it is unnecessary to reduce the external noise to inaudibility. The residual levels can be related to absolute levels, as given in BS 8233.[1]

The building envelope is selected to reduce external noise to a level that, when combined with the building services noise, will be in the following ranges:

- Open plan offices   45 – 50 dBL$_{Aeq,T}$
- Cellular offices   40 – 45 dBL$_{Aeq,T}$
- Conference rooms   35 – 45 dBL$_{Aeq,T}$ (subject to size*)

* the greater the distance between the speaker and the listener the lower the criterion should be.

See end of chapter for a description of acoustic terminology.

Previous to 1998 if the Building Research Establishment Environmental Assessment Method (BREEAM)[2] credit for indoor noise was sought, the low end of the dBL$_{Aeq,T}$ ranges given above had be met. Since 1998 it is necessary only to meet the recommendations of BS 8233, and the ranges given above will satisfy these.

The specification for the building envelope performance should often include octave band sound reduction indices, particularly at low frequencies, to cater for dominant frequencies in the external noise. The octave band requirements can be determined using the following approach. Previous experience has shown that with predominantly road traffic noise (as described by the noise level exceeded for ten per cent of the time, i.e. L$_{10}$) the residual external noise can exceed the building services noise (as described by the noise rating, i.e. NR).

1 BS 8233: 1999. *Sound insulation and noise reduction for buildings. Code of practice*, British Standards Institution.
2 Building Research Establishment Environmental Assessment Method, *BREEAM Offices*, September 1998, Building Research Establishment.

The acceptable excesses are given in Table 1, and illustrated by applying to a building services noise criterion of NR35:

Table 1 Acceptable noise excesses

	Octave band centre frequency, Hz							
	63	**125**	**250**	**500**	**1k**	**2k**	**4k**	**8k**
Building services criterion, NR35	63	52	45	39	35	32	30	28
Acceptable excesses of external noise, L_{10}	+5	+4	+2	+3	+3	+3	+3	+3
Maximum residual external noise, L_{10}	68	56	47	42	38	35	33	31

Where the external noise is dominated by road traffic the relationship between L_{10} and L_{eq} can be taken as:

$$L_{eq} \approx L_{10} - 3 \text{ dB}$$

It has been found that when external noise is controlled in this way it is audible but remains below the level at which it is disruptive, and it is also reasonably compatible with the recommendations of BS 8233.

Both of these approaches should lead to indoor ambient noise levels that allow easy verbal communication between people at distances appropriate to the use of the space.

The choice of materials for the building envelope will influence the maximum sound insulation that can be achieved. Concrete, stone and brick used in traditional constructions are capable of substantially higher sound insulation than curtain walling systems and lightweight roofing systems, and they usually provide better low frequency performance. This is important as traffic noise is usually dominant in the lower frequencies.

Curtain walling systems often consist of large areas of glazing with minimal areas of mullion and spandrel. Even the highest performance sealed, double glazed unit can only reach about R_w47, whereas when the lightweight spandrels and mullions are allowed for a maximum performance of R_w45 might be more realistic, even with every effort being made to maintain the overall performance. A heavyweight, wet wall solution can reach R_w55, and with reduced areas of window can achieve a similar performance to the highest performance curtain walling system, using a glass construction with a lower performance.

A thermal, double glazed construction of 6 mm glass, 12 mm air gap and 6 mm glass, which is often specified for facade systems, is expected to have a sound insulation performance of not more than Rw33. This may be quite inadequate to maintain the selected internal design targets when the building is in a busy urban environment. It is also important to understand that the noise exposure on the face of a building may not reduce with height. As the elevation of the facade increases it is exposed to more noise sources, i.e. greater lengths of the adjacent roads and neighbouring roads that are not visible at ground level. Sometimes the noise level can increase with height, although as it consists of mixed multiple sources it can be less aggressive in character.

Lightweight roofing systems can provide a wide range of sound insulating performances which can, in Rw terms, perform better than a reinforced concrete roof slab – although these can be costly and at octave bands of 125 Hz and below, are likely to perform less well than a concrete slab. This is particularly important when considering the exclusion of noise from roof mounted mechanical services equipment, as well as traffic noise.

The ability to use naturally ventilated, or mixed mode, building service systems is often limited as adding attenuation to the air routes through the facade also adds resistance to air flow. In busy urban environments maintaining the relatively high sound insulation necessary from facades that face onto busy thoroughfares reduces the natural ventilation available to amounts that are ineffective. Dependence on openable windows for ventilation also results in little control over external noise.

It may be appropriate to accept higher internal noise levels in naturally ventilated offices, although the client (this may be the developer or occupier) must be made aware of the implications of this.

Vibration and structure-borne noise control

The control of perceptible vibration and structure-borne noise in a development requires a vibration survey of the site, from which the various coupling losses to and amplification in the structure can be applied and the residual levels assessed. The residual levels when compared to design targets may indicate the necessity to structurally isolate part, or all, of the building to limit the effects to acceptable levels.

Vibration levels in office areas, as a result of internal and external sources, should be limited to Curve 4 of BS 6472.[3] More sensitive spaces may require a better standard.

3 BS 6472: 1992. *Guide to evaluation of human exposure to vibration in buildings (1 Hz to 80 Hz)*, British Standards Institution.

Structure-borne noise, i.e. noise generated in the building resulting from vibration of adjacent road or rail traffic, etc should be limited so that the maximum level regenerated should not exceed the following criteria:

- Open plan offices   50 – 55 dBL$_{Amax, (slow)}$
- Cellular offices   45 – 50 dBL$_{Amax, (slow)}$
- Conference rooms   40 – 45 dBL$_{Amax, (slow)}$ (subject to size)

These limits have been derived from involvement in many projects and found to be satisfactory.

Elastomers and helical steel springs have been used in bearing assemblies to isolate buildings from adjacent vibration sources. The design of bearings should result in a natural frequency sufficiently below the dominant frequency of the disturbing vibration to give the necessary isolation, and limit the bearing deflections to avoid constructional complications.

Figure 1 shows one of the spring isolation assemblies installed beneath the Bridgewater Concert Hall, Manchester to reduce the effects of the adjacent Metrolink light rail system. Although this example is for a performance building there are many isolated office buildings near, or over, rail systems.

Figure 1: Spring isolation assemblies at Bridgewater Concert Hall (flexible 'skirt' which protects springs raised for photograph only).

It is vital that there are no rigid connections across the line of the building isolation, linking the isolated and un-isolated parts of the structure. In particular, care must be taken with the routing and support of the building services as these offer great potential for degrading the isolation.

Noise emission to the neighbouring environment

Noise emissions from the development itself also need to be limited to levels that are appropriate to the surrounding environment so that they do not lead to noise nuisance claims. The local authority usually has standard conditions to be complied with, often based upon BS 4142.[4] This standard gives a method for rating industrial noise affecting mixed residential and industrial areas but it is used as a yardstick against which the effect of new noise sources can be assessed.

Usually, local authorities will have an established policy for noise limitation in the standard planning conditions. If it does not, controlling the noise emissions from the development to a level 5 dB(A) less than the existing background noise level (described by the L_{A90}), through the operational period of the new noise sources, will ensure that there is an imperceptible increase in the background noise. If the new noise sources are tonal or impulsive the noise emission limit should be 10 dB(A) less than the existing background to compensate for the character. It is advisable to agree the approach with the local authority in the early stages of design.

Office environment

Offices need an environment that enables reliable communication between people whilst intrusive speech from adjacent areas is screened. The provision of this condition requires consideration of a number of design elements.

Background noise

The control of background noise is important as within an appropriate band it allows reliable speech communication at moderate distance but screens residual speech from adjacent areas. Residual external noise and building services noise combine to give the background noise and this should be tailored to the type of space. In open plan office space a higher background noise level is desirable than in cellular offices or in a boardroom. Examples of suitable building services noise levels are given in a number of standard texts, including BS 5720[5] and the *Guide to Current Practice* from the Chartered Institution of Building Services Engineers[6], and some common examples are given below:

- Open plan offices   NR38
- Cellular offices   NR35

4 BS 4142: 1997. *Method for rating industrial noise affecting mixed residential and industrial areas*, British Standards Institution.

5 BS 5720: 1979. Code of practice for mechanical ventilation and air conditioning in buildings, British Standards Institution.

6 Chartered Institution of Building Services Engineers, *CIBSE Guide A Table 1.17*, 1999.

- Conference rooms   NR25 – 35 (subject to size)
- Entrance halls and toilets   NR40

Providing there are no other contributing noise sources, the noise ratings given above should be determined by L_{eq} octave band measurements. Should other, intermittent noise sources be present, L_{90} octave band measurements will remove the influence of these and indicate the steady, underlying building services noise.

It is important to realise that conditioning systems that rely on reducing amounts of air to cater for reduced loads also result in reduced background noise. In some circumstances, where maintenance of the background noise is essential, it may be necessary to consider the use of a masking sound system to compensate for this effect. For mixed mode systems the background noise from mechanical components may only be available for part of the time.

Masking sound can be provided unintentionally by a variety of means, e.g. the cooling fans of computer processors, aerators in aquaria, recorded music, water features, etc but ideally should be broad band, bland sound very similar to well designed air conditioning noise. This is usually produced by a distributed sound system, which provides an even spread of unintrusive, shaped sound that is usually not noticeable, unless switched off during occupancy. Self-contained masking sound units, consisting of sound source, amplifier, loudspeaker, etc. are available which enable localised treatment where the control of larger areas is not justified.

Office acoustic

The control of reverberant noise in offices spaces is an integral part of environmental control and is traditionally provided by carpet and an acoustically absorptive ceiling finish. The increasing use of passive services systems that rely on the exposure of a significant part of the concrete soffit severely limits this control. The effect is most marked in open plan arrangements where the general reverberant noise can build up and the acoustically hard ceilings can result in greater propagation of intelligible speech between workstations, regardless of the screening arrangement. The geometry of the exposed soffit can also contribute to unwanted reflections and focusing. This should be reviewed in the early stages of design. It is usually necessary to include some acoustic absorption at high level to limit the impact of the omission of the 'standard' absorptive suspended ceiling and this can be provided by patterns of vertically hung acoustic panels or integrating absorptive elements into light fittings. The illustration below shows a cross section of the luminaire installed in the new Arup Campus office, Solihull.

Nevertheless, the effects of these approaches do not usually provide the same control as a suspended absorptive ceiling.

Perforated sheet metal 'wings'
overlaid with acoustic absorbtion

330 mm

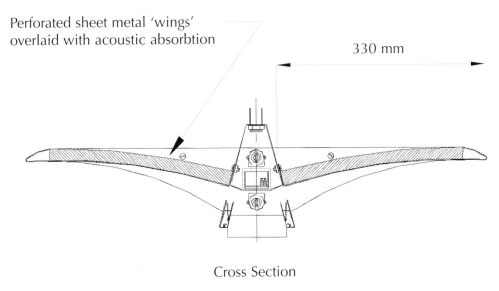

Cross Section

Figure 2: Cross section of luminaire installed at Arup Campus office, Solihull

Figure 3: Luminaire in situ

Other factors involved in adequate acoustic separation between adjacent offices or between adjacent workstations in an open plan arrangement are as follows.

Adjacent offices

The standard of privacy between adjacent offices results from a combination of the sound insulation maintained between the spaces (or sound level difference) and the background noise level. The background noise level is important because it screens the residual speech levels from the adjacent office, after it has been reduced by the sound insulation between.

A general indication of the standard of privacy obtained between two offices can be obtained by comparing the sum of the NR from the building services noise in the room of the listener and the weighted level difference between the offices (i.e. D_w) with the subjective descriptions below:

Speech at normal voice levels	D_w + NR
Intelligible	< 65
Audible, could be intelligible if the speaker and/or the subject is well known	65 – 70
Audible but not intelligible	70 – 75
Just audible	75 – 85
Inaudible	> 85

To obtain a standard where normal speech levels may be audible but not intelligible when the background noise level in the receiving room is NR35 the sound level difference, or sound insulation, between the rooms must be in the range of D_w35 to 40. Where office partitions span between a raised floor and a suspended ceiling a level difference in the range of D_w35 to 40 is the maximum practicable. To maintain the same level of privacy between offices the sound insulation must increase as the background noise level reduces.

If the standard is to be achieved with raised voices the sum of the D_w + NR should be increased by five.

The sound level difference between offices is controlled by the sound insulation of the separating partition modified by the flanking routes at the junctions with the facade mullion, the interior partition, with the floor or raised floor and with the soffit or suspended ceiling. Figure 4 illustrates these routes.

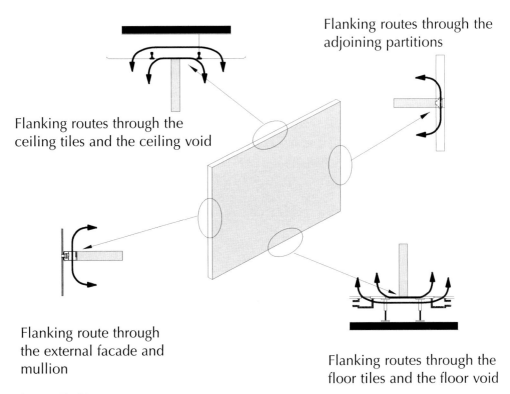

Flanking routes through the adjoining partitions

Flanking routes through the ceiling tiles and the ceiling void

Flanking route through the external facade and mullion

Flanking routes through the floor tiles and the floor void

Figure 4: Flanking routes

An example, using typical performances, of how these flanking factors can influence the overall sound insulation of the partition is given below. The performances of the individual elements are combined by 'logarithmic subtraction' to give the 'apparent sound reduction index' of the partition.

Element	Element performance	Logarithmic subtraction to total		
Partition	45	45		
Junction with facade	45		41	
Junction with other partition	50	44		37
Junction with suspended ceiling	40		39	
Junction with raised floor	45	39		

This is a crude assessment, which takes no account of the surface area of partition and perimeter length, etc but is usually within 1 dB of the answer given by the full calculation. The performance descriptors, or units, have been omitted for simplicity. It can be seen that the overall performance of the partition, at 37, is lower than the weakest route for noise through the junction and void of the suspended ceiling.

To achieve a particular standard of privacy between adjacent spaces usually requires specific requirements for the sound insulation of the building facade, partition system, raised floor and suspended ceiling.

The junctions of the building facade and the floor slabs also need to be considered in maintaining the sound separation between floors.

The use of floor and ceiling voids for services air distribution will require void barriers or attenuation of the air routes and an appropriate acoustic performance of the ceiling to maintain higher standards of separation.

Standards should not be adopted in the design without agreement with the client.

It is often difficult to explain, verbally, what the different privacy standards mean in practice. On rare occasions it has been possible to demonstrate using an existing building with a similar condition, when the client can hear what may be expected in the proposed building. However, finding a reasonable match is difficult but relatively recent innovations in computer techniques enable 'auralisations' to be produced. Although these techniques were originally developed for performance spaces they enable the effects of different background noise levels and separating sound insulations to be demonstrated in terms of audibility and intelligibility. This approach often drastically shortens decision times as many uncertainties are avoided.

Open plan office

Obtaining standards of privacy between open plan workstations also requires the consideration of the same principles of the level difference between speaker and listener, and the background noise level, as for the separation between cellular offices.

The ability to provide standards of privacy between open plan workstations is more limited, but some of the lower standards can be achieved by consideration of the following:

- distance between workstations (this factor is affected by an acoustically reflective soffit);
- orientation of workstations;
- height of screening;
- background noise level (a masking sound system may be necessary);
- sensitivity of users of the workstation to intrusive noise;

- the level and character of intrusive noise sources;
- acoustic absorption within the workstation.

Most of these factors are not relevant to speculative office buildings but attention to them will be necessary at some stage if any control is to be exercised.

New occupants of open plan offices can often be dissatisfied with the environment when they have been used to smaller offices in older, more heavily constructed buildings. The provision of local 'quiet spaces' can help during the transition period as well as providing permanent refuges for the occasions when occupants need more privacy than their workstation provides.

Plant rooms

The size and location of building services' plant rooms should be selected to avoid conflicts with noise and vibration sensitive areas and to allow the installation of appropriate amounts of sound insulation and attenuation.

Too often plant rooms are positioned in 'space left over in the planning exercise', referred to as SLOPE, increasing the cost of noise control – if there is room for the necessary treatment. Sometimes the noise can be impossible to control in the space allowed. Optimum plant location can save time, money and lead to more confidence in the final outcome.

Particular care is necessary with the location of chillers and electrical generators, as these are likely to be the noisiest items of equipment installed. Noise levels within generator rooms can be 105 to 110 dB(A), or more. Levels of this magnitude may require box-in-box constructions just to ensure that the increase in services noise levels in adjacent occupied space is no more than 10 dB above the design criterion.

To be safe, the noise breaking out of plant rooms for normally operating systems should be 10 dB less than the noise criterion of the adjacent space. Although not exact, for an NR38 space this can be taken as NR28.

Plant room walls can be constructed of block or plasterboard, or a combination of both. Thickness and density of block or plasterboard detailing will depend on the noise levels generated by the plant housed and the sensitivity of the adjacent spaces. Clearly, a noisy plant room close to a sensitive space will be more complicated to design and build than one surrounded by store rooms etc.

Floor slabs are usually dense concrete and may need to be increased in thickness to improve sound insulation. Note that doubling the mass of a slab will increase the sound insulation by about 5 dB. Having reached the practical limit on slab thickness, adding a floated concrete slab is usually necessary for further improvement.

Weak spots in the plant room envelope are service penetrations, particularly ductwork, return air routes if the plant room is used as a return air plenum, and, of course, doors. The plant room door may need to be a specialist acoustic door set, where the door leaf, frame and seals are provided and fitted as a package, with laboratory test data to confirm performance where demanded by the required sound insulation. Sometimes a specialist door set can be avoided by using a lobbied arrangement.

Vibration isolation of equipment and connecting services within plant rooms is usually necessary to avoid perceptible vibration and structure-borne noise in adjacent occupied space.

Base build and fit out

What is provided in the base build can vary from the 'shell and core' where bare concrete slabs and soffits, together with connections to building services at riser positions are provided to the tenant to a Category A fit-out where raised floors, suspended ceilings and building services are installed. With the latter, more of the fit-out issues must be considered in the base build design to enable tenants to obtain their chosen standards.

A Category B fit-out would include the installation of internal partitioning and upgrades to the base build and Category A fit-out, etc. Refer to *BCO 2000 Guide*[7] for a fuller description of fitting out categories.

It must be clear, in the early stages of design, what standards a prospective tenant will be able to achieve during the Category B fit-out, without modifying the base build and/or Category A provisions, and these should be made clear in the tenancy agreement. Where boardrooms, video-conferencing rooms and rooms of similar standard are to be included, it is usually necessary to install the partitions from slab-to-soffit to achieve the necessary sound insulation.

The office floors in speculative buildings are often designed to be suitable for open plan layouts but most tenants require some cellularised space, with the flexibility to change. This has several implications in the building design.

Suspended ceilings

A suspended ceiling in an open plan office should provide effective sound absorption, to give the major element of reverberant noise control, with a requirement for minimal sound insulation.

---

7 British Council for Offices, *BCO 2000 Guide*, October 2000.

Where cellular space is created, by installing partitions between raised floor and suspended ceiling, the sound insulation of the suspended ceiling becomes important. Without increasing the sound insulation the standard of privacy available is likely to be very poor, with speech clearly intelligible in the adjacent office.

This can be corrected by installing a suspended ceiling with the necessary sound insulation throughout the project, which is expensive and often unnecessary, or ensuring that the system installed can accept a proprietary acoustic overlay in the necessary areas at the time of fit-out.

If the ceiling void is to be used as a return air plenum it may be necessary to add attenuating devices over the air routes, e.g. grilles, diffusers or luminaries, to avoid significant reduction of the sound insulation of the ceiling. These devices are often constructed by the ductwork fabricator, using sheet metal and absorptive duct lining.

Alternatively, void barriers, on the partition lines, can be used but these are more difficult to fit, to move later and they complicate the patterns of return air.

Raised floors

Usually, raised floors are of little concern within office fit-outs unless the floor is being used as an air plenum, for either supply air or return air. To achieve the maximum practicable standard of privacy between cellular offices will probably require the addition of attenuation to the underside of the air outlets. This attenuation is also often fabricated from sheet metal and absorptive duct lining, in a box form with a short, ducted connection. Rearrangement of the floor tiles, with the outlet and attenuating box attached, is simple.

Interface with facade

The interface between the internal partitions and the building facade must provide sufficient sound insulation to maintain the standards of privacy offered to the tenant.

To enable particular standards of privacy to be obtained, the flanking sound performance of the facade, on the lines that junctions may occur, must be specified. Without specific measures the facade mullions often cannot maintain the potential sound insulation of the abutting partition and retro-fitting additional treatment to the facade is difficult, or impossible.

Building services noise levels

Air conditioning systems in office areas are often designed to suit open plan arrangements in speculative developments, with a noise criterion of NR38 to NR40 commonly used. However, when selected areas are fitted out with cellular accommodation, conference rooms, boardrooms, etc NR38, or more, is too high.

The introduction of a boardroom, or the larger conference room, is likely to require extensive changes to the base build provisions, including stripping out the raised floors and suspended ceilings to install slab-to-slab partitions, and adding enhanced air conditioning. Modification of the base build building services is usually only necessary for cellular offices and the smaller conference rooms, and reduction of the base build criterion to NR30 or NR35 is recommended. The base build services design should allow for the modifications necessary to introduce appropriate noise control measures. Remember the balance between the background noise and the sound insulation in achieving the desired acoustic separation.

An alternative approach could be to select a compromise noise criterion for base build design that suits the upper end of the range given for cellular offices and the lower end of the range given for open plan space. This would suggest a building services noise of NR35 and, based upon BS 8233, a total noise level of 45 $dBL_{Aeq,T}$. This approach has cost implications that must be reviewed on a case-by-case basis.

Multi-tenanted buildings

A multi-tenanted building introduces additional concerns, particularly where there is mixed use. For a development incorporating offices, retail and residential space, adequate separation between the different tenants is essential.

In multi-tenanted office buildings, there must be adequate separation at tenancy walls and between floors. For walls a minimum weighted level difference of D_w45 is recommended and this will require a slab-to-soffit construction. The flanking performance at the building facade will have to be higher at junctions with separations between tenancies than for separations within tenancies.

An atrium is often a potential source of disturbance. Many newer office buildings include office floors open to an atrium. This has advantages in a single tenancy in that the atrium acoustic response can be reasonably well controlled, as the openings to the office floors act as absorption to reverberant noise in the atrium, whilst the occupants of the office floors enjoy a feeling of community. However, this can be offset by activity in the atrium disturbing the office occupants and activity carrying over from one office floor to another.

To minimise the effects of disturbance from other office floors the factors involved in open plan office planning, referred to in an earlier section, can be utilised.

Glazing-in the office floor introduces a means to control disturbance but reduces the feeling of community and creates a reverberant atrium. The addition of significant areas of acoustic absorption to the atrium may then be necessary to create a pleasant atmosphere.

Should a voice alarm system be installed in the building, specific control over the reverberance may be necessary to achieve intelligibility.

To allow for the possibility of multiple tenancies the ability to glaze in the office floors at a later date is useful in a speculative office development for both acoustic and security reasons.

With the possibility that one tenant may have use of the atrium, but several may be overlooking it, it is necessary to consider the range of possible atrium uses and the sound insulation necessary to separate the offices from the atrium and reduce the disturbance. The limitations on sound insulation of standard, double glazed constructions may limit the activity in the atrium during times when occupation is expected in the offices.

The unconventional

The pursuit of unusual geometries and materials in the building form, innovative approaches to the provision of office facilities and revolutionary use of office space necessitates more detailed examination of all aspects of acoustic design, as none of the usual assumptions or solutions may apply.

The 'unconventional' will require more time to develop than the conventional and result in greater expense, as newly developed products or designs will not have established performance data and must be proved, usually by testing. Suitable provisions should be made in the planning to allow for this.

An architect's quick acoustic checklist for commercial offices

Ideally, the acoustician should be involved in the design of a project from a very early stage, usually beginning in RIBA Work Stage B – Feasibility. In each of the subsequent Work Stages there are acoustic considerations, and indications of these are given below.

Work Stages B, C and D
Feasibility, Outline Proposals, Scheme Design
- Noise survey of the site to identify building envelope sound insulation and noise emission limits.
- If there are vibration sources close to the site, a vibration survey may be required to determine whether building isolation is necessary.
- Re-planning of the masterplanning or building planning can avoid conflicts between noise and vibration producing areas and noise and vibration sensitive areas, which can be expensive to design and uncertain in final outcome.
- Review design options for most effectiveness and economy.
- Establish acoustic design targets for sound insulation, room acoustic response, noise emission and building services noise for base building areas.

- An emergency voice alarm system, instead of a fire alarm sounder system, may require treatment in addition to that necessary to create an aurally pleasant space.
- Establish the standards that are required by the end users or to be offered to the tenants and ensure that the provisions in the base build will support them.
- Identify types of constructions and finishes that can satisfy the acoustic design targets.
- Ensure that the location of building services' plant and routing of the distribution does not result in difficulties in meeting the design targets or the requirement for expensive solutions.
- Identify the need for specialist acoustic items, e.g. operable walls, specialist door sets, floated floors, resiliently suspended ceilings.

Work Stage E, Detail Design
- Identify sound insulation requirements of building envelope and develop the design of glazing, curtain walling, lightweight roofing, etc.
- If necessary, develop the design of building isolation to control perceptible vibration or structure-borne noise from internal or external sources.
- Develop wall, partition and floor construction designs to meet the internal insulation requirements, including plant rooms and building services penetrations.
- Develop the detailed performance requirements and locations of acoustically absorptive or reflective finishes and the geometry of specialised spaces to provide the optimum acoustic response.
- Recommendations for treatment of specialist equipment, e.g. refuse compactors, adjustable lorry dock, etc.
- Identify details of specialist acoustic constructions, e.g. specialist acoustic door sets, floated floors, operable walls, etc.

Work Stage F, Production Information
- Provide specification clauses for acoustic aspects of detailed design for inclusion in the appropriate tender documentation.

Work Stage H, Tender Action
- Review acoustic aspects of tender returns where doubt exists regarding compliance.

Work Stage K, Operations on Site
- Advise on acoustic aspects of submissions from contractors.
- Witness laboratory or factory testing of acoustic elements and critical items of equipment to ensure compliance.
- Visit site as necessary to check on specific acoustic constructions.

Work Stage L, Completion
- Attendance during commissioning to confirm acceptability of method and reliability of results.

Acoustic terminology

dB
The decibel, a convenient scale that compresses a wide range of amplitude values into a smaller range of numbers. In acoustics, the dB is ten times the logarithm of the ratio of the measured sound pressure (detected by a microphone) to a convenient reference level (the threshold of hearing). Thus L_p (dB) = 10 log $(P_1/P_{ref})^2$ where P_{ref}, the lowest pressure detectable by the ear, is 0.00002 Pascals (i.e. 2×10^{-5} Pa). The threshold of hearing is 0 dB, while the threshold of pain is approximately 120 dB. Normal speech is approximately 60 dB(A) or more and a change of 3 dB is only just detectable. A change of 10 dB is subjectively twice, or half, as loud.

dB(A)
The unit used to define a weighted sound pressure level, which correlates well with the subjective response to sound. The weighting used follows the frequency response of the human ear, which is less sensitive to low and very high frequencies than it is to those in the range 500 Hz to 4 kHz.

L_N
The dB(A) level, or octave band dB level, exceeded for N per cent of the time period of measurement e.g. L_{A01}, L_{A10}, $L_{A\,50}$, $L_{A\,90}$, $L_{A\,99}$ or L_{01}, L_{10}, L_{50}, L_{90}, L_{99}. Where a time period for the measurement is defined it is shown by $L_{A90,T}$, e.g. $L_{A90,5\,minutes}$. Where the response of the sound level meter is specified it is shown by adding the detail in brackets e.g. $L_{A90,\,(slow)}$.

L_{eq}
The equivalent continuous sound level, in dB(A) or dB for octave bands, is a notional steady sound level which would produce the same sound energy over a given time period as the measured, time varying sound, denoted by L_{Aeq} or L_{eq}. Where a time period for the measurement is defined it is shown by $L_{Aeq,T}$, e.g. $L_{Aeq,1\,hour}$. Where the response of the sound level meter is specified it is shown by adding the detail in brackets e.g. $L_{Aeq,(slow)}$.

L_{max}
The maximum sound pressure level reached during the time period of measurement. Where the response of the sound level meter is specified it is shown by adding the detail in brackets e.g. $L_{max,(slow)}$.

Noise rating (NR) curves	Noise rating (NR) curves are a set of internationally agreed octave band sound pressure level curves, based on the concept of equal loudness. The curves are commonly used to define building services noise limits. The NR value of a noise is obtained by plotting the octave band spectrum on the set of standard curves. The highest value curve that is reached by the spectrum is the NR value.
D_w	A single figure, weighted sound level difference covering the 16 third octave bands from 100 Hz to 3150 Hz. Measured on site in accordance with BS EN ISO 140-4[8] and rated in accordance with BS EN ISO 717-1.[9]
R_w	The sound reduction index, R, (or transmission loss) of a building element covering the 16 third octave bands from 100 Hz to 3150 Hz, measured in a laboratory in accordance with BS EN ISO 140-3.[10] It is a measure of the loss of sound through the material, i.e. its attenuation properties. It is a property of the component, unlike the sound level difference that is affected by the common area between rooms and the acoustic of the receiving room. The weighted sound reduction index, R_w, is a single figure description of sound reduction index, using the third octave band data and rated in accordance with BS EN ISO 717-1. The higher the figure the better the sound insulation. When the R_w is calculated from site measurements it includes the effects of the flanking routes and is referred to as the apparent weighted sound reduction index, R'_w.
Ambient noise	Totally encompassing sound in a given environment. Background sound forms part of the ambient noise and is described by the L_{A90}.

---

8 BS EN ISO 140-4: 1998. *Acoustics. Measurement of sound insulation in buildings and of building elements. Field measurements of airborne sound insulation between rooms,* British Standards Institution.
9 BS EN ISO 717-1: 1997. *Acoustics. Rating of sound insulation in buildings and of building elements. Airborne sound insulation,* British Standards Institution.
10 BS EN ISO 140-3: 1998, BS 2750-3: 1995. *Acoustics. Measurement of sound insulation in buildings and of building elements. Laboratory measurements of airborne sound insulation between rooms,* British Standards Institution.

Author profile

Malcolm Wright CEng MCIBSE MIOA, Associate Director
Arup

Malcolm Wright has been involved in noise and vibration control in the construction industry for over 30 years. For the last 18 years he has specialised in acoustics and is currently an Associate Director with Arup Acoustics, where he is responsible for a wide variety of projects. Arup Acoustics has been involved in many office buildings including the new headquarters for the Hongkong and Shanghai Banking Corporation in Hong Kong, City Hall for the Greater London Authority, the new European Headquarters for Merrill Lynch, and the Lloyd's Register of Shipping building.

15 Interior design

Simon Jackson
Gensler

> People think design is styling. Design is not style. It's not about giving shape to the shell and not giving a damn about the guts. Good design is a renaissance attitude that something that the world didn't know was missing.[1]

Introduction

People today have unprecedented choice as to where and how they work. Not surprisingly, they favour the settings that best support them in their critical activities. The best settings are knowledge centres, tailored to their users' culture, workstyle and process while remaining flexible and open ended, which recognise the speed of change. They give physical form to an organisation's business plan through its property strategy, its building and facilities, and every workplace project that grows out of them. The interior and exterior environment must coalesce to not only serve the needs of the user in terms of function, comfort and cost, but also to enhance the user's experience inside and outside the structure.

> The experiences we have affect who we are, what we can accomplish, and where we are going, and we will increasingly ask companies to stage experiences that change us.[2]

Is the interior designer a scientist or an artist, a psychologist, a technologist or an anthropologist?

As designers, we can enhance the success of our clients' companies by understanding how the design of physical space can support the learning, collaboration, knowledge creation, and communication necessary to enhance creativity and innovation.

The most important directive in workplace design is: 'Know your client and know your client's business.' As designers of ideas and designers of solutions, our passion is to create work environments that facilitate the client's business process and support the efficient, cost-effective delivery of their goods and services.

---

1 Paola Antonelli, Curator of architecture and design, Museum of Modern Art.
2 Joseph Pine II & James Gilmore, *The Experience Economy.*

As avid observers of the business world, designers see companies today being bombarded with change on numerous fronts: organisational restructuring, demographic concerns, technological innovations, environmental and health issues, and economical fluctuation. The spirit of change is permeating business, and for us change is not a simple one-time event but an ongoing journey. In order to stay competitive, companies are restructuring themselves to be more dynamic, more innovative, more flexible and, most importantly, to be agile.

Strategic business plan projections are becoming less predictable – the only certainty is change or perhaps, more appropriately, evolution.

The organisations of agile companies allow them to thrive on change and evolution, and their structures, including the workplace, must be flexible enough to permit rapid reconfiguration of both people and space, keyed to the needs of their customers.

Design solutions for the workplace are not finite or static. They must embrace change, ready to adapt to the future prototypes within a company's business evolution.

Unfortunately, the determining factor of 75 per cent of today's design and planning work is not increasing productivity or enhancing interaction, but saving real estate costs and, ideally, creating more flexibility in the work environment and reducing the cost of churn and change.

The challenge to interior designers of today is to raise the discussion about place to a higher level of intellect.

As workplace design professionals we must approach our evolving worlds from a new perspective, helping us to understand the changing nature of work and the issues that surround it.

The key issues according to CEO's in creating productive workspaces, are in order of priority:

Human resources	1
People performance	2
Technology	3
Designed environment	4
Workflow	5

Therefore, CEOs see human resources' support and people performance as major issues.

80 per cent of the reasons why people do not perform reside in the work environment.[3]

3 Geary Rummler, specialist in human performance.

Quality of life, productivity and sustainability will also drive future work environments.

The mission is clear. Interior designers must understand people's needs and desires, as well as the sociological processes of human interaction. Along with efficiency in office design, particularly with the increased importance of technology, we must continually build our expertise in understanding the effects of the spaces we design on personal interaction and creativity. We must put ourselves in our clients' shoes as we design, trying to live as they do, worry about the things which concern them, and anticipate the physiological responses that are fostered by the places we create.

This chapter concentrates on the interior design process and demonstrates, through case studies, solutions to some of the key drivers within a project.

Firstly, however, we need to redefine the design process to compliment 'agile' clients' businesses.

The way forward is paradoxically to look not ahead, but to look around.[4]

Business today and tomorrow needs a new design process. The traditional, linear approach to design briefing, concept, scheme and design development, etc does not serve the needs of organisations in a complex, changing world. It fails to meet today's business pace, and fails to include adequate input from appropriate sources.

Information gathered becomes obsolete due to the nature of the design process and thus, design solutions are often inappropriate to be able to create the kind of dynamic, open-ended solutions that will best serve our clients in a world of change.

The design profession must link its thinking to the needs of business. That means expanding its knowledge base to include issues and topics that historically have not been considered by the design profession, such as: organisational psychology, behaviour modification, cognitive ergonomics, economics, telecommunications technology, group communications dynamics, and demographics.

Not only do businesses, and ultimately designers, need to expand their awareness of these various subjects, but they also need to evolve processes from linear to organic and embrace the following:

- shared goals and expectations;
- mutual respect and trust;
- established rules;
- decentralised decision-making;

---

4 John Seely Brown.

- dedication to learning;
- commitment to ongoing testing and refinement.

As the approach to design becomes more integrated, participatory and less linear, the role of the designer is increasingly that of a facilitator. Progress depends on the ability to facilitate direct inputs and orchestrate the actions of the myriad of players and perspectives involved in any project.

Designers share responsibility for the growth and development of our professional knowledge base. Participation in the development of new processes and areas of research are critical to the long-term viability of the profession and the contributions we make to the success of business – our own as well as our clients.

It is always rewarding to design for clients that believe design will make a difference to their business.

We should continue to investigate collaborative methods of delivering design services that respond to the accelerated demands of the marketplace. New methods must be organised around integrated 'systems' platforms (such as Electronic Data Management Systems) and should include the perspective and expertise of multi-disciplinary inputs (i.e. suppliers, construction trades, anthropologists, behavioural scientists, futurists, MBAs).

A future-proof work environment is one that has been designed to take account of changes in the occupants' needs over a number of years. Future-proofing requires architecture, engineering, interiors, construction and management collaboration that ensures flexible infrastructures.

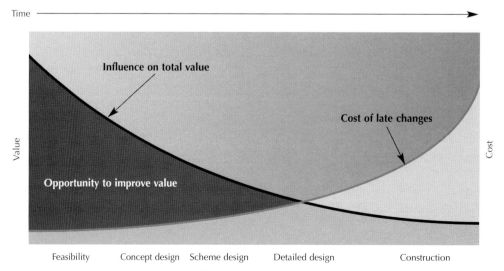

Figure 1: Maximise value – operational; Minimise risks – investment

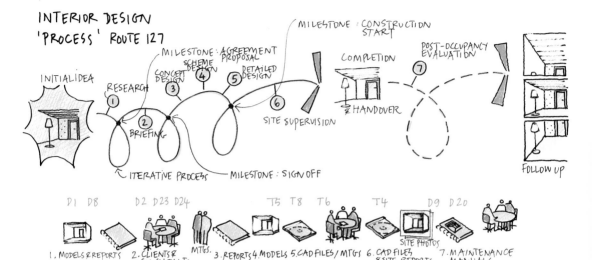

Figure 2: Interior design process route

This collaboration should be highly visible at the earliest stage of the project – pre-design! Effective pre-planning minimises the likelihood of costly change in the later stages of the process or throughout the lifecycle of the facility (as described in Chapter 18: The End Game, we should view implementation as only part of the story).

Project process

The significance and valuable contribution design plays in a facility's lifecycle is to establish at the earliest point the solutions – the pieces that allow for effective business evolution and create a platform for creative, innovative and productive performance.

As interior designers, we move through a series of design and implementation stages which overlap and merge, interlock, influence and inform, where the collaborative and coordinated result is the successful project.

Envisioning the strategic client brief

Envisioning sessions with the thought leaders, integration meetings and executive presentations all bring together people that may have never sat together at the same table before – and certainly not while sharing a common interest.

High on the corporate agenda is productivity gains – a complex series of issues make up the influences on productivity. Project success is ultimately only realised if the client's core business has benefited from the experience. How you judge and measure whether a project has been successful in raising productivity and/or performance can only happen if the criteria is established before or during the briefing phase.

The ten project drivers we consider most influential on success are:

- growth;
- risk and opportunity;
- cost;
- technology;
- organisational change;
- competitive advantage;
- flexibility and adaptability;
- environment and quality of life;
- work patterns;
- and image and identity.

A key issue to be resolved in creating an integrated workspace is how to express the firm's unique mission and individuality in the physical design. Beneath the physical embodiment of the design lies the process of developing the client brief. This involves focusing attention on a comprehensive, unbiased evaluation of the company's business goals and to whom they relate to in terms of workstyles, staffing and adjacency needs, for the present and the future. This analysis serves as the basis for checking the efficiencies of a space plan against the client's needs – a critical factor when determining the appropriateness and value of a lease.

Gathering the data or knowledge to inform the design which will follow can be done in a number of ways. Increasingly, electronic forms of data capture, such as web surveys are used to gather microinformation such as filing counts to substantiate the high-level macro ideas of the Executive and Project Steering Committee. *Forward Thinking* utilise a series of envisioning workshops to bring together the key parties and their ideas – the result being the strategic briefing report or accommodation model. The basic discussion about filing could turn out to be a development of data capture and retention generally.

From strategy to delivery . . . and beyond

Nothing can tear down silos and align domains like focusing on a tangible reality such as the workplace, and therein lies its most strategically important contribution. Properly mandated and facilitated, a workplace initiative can be highly effective in helping to achieve alignment at all levels.

Case study: Smith & Nephew

The senior executive and thought leaders at Smith & Nephew understood the value of embracing change management.

Smith & Nephew, a leading worldwide healthcare group recently decided upon a major organisational restructure. Part of this restructuring involved the relocation of

Figure 3: Smith & Nephew breakout area

their corporate headquarters operations. Their previous headquarters were located at Temple Place, Embankment in London, and were situated in a building that is a classic example of Victorian architecture, once the London residency of Lord Waldorf Astor. The interior, although spectacular, was not conducive to departmental communication, nor did it accommodate the demands of a modern office.

Smith & Nephew relocated its headquarters to Heron House, a newly constructed building at 15 Adam Street, off the Strand. Gensler was approached to develop a strategy to transform Smith & Nephew's new headquarters into a workplace that would support and empower its evolving practice whilst maintaining an appropriate link to tradition and history. The move has been part of a complete change in corporate culture.

The new office has been designed to promote staff integration and communication. The reception area with a café bar and breakfast area has become a 'corporate hearth' – a business lounge concept creating a focus for visiting executives to head office. An open plan environment and fully glazed offices have improved staff communication and executive visibility, as well as creating a new culture to take the company into the millennium.

Change management as the new business driver

By aligning the different components of an organisation with the business strategy, change management can deliver an integrated approach that specifically addresses the unique nature of people, systems, processes and workplace.

Change management directly concerns itself with the crucial question, 'how?':

- How can an organisation embrace change across the board?
- How to develop the information channels to communicate effectively with employees about upcoming change?

- How to secure widespread support and co-operation?
- How to help employees master new workstyles and settings?
- How to implement changes that will enhance satisfaction, productivity and performance?

A change management programme is tailored to the client's unique needs, culture and available resources. Initiatives can involve:

- internal and external communication plans;
- materials and communications for both pre- and post-occupancy;
- focus groups;
- a website with ongoing updates;
- brand and reputation management strategies;
- ongoing facilitation and coaching;
- environmental orientation and system training;
- and information technology, transparency, resilience and agility.

The role of the interior designer throughout the briefing process is to challenge convention, and to ask 'how?' and 'why?'. Through the process of envisioning and integration, the project picture – or jigsaw – begins to materialise. Getting it right at the beginning ensures a smooth process to follow.

Concept and scheme design

Factors which continue to influence workplace settings include: increasing cost of space, fluctuating space requirements, changing employee expectations, dynamic organisational structure, new information technologies, and competition for the most qualified staff. These factors generate the need for significant innovation in how facilities are planned, designed, managed and used to enable organisations to achieve their fundamental business objectives.

We are observing a movement towards combining the efficiencies of 'universal planning' with a variety of non-conventional workplace settings, including:

- Shared offices: a desk, office or workstation is intended for use by different people at different times (shared-assigned, non-assigned, non-territorial, hoteling, just in-time, 'landing pad' concept, free-address, etc.).
- Satellite offices: offices beyond the office that respond to individual employee schedules, sales force recruitment and retention, ride-share programmes to improve outdoor air quality, telecommuting, etc.
- Collaborative environments: group settings to promote team-oriented work and facilitate interaction among employees (clusters or workgroups, caves and commons, team rooms, breakout areas, etc.).
- Mobile working.

Figure 4: IBM e-business innovation centre

Case study: IBM

For IBM, becoming a true frontier e-business organisation implied a rethinking of the traditional view of workplace design. Gensler's response was a concept developed with IBM's e-business innovation initiative 'ebii'. The ebii prototype concentrated on the creation of workplace that not only accommodated changes in growth, work processes and client interfaces, but actually engendered creative thought processes.

By breaking the mould of the work environment, IBM hoped to liberate the creative and pioneering spirits that existed within. There was a willingness on behalf of the client to experience and take risks with new ideas in order to create something different and provocative. This was exemplified by the construction of extreme spaces such as the 'experience theatre' and 'think tank', to stimulate and to provide an attitude shift away from the traditional work environment.

I want to work here – I want a job in this creative environment.[5]

In addition, non-dedicated offices, universal workstations, increased shared facilities, team rooms and drop-in areas became signature IBM 'e-place' features that described the new departure from conventional office design.

High-tech electronic presentations such as holographic projection screens, plasma and computer-controlled lighting sequences were used with low-tech, tactile presentation tools such as over-scale models and writing tablets. This all helped to create a fun working environment, generating energy and enthusiasm while improving staff recruitment and retention.

Gensler sees the Centre for IBM e-business innovation space as representing a trend to a more casual and open working environment that engenders communication, collaboration and idea generation.

Rejuvenating and re-invigorating existing buildings, as in the IBM case study, is one challenge – designing from the inside out is another matter, but one which is highly rewarding because it allows for an integrated group of design disciplines to work with a somewhat blank canvass. It is an enjoyable process, helping a client to make a building really work for them. The interior design concept is woven through every detail of the facility with architecture, technology and engineering fully co-ordinated into a singular process.

Case study: Schroder Investment Management

The Schroder Investment Management (SIM) project included building design consultation services which moulded the architectural design for more appropriate use by the end user as well as considering the commercial 'best practice' aspects.

Planning grids, core locations and general floor plan configuration were optimised and the result was a highly efficient building. As well as the space planning aspects, the interior design concept was overlaid on the building's internal elements so that the overall image was seamless between 'shell and core' and 'fit-out'.

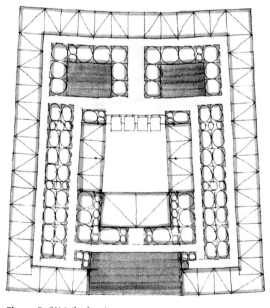

Figure 5: SIM (before)

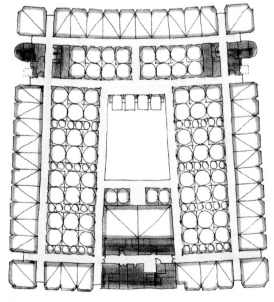

Figure 6: SIM (after)

Figure 7: SIM completed project (boardroom)

Building Design Consultation

Building Design Consultation is a specialist service provided by Gensler for developers, agents and end users. We seek to establish the most appropriate building or development for a variety of (hypothetical) users. The success we have achieved in improving net and usable efficiencies, improved building configuration and optimised space utilisation creates a win-win situation for tenant, developer and landlord (*see* Figures 8 and 9).

Building Design Consulation Services were implemented to affect improvements in a recently completed major London building.

How can we create an integrated building that supports the workplace and projects the appropriate exterior image? By approaching architectural design from both the inside out and the outside in, designers can place design emphasis where it matters. Finding a balance between the requirements of the interior and the exterior leads to an integrated architectural design solution.

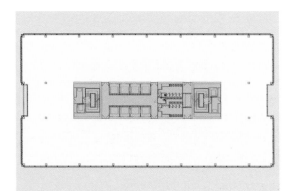

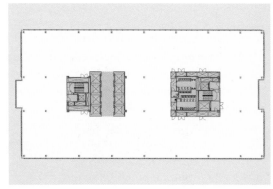

Figure 8: Floorplate (before)

Figure 9: Floorplate (after)

Figure 10: 90 High Holborn

Case study: 90 High Holborn

Gensler was appointed by the client to design a landmark development in Holborn with distinguished high-quality architecture. The brief specified that the design would be a statement building that would attract high profile tenants. The client's objectives stated that they 'wanted a state of the art piece of architecture that will raise investment values to a record in that area'.

Gensler also designed the interior space for the principal tenant, Olswang, who occupy 140,000 sq ft of the building.

Design development/detailed design

The interior scheme design needs to be refined and revised into a scheme that can be implemented. This stage of the process is primarily concerned with the coordination of the various design, technology and engineering elements.

There are seven basic infrastructures that every occupant/workstation needs individually:

- fresh air;
- temperature control;
- lighting control;
- daylight and view, reduced isolation from outdoors;
- privacy and quiet working;
- network access: multiple data, power, voice connections;
- and ergonomic furniture/filing storage systems and environmentally appropriate finishes.

It is clear, however, that the dynamics of space and technology in today's work environments cannot be accommodated through the existing building infrastructures or the linear design processes that create them – neither the blanket systems planned for uniform, open plan configurations, nor the idiosyncratic systems planned for unique office configurations. What is needed are flexible grid, density and closure systems – a constellation of building systems that permit each individual to set the location and density of ventilation and thermal conditioning, lighting, telecommunications and furniture, including the level of workspace enclosure.

Only the commitment of the full architecture/engineering/interiors/construction and manufacturing team to collaboratively deliver re-locatable user-based infrastructures will create new and retrofit future workplaces capable of supporting and encouraging productivity, organisational flexibility, technological adaptability and environmental sustainability. Only a flexible workplace infrastructure – from servicing systems to furniture – will support the constant demand for the regeneration of workgroup and workstation solutions.

Flexibility means change, and change, or evolution, should be encouraged. Change involves implementing standards in the work environment. However, a number of obstacles can arise and many barriers exist to achieving efficiency and standardisation in a workplace:

- economics;
- spatial arrangements and building deficiencies;
- technological deficiencies that inhibit interaction;
- training or lack of understanding on how to use standards;
- individuals who are reluctant to share power, credit and recognition;
- communications.

The planning module dimension is a critical factor in efficient interior space use. It is the common denominator for all office sizes and planning concepts. The best office module for each client is the module that is the most suited to office requirements, provides good interior circulation, is compatible with efficient open plan furniture systems for administrative and support personnel, and is easy to work with in the construction of doors, partitioning and other interior components and their integration with the building fabric and infrastructure. Conversely, as we have mentioned, in new construction it is essential that the research into office standards be initiated early in the design process so that the building module and structural bay can be integrated with these in mind.

One approach is to develop fundamental space planning and finish standards that use common repetitive elements to respond to the client's desire for an overall unity from floor-to-floor or building-to-building. This would include incorporating design criteria for colour palettes, lighting concepts, interior landscaping, furnishings and finishes, as well as recommendations for improving the facility's environmental systems and the updating of the company's graphics programme. Standardised office configurations enable the freedom of rearranging people as well as furniture.

The most fundamental criteria is flexibility to reconfigure work teams, to incorporate or remove subsidiary groups as companies merge or spin-off and, in general, to adapt the facility to conform to a company's aggressive churn rate. Flexibility is most easily accommodated by standardisation.

The process of standardisation can also become a vehicle for supporting – rather than restricting – the aesthetic component, incorporating standards within workplace design and integrating opportunities for enhancing a space through colour, form and materials as well as for accommodating equipment and systems. Standardisation sets the stage for an environment of simplicity, strong forms and clarity, where employees' personalisation of a space adds to the ambiance of structure rather than contributing to a feeling of chaos.

Gensler was able to draw on its vast benchmarking knowledge and extensive experience in accommodating local work practices and differing cultural influences. We were able to effectively direct Shook Hardy & Bacon, a Kansas City based law firm, in employing a universal office size for single partners and double associates, as well as introducing an open plan approach for paralegal and analyst staff. This approach meant that Shook Hardy & Bacon was able to efficiently manage its space requirements as well as having a great degree of flexibility in its recruitment strategy.

The design of the space was a great success. Shook Hardy & Bacon challenged Gensler in their wish to 'spread the design' to all areas of the space. This meant that client and practical spaces were dealt with in an egalitarian manner. Clients and visitors are therefore encouraged to step beyond the front-of-house to equally handsome working areas. Shook Hardy & Bacon's new premises not only meets and

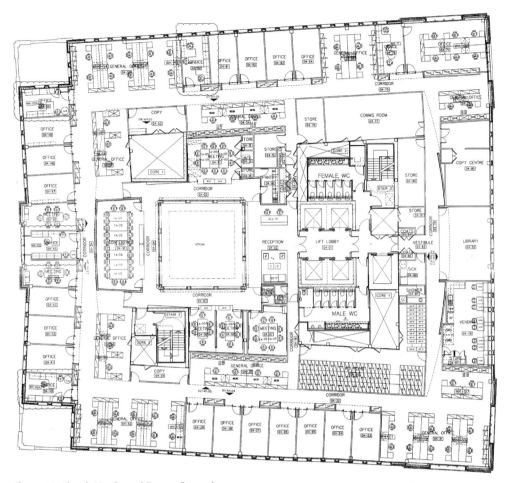

Figure 11: Shook Hardy and Bacon floor plan

exceeds its space utilisation needs, it also offers staff an efficient working environment of which to be proud.

Implementation

The contractual approach to project realisation can be varied. This variety of approach places differing 'demands' on the drawing packages required by the contractor. Generally, the best method is based on partnership and collaboration between design and construction in either formal or informal relationships.

Cost and programming certainty, as well as buildability and ease of variances can be best achieved in a non-adversarial relationship. Leading up to implementation, the interior design team produces tender and construction documentation (working drawings and specifications) and gains planning, building control and statutory approvals, and other permits.

During construction and installation, the team reviews submittals of shop drawings and samples, and clarifies and interprets the drawings and specifications for the contractor. Regular visits to the site ensure that the work is progressing in accordance with the construction documents. Upon substantial completion of the project, a final review is conducted and a final snagging list of incomplete or incorrect items is prepared and submitted to the contractor. The designers then work with the client to schedule the move-in.

Increasingly, there is pressure by clients for shorter design and construction programmes – dynamic companies demand dynamic responses from all parties involved in the process. It is essential that a project which requires 'speed to market' has all team players together at the outset – this ensures that respective concerns and issues are addressed at the earliest point and that the project strategy is established and agreed, which will enable the shorter timescale to be achieved.

The Smith & Nephew project was achieved within a design and construction programme of 21 weeks, when normally a project of this type would take 9 months.

The pervasive influence of design

As the visual signature of a company, the influence of design is pervasive. Design can mirror and project corporate strategies and can play an integral part in shaping those strategies. By communicating the company's respect for its employees, design can stimulate their best efforts. As the practice of business evolves, so do the considerations and criteria for designing appropriate work environments. As designers, we have to be ahead of the cycle. We have to know where business is heading and think about business operation in the same way as the client. Our job is to respect the intelligence and flow of the business world, provide thoughtful and appropriate design and planning services, and create work environments that allow employees, management and customers to interact in the most positive and productive way. Businesses are concerned with achieving the appropriate workstyles with the most efficiency, comfort and flexibility. When we begin the process for each new workplace project, we must bring to it all our experience, ingenuity and resourcefulness. Anything less will not be enough. The process of developing a facility is always challenging, but keeping the client happy means continuing to work with them after occupancy to help them maximise the value of what we designed and to adapt to the changing business world.

Interior designers create the workplace to fit the client's culture. It is not just about the floor plan, the type of workstation and associated storage, the colours and the finishes.

The number one issue that needs to be resolved in creating the integrated workspace is how to express your client's unique mission and individuality in the physical design.

Figure 12: Pricewaterhouse Coopers' flexible workspaces

Interior designers need to define the visual signature of a company. A well-designed work environment becomes the envelope for a compelling brand experience, communicating the unique story. Brand strategies can be brought to life through the use of words, colours, places and products, as reflected in a personalised and appropriate workplace.

The best way to begin the process is through the visioning session, where the client-design team synthesises key messages and sets a clear direction for extending that vision into the built environment.

Pricewaterhouse Coopers, for example, accommodates experts from across the firm's global practice in an environment with a variety of function-orientated spaces, flexible workstation configurations and sophisticated technology provided through carefully coordinated infrastructure, wiring and furniture. Consultants work through solutions with their clients who now fully understand what they will take back to their companies. The result is effective collaboration, which ultimately leads to enhanced creativity and stronger relationships.

Design represents the process of generating planning solutions to what are essentially dynamic problems – people, relationships, workflow and communication. The interior design process should result in a space that is practical, efficient, dynamic, personal, functional and flexible. It must be organised and equipped to support the way people work. As an architect of the workplace, the designer's role is to help clients to achieve their goals through design.

Designers are generally objective observers who provide an outside, unbiased perspective and can translate the corporation's management style and culture into a physical environment. Throughout the project process, the team maintains an eye keenly focused on the appropriate utilisation of space and the resulting aesthetic and functional effect.

The implications of social interaction are just beginning to be analysed in various new workplace settings. At some companies, self-motivated employees do not need to physically work at the office at all, except for the collaboration and interaction it provides. A tremendous challenge is to nourish and propagate the corporate culture to new employees when part of the staff is working elsewhere. Likewise, the spontaneous interaction that takes place in the coffee room or in the hallway is extremely beneficial to reinforcing a sense of teamwork. Managers have to explore new ways to lead and work with off-site staff. Many working environment concepts lend themselves to an easy encounter management style. However, the number of team spaces, huddle rooms and conference rooms usually increase in order to provide areas for scheduled, as well as spontaneous, meetings.

In order to define a new workplace concept, the design team must understand the specific requirements of the user group. This requires close examination of physical, technological and psychological issues. First, one must explore specifically what is expected of the workspace, since these objectives establish the measure of performance against which the success of the new environment will be measured. Functional requirements define space and adjacency, and workflows define relationships between space.

Dr James Moore, corporate strategist, CEO of GeoPartners Research and author of the critically acclaimed *The Death of Competition*, talks with Peter Lawrence, Chairman of the Corporate Design Foundation:

> Like most people, I think of the relationship between design and business in terms of product design. A business creates a physical product that needs to be designed for effective use, or it develops a service, which is essentially a process relationship, that also needs to be designed. But a deeper way that design is important to business is through the process of designing itself, which good designers embody in their work. It has a lot to teach business people, who more and more are designing and redesigning their products, businesses and industries. In my management consulting practice, design is a way of thinking about human and material resources, and how they interact to improve functionality in a specific domain.[6]

In the book, *Workplace, by Design,* Franklin Becker and Fritz Steele state:

> It takes a fundamental paradigm shift to identify and implement workplace strategies that alleviate the pressures organisations are facing as they struggle to become more

---

6 'James Moore on Design' in *@issue*, a publication of the Corporate Design Foundation, vol. 3, no. 1, www.cdf.org/frameset.html

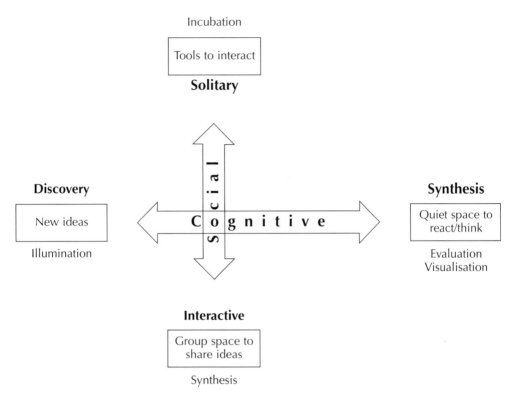

Figure 13: Components of creativity

competitive. In this shift the workplace becomes a dynamic tool for supporting and even stimulating new ways of working, rather than a fixed asset whose performance is assessed primarily in terms of how much money it costs or generates.[7]

With clearly defined objectives, companies understand how change in the physical environment – along with changes in culture, technology and business processes – can be factors in achieving their goals. Businesses have moved towards providing more collaborative environments in an effort to help workers communicate more effectively and function better in teams. Some managers have abandoned their private offices to relocate in more open spaces where they can be more accessible to staff. The new designs emphasise working together over working apart, as companies integrate the space plan, design and communications strategies to support organisational objectives.

Companies can use the work environment to enhance productivity, express the corporate culture, and signal and support changes in culture to help flatten hierarchies.

7 Becker, Franklin and Fritz Steele, Workplace by Design: Mapping the High-Performance Workscape (1995), New York, Jossey-Bass

Organisations continue to build physical work environments and technological infrastructures that support the processing of information rather than its creation, and that focus on individuals rather than the relationships. Facilities design can create significant barriers to the type of activities that true collaboration requires. Alternatively, the environment can be used to create settings that support the behaviours and relationships that create innovation, leading to an enhanced product, service and bottom line.

Discover the synthesis

Creativity has always been the domain of the designer. 'Creativity is power', as John Kao says.[8] It is no longer enough to possess knowledge. The edge comes from innovation constantly offering 'new and better' products and services to the marketplace. Productivity today is not just about delivering more for less but making sure that what is delivered is measurably better than the competition. Quantity still matters, but real and qualitative differences are what distinguish winners from losers. The great teams that have delivered significant innovations have all the following in common:

- a shared vision;
- great people and a distinctive culture;
- access to needed communities of practice;
- a creative process that is fully supported by place and technology.

That 'place' is crucial to innovation is a new economy insight that is persisting, despite the downturn. In their heyday, dot.com and start-up companies realised that their most valuable real estate was any space that spurred the creative process. This led them to push the boundaries. How do we want to work? Posing this question seriously led them to throw out the rulebook and evolve settings that supported fast moving collaboration.

Place and innovation

Innovation is not just collaboration, however. It involves cycles of divergent and convergent thinking and of individual, focused work and collaborative teamwork.

Place is crucial to this iterative process. It must support all of these different ways of working and, at the same time, support the transfer of tacit knowledge (that is, knowing how as opposed to knowing about.) Conveying tacit knowledge depends on face-to-face interaction in a setting that encourages it to happen. Gaining tacit knowledge requires experience: being there. Casual conversations, notes scratched in the margins, body language – it all matters. Technology can augment it, but never wholly replace it.

---

8 Kao, John, Jamming: The Art and Discipline of Business Creativity (1997) London, HarperCollins Business

As place and technology converge, the ability to capture, hold and retrieve information will be a measure of how well a given setting supports the innovation process.

Interior design is the most critical aspect to integrating place with business and cultural aspirations. To keep pace with the market, designers need to fully understand their clients and the way they work, using this knowledge to lead their clients to places they did not know they wanted to go. Designers constantly need to be responsive to changes in the workplace. A rigorous collaboration with clients becomes, like all architecture, a reflection of a larger cultural position.

Business practices have diversified dramatically in the last 30 years and, as a result, workplace design has become a highly specialised discipline that needs to respond to a complex set of social and business requirements. On some level, all the work presented here addresses the new management techniques that have guided a transformation of the workplace into a more agreeable world with a newly found focus on the individual.

Designers have been challenged not only by the necessity to create design solutions that can accommodate the rise in company cultural engineering, but to stimulate and support it.

As large corporations and companies have attempted to occupy the role of the 'helpful relative' with regard to employee problems at both work and at home, total quality calls not only for a 're-skilled' worker, but also for an 'enriched' workplace. As a consequence, today's workplace is quickly becoming the centre of many people's lives. As the sense of community in our cities and suburban areas seems to be diminishing constantly, the 'community' of the workplace has grown even more important. The more aware interior designers understand that it is more likely that we participate in the lives of our co-workers than in the lives of our neighbours across the hall or down the street; they also understand that many of their clients must address this absence of external community by establishing strong internal corporate culture. In the presentation of these projects, you will often encounter references to concepts such as 'establishing a sense of community', 'fostering the corporate culture', or 'creating neighbourhoods within the space'. When the interior designers use these devices, they are involved in an architectural strategy that is 'political' in nature as it responds directly to the needs of the people occupying the spaces, the needs that go well beyond a pre-established business plan. Intelligent architects and designers understand that the workplace is in a dramatic state of change, but also understands that it is our larger culture that is the catalyst for these changes.

Good designers understand that people are working in increasingly diverse ways, and as architects of the workplace it is their job to orchestrate this diversity. The traditional office that once hosted a standardised nine-to-five work structure is rapidly giving way to other work patterns: employees are out of their workplaces a good deal of the time

– on the road, in meetings, or on site with clients. As a result, Gensler, for example, is redesigning, rethinking and re-planning the traditional work environment of single occupancy workstations and private offices. They have planned a vast number of alternative work environments, each designed to accommodate new work patterns, some of which are documented above. At the same time, designers understand that people still need to work together in a community orientated atmosphere. Therefore, their projects often call for the creation of specific areas for different activities: project rooms, quiet rooms, guest areas, as well as collaborative environments that promote teamwork and facilitate interaction among employees. At times this might mean the creation of small groupings of employees; or at others, it might mean the creation of a large, visually open area where employees can 'feel' the contact of their co-workers and observe the entire team at work.

Scientist? Maybe; Artist? Yes; Psychologist? Perhaps; Technologist? Increasingly; Anthropologist? – The Designer's Challenge!

Every business organisation has a unique past, present and future, and a good design firm therefore tailors its solutions to the unique and individual qualities of each client. There is an awareness of the forces of change affecting the way people work, and consequently, how office environments should be planned and designed. For all designers, the biggest challenge lies in understanding the client's business and to forming a partnership in order to accurately meet the facilities' needs. Practices such as Gensler have worked carefully on the creation of standards which are then applied to field specific workplaces, such as law firms, for example. But while such standards can be quite useful, they can only be applied in certain areas of their work. As the business world moves at an accelerated rate, designers are challenged by the requirements of some of the world's fastest growing companies that are expanding into completely new territories where office standards simply do not exist.

From now on, our mission is not simply to design appropriate buildings and settings to support our clients, but to use design to help them evolve and improve as organisations and the individuals therein to measure the results of our efforts.

As we embrace this new paradigm of 'performance consulting' we have to rethink our roles, responsibilities, skills, procedures and tools.

It means developing a new vocabulary that speaks even more clearly to this emphasis. Clearly, I hope this chapter encourages the reader to consider the interior design process in the appropriate holistic manner.

Author profile

Simon Jackson, Vice President and Studio Principal
Gensler

Simon Jackson joined Gensler in 1995. He has been responsible for many award winning schemes and at Gensler as a Vice President and Studio Principal he plays a key role in workplace design and strategic planning.

Simon's central concern is design excellence at every stage of a project and he is a mentor for the design and delivery process. Simon is a keen supporter of Gensler's inside-out approach; he is widely sought by clients for advice on building design efficiency and ways to maximise a building's potential through design. Simon heads up Gensler's local Strategic Planning and Building Design Consultancy groups and is recognised as a designer who challenges clients to think about their projects in new and innovative ways.

Simon's vast project portfolio includes work for clients such as: British Gas, Citibank, Defence Evaluation Research Agency, Johnson & Johnson, J Sainsbury plc, Legal & General and Warner Bros to mention a few.

Gensler is an international architecture, design, planning and strategic consulting firm with offices in London, Amsterdam, Hong Kong, Tokyo and throughout the United States. Gensler's work covers a wide range of buildings and facilities owned or used by businesses, institutions and public agencies. The firm's services engage the full development cycle from initial planning through design, implementation and management. The focus of the practice is on client issues and challenges.

A strong belief in the effectiveness of design to enhance clients' performance, provides the impetus for creativity and innovation. Gensler's refreshing approach produces work that defies a stylistic signature. Recently, Gensler has been named as the top interior architect for commercial office space in the 2002 'Inside Out' report on the central London office market.

16 Risk management

Mark Dillon, Sheppard Robson
William J. Gloyn, Aon Limited

There is no doubt that insurance for some buildings is now a problem area. However, it is not just an issue for buildings but a major problem for all businesses. Like many other sectors of industry and commerce, the horrific events in the United States have been a catalyst for rapid changes within the insurance market. These changes were, however, already underway before then.

It is necessary to think of insurance as just one part of a four-part risk management process. The need for increasingly sophisticated risk management has been emphasised by some of the events in the world financial scene during the past few months. It is a buzz phrase but is still not widely understood.

The basic elements of risk management are:

- Risk analysis and quantification.
- Risk reduction or elimination.
- Risk retention or transfer.
- Constant review.

Of these perhaps the most important is the ongoing need to review the situation. It is interesting to note from a risk financing review, carried out by Aon from research amongst 500 leading UK companies, published in summer 2001, that terrorism was not identified as one of the top ten key risks, although it had been number 8 in both 1995 and 1997. In 1997 it was also the second highest concern in terms of the availability of adequate insurance cover but had since dropped out of the charts[1].

This chapter is broken down into six key areas:

- Security.
- Fire protection.
- Support facilities – assessing reliability and risk.
- Disaster recovery planning.
- Data storage.
- Insurance.

---

1 For further information visit www.aon.com

Security

This section outlines the key demands of good practice in relation to the location of the building on the site and the layout of the building itself. It is sensible to incorporate the key requirements of good security planning into the design at the early stages, as retrofitting is usually more expensive and less effective.

Assessment

As in all sections of this document, the key to good risk management is risk identification, and the implementation of appropriate control measures. In addition, areas of risk will only be identified when an individual is tasked with the job of doing so.

Anti-crime/terrorism

Early design decisions will greatly effect security. The following should be considered:

(a) Sitewide
- Location of building in relation to site boundary and the provision of external wall or fence to provide the principle of 'defensible space'.
- Single, monitored/manned point of access to site preferred.
- External CCTV coverage to entry road/building approach/loading bays.
- Car parking area to be fully segregated from remainder of building.
- Car parking area to be well lit, covered by CCTV camera and have access rigorously controlled.
- Security patrols to external and internal areas.
- All vulnerable external spaces to be well lit, including access doors, external doors and windows.

(b) The building itself
- Single point of secure access to building.
- The number of recesses and re-entrant corners to be minimised or covered by CCTV cameras.
- Minimal number of opening doors and windows at ground floor level.
- Install conduit to allow tenant to install CCTV coverage to all common areas. Film to be recorded in security room and stored for required 30 days. Video cassettes to be regularly changed.
- Adequate signage, both internal and external, to notify people of the levels of security in operation.
- Contact should be made with the local Crime Protection Officer.
- Core designed to allow isolation of individual floors.
- Occupant profile.
- Consideration should be given to the benefit of constructing safe areas within the fabric of the building for use in the event of a terrorist emergency.

Fire protection

This section sets out the levels of good practice for base fire protection systems and required levels of structural fire protection[2]. In addition, the benefits of a holistic approach given by fire engineering are also noted.

Detection and alarms

In the UK the usual standard that is quoted for fire alarms is BS5839 Part 1 1988 but there are others such at BS5839 Part 6, Part 8, EN54 and various building regulations. Even within these standards there are sub standards such as type L1, L3, P2, LD1 and Grade A. In this instance we are concerned with L1 and L2.

An L1 installation calls for the installation of alarms throughout the building. L2 limits the provision of alarms to defined parts of the building. L stands for 'LIFE'. In addition there are also P1 and P2 installations which relate to property protection.

It is recognised that voice alarms motivate people to leave a building more quickly. These are essential for phased evacuation but should be considered for all installations. In addition, a fire engineered solution may be more flexible if higher levels of alarm and detections systems are installed as part of the base scheme.

Sprinklers

Sprinklers are an effective way of controlling the speed of fire and minimising the damage to the building.

The need for sprinklers is governed by the height of a building, the size of a compartment or the degree of hazard within the space. These are all confirmed by the Building Regulations[3] and Section 20 of the London Building Acts[4], and should be installed to the relevant British Standard.

Providing sprinklers where not required by the above will normally improve safety and reduce insurance premiums. In addition, providing more than the minimum base build Category A provision will improve flexibility and simplify space planning for the occupier. This additional provision should be considered. Category A refers to the level of fit-out undertaken to the base building. A Category A fit-out normally includes the installation of the following: suspended ceilings, raised floor, basic mechanical and electrical services, i.e. lighting, heating, ventilation and cooling, finishes to the core and basic safety signage.

---

2 For more detailed information on fire protection visit www.bfpsa.org.uk
3 The Building Regulations 2000 (Approved Document B – Section 1 – Fire Alarm and Fire Detection Systems), HMSO. Also availaable at www.safety.odpm.gov.uk/bregs/brads.htm
4 S.I. 1987 No 798, The Building (Inner London) Regulations, HMSO.

Where conventional sprinklers are not appropriate, consideration should be given to foam, water mists or gas systems.

Specialist IT installation require specialist solutions in terms of alarms and protection.

Hose reels/dry or wet risers

The need for hose reels has been questioned by fire safety managers in that it encourages staff to stay and fight the fire. Current advice is they should not be installed, although this should be agreed with individual Building Control officers at the outset.

Fire engineering

Consideration should be given to the relationship between active and passive fire protection systems when formulating the design of a building. The use of mechanical smoke extract systems and pressurisation systems needs to be carefully considered with respect to construction detailing. The combination of all aspects of life safety should be considered as a whole as opposed to element by element.

Structural fire resistance

Part B of Schedule 1 of the Building Regulations 1991 states that 'The building shall be designed and constructed so that, in the event of a fire, its stability will be maintained for a reasonable period.'

Aspects of Approved Document B 1991 fire resistance periods are based on height only:

9+ storeys	(>30m)	120 mins
8-9 storeys	(<30m)	90 mins
5-6 storeys	(<20m)	60 mins
2 storeys	(<5m)	30 mins

The figures in minutes refer to the levels of protection that elements of structure are required to be fire protected to, i.e. a beam rated to 90 minutes should be able to withstand full fire conditions for 90 minutes before collapsing.

Reduce all periods by 30 mins if provision is made for sprinklers.

- 'A fire safety engineering approach that takes into account the total fire safety package can provide an alternative approach to fire safety.'

- Section Factor and Protection Thickness Assessment

$$\text{Section Factor} = \frac{\text{Heated Perimeter (H}_p)}{\text{Cross-sectional Area (A)}}$$

Section factor is a measure of the 'massivity' of a section.

Proprietary passive fire protection can be determined from the manufacturer's published data, for example, the *Yellow Book: Fire Protection for Structural Steel in Buildings*, published by ASFP and SCI[5]. Manufacturers relate thickness of protection to H_p/A ratio.

In general, protection thickness recommendations are derived from the BS 476 Standard Fire Test[6], and are designed to restrict steelwork in a fire to a limiting temperature of 550°C.

Site applied protection materials

- Boards (rigid).
- Sprays.
- Thin film intumescent coatings (swells to provide a charred layer of low conductivity material at temperatures of approximately 200-250°C).
- Flexible/blanket system (foil-backed).
- Concrete encasement.

Off-site fire protection

- Thin film intumescent coatings.
- Off-site applied spray (rare, generally restricted to the petrochemical industry).

Steelwork fire resistance

At 550°C structural steel retains 60 per cent of its room temperature strength. Permissible stress code used a 60 per cent limit, and therefore 550°C has become the 'critical' temperature.

In fact, the failure temperature of a structural steel element varies according to:

- temperature profile;
- load.

5 *See also* British Steel (1997), *Fire Resistance of Steel Framed Building*.
6 Available from www.bsi-global.com

Effect of temperature profile

If a member is not uniformly heated then, when the hotter part of the section reaches its limiting temperature, it will yield plastically and transfer load to cooler regions of the section, which will still act elastically. E.g. a concrete slab protects the top flange of a beam from the fire and acts as a heat sink. This induces temperature differences of up to 200°C between upper and lower flanges in a standard fire test. Test data shows that the limiting (lower flange) temperature of a fully loaded beam carrying concrete slab is about 620°C.

Effect of load

At low loads, fire resistance is increased.

From BS5950, Part 8:

$$\text{Load ratio} = \frac{\text{load at fire limit state}}{\text{load capacity at } 20°C}$$

For example, a fully loaded beam in bending has a load ratio of 0.5:0.6. A beam with a load ratio of 0.25 (which is simply supported, carrying a concrete slab) will not fail until steel reaches 750°C.

BS 5950 Part 8: Code of Practice for Fire Resistant Design

The Code of Practice contains two basic approaches to assessment of fire resistance.

- From tests – in accordance with BS476.
- By calculation, in accordance with:
  - the limiting temperature method;
  - the moment capacity method.

The limiting temperature method assesses the need for fire protection by comparing the temperature at which the member will fail (the limiting temperature, which depends on load ratio) with the temperature of the hottest part of the section at the required fire resistance time (the design temperature, determined from BS 476 Standard Fire Tests).

The moment capacity method assesses the fire resistance of a beam by calculating its moment capacity using the temperature profile at the required fire resistance.

Cardington full-scale fire tests

During 1995 and 1996, a major fire test programme was conducted on a full-scale eight-storey steel-framed building.

The following conclusions were drawn by the BRE[7] from the tests:

- No collapse was evident, even though the unprotected beams reached temperatures over 900°C. (Existing fire design codes predicted structural collapse at 680°C.)
- The behaviour of the structure was different and better than that shown in standard fire tests.

Off-site protection

- Thin film intumescent coatings.
- Off-site applied spray (rare, generally restricted to the petrochemical industry).

Increased knowledge of how real structures behave in fire means that improvements in fire protection may be possible in many instances by adopting analytical approaches.

Fire safety engineering is an integrated package of measures designed to achieve the maximum benefit from the available methods for preventing, controlling or limiting the consequences of fire. In terms of structural stability, fire safety engineering is aimed at adopting a rational approach which ensures that fire resistance/protection is provided where it is needed, and expense is not incurred needlessly in giving an illusion of safety.

Support facilities – assessing reliability and risk

The purpose of this note is to provide an outline description of the analysis that can be carried out to ascertain the reliability of the M&E systems serving business critical systems and propose Good Practice Standards for selection and design of key M&E equipment. The analysis is normally carried out in two initial stages:

- review of fault tolerance;
- review of common mode failure.

For systems that require a very high degree of reliability, such as financial services trading operations, an additional statistical analysis of the availability of the M&E systems could be carried out. The statistical analysis is often referred to as an 'ARM study' (availability, reliability, maintainability).

At all stages it is vital that the analysis is business driven and therefore client led. The correct analysis of the business requirements will enable both an appropriate level of

---

7 BRE (April 1999), *The behaviour of full-scale steel-framed buildings subjected to compartment fires*, UK, The Structural Engineer.

standby plant to be provided and an appropriate level of reliability and availability specified. In addition, the inter-dependability of the systems should be considered to ensure that an appropriate level of resilience is provided at the point of delivery of the business critical system to the end user.

Assessing risk

In assessing the risk to M&E systems in buildings, it is necessary to have in mind the potential effect of the likely threats to the occupier's business. Typically with modern, IT intensive business, the areas under risk can be categorised as follows:

- Any threat to the M&E services that would pose a risk to IT services supporting the business operation.
- Any threat to the M&E services that would place the occupation of the space containing the business operation at risk.

Using this criteria, the failure of air conditioning to an office space would not be considered critical whereas a similar failure in an IT area would be critical. On the other hand, the maloperation of a fire alarm system causing evacuation of an area of the building would not be significant to an unmanned IT server room but would be critical in an area dealing with, say, direct telephone sales.

The threats posed by failure or maloperation of M&E services can be placed in categories related to the time period (T) in which they are likely to have an impact on the business operation:

- T1:   Over a period of days or more.
- T2:   Over a period of hours.
- T3:   Over a period of minutes.
- T4:   Instantaneous.

Loss or failure of a critical electrical system directly supporting the business would cause an instantaneous interruption to the business operation. The effects of a similar failure of a critical heating, ventilating or air conditioning system, or power supply to it, is less likely to cause a similar immediate effect.

In addition to identifying the impact of the failure of an M&E service in terms of period of disruption to the business, it is also possible to quantify the risk in terms of the likelihood of occurrence. Typically the following criteria is used:

- Low: Failure of one in 20 years or more.
- Moderate: Failure of one in five to 20 years.
- High: Failure of one in five years or less.

Below is a list of a number of broad, generic threats that are common to many M&E services:

- incoming utility failure;
- plant failure or maloperation;
- lack of maintenance;
- fire;
- environmental disaster;
- electromagnetic interference;
- software failure;
- faulty or inappropriate design;
- inappropriate specification;
- change of use and lack of adaptability for churn;
- over complexity leading to a decrease in reliability;
- lack of fault tolerance;
- single point of failure;
- inappropriate redundancy criteria.

The last three items require careful assessment to match business needs. The following review and analytical techniques are often used.

Single point of failure

In parallel with the review of fault tolerance, a review of the M&E networks should be carried out to ensure that the resilience offered by the standby and redundant plant is not compromised by the failure of a single component at a critical node in the networks.

Arm study

At a point in the design (normally during the detailed design of the fit out) when not only the systems but also the M&E components have been identified with some certainty, an 'Availability, reliability, manageability' (ARM) study could be carried out.

Good practice

The reliability and availability of M&E systems can be improved by enhancing the constituent parameters by a combination of factors during the design, installation, maintenance and operational stages of a project. This good practice can include the following:

- Providing alternative sources of supply for utility services.
- Assessing the reliability and quality of the electrical supply, and making suitable provision for tenant's generators and uninterruptible power supplies.

- Alternative sources of supply should be well separated when they enter the building, preferably on opposite sides of the building.
- Over-sizing of main plant and running them at a percentage of full load in multiple configurations to provide an 'N+1' or better installation for critical plant.
- Providing a flexible distribution network to allow the shedding of non-critical loads when required.
- Specifying high quality equipment providing a good mean time between failure, i.e. a high level of reliability.
- Siting of normal and standby plant in different fire compartments, floors and aspects of the building.
- Siting of M&E plant supporting critical business operations to mitigate the risk of flooding from either natural or manmade disasters.
- Assessing the likely impact of the harmonic spectrum of the occupier's IT equipment on the electrical distribution network and power supply quality, and taking appropriate mitigation measures, e.g. double rated neutrals, de-rating of transformers and generators, use of active filters or isolation transformers etc.
- Commissioning a site survey of the ambient electromagnetic fields. Sensitive kit should be positioned away from areas likely to experience high field strengths or install mitigation measures such as screening.
- Taking precautions to mitigate the likely problems caused by electromagnetic interference generated by electrical systems installed in the building.
- Adequate commissioning of systems.
- Provision of adaptable systems to limit the impact of changes.
- Providing early detection and alarm of environmental factors including fire and water.
- Adopting condition-based maintenance by closely monitoring plant operation. This ensures early detection of potential savings, avoids consequential damage and makes full use of the life of the plant.
- Providing suitable maintenance facilities and design of plant for ease of maintenance and repair.
- Designing distribution networks so that standby and redundant systems can be tested on load without disrupting the occupiers, or making provision for the installation of test loads.
- Increasing the frequency of maintenance, planned tests and inspections. The duplication of major items of plant allows these to occur without system downtime.
- Specifying equipment with short repair times.

Disaster recovery planning

Given the impact of the September 11th terrorist attacks, the following assessment in relation to a catastrophic event needs to be considered in detail.

a) Disaster recovery planning risks that will be identified include:

- IT failure – both hardware and software problems.
- Natural disaster, e.g. floods.
- Fire.
- Terrorist activity, both directly against the occupier and indirectly via action against other adjacent targets.
- Fire and explosions.

b) Risk assessment is a product of two elements:

- Likelihood of the risk occurring. This can be dependent on issues including location (for example, likelihood of flooding or proximity to likely terrorist targets) and the type of user – occupiers with high IT dependency are more likely to suffer business interruption than those with little dependency.
- The impact of the risk on the business when it occurs – losses in terms of money, personnel, adverse publicity, action by regulators, etc.

Major occupiers tend to categorise their buildings into three levels of importance:

- Critical to whole/business.
- Critical to regional or local business.
- Not critical.

Business considerations are:

- Operations – loss of income, profit, opportunity.
- Legislative – breaking the law.
- Reputations – loss of credibility/standing in market and hence share price.

Use of risk assessment methodology will allow risks to be ranked in order and then appropriate control measures and contingency plans will be implemented.

c) Control measures

The range of control measures available to the building developer and occupier are significant but not without cost – it would be reasonable to assume that the greater the risk to business continuity, the more the user should be prepared to pay to avoid business interruption.

The following measures need to be considered:

(i) Building design and use. This could be viewed in three distinct sub-sets.

- Basic design measures that should be incorporated into all buildings:
  - Appropriate location of plant rooms to avoid risk to services, e.g. sensitive building services equipment should not be placed in basements in locations prone to flooding.
  - Backup of service provision, e.g. two telecomm feeds to the building coming in from different locations.
  - In large buildings, provide distinct separation between the structure to enable one part to operate independently from other sections.
  - Blast protection to buildings should be located near potential terrorist targets.
  - Adequate levels of fire detection and fire fighting equipment.
  - Adequate levels of security, e.g. CCTV, card access systems.

- Design for specific users. Dependent on the user this could include:
  - Provision of standby generation and uninterruptible power supplies (UPS). Consideration would need to be given for fuel storage, floor loadings to support battery packs, location of generator exhausts (avoiding air intakes and fire detection) and materials in UPS rooms which can withstand accidental battery discharge.
  - Distinct separation of comms rooms (e.g. for file servers, intermediate distribution frames) from telephone switch rooms so that a problem in an IT room does not cause a failure in voice communications.
  - Provision of adequate security to comms and telephone switch rooms, e.g. CCTV, card access systems.
  - Installation of very early smoke detection (VESDA – Very Early Smoke Detection Apparatus) and fire suppression systems, e.g. sprinklers, gaseous systems. VESDA is a system of small pipes, spaced about a room, that suck air from within a space and draw it over a sensor. This will raise the alarm quicker than waiting for the smoke to naturally make its way to the detector.
  - Leak detection systems in sensitive areas.
  - Blast protection in buildings housing mainframe computers.

- Maintenance and testing. This would include:
  - **A rigorous programme of planned preventative maintenance,** e.g. regular maintenance of standby generators and uninterruptible power supplies (UPS), maintenance of HVAC systems to minimise the risk of leaks, testing of fixed wiring installations and portable appliances to minimise the risk of fire, etc.
  - **Testing of control measures on a regular basis,** e.g. load testing of generators, testing of fire alarms, etc.

(ii) Business continuity planning. The following should be considered:

- Production of detailed plans by the business (or individual business areas if a larger user) to allow them to manage an interruption which should include:
  - **Business impact analysis** – what would actually happen to the business if interruption occurs. This will allow the criticality of the business to be identified and, if appropriate, ranked against other business units occupying the same building. The analysis should also identify the timescales in which the business needs to be recovered to minimise adverse affects. This process also assists in defining which of the available recovery options is most suitable (see below).
  - **Identification of critical components required to allow the business to function** – from IT software/hardware to stationery requirements – and how these would be provided in the event of a business interruption.
  - **Actions plans** – task lists identifying who would do what in the event of a business interruption.
  - **Names of key contacts** with work/home/mobile/pager numbers – both internal staff and external customers/suppliers.
  - **Means of testing the plans** – desktop scenario tests, testing of telephone contacts, actual testing of any off-site recovery facilities, etc.
  - Selection and upgrading of alternative locations to provide 'Business Continuity Centres' which would be easily used in the event of an emergency.

- Formation of a core team, of a size appropriate to the business, to manage any business interruption. Functions that require to be considered would include:
  - **A central manager** to co-ordinate the activities of the team.
  - **Accommodation** – ensuring the affected building is safe/secure, salvaging equipment, records, etc and managing any building recovery activity.
  - **Personnel** – ensuring evacuation occurs, accounting for all building users, liaising with the emergency services (if they are involved) and managing issues arising from casualties.
  - **Communications** – ensuring that appropriate and timely information is given to staff, customers, suppliers and the media.
  - **IT** – ensuring recovery plans are implemented in an effective manner.
  - **Insurance** – ensuring loss adjusters are involved as soon as is feasible and maximising the recovery of monies from insurers.

- Identifying and, if necessary, procuring recovery options: these may include:
  - **Doing nothing** – there may well be some scenarios where it is appropriate to 'ride out the storm', e.g. short term loss of power. However, these scenarios must be identified, agreed in advance and documented in contingency plans.
  - **Working from home** – some business areas may be able to function from home for short or even prolonged periods of time. Again, these areas should be identified and appropriate action agreed in advance, e.g. provision of ISDN lines to staff homes.

- **Switching operations** – for organisations with a multi site operation this may be a feasible option. However the switch needs to be planned in advance (e.g. ensuring phone calls can be diverted, staff in alternate sites have the correct skill sets to deal with the diverted business, etc) and it must be recognised that this may only be a short-term solution. The site to which business has now been switched can become quickly overwhelmed with a potential for income loss.
- **Using off-site facilities for critical businesses and functions.** These may include work area recovery site where desks, IT, telecommunications etc are provided by a third party supplier, or mainframe recovery where IT processing functionality is transferred to a third party supplier. These options are expensive and thus tend to be reserved for critical operations where any business interruption would involve significant losses. Off-site facilities must also be carefully set up, regularly tested and maintained which, in itself, can involve considerable cost.
- **Using alternative accommodation** – including displacement of less critical business areas to allow critical occupiers to use their space, use of non-critical space (e.g. meeting rooms, training areas, rest areas and staff rooms/canteens) and acquiring/fitting out alternative premises although this latter option must be recognised as expensive and to be used in times of prolonged business interruption/building loss.

- **Ongoing programmes to maintain and test recovery plans.** Businesses continually change and their continuity plans must change with them; untested plans are likely to be unworkable plans.

Data storage

Extent of storage requirements

Current computer data storage facilities require much of the same infrastructure as other data centre building types. Redundancy of services, resilience of structure, flexibility of use and redundant diverse facilities are all key elements that must be accounted for in a storage facility.

Worldwide data storage capacity is estimated to be 3.4 exabytes today and anticipated to grow to a staggering 43 exabytes in 2005. Up to 80 per cent of worldwide storage capacity is not new data but copies of primary data. There are a number of reasons for the pervasive growth of copies of primary data, including disaster recovery, backups, intra-departmental data sharing, and application staging. Each of these functions are components of a business continuance strategy, and the business goal of data storage.

Data is not only growing in size but in importance as well. Large enterprises have been protecting their primary data for years. Much of this has been for mainframe data, but open systems Unix and NT based data is increasingly becoming mission-critical and the same requirements apply. Data replication is a key component of business continuance but increases the amount of storage needed. This puts an enormous strain on existing storage infrastructures. Special purpose storage appliances, facilities and management regimes are needed to optimise storage networks.

Fibre and Storage Area Networks (SANs) are being deployed at an ever-increasing rate to assist in the movement and management of mission critical open systems data. Estimates indicate the SAN component market at £1.00 bn in 2000 growing to £10.88 bn by 2005.

Current methods

Business continuance is the set of tools and processes that enable an IT organisation to continue operations during planned service outages and unplanned events (e.g. site disasters, system failures). For years, mainframe environments have implemented business continuance solutions that include host based data replication, disk based mirroring, remote tape vaulting, near instantaneous backup, and near instantaneous restore. Each of these technologies has one goal in mind: to create and maintain secure and consistent copies of data while applications remain online and available.

There are different levels of disaster. A relatively minor disaster could include a single disk failing. Or an entire storage sub-system could fail. The worst case is if there is a catastrophic site disaster.

Consider how a couple hours of downtime to Amazon's online order entry system site would have a huge cost due to lost sales and goodwill. If Amazon used data replication technology, some transactions could get lost during a failover to a secondary site but the costs would be manageable.

In order to get operations up and running quickly, you need a restart, not a recovery. There is a big difference between these. A recovery can take from hours to days, and possibly up to a week. A restart is performed using duplicate copies of the data maintained on a storage system at another site. This data would be accessible almost immediately and, depending on what remote mirroring solution is used, it would be an exact copy of the primary data.

One of the most common methods of online replication between data centres is to extract data from an application at a primary data centre and send it to a secondary data centre. For those applications where the cost of downtime is very high, a hardware based approach that mirrors data between a primary and secondary site should be used.

The high cost of such a business continuance solution includes the cost of twice the storage capacity, the networking cost between the two data centres, and usually the added cost of hardware and mirroring software.

(a) In house, owner occupier facility

The most obvious reason for not locating data storage facility on site is the possibility that events leading to the collapse of the core business would also affect the data centre. There are, however, reasons for doing so. Data transfer is most efficient over short distances. Monitoring of the facilities and other shared building services can be located at the same site, often costing companies less.

In almost all cases, however, where a local data centre is used there is an argument to locating a business continuity data centre/data storage facility remote to the core business site.

(b) Remote, occupier facility

In all cases a level of risk must be determined before continuity schemes can be put in place. Companies will need to determine how much money it will cost the business as a result of information/communication downtime and how long before services are restored. This cost would be balanced with the cost of the data recovery scheme to be implemented.

Increasingly, companies are realising that downtime is more costly than duplicate facilities and additional measures of redundancy/security. Remote data centres are most effective when data can be stored and updated mirroring the local data site, or as close as possible to real time. This requires a fibre network, which currently has proximity limitations on the order of 30 miles. In some instances this may be too close to provide adequate security as natural disasters often span regions of several 100 miles. In these instances, data recovery would have to be managed differently and possibly as a backup. Businesses would have to account for the retrieval of data in cost projections.

(c) Fully serviced tele-hotel

The tools required to deliver storage as a service differ slightly from the tools required to manage data or the infrastructure itself. Businesses are increasingly opting out of the data business for managed data services. It is one thing, for instance, to operate a power generation plant, quite another to operate the electrical distribution network, and still another to operate the customer service aspects of a delivered electric utility. Each function requires specialised tools.

This is similar to operation of an in-house data centre and business continuity facility. Businesses will be required to maintain robust facilities while managing networks and storage space for departmental use. Serviced data centres provide high levels of business expertise, relieving the core business of the burden of an often complex and expensive peripheral department.

In any case the facility is the same: the service management, of the facility, offers the appeal.

Table 1: Pros and cons of existing methods

	Pros	**Cons**
In-house, owner occupier facility	• Proximity to core business users. • No long distance networking. • No duplication of office and IT facilities.	• Circumstances that would effect the core business to stop will often affect the data retrieval business. • Security needs to control personal between the office areas and data centre.
Remote, occupier facility	• Separation of core business activities from data/records storage. • Build-to-suit facilities use space more efficiently. • Data storage can be located in less expensive area.	• Increases networking costs. • Duplication of certain internal business elements (i.e. facilities departments, IT departments).
Fully serviced tele-hotel	• Same as remote occupier facility. • A specialist company, allowing the client to focus on core business activities, provides data facilities maintenance. • Capital expenditure for a new occupier facility is removed.	• Service costs are not always cheaper than an occupier facility.

Future developments

(a) New methods of storing information

Current data storage involves magnetic media as the industry standard. Ease of data writing and retrieval make magnetic media the easiest to use in business continuity situations.

Traditional tape-based backup solutions, in fact, no longer can meet the backup/restore requirements required by the growth of installed disk capacity or demands for 24/7 web operations and e-commerce-based applications. Disk-based, continuous replication is becoming the norm. Having a live replica on disk means you do not have to restore; you just use the replica.

Moore's law describes the prediction that the processing power of computer chip will double approximately every 18 months. (Moore was a scientist who predicted that the capacity of processors will double every 18 months. This has generally held true.) Similar comparisons can be made to data storage. Magnetic media is nearing its physical limits and new storage media will need to be developed.

Imagine being able to record 100 movies on a disk the size of a CD, or one day recording the contents of the Library of Congress on a single CD disk. These are the promises of holographic data storage.

Holography enables storage densities that can far surpass the limits of traditional magnetic and optical recording. Holography can break through these density limits because it goes beyond the two-dimensional approaches of conventional storage technologies to write data in three dimensions. In addition, unlike conventional technologies which record data bit by bit, holography allows a million bits of data to be written and read out in single flashes of light, enabling data transfer rates as high as a billion bits per second (fast enough to transfer a DVD movie in about 30 seconds).

With its powerful combination of high storage densities and rapid data transfer rates, holography stands poised to become a compelling choice for next-generation storage needs.

(b) Impact of property requirements design.

Dillon's law (not really) is that the cost of technology facilities doubles every generation.

By definition, 'protecting' data means making multiple copies. The key questions to be answered by companies are how many, where do you put them, and how often do you update them?

Insurance

In a property context, as in many others, insurance has traditionally taken a low priority. Although risk transfer is important, it has for many years been so simple for commercial property owners. The price has been cheap and it was easy to arrange the cover needed. The same has not always been true for other business sectors. For instance, in the mid 1980s there were tremendous difficulties and high costs associated with professional indemnity insurance for architects in the UK. This led to the formation of a mutual/captive insurer – the aptly named Wren. Interestingly, there is only a minor insurance element to the Wren's activities. In the main they are concerned with risk management, in particular avoiding the assumption of risk by their architect members through careful contract drafting.

Even when insurance is required by contract or by statute, it involves a degree of uncertainty if the insurance company is not chosen with care. The last few years have seen a number of major insurers disappear as a result of insolvency or financial problems. Many left behind long tail liability covers, such as public liability and employer's liability. If those who expected to benefit from these policies have not kept a close, watching brief on the insurance market they may find themselves without protection in the event that a claim surfaces in the future. If sufficiently large, like the asbestosis claims still coming from the US, the absence of insurance can threaten the financial stability of the policy holder.

For building owners, tenants and funders this is particularly important when relying on professional indemnity insurance. As the cover is on a claims made basis, it is the policy in force when the claim is made that is the one that responds, rather than when the negligent act occurs, as is the case with public and employer liability insurance. It is therefore vitally important to monitor the ongoing existence of the cover and certainly essential if any great reliance is placed on seeking financial redress from it in the event of a building defect.

Unfortunately, post 11 September, there is little doubt that the solvency of some parts of the insurance industry are in question. As already stated, this situation is not totally as a result of that terrorist action. The cost of re-insurance – essential to lay off the risks accepted by the primary insurers who issue the policy – has been falling for almost ten years. In the same way, the cost to the insurance buyer has also been falling and in no sector has this been more the case than in the profitable commercial property sphere. The cost per £100 of purchasing all risks cover for an office is only 30% of that which would have applied 20 years ago. This has to be countered against a scenario of increasing levels of insured losses that in turn have left many insurers with operating deficits for many years.

Since 11 September the market has become much harder. Some insurers have actually cancelled terrorism cover where they had the right to do so under the policy terms. Now, without reinsurance from 1 January 2002, others have been forced to follow suit – even if they do not have the contractual right to do so. To do anything else would actually be trading in a way unlikely to be acceptable under corporate legislation, exposing shareholders to a complete collapse of the company. What is increasingly apparent is a return to the basic principles of underwriting rather than the relaxed conditions of the soft market we have experienced in the last decade. For property owners this is likely to have all the effects outlined earlier and in addition, as already experienced when recently attempting to place new risks in the market, a particular focus on design and protections incorporated into the property.

With the continuing uncertainly about the full financial impact of the New York attacks on the global insurance market, there are still many issues to be resolved. In addition to war, terrorism and sabotage attacks are now being completely excluded from insurance and reinsurance contracts of any kind, except those specifically designed to cater for those risks. In addition, we are seeing the application of exclusions to this effect on some policies with little real exposure to such incidents. As a result of the fear of financial insecurity and the need to achieve comfort at any price, there is a flight to quality and a desire to have protection provided by an insurer of adequate credit rating. Finally, at least in my summary, insurers will be looking to withdraw or reduce their exposure to complex risks.

This inevitably brings us to 'tall buildings', or rather any large buildings for why should tall building be different to any other complex structure?

The big issue for the insurance market is now one of accumulation of risk. Inevitably, tall buildings equate to high-value buildings. The changed structure of the insurance/reinsurance market means that the primary insurer will be able to absorb less risk in value terms and will also be analysing that risk to identify the real maximum exposure. As a result, it is likely that many property owners' policies which have previously been insured 100 per cent with one insurance company will have to be scheduled over many insurers, each of whom retains a small percentage of the risk. This, interestingly, is exactly how things were arranged 20 years ago before the primary insurers put much bigger reinsurance programs in place and also, quite frankly, started taking a much more relaxed attitude towards underwriting. For the property owner this should not pose a problem although for the broker it will mean far more work in securing full coverage.

Under the terms of the agreement to lease, the lease and the funding agreement, the building owner has an obligation to insure the property. It is likely that the risks to be insured will be specified within those documents and highly likely, at least in any negotiated in the UK during the last ten years, that terrorism will be specifically stated. As the repairing covenant of the tenant would specifically exclude damage from insured risks, whether or not the landlord has been able to arrange cover, the building owner and funders will be exposed for the uninsured damage and subsequent consequential loss.

It is therefore vitally important that specific terrorism cover is arranged, as indeed it had been in the UK since the Association of British Insurers introduced their standard exclusion of such damage effective from 1 January 1993.

With the exception of a relatively small alternative market, the Pool Re has exclusively provided terrorism cover in the UK since 1993. This is a mutual insurer comprised of over 200 insurance companies and Lloyd syndicate members which was effectively organised by the government in the face of the loss of terrorism cover. There is still some uncertainly over the workings of the Pool Re and the cover it gives, but it has proved itself efficient over the past nine years. The government stands as re-insurer of last resort behind the Pool Re's own funds – in 2001 some £1.2 bn – and a government-guaranteed bank facility of £0.5 bn. Despite some complicated rules, all of which must be observed if cover is to be guaranteed, the Government has on many occasions confirmed that it will stand by the Pool Re until a viable commercial alternative arises. In light of 11 September, that seems to be a very remote possibility for many years to come!

The major issue now facing UK policyholders is the gap between the fire and explosion cover provided by the Pool Re and the total exclusion of any damage applied by the insurance market. The Treasury, who determines what the Pool Re can do, is considering the extension of cover within the terms of the legislation which set up the company in 1993. This will leave some gaps in cover and in the definition of what constitutes an act of terrorism. The insurers have extended this beyond political acts to those with ideological and religious motives – something not catered for in the Act.

Tall buildings do indeed present their own insurance problems but they are not to be viewed in isolation from the whole of the commercial property stock. Despite the vulnerability of the insurance market since 11 September, it is a sophisticated sector of the business world and will continue to respond to the requirements of property owners. What is, however, certain is that property owners and their consultants will also have to wake up to the problems of the insurance market. Far more attention to insurance issues will be needed in order to preserve the financial security essential to underpin the investment and ownership of this asset class.

The importance of insurance

Insurance does, however, have a very important role to play in business life in general. If matters go smoothly it is rarely apparent. Unfortunately things do go wrong and that is when it is needed. Insurance cover provides the financial resources required for legal obligations to be met, damaged property to be replaced and the income needed to sustain a business to be maintained. This protection is especially important when undertaking a project in an unfamiliar territory, one where business practices, often taken for granted in Western Europe, may not always be encountered.

Insurance repays careful preparation. Unfortunately this does not always happen and the resulting shortcomings of a policy are only detected once a claim arises. Extreme diligence and caution therefore needs to be exercised, both professionally and personally, in the handling of insurance affairs. There is a need as never before for specialist and expert advice – insurance today is not for amateurs. It demands detailed consideration by the client, consultants and contractors to ensure that each one is adequately protected against their own risk exposures.

The changing appetite to accept risk has an increasing relevance to the commercial property world. The landlord has traditionally transferred many risks to the tenant, using the mechanism of the service charge as a buffer against unexpected cost increases and expenditure. The introduction of PFI concepts into letting deals often changes the balance. The same is true for the serviced office provider.

Many of the new risks can be absorbed within an alternative risk transfer vehicle. This is usually set up off-shore and can be similar to the captive insurance companies that have been around for many years. With the benefit of sophisticated reinsurance arrangements they can absorb much of the business risk associated with today's new leasing structures, including credit enhancement and premature life cycle failures.

Many organisations, after adequate thought, are well able to absorb a certain amount of risk. This is often more cost effective than effecting insurance which involves paying for a service (including a theoretical profit element) to a number of other parties. For many larger organisations this risk absorption is achieved by means of their own captive insurance company. For others, the answer may lie in a mutual insurer as many firms of major UK architects discovered when they set up the Wren to insure their professional indemnity risks. Yet another option is merely to expose the profit and loss account. It is, however, when a particular risk exposure is great enough to threaten the stability of the balance sheet that some other form of risk transfer may be considered. Insurance may, of course, be a contractual obligation not a matter of choice; leases, funding agreements and building contracts are typical examples. Another possibility is the statutory imposition of an insurance requirement, as found under the Road Traffic or Employer's Liability regulations.

Insurance – chain mail or string vest?

The four principle types of insurance policy in a commercial property context are:

- Property damage.
- Consequential loss.
- Legal liabilities.
- Personal protection.

The first of many likely complications comes from the fact that not all of them will be arranged by the party that suffers the immediate loss. It is indeed possible that none will be so arranged. As a result, there is unlikely to be a commonality of interest between the insurers, the insured and the claimants. This is bad news for those who suffer the loss, and aggravation or worse for most of those involved. It is, however, extremely heart warming for the litigation industry. Taking one particular type of insurance as an example, The 1988 Liekerman Report on professional liability, published by HMSO, suggested that upwards of 80 per cent of claims payments under Professional Indemnity policies were needed to pay the cost of the litigation process itself. Only 20 per cent of the money paid by insurers actually went to satisfy the claims of those who suffered the loss!

Before examining some of the policies in a little more detail, it is worth considering some of the legal principles which help to frustrate the claims process and help to underpin the concept that insurance is not a subject for conversation at polite social gatherings.

Some of the commercial and legal principles examined
With so much money going into the litigation process, it is hardly surprising that it is legal issues which come to the forefront rather than practical ones which seek to address the problem. There are some interesting nuances which serve to assist this process very effectively.

(a) Utmost good faith
It is a basic principle that insurance is a contract of good faith. This requirement at least applies to the insured who has many duties but particularly that of disclosing all material facts. Unfortunately, there is no clear way of identifying what these might be, at least not until the claim arises. The duty upon the insured is to disclose to the insurer all facts that would affect a prudent underwriter's assessment of the risk. Failure to do this, or to misrepresent facts, generally gives the insurer the right to avoid the policy. It does not matter that the claim is not connected with the fact; for instance, incorrect information about the previous history of flood damage can give rise to the insurer's right to avoid a fire claim. There have been a number of high-profile international court cases on this subject over the past few years but these have done nothing to relieve the insured of a total obligation.

(b) Material damage proviso
It is important to note that the failure of a material damage claim can also lead to the avoidance of a consequential loss claim. It is a fundamental proviso that a successful claim for the former must precede the other. This is to ensure that funds are available to repair the physical damage which gives rise to the consequential loss, thereby minimising the period of that loss.

(c) Inter-relationship of insured parties
There is continued confusion over the rights of a party whose interest is noted on a policy. It is still a frequent requirement but in reality means little or nothing. The only real protection that can be obtained is to be joint-insured under a policy. Also required is an express provision of severability to avoid the contract-breaking actions of other parties, including joint insured, prejudicing any interest in the contract. Otherwise all parties to the contract will be affected by the actions of another, such as non-disclosure of a material fact, thereby giving the insurers the opportunity to avoid the claim in its entirety, not merely for the interest of the offending party. The joint insured party is entitled to a share in the control of the claims procedure and subsequent proceeds together with rights of notification of the

cancellation of the policy. It should be noted, however, that without an express provision there is no right to be notified of the non-renewal of an expired policy.

It may not come as a surprise to learn that claims involving a number of joint insured may themselves be difficult to negotiate. Insurers have no duty to act as arbitrators between disputing insured. They are likely to seek to satisfy policy liability by issuing a cheque in joint names leaving it to the parties concerned to fight it out amongst themselves. If one of those parties becomes insolvent it will be even more difficult, if not impossible, to use the claims proceeds for the intended purpose.

(d) Subrogation rights

After playing all the other cards, if an insurer is forced into the position of having to pay out will the matter stop there? It most certainly will not! Indeed, here is perhaps the nub of why insurance is so important but often unrecognised. Under a contract of indemnity, and following payment of a claim to the insured, the insurers have the right to be placed in the position of the insured in pursuing rights and remedies against third parties. Insurers have no subrogation rights against a joint insured, who is therefore not a third party, another good reason to seek this status. Insurers may agree to waive their rights against specified parties, for instance contractors working in an existing building for a fit-out contract, often on payment of an additional premium.

These are, however, exceptions rather than the rule. Material damage and liability insurers will seek to find another party to at least partially repay their loss. The only way they can do this is using the threat of litigation, a threat that often extends to the courtroom door and beyond. It tends not to be an area in which gentle persuasion is terribly effective.

As previously stated, there are four major classes of insurance which might be encountered in a serious incident which affects a building or construction project.

Property damage

During construction there will be a contractors all risks policy effected in accordance with the contractual requirements of either a recognised standard form or some bespoke wording prepared by the client's professional advisers. Following completion of the building, contract cover will be transferred to either a commercial all risks policy or a fire and specified perils cover. There may also be an engineering breakdown insurance which is often coupled with a statutory inspection contract. This provides the periodic inspections of lifting equipment, pressure vessels and other assorted plant, required by various health and safety regulations, normally on a six-monthly or annual basis.

Within the building there are likely to be contents. If they belong to the building owner they may be covered under the same all risks policy as the buildings but a separate policy may exist. A tenant will obviously have a separate contents insurance, possibly on an all risks basis and possibly with theft insurance included or as a stand-alone policy. There is sometimes tension between landlord and tenant regarding the insurance of fit-out works. A well-drafted lease should make the responsibilities clear.

A particular form of insurance becoming more common in this country provides cover for the building owner in respect of latent or inherent defects. Failures in design, workmanship or materials are specifically excluded from almost every other type of insurance. A combination of the prudence of the building owner and the lack of confidence of tenants and funders has created a surge in interest in this cover for commercial properties. Decennial insurance in France and some other Napoleonic Code countries is a statutory requirement designed to give direct protection to those who suffer damage who might otherwise only have legal and contractual remedies to rely upon. As the damage may only become apparent some years after practical completion, and after changes in ownership, those remedies can be diluted by time or dissolve completely following insolvency. It is becoming widely appreciated that the reliance on collateral warranties, to meet the cost of rectifying latent defects, is largely misplaced. They depend upon professional indemnity insurance which, as outlined below, may not be in place to protect those who suffer the damage some years after the design work was completed.

Latent defects insurance is usually placed on a ten year non-cancelable basis, although 12 years is now possible. The cover is for the rectification of defects in the structure which become apparent after practical completion. Additional protection can be purchased for weather and waterproofing, defects in mechanical and electrical plant, together with loss of rent and other consequential losses.

Consequential loss

This cover comes in many guises. In essence it is designed to protect against the financial consequences of insured damage to property. As previously stated, the cover must follow the same basic provisions as the material damage insurance and may provide for loss of rent and service charge, or for the tenant's or occupier's loss of profits. It may be on a wider business interruption basis providing an amalgam of various protections including increased costs of working. The cover may be on an anticipated basis, for buildings under construction; it can reflect turnover at historic levels or perceived expenses. Whatever the basis, it will be for a set indemnity period, often quite short for profits, perhaps 12 or 24 months, but much longer for loss of rents where periods of five or seven years are not uncommon.

Legal liabilities
We all have a tendency to look for blame in others if something goes wrong. As a result, there are a selection of liability insurances designed to give protection, both in respect of costs and damages awarded by the court following the establishment of a

legal liability and also the costs involved in attempting to avoid that uncomfortable situation. Public liability insurance gives protection in respect of injury or death to third parties and damage to third party property arising out of the business of the insured. A variation on this is property owner's liability cover which obviously limits the activity to ownership of property although facilities management and other peripheral issues may also be covered. Products liability insurance is protection for the supplier of a defective product although this does not include any responsibility for the replacement or repair of the product itself, merely the consequences. A rare example of a statutorily imposed insurance requirement is that for employers liability insurance. This provides protection for the employer in respect of legal liability arising to an employee following injury, disease or death. Unlike workmen's compensation, as required in some other countries, it does not pay an immediate benefit to the employee but merely provides the financial wherewithal to allow the employer to do so if found legally liable.

Environmental impairment liability is a relatively new area in the UK. The vast majority of liability policies now exclude gradual pollution. This is seen as a matter than can be controlled by good management. Sudden and accidental pollution is still covered.

With the advent of the new contaminated land regime, property owners, tenants and funders may find themselves liable for clean up costs even if they did not cause the contamination, did not have an interest in the land when it occurred and have not been negligent. Such is the way with strict statutory liabilities.

The insurance market is responding with a wide variety of covers to provide protection to the various parties concerned. All the options require detailed site investigations. The cover can, however, often be transferred to future owners and give considerable comfort to those concerned about the long-term ability of consultants and contractors to meet their contractual obligations – even after the most expensive and extensive remediation programmes.

An important element of any property development insurance programme will be professional indemnity (PI) insurance. This is designed to protect the professional in the event that their activities create a liability arising from error, omission or neglect in the provision of professional services. Unlike the other liability policies examined, PI cover is on a 'claims made basis' – the policy in force when the claim is made is the one that responds rather than the one that was in force when the incident occurred.

PI cover is relatively new, compared with the other forms of public liability protection. The insurers introduced the alternative basis of settlement to avoid the claims which could otherwise surface many years after the policy period in question. They therefore have the ability to avoid further claims by refusing to renew a policy or to impose higher levels of excess if the claims experience in any one year becomes unacceptable. This adds to the risk that a building owner, relying upon a consultant's PI insurance to underpin a collateral warranty, may find that there is reduced cover or that it has ceased entirely. PI therefore has to be kept in force for as long as a potential liability exists. The terms and conditions of the cover can also change at any renewal. This may turn out to be an unpleasant surprise if care is not taken to monitor the cover. Although provision for the client to monitor the design consultant's insurance is usually included in professional appointments and warranties, in practice it is rarely undertaken.

Liability policies have an important factor in common. They are designed to protect the insured against whom some legal liability is being alleged. They do not provide direct protection to the party who has suffered the loss.

The final suite of liability covers that might be needed can be classified as legal indemnities. They include an assortment of contingency protections aimed at providing indemnity for the breach of a legal obligation or restriction, together with the additional costs that certain situations can create. Generally tailor-made to fit a particular property or development scheme, they are often demanded by a funder, potential tenant or purchaser. As a result they are usually assignable to future owners, sometimes at a nominal additional premium.

Examples are:

- Restrictive covenants – designed to provide defence costs and indemnity against an award for the breach of a known covenant that does not appear to have any surviving beneficiary when placing the cover.
- Defective title – again costs and defence for claims from a third party against the use of land for which no title can be proved at the time of effecting the policy.
- Archaeological remains – possibly defence costs but more likely the consequential losses which occur from a delay to a development caused by the discovery of unexpected remains which give a relevant authority the right to halt works and possibly demand re-design.

Within the same generic group we should briefly consider bonds. These come in various guises. Well known is the performance bond required of a contractor to meet the additional costs of engaging an alternative if the job is not completed. A developer may also be required to deliver a road bond to guarantee compliance with planning obligations to construct and maintain public infrastructure to support a development.

All bonds require the production of detailed financial information to insurers, who act as sureties, together with back-to-back indemnity from the bonded party. The main benefit of using an insurance bond is the freeing up of lines of credit which would otherwise be frozen if a bank bond was used.

Personal protection
Many private individuals and employees will be covered by life assurance. There may also be personal accident and sickness cover, often coupled with private medical expenses insurance. Although individuals may take out these covers, they are at least as likely to be provided as part of an overall employee benefit package. Within such cover there may be protection for the employer to mitigate the costs of absence from work, either temporary or permanent, of key staff.

Premiums
In the current volatile market it is virtually impossible to give even a rough guide to the premiums which might be expected to apply to the varied selection of insurances referred to above. Setting a premium depends on so many factors that any indication will be inaccurate for too large a proportion of individual cases. To be taken into account are underwriting considerations, such as previous claim experience, building construction and location, occupation or business, loss control measures in force and physical protections such as a sprinkler system or intruder alarms.

Also to be considered are moral hazards, the state of the market and the appetite of a particular underwriter for the business in question. Part of the skill of the broker is to weigh up all these components and produce a tempting proposition to secure the most attractive deal for the client.

With a totally free market, now including such a wide variety of overseas insurers, the range of responses can often be astounding. But arranging the cover to the client's satisfaction is just the beginning. It provides the opportunity to make a claim and that can be an entirely different story.

Claims management
Major incidents, it is true, do not happen that frequently. As a result, they often find the various insured concerned ill prepared.

On scanning through the above list it is easy to see how many separate contracts arranged by a wide variety of parties might be involved in even a relatively small incident. Serious damage to a multi-occupied property involving death or injury to third parties as well as the employees of the responsible party with subsequent interruption to business could involve literally dozens of separate contracts of insurance. The basic provisions of them all will have to be satisfied before claimants feel that they have obtained a satisfactory settlement. The fact that this does not always happen is very often the responsibility of the claimants themselves.

Often the insured will have arranged cover with the assistance of a broker. Immediate advice and support should therefore be at hand, provided by an experienced claims team for whom such an incident is not a one-off experience. Some insureds, admittedly, find comfort in dealing direct with their insurers. It is sometimes in the event of a major incident that their confidence may be undermined – remember the profit and loss account. No matter what the circumstances, it is important to give immediate notice to the insurers of any circumstances that are likely to give rise to a claim. The mechanics of doing this are generally clearly set out in the policy document and form part of the conditions of the contract. Failure to comply with them will offer yet another potential route to the insurers for avoiding a claim.

It is quite likely that the insurers will appoint their own professional advisers. Amongst these will be a loss adjuster in respect of material damage, consequential loss and liability claims. The latter are also likely to see lawyers appointed as will a damage claim if the circumstances begin to give any cause for hope that a plea for avoidance may be justified. Any of these parties may well call in an expert to conduct a forensic investigation.

Recalling the basic requirements for the acquisition of subrogation rights, it is only when claims have been paid that the insurers have a right to seek recovery from third parties. In practice, however, this process is likely to start at an earlier stage, especially if the sums are big enough.

Conclusion

Office buildings do indeed present insurance problems but they are not to be viewed in isolation from the whole of the commercial property stock. Despite the vulnerability of the insurance market since 11 September, it is a sophisticated sector of the business world and will continue to respond to the requirements of the wider business community. What is, however, certain is that property owners, tenants and their consultants will also have to wake up to the problems of the insurance market. Far more attention to insurance issues will be needed in order to preserve the financial security essential to underpin the investment, occupation and ownership of this important asset class.

Author profiles

Mark Dillon, Partner
Sheppard Robson

Mark Dillon has been with Sheppard Robson since 1987 and was made a partner in 1998. Mark has specialised in design and implementation of large commercial offices on a countrywide basis.

The occupier has made security a key issue in the design and maintenance of the majority of these buildings. In addition, Mark's recent involvement in data centres (internet hotels) has raised the issue of building security to a new level. The preceding documentation is a summary of key issues that should be considered in the design of any new office.

Sheppard Robson Architects are a 260-strong company based in London and Manchester. Founded in 1938, Sheppard Robson has gained extensive experience in educational, R&D, hospital and more recently, over the last 30 years, the design and implementation if large commercial office buildings.

Sheppard Robson believe in working closely with the client to produce architecturally outstanding buildings that are delivered to agreed programme and cost targets.

William J. Gloyn, Chairman and Account Director
Aon Limited

Bill Gloyn is the Chairman of Aon Limited, UK Commercial Property Practice Group. The team, which he set up in 1983, specialises in the insurance and risk management requirements of the commercial property owner and developer. Numbered amongst its clients throughout the country are public and private property companies and also institutions, charitable organisations and the management portfolios of several major firms of Chartered Surveyors. As Account Director he maintains an active role in a number of the Division's accounts, including some for global property-related clients with international investments. He chairs the Aon European Real Estate Practice Group, which he formed in 1999, that has representatives from all major European territories.

He advises the British Property Federation on insurance matters and is Chairman of the BPF Insurance Committee and the BPF representative on the JCT Insurance Committee. He was a member of the Advanced Study Group of the Insurance Institute of London that produced a widely acclaimed guide to Inherent Defects Insurance.

Bill is an external tutor for the Masters degree in Construction Law at Kings College, University of London. He also lectures for the Continuing Professional Development Foundation based at the University of Westminster as well as conducting in-house CPD seminars on insurance and risk management related topics for lawyers, surveyors, accountants and other professional firms.

17 Occupier issues

Philip D. H. Brown, Martyn Hayward and Paul Brown
DT2, Debenham Tie Leung

Introduction

The aim of this chapter is to highlight to the occupier a number of issues and pitfalls that can be avoided by early planning and asking the right questions of the developer and consultant team. Some have been touched upon in other sections and we seek here to give more detail and relevance subjects such as costs in use, outsourcing and of health and safety issues.

In line with best practice the provider of space can no longer walk away from his product expecting the occupier to take on and deal with all the pitfalls. For this reason a greater reliance on feedback and dialogue between all parties is to be encouraged.

In an ideal world, the developer aspires when creating an asset to achieve a pre-let and in so doing maximise development return. Clearly this can only happen with the right product, design, location and flexibility, all of which are paramount if a developer's building is to be chosen by an occupier over competing buildings. At an early stage, any prospective occupier should be engaged in dialogue to ensure that the developer provides what is required at the most economical price and, crucially, the resolution of any differences of opinion. Far too often buildings fall short of the realities of occupation due to a lack of understanding, which results in many facilities having to be retrofitted to enable the continued smooth running of the building.

Whole Life Costing

So what is whole life costing? Whole life costing (WLC) is a process for assessing the costs of constructing (or installing) and operating and/or maintaining an asset over its life, sometimes known as Costs in Use.

The principal use of whole life costing is to facilitate long-term decision making between one type of asset specification and another. The WLC technique has been extensively used on PFI schemes to enable bidders to assess their costs for constructing and running properties over anything from 15 to 30 years.

Whole life costing can have a key role in deciding the choice of particular plant, materials and finishes. Whilst it is not always the case that increased capital expenditure will result in lower maintenance or operating and replacement expenditure, it is true that this is often the conclusion. However, as in life there have to be compromises as access to unlimited capital is not always available.

Clearly from an occupier's viewpoint a property where WLC has been carried out should lead in the longer term to a reduction in the overall costs. However there is not a widespread take up of WLC for the following reasons:

- WLC is only effective in looking at specific elements such as marble finishes and air conditioning – carrying out WLC on all aspects of a property would generate an enormous number of factors to consider including interaction between one element and another.
- WLC can only provide a guide as to the best value solution rather than exact cost.
- The level of information available on the long term behaviour of materials is not extensive.
- Differing occupiers have differing fiscal policies and it may be beneficial in some cases for the occupiers to have higher running costs and lower capital expenditure.
- For the landlord, each occupier will have a different way of using the building, which would be almost impossible to predict.
- The way occupiers want to use their property is changing at an ever-increasing rate, which limits the effectiveness of WLC.

Despite these drawbacks it is clear that WLC has a role to play and the increasing introduction of professional Facilities Managers will assist in adding more information to the WLC database. The growing use of performance based contracts will ultimately enable optimum operating and maintenance benchmarks to be established for the various materials and design techniques used in construction. This will assist in reducing some of the anomalies that presently exist in WLC.

From a tenant-occupier perspective the use of sinking funds and apportionment of capital expenditure is always complex and commercial pressure on landlords to offer a competitive rental level controls the level of capital expenditure to be invested in the construction phase of a property. Having said this, where long-term leases are being negotiated the occupier would benefit from the WLC process, as indeed would owner-occupiers.

Any long term forecast technique such as WLC engenders a degree of risk and it is therefore necessary to consider a risk management model alongside WLC to assist in formulating a complete understanding of the financial position.

Outsourcing

Outsourcing as an option for procuring Facilities Management services is now well established, and although similar to sub-contracting, outsourcing requires the agreement of three parties, namely the client, the supplier and the staff. The third dimension, that is to say the staff, is brought about by the transfer of the in-house staff to a third party supplier. The duration of an outsourcing contract can range from three years to thirty years, whilst the norm for commercial occupiers is three years extendable to five, outsourcing projects initiated through the Private Finance Initiative (PFI) are more likely to be fifteen to thirty years in duration. PFI contracts in simple terms sees the government transferring the risk of property/asset ownership and management to the private sector in a similar way that a corporate occupier of property might undertake a sale and lease back. Successful examples are Princess Margaret Hospital in Swindon, and ironically an unsuccessful example is the Treasury property.[1]

The occupier's desire to outsource should in theory be driven by three main factors – cost, quality and business need. However in practical terms it is the cost case that motivates the occupier to consider outsourcing. The ability of suppliers to be able to reduce costs is driven by a number of factors and these are listed below:

- They are specialists in the chosen outsourcing field.
- Their central costs can be spread over a number of clients.
- They have invested in infrastructure to ensure efficient operation.
- They can optimise resource levels needed to provide any specific service.
- They are able to introduce best practice from their specialist chosen area.

Conversely, most occupier's core business will not be in the specialist area to be outsourced. From the supplier's viewpoint, their ability to deliver the benefits listed above and successfully provide an outsource solution is dependent on two key factors - firstly their overall management structure and approach, and secondly, their ability to successfully integrate the transferring staff into their organisation. It is this latter factor, driven by cultural fit, which will determine the long-term success of an outsourcing route.

TUPE legislation

A section on outsourcing Facilities Management would not be complete without touching on the area of TUPE (Transfer of Undertaking Protection of Employment) legislation. Occupiers should be aware that outsourcing, and that is to say transferring their existing in-house staff to a third party supplier, is covered by TUPE legislation.[2] In general terms the legislation is designed to protect the rights of transferring staff and increasingly it ensures the continuation of benefits. For instance, pensions which up

---

1 For more information on PFI go to www.privatefinance-i.com
2 For more information on TUPE visit ww.dti.gov.uk

until recently had not been covered under TUPE legislation, are now to be brought under TUPE which means the pension benefits presently enjoyed by existing in-house staff will be transferred to the third party suppliers. Whilst this increased protection addresses some of the issues transferring staff have with the outsourcing approach, it also reduces the supplier's ability to reduce costs simply by reducing the benefits offered to transferring staff. This will force suppliers to concentrate on their management structures and infrastructures to deliver the efficiencies required by occupiers. It is the direction and management of a supplier that will ensure that an occupier's cost, quality and business need requirements are fulfilled.

Securing an outsourcing solution can be achieved either by tendering or through negotiation. Whilst tendering ensures that the lowest price is secured, the complex nature of an outsource solution means that cultural fit will be as equally important to an occupier as the cost if a long term successful solution is to be provided.

Whether an occupier selects a negotiated or tendering route one of the key fundamentals is to convey to the supplier the needs of the occupier's core business. For many occupiers this will be one of the more difficult parts of the process. Defining the tasks is probably not that difficult. However, defining the performance surrounding that task will be key. It will be necessary to define both service level agreements and key performance indicators for each task to ensure that the supplier has a real understanding of the occupier's needs. Fortunately for occupiers there are now a number of specialist consultancies who are able to assess such issues and prepare the documentation necessary (such as DTZ Pieda Business Consulting).

Another factor for occupiers to consider is the ongoing management of the outsourcing solution. It is a common misunderstanding that through outsourcing you no longer need to manage the specialist area to be outsourced. It is fundamental to the ongoing success of the outsource solution that the supplier has an understanding of the changing requirements of the occupier in terms of his business. Therefore any changes in the occupier's core business should be clearly communicated to the facilities mangement supplier and ideally with advance notice.

It was noted earlier in this section that most occupiers consider outsourcing when they want to reduce their cost base, which inevitably means that the timing of any outsourcing will normally coincide with the downturn in the occupier's core business. Again another myth is that by outsourcing an occupier can avoid redundancy costs, this is not the case. If an occupier believes that he is overstaffed it is better to bite the bullet and make those staff redundant before they consider an outsourcing solution.

So to conclude this section on outsourcing, there are clearly a number of benefits to selecting an outsourcing solution. However there are a number of fundamental parameters that need to be met by the occupier if a long term successful solution is to be achieved. The success of any outsourcing will in most cases be proportionate to the level of up-front input the corporate occupier is prepared to put in to making the outsourcing work. The misunderstanding by many corporate occupiers that outsourcing means that they do not have be involved will lead to an unsuccessful working practice.

Importance of feedback loops

It is perhaps one of the most interesting points about the property industry that buildings are designed, constructed and let by companies who have little experience or knowledge of the occupier's business needs. To make matters worse, many occupiers do not really know what they want, or even understand how the design of a building could affect their core business.

So is the information not available that would address this problem? Well no, there are a number of sources available to the occupier and to those who design and build properties, it is just a case of knowing where to look.

The primary sources of information are:

- Help Desks.
- Logbooks.
- Occupier's staff.
- Feedback surveys.

The Help Desk

The Help Desk is increasingly accepted today, as the standard management tool for dealing with Facilities Management issues. The Help Desk can be used as a control point for dealing with both proactive tasks as well reactive and for the occupier, it is a means of communicating any issues in the most efficient manner.

For the Facilities Manager it assists in resource allocation, helps to deal with issues as they arise and most importantly it acts as a database recording all the issues and their solutions. Many companies will link service level agreements to the Help Desk and will use it to measure and monitor the performance of those undertaking tasks, whether it be an in-house team or an external supplier.

The database aspect of the Help Desk can provide both the occupier and supplier with a useful source of information. By analysing the types and frequency of calls it is possible to formulate a picture of what is going on. Recurring problems are more than likely (assuming it is not a recurring performance issue with the service supplier) to stem from the way in which the occupier's business is interfacing with the property. This type of information is equally as beneficial in assisting to reduce current cost levels for the occupier as it is in highlighting inherent issues with the design and specification of the building.

The Building Logbook

Managing the facilities of a building entails completing some form of logbook. This is occasionally produced manually, but more often than not information is stored electronically, and has commonly come to be referred to instead as Computer Aided Facilities Management (CAFM) systems. The Logbook not only records what tasks have to be fulfilled and when based on the design, material selection and services required for that building, but also the reactive tasks undertaken in the course of managing the building. The Logbook like the Help Desk provides a complete information database specific to that building.

The benefits of this information can be looked at in the short, medium and long term. In the short term, by analysing the reactive tasks which have been carried out over a twelve-month period, an occupier can begin to understand some of the issues that need to be addressed through either a change in process or even a capital expenditure. Analysis may reveal that the operating hours of the building need adjusting, by examining when people are booking in and booking out and understanding which departments and which areas of the building they operate in.

Over the course of time the amount of information stored on the Logbook will increase, and so will the degree of understanding of the property and how best it should serve the needs of the occupier's core business. In the event that a new property is sought, this valuable source of information can be used to define the type of building, its shape and the functional space required in order for it to meet the occupier's business requirements.

The Logbook assimilates an enormous amount of information, which over the course of time reflects the changing requirements of the occupier's business needs. Going back no more than three years will ensure that relevant information only is extracted. In terms of extracting the information, this is probably best done under generic service headings such as cleaning, maintenance, services maintenance, utilities, landscaping, projects, etc. The information should be looked at not just from a negative perspective but also from a positive. For instance, what were the parts of the building that did work well for the business? In undertaking this sort of information extraction it may also be beneficial to look at the information in the light of any benchmarking exercises that have been carried out as well.

Occupier user groups

Some occupier organisations have created user groups who would in the ordinary course of events liaise with the facilities management team. These groups provide direct feedback from the users about the building, where it works or doesn't in terms of meeting their business needs.

When an occupier is looking at a new building, then the creation of a user group, representing a cross section of staff who will work in the building, is extremely valuable. However, the user group needs to be clearly directed as to the parameters within which it must have to work, particularly in terms of time and costs. Although the user group is more likely to focus on specific areas of the building – such as meeting facilites and rest areas.

In addition some occupier organisations may have conducted a facilities requirement survey of all their staff and again this will provide a valuable source of information.

Occupier surveys

With best practice in mind the developer, agent, construction team and building management should all be interested in courting occupier feedback through questionnaires and regular meetings with the relevant personnel. The person to speak with will be dependent on the nature of the feedback sought but is unlikely that the degree of information required will be obtained if, for example, just the director was asked. Greater benefit can be achieved by dealing with staff working directly with the Facilities Manager and technical teams on a day-to-day basis and who generally have a better understanding of the realities of their business needs. The building owner and agent should not be frightened to seek feedback as to the level of service being delivered. Any survey of the occupier's satisfaction with the service provided should, if nothing else, cover key areas such as:

- The clarity of information provided to date.
- The occupier's preferred format and regularity of communication, i.e. by letter, telephone, email, etc.
- The requirements of health and safety and environmental policies.
- The standard of maintenance – cleaning, mechanical and electrical, etc.
- The standard of concierge services if delivered and if not whether they would they be of interest.
- If there are any future occupation needs.

Clearly, if frequent complaints are received from occupiers based in one part of the building then this must be indicative of problems – say with air conditioning that requires rectification.

A number of professional agencies, such as DTZ, have formulated their own occupier surveys which obtain feedback from occupiers and enables their future needs to be considered as well as assisting the building owner to formulate their future building and management strategy.

There are also firms who specialise in tailoring reports to meet specific needs and will carry out one to one surveys (such as Kingsley Lipsey Morgan *www.kingsleylipsey morgan.com)*.

435

Minimising designer pitfalls

Whilst it is understood there are commercial constraints to constructing a building, designers and builders should also be guided by the way in which occupiers use buildings. Through understanding the issues occupiers face in trying to operate in a building will assist developers and owners alike to create a desirable property.

Increasingly the way that occupiers use their buildings is changing at an ever-increasing pace. New working practices such as home working are rapidly becoming the norm, facilitated by ever improving technology. It can only be a matter of time before the location of a building is no longer the main driver for occupiers allowing them a greater choice in the buildings they occupy.

Feedback, research and the ability to communicate and listen are therefore key. Many problems can be overcome by putting in basic services, which might appear more expensive initially, but in reality reduce the set up costs and aid a smooth transition from a building site to a well thought out and run building. An example of this is where a fire alarm system is installed which has the ability to act as a tannoy, but only has the basic speaker specification. For minimal cost this can be upgraded to allow live voice-over which then enables the system to be used for bomb evacuation procedures, which in today's uncertain world must be considered essential. It is all about creating a flexible system that can be adapted easily in line with an occupier's changing needs.

Compromises are always made between the developer, who needs an adequate return to enable construction in the first place, and on the other hand the occupier who would like the world at no extra cost. Simple design changes can usually be catered for in most cases if discussed at an early stage, such as security, CCTV and finishes, and the effect that these may have on costs in use.

It is more cost effective at the design stage to install, not only the cable trunking, but also the CCTV installation itself. Consideration should also be given as part of the base building management system to incorporate a dedicated landlord's computer terminal at reception with slaves to each floor to enable instant delivery of building information and facilitate self-help for the issuing of access passes, concierge services, newsletters etc.

Material selection for ongoing maintenance can have a big effect on cost in use. For example, when considering the finishes to apply to an emergency staircase, there is always the debate of carpet versus vinyl flooring. From a cleaning perspective, it is easier and cheaper to vacuum the carpet as opposed to regular mopping and sealing of the vinyl floor finish. In terms of presentation carpet gives a more upmarket finish for little or no extra cost and with a reduced maintenance regime. Floor and wall finishes also play an important role in this, paint or vinyl wallpaper versus polished plaster or marble. Colour and material selection are also key. Due to changes in fashion, even the most expensive finish will often be replaced after 10-20 years. It is not uncommon for a corporate occupier, when designing and specifying a building for their own occupation to choose a higher standard of finish. Whilst this may be more expensive, it will prove cost effective over the life cycle of the building. Developers have a habit of compromising in this area when specifying on a speculative basis.

With the advent of radio communication for computers, the debate must be had as to whether the raised floor is dead, as the need for extensive cabling is negated. This of course must be contrasted with the need to give a number of service providers the ability to offer services. Consideration must be given as part of the base build to the installation of satellite systems.

Commissioning and handover

When nearing Practical Completion pressure is always put on the contractor to complete and the architect to issue the Certificate of Practical Completion, this is especially the case in a good market with the opportunity of pre-letting. In a poor market however the reverse can also be the case with the developer seeking to delay practical completion for clear financial reasons.

The management and resolution of defects is an important issue and one, which could be made more easy if practical completion was given more honestly. Building management is often left having to manage the process especially when it comes to meeting air conditioning design criteria and the fine tuning of the building management systems (BMS) for example.

To ensure a smooth transition from building site to an occupied and well run building, work needs to start on the production of a critical path analysis of fundamental building management issues that will occur as the project progresses and the appointment of key personnel (if appropriate).

It is advisable at the time of handing over premises to an occupier, assuming that the snagging list has been completed and dealt with, to go through a bespoke building checklist which needs to incorporate the following:

- Condition of the premises.
- Areas for which the the occupier will be responsible.
- Areas at the time of handover that the occupier is not happy with.
- An agreed action plan for resolution.
- Utility meter readings to be taken as appropriate.

Later confusion can be avoided by a clear understanding of what is included within the completion and what is not and an agreed action list of items requiring attention with a timescale of completion and by when and whom.

An occupier should obtain copies of various manuals appropriate to the completed accommodation, obviously for buildings let as a whole considerably more information

Table 1 Critical path and management issues to be considered

• Implementing an ongoing building management structure	• Occupier manuals
	• Sub-division arrangements
• Procurement of maintenance contracts	• Branding
	• Building website
• Staff recruitment	• Health and safety
• Security	• Signage
• CCTV and Access Control Systems	• Evacuation procedures
• Building management operational needs	• Document storage
	• Building rules and regulations
• Building management system (BMS)	• Managing defects
	• Concierge and hotelling opportunities
• Occupier fit-out	

will be required than if the occupier is only taking part of a larger building. The information sought at the time of handover should include O&M manuals, building rules and regulations as laid down by building management and the owners, and procedures and practical advice on the actual implementation of lease terms, such as the procedure to be adopted on an assignment and how to obtain consent for alteration works. For ease of use it is recommended that all relevant information be compiled into a single guide for the occupier's use.

The guide should spell out to whom the rent and service charge is to be payable. Occupier's should be aware of any tenant forum and to nominate an appointed person from their company to attend various meetings. Guidance should be given as to how to carry out alteration works both initially as part of the tenant fit out process and alterations during the course of the period of occupation. The occupier needs to know how to obtain approval, how many copies of plans and specifications are required and have a general understanding of the need for this information. The occupiers need to be aware of the various forms of maintenance contracts that need to be entered into and thus to whether economies of scale can be obtained with reference to utility procurement by using the building owner's suppliers and performance based contracts.

In multi-let buildings where occupiers require their own security systems it is generally imperative that these be capable of linking into the main building systems. In today's technological world, communication between building owners and managing agents is more often than not via the building's specific website or intranet.

Occupiers also need to ensure that they are fully aware of the bomb procedures and evacuation procedures for the building as well as be aware of the building disaster recovery plan and ensure that their requirements are incorporated within this document. This should be distinguished from an occupier's own business continuity plan, as the building owners will be responsible for ensuring that in any disaster contractors are called upon to make the building safe, instruct the insurers and put in to motion the necessary works to reinstate the building. It may also well be advisable to create a specific disaster recovery plan. Names and addresses will also be required for inclusion and key personnel within the building owner's own plans, for if best practise is being adopted they all will also notify occupiers, agents and contractors should a disaster occur to their own operational premises so that communication can be maintained at all times. Subject of course to compliance with the Data Protection Act 1998.

Facilities management and training

Increasing awareness and understanding of the importance of facilities management not only by occupiers but also by the industry itself has led to an increase in the demand for a more professional approach by those offering FM services. Within this fast growing professional discipline, facilities managers have extensive responsibilities for providing, maintaining and developing a myriad of services. These range from property strategy, space management and communications infrastructure to building maintenance, administration and contract management.

The skills now expected from a professional facilities manager are very varied, and whilst in the past the facilities management services may have been the domain of the maintenance manager this is no longer the case.

The FM industry's governing body in the UK is the BIFM (British Institute of Facilities Management)[3], who have recognised the occupier's need for greater professionalism within the industry. There are now a number of professional qualifications which facilities management staff can attain. In addition there are also a number of universities who offer either a diploma or post-graduate qualification in Facilities Management.

The BIFM promotes the highest standards of professional conduct through its stated objectives, which are to:

- Promote and develop the science and understanding of facilities management.
- Provide a national professional qualification – BIFM (Qual).
- Provide support through training, education, information and research.
- Provide continuing professional development through presentations, meetings and visits.

The facilities management industry itself has also recognised the need for better training and indeed better research and there are now a number of leading companies within the industry who sponsor research programmes for the further advancement of best practice. Without this focus on training and research the occupier's requirement for innovation, and the need to maintain best practice could not be fulfilled.

3 Further information on BIFM visit www.bifm.org.uk

Perhaps one of the more interesting aspects of Facilities Management is that a number of its suppliers are increasingly becoming global players, and as such they are able to draw upon best practice on a global scale. The increasing use of the internet means that ideas and views can be exchanged very easily on a global basis, which means the speed at which new ideas are being discovered is increasing.

For those occupiers who retain an in-house staff to provide their facilities management services, it is essential that their employees are provided with the opportunity to attain a facilities management qualification. It is as much the process of attaining the qualification as the qualification in it's own right that will ensure employees are introduced to new ideas and new practices that can benefit the occupier's core business.

Benchmarking against best practice

The use of benchmarking is an established tool for driving best practice and is part of a modern management approach. However there are still many companies who use benchmarking to provide a tick in a box, rather than as a tool for continuous improvement.

Many occupiers benchmarking their facilities management services invariably measure only the cost and the most common metric being cost per square foot or per square meter. Whilst this provides a level of information, it can lead to lack of action, the occupier who does nothing seemingly has the lowest cost and thus becomes the best performer. The action itself will be driven by a number of factors such as type of business, legislation warranties. By way of an example cleaning of cladding may need to be done once per year to meet the requirements of the warranty, but because the property happens to be the corporate headquarters of an organisation, the owner decides to clean the cladding six times per year. So it is vital to understand the action when comparing costs.

The increasing use of performance based contracts in the facilities management industry provides us with a real opportunity to consider both the cost and qualitative aspects of a service and thus be able to benchmark the real added value of what is being delivered.

The success of a benchmarking process will depend upon careful planning to establish:

- What it is you want to measure and why?
- The basis on which you will measure.
- What data is available both internally and externally to your organisation?
- How the data will be validated?
- The implementation plan for taking action once the benchmark data has been achieved.

There are now an increasing number of sources which occupiers can use for undertaking a benchmark exercise, such as Jones Lang LaSalle's 'Oscar benchmarking' which provides benchmark information on service charges, and Johnson Control's 'Occupancy Cost Index', 'BCIS Cost in Use data.' and 'OPD – Occupiers Property Database'.[4]

For those occupiers really looking for best practice, one of the ways to achieve this is to identify a task and to look across other industries, examining how similar tasks are undertaken. For example, looking at the way Formula 1 racing creates pit-stop teams that are able to work very efficiently under extreme pressure, may be useful for catering teams or postal services teams. Clearly this approach requires considerably more planning but the results could lead to a fundamental improvement in the process.

One of the fundamentals of benchmarking is that customer and client needs for improved performance, either through reduced costs or improved quality, means that as businesses we all have to instigate best practice. And this should not be as a one off event, but an ongoing exercise within facilities management providers.

Complaints as a marker of building performance

Facilities providers who believe that silence from the occupier is a tacit indication that all is well – are making a dangerous assumption. When complaints are received, dependent on their nature, it is not necessarily an indication of poor building performance. Negative feedback from an occupier has to be viewed in context, having regard to the nature of the complaint, age of building and the like. Most complaints result as a consequence of poor communication.

Best practice is to continually:

- ask questions;
- update;
- and monitor and improve service.

This is far removed from the old idea that the landlord handed over completely when the occupier moved in, only to be seen again at the end of the lease.

Health and safety – the challenges ahead

In the UK, health and safety has always been subject to intense legislation and enforcement, yet despite these measures a large number of people still die as a result of business activities every year. As well as being distressing to the families of those involved, these tragic events also result in a huge cost to society, both directly and indirectly.

---

4 See www.joneslanglasalle.com and www.johnsoncontrols.com

Very often, those responsible for these deaths are not held personally accountable for their failings, and the use of fines for retribution is seen as a soft option as they do not reflect the seriousness of the event and many companies can write these off as an inconvenience.

In 2000, the Government launched its 'Revitalising Health and Safety'[5] strategy, which is a 44-point plan designed to reduce the incidence of work-related deaths, injuries and diseases by 2010. So far this campaign has resulted in two key initiatives which are designed to inject a new impetus into the whole health and safety sphere, and to re-focus business leaders into taking a more proactive approach to health and safety management. The first, 'Corporate Killing' is a proposal to make business criminally responsible for deaths that result from their activities. Those at the top of the organisation could be made to pay for failings within their company, whether under their direct control or not. To help senior directors prepare for this challenge, a code has been published, which spells out their health and safety responsibilities and the measures they should adopt to help minimise health and safety risks throughout the business.

Corporate killing

The failure to bring to justice those deemed responsible for tragic, and often high profile, disasters has prompted calls to change the way in which deaths resulting from business activities will be punished. Under its 'Revitalising Health and Safety' campaign, the Government is proposing to introduce a new offence of 'corporate killing' to enable companies to be charged with manslaughter for such occurrences. This offence would apply to companies in both the public and private sectors.

Is this something new? Well not entirely, the Health and Safety at Work Act already makes provision for making both companies and individual employees accountable for serious health and safety failings. However, the severest penalties under the Act (unlimited fines and up to 2 years in jail on indictment) often do not bear resemblance to the nature of the incident. Although existing criminal liabilities, such as involuntary manslaughter, do offer higher scales of punishment, it is very difficult to gain a successful conviction, particularly in large and complex organisations. The difficulty arises because before a company can be convicted, the individual who is deemed to be in control or represent the 'embodiment' of the company must himself be guilty of manslaughter. If this cannot be proved, then the charge against the company will fail.

For example, following The Herald of Free Enterprise incident, prosecutions were brought against seven individuals and the company. The case failed because blame could not be attributed directly to any of those individuals. Similarly, as a result of the Southall rail crash, Great Western Trains were fined a record £1.5m for breaches of

---

5 Visit www.hse.gov.uk/revitalising/progress/summary.htm

the Health and Safety at Work Act, but the manslaughter charges were dropped, as a specific individual could not be identified as being negligent.

Very few successful prosecutions for manslaughter have been brought against corporate entities, and these were all small companies where the key individuals could be easily identified and held responsible. The aim of the new proposal is to make that process easier and to ensure that punishments for deaths resulting from poor health and safety management reflect the seriousness of the offence.

The recommendations put forward by the Government include:

- Creating the new offence of Corporate Killing, which will equate to the similarly proposed offence of 'killing by gross carelessness' for individuals.
- The offence will only have been committed if the conduct of the corporation, leading up to the death, fell below that which could reasonably be expected.
- It would be irrelevant whether the risk of the event was obvious or not, or whether the company was aware of it or not.
- Any death will be regarded as being caused by the company if it results from 'management failure' to control health and safety risks for those affected by the business activities.
- Such failure will be regarded as the cause of a person's death even if the cause can be attributed to an act or omission of an individual.
- Individuals within the organisation could still be held liable for 'reckless killing' or 'killing by gross carelessness' as well as the company being liable for 'corporate killing'.

There are concerns however, that these new offences are designed to create a fall guy, and that those at the top of organisations will be held accountable for failings 'down the line'. If a group of people on the street are involved in a serious crime, then it is only those who perpetrate that crime who are held liable, not the whole group. However, as you will see from the next section, those in charge of a responsible organisation should be directly involved in the management of health and safety throughout the whole business and would therefore be able to provide adequate resources and prevent failings.

Directors' responsibilities

Another major step in the strategy to revitalise health and safety has been to influence company directors that they must take a more active and positive role in the management of health and safety issues.

Although the Turnball Report[6] already requires businesses to annually review their risk management controls, a new Code has been issued by the Health and Safety Commission (HSC), which outlines specific responsibilities Directors should follow to establish effective health and safety management systems within their organisations.

There are five key Action Points outlined in this code, and whilst they only reiterate what is already required under existing legislation, make clear that Board Directors cannot just sit back and delegate their liabilities to others. The first responsibility is that the board must accept its collective leadership role and ensure that the business is committed to continuous improvement in risk control. These intentions must then be drafted into a written statement, along with details of the organisational structure and the arrangements in place needed to ensure that the policy can be delivered. Obviously, this message has to be communicated to all employees and regularly reviewed and updated to ensure that it remains valid.

Clearly the weight of this message would be seriously diluted if the actions and decisions of individual directors did not match those of the company. How often have we seen financial or management controls being imposed, which prevent good health and safety practices being followed? As such, Directors must be aware that they also have a personal responsibility to reinforce the overall company message through their attitude, behaviours and actions.

Even with a top-level commitment to health and safety, many problems often arise at the operational level due to poor planning and foresight. Often decisions are made to invest in new technology or processes without thinking about how health and safety controls will be achieved once in place. More often than not the costs for remedying these problems after the event are far more expensive than if these issues were considered at the design stage. In addition, the company may do business with other organisations, including contractors, whose own health and safety standards may have a detrimental impact on those set by the Board and could lead to a damaged reputation. Therefore directors must ensure that all business decisions are in line with the values and commitments set by the company.

The involvement of employees, in all business matters, has long been recognised as a key element in operating a successful business. Regulations are already in place which require businesses to consult with employees on health and safety issues, however the Board must recognise the importance of employee involvement and ensure that there is top level representation in the process so that improvements can be taken forward.

Finally, the Board must ensure that it is always up to date with current health and safety requirements and risk management techniques. It is strongly recommended by the HSC that one Board level Director is appointed as being responsible for championing health and safety issues. This health and safety director will then be responsible for ensuring that risk management issues are implemented throughout the whole of the organisation. Continual reviews and audits of the management system and overall health and safety performance must also be undertaken to ensure that it remains relevant to the business needs.

---

6 Visit www.icaew.co.uk to view PDF version of the report.

Whilst this code has been put into place, it is important that businesses don't just follow the guidelines blindly without understanding or appreciating the overall benefits such practices would provide. Effective management of health and safety will almost certainly help to reduce the number of work-related accidents and the obvious consequences that may follow such events. Aside from the legal penalties, the hidden costs that result from accidents, such as bad press, lost productivity, staff absence and (more increasingly) litigation, may cause serious financial damage. Good health and safety management may also help to win business from other companies who do take such matters seriously. Increasingly, organisations are adopting high moral standards when choosing who they do business with!

The Health and Safety Executive have published an extremely useful guide to help businesses adopt good health and safety management practices. Entitled 'Successful health and safety management'[7] (Reference HS(G)65 and available from all good bookshops), this document outlines the key steps to implementing an effective strategy to help minimise health and safety risks and should be essential reading for anyone who is involved in the running of a company help them meet these new challenges.

Establishing a successful occupation strategy

This chapter has highlighted for the occupier of commercial premises some of the problems and pitfalls that can occur in taking on new workspace, or in running existing premises, but which with foresight and by planning ahead can be avoided.

Whilst the major operating expense of any business is the cost of employing staff, ensuring that quality and effectiveness of the workspace is maintained will enable staff to work efficiently, reduce absenteeism and so enhance workplace productivity.

The increasingly influence of Health and Safety Regulations and impending directives on the use of energy in buildings will place a greater premium on dealing with these issues in a productive way. Establishing, and then implementing, an occupational strategy is an effective way of both ensuring compliance and maintaining the operational efficiency of the workspace.

---

7 Health and Safety Executive (1997), Successful Health and Safety Management, London, HSE.

Author profiles

Philip D H Brown BSc FRICS, DT2

Phil Brown is director responsible for the overall management and strategy of the focused property company management team at DT2 Debenham Tie Leung. Phil has had experience in most property disciplines including: management, rent reviews, leasing, refurbishment, sales and development and has led teams of consultants and other professionals to maximise the investment and rental value of property portfolios in line with clear business plan objectives. Phil was a Director of Hammerson UK Properties Plc and has been part of the management teams at Randsworth Trust and Brixton Estate.

Phil is a Director of the British Council for Offices, and has served on the Conference and Awards committees. Is a member of the Chartered Surveyors Livery Company and Freeman of the City of London.

Martyn Hayward BSc,MRICS, MBIFM, DT2

Martyn Hayward is currently the director responsible for facilities management with DT2 Debenham Tie Leung's Property Management division. His Facilities Team manages some £125million of expenditure per annum and over 90m sq ft of property across the UK. Martyn's area of specialisation is performance measurement and management, which is now a fundamental feature of the management approach DT2 provide to its clients.

Paul Brown MIOSH RSP, DT2

Paul Brown is DT2 Debenham Tie Leung Group Health and Safety Manager and has wide experience in all matters relating to health and safety management. Expertise has been gained in both enforcement and a consultative role, for service related industries. Paul is involved in the setting of company wide policies and ensuring that these are implemented throughout the UK at all of the DT2 offices.

18 The end game

Matthew Giles and Alister Harwood
Interior Services Group

Synopsis

We want to take you on a mental journey forward to the end of a typical commercial office project. From that vantage point, we invite you to look back at some of the factors influencing the success of your project. As members of a group of companies which specialise in different aspects of delivering and advising on built space, we are in quite a unique position. Each week, we solve issues to do with managing our clients' risks, inspiring trades to deliver their best work, and providing the right space on time and at the right price. From the variety of assignments we undertake, we also see trends in office use and in essential parts of an operational office environment such as IT solutions and furniture.

We then invite you to look forward and imagine how the completed space will be maintained and serviced during its lifetime. Having spent so much effort achieving a high-quality, defect-free facility, every owner, occupier and property manager will want to keep their office functional, efficient and clean. We explore some of the options for managing the facility after completion. You could think of the office's life cycle in terms of a clock (*see* Figure 1 overleaf).

The users are at the heart of the process, and most occupancies are geared to a 25-year lease period. Representative periods for building and fitting out the office – creating the facility – are shown on the clock face above. The remainder of the time is spent managing the facility. Any point in time during the lifetime of the space is represented by the position of the hands. The clock face model also indicates the likely relationship between initial capital expenditure and life cycle costs.

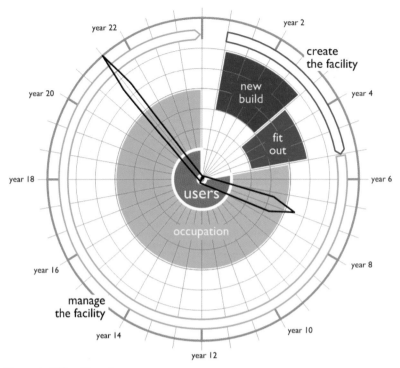

Figure 1: Office lifecycle

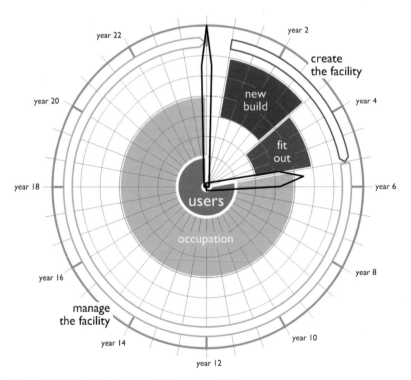

Figure 2: Office lifecycle – end of fit out period

Introduction

Imagine you have just completed your new office. It was handed over last week, with no remaining defects – a first in your experience. On the clock face, the hands are just after the end of the fit out period (*see* Figure 2).

You are at your new workstation, reading the latest e-mail from one of the board directors congratulating you on the move, on the quality of her team's new working environment and the opportunities it gives them for interacting. It is only one of a number of communications from delighted staff. They have all commented on how much better their new surroundings are and how painless the move has been. Of course, there were a few adjustments to be made to the furniture, but the installers were on hand to make them efficiently.

At some point this morning, you must review the text of a nomination for a prestigious award recognising the merits of the design and the many successful innovations the project has embodied. The office has already featured in a number of upmarket journals and attracted some very favourable comment. It is seen as symbolising a fresh, new approach by your company, combining value for money with an emphasis on working flexibly. The HR director has commented that the high profile of the project has already started to attract a noticeably higher calibre of candidate to the company. As you reflect on the success of the project and your own part in it, you remember the many hurdles the team had to overcome. Some of them seemed almost insurmountable at the time, and caused you some sleepless nights. But good teamwork, trust in each other and a steady nerve got them solved, and the final result is, in fact, better for them.

At every stage, you were able to keep your board fully informed of the progress towards the cost and programme goals, and of the impact of the changes that the business unit heads requested. Together, you could take the best decision for the business needs based on firm information. This allowed you to react to the quite major change in the company structure that happened about halfway through the programme. Is that not how all projects should run? Do we not all want to be part of that kind of experience? With the right team, and the project set up in the right way to reward trust and teamwork, it can be.

The trouble is, some of the existing processes and attitudes do not contribute to creating this kind of atmosphere. The initiatives stimulated by the Egan and Latham reports are highlighting new approaches. It will also take new kinds of organisation in the construction and property sector to implement these approaches and work with clients in a holistic, business-focused way. The best of these organisations will have processes in place for learning from the diverse experiences of their professionals at various points on the clock face, and then feeding the results back into other connected activities and decisions.

The beginning of the facility

As you stand at the end of the project that delivered the space, you are now faced with the ongoing management of the facility. We now fast-forward five years.

The initial project will be a distant memory. You will have had to face a new set of challenges:

- making sure the building functions as planned and maintaining it;
- managing the facilities team – in-house or out-sourced – to deliver a service which supports the core business units in the critical areas;
- managing change and alteration to keep pace with changes in your business.

Your board may have asked you to look at ways of rationalising the entire property portfolio, or how to get the property costs off the balance sheet. You may already have disposed of the building. How easily and advantageously this happened depended on many of the decisions you took as the office was first designed. Luckily you have a strong, trust-based relationship with the people that designed and delivered the space in the first place. They have been able to implement changes efficiently, with minimal lead-in, that have added significant value to your business. They have kept the information resource on the space and its systems up to date, eliminating unnecessary surveys and errors. They have pro-actively suggested improvements based on their overview of the industry and space utilisation.

The end of the office

Now imagine yourself another 15 years into the future. Some of the trends towards an office-free future that were forecast at the beginning of the century have not come to pass. Others have had a different outcome than predicted, and have still had an effect on the way your organisation does business. Whatever the reason, despite being a highly adaptable and durable facility, the office building you created no longer fits the needs of the business. It has to be replaced. We are back at the beginning.

A choice of product

Every month, we see a variety of uses of office space and how it is configured to suit different clients. A few years ago, there were really only two routes a client could choose: spec office or built-to-suit. Now, you can choose from a range of products:

- Purpose-built (typically owner-occupied).
- Pre-let leasehold development (typically one to 20-year lease; from 50 sq m upwards).
- Traditional leasehold office (typically one to 20-year lease; from 50 sq m upwards).
- Quasi office (e.g. combined light industrial and office – B2 – space).

- Flexi-lease office (typically six-month to five-year lease; 100 to 2,000 sq m; space and service adapted to tenant requirements).
- Serviced office (typically three-month to two-year lease; 10 to 200 sq m).
- Corporate PFI solution (typically 25-year agreement; from 10,000 sq m upwards).
- Virtual office (e.g. tele-working).

The choice can be made according to the work function to be accommodated, how close it is to the core business, its likely duration, and what level of commitment you would like to make to that space. Many organisations adopt a mixed approach, housing core functions in a built-to-suit head office, with peripheral teams in less permanent space and serviced offices.

If you are thinking about leasehold space, there are decisions to be made on the state in which you will take the space and the route to bring it to your required standard. Buildings are commonly let in one of two states: shell-and-core or developer's Category 'A'. Our understanding of the meanings of these terms are:

- Shell-and-core – structure, main services plant, envelope and cores complete together with core areas (reception, lift lobbies, toilets, etc) fitted out but general floor areas left with bare structural floor and ceiling.
- Category 'A' – as above, plus general floors fitted out with ceiling, high-level services to suit open-plan occupation, and raised floor.

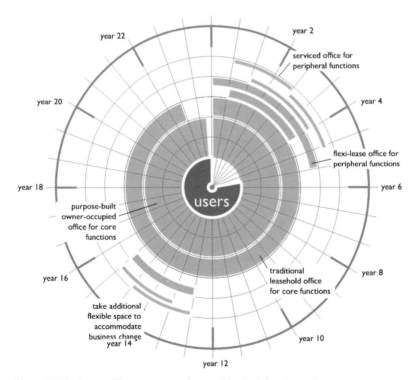

Figure 3: Choice of office space product and typical duration of use

Often, they can be a mix of both – category 'A' on the floors likely to be predominantly open-plan office space; shell-and-core in areas which may have more special uses – restaurants, computer rooms, etc. Case study 1 outlines how one of our clients took a pre-let on a developer-specification building and tailored it to their needs in an efficient way.

Case study: Taking a pre-let

Law firm Slaughter and May thought long and hard about relocating to a new headquarters on the boundaries of the City of London. A potentially suitable development was planned nearby, in the right location. Slaughter and May took an early pre-let option with the developer which enabled them to influence many of the important features of the building and get them incorporated into the base build, saving time and money. These features included:

- Single inclusive planning consent for base build and fit out.
- Building on a 1,350 mm grid module in lieu of 1,500 mm resulting in a ten per cent increase in space efficiency.
- Selection of external stone cladding.
- Additional entrances into building.
- Deferring completion of landlord's common parts and main entrances for inclusion in the fit out.
- Selection of key finishes for other landlord areas.
- Knock-out panels for future risers.
- Base build power generation sized to suit Slaughter and May's needs.
- Joint validation of, and enhancements to, central plant and equipment.

The right standards

A lot of work has been done on the optimum building module and the specification for a standard office, much of it supported by the British Council for Offices (BCO). The papers they have published address the dangers of over-specification, for example of small power.

As you plan your building, it is worth interrogating each feature against the BCO standard, and deciding on the real value of any departure (*see* case study 2, below).

Efficient and effective space

A useful distinction can be made between efficient and effective space. An office is efficient if it generally runs well, has high utilisation rates and the operating costs are reasonable. Space is effective if the people working in it are satisfied and work productively. Factors include:

- good lighting;
- well-designed and well-maintained air conditioning;

Figure 4: Interior space, Slaughter and May

- good spatial layouts;
- well-chosen.

You will also want to assess the likely response of the building to potential changes in use that your evolving business may demand. It may be helpful to distinguish between two concepts:

- Flexibility – built-in features which increase the ability of the space to be used in different ways, e.g. main plant sized to accommodate high occupation density.
- Adaptability – the ability of the space to be altered for different uses, e.g. space in plant areas ready to accommodate additional plant if necessary.

The key difference is that you may pay for flexibility without necessarily being able to use it. On the other hand, if a building is not adaptable, it may take significant cost to alter.

Build-to-suit solutions

If you a are client thinking about building an office from scratch specifically to suit your needs, it is likely that your company:

- is large;
- occupies a number of buildings in many locations.

These represent the most typical characteristics of organisations who commission purpose-built offices. The reasons why organisations do this are varied:

- the debate between property assets on or off the balance sheet;
- a need for certainty of the quality of the finished space;
- triumphalism.

The challenge is to balance the specific needs of your own organisation with proven generic office standards. If the balance is too far towards your company, you run the risk of creating a one-off facility which may not be able to react to any changes in your business.

If you get it right, you will create an asset. It will be able to accommodate various styles of working, and different work functions as your business changes. If the need arises, it could be let to another company. In that case, your building will be competing against all the others on the market, and will be assessed by potential tenants (*see* case studies below).

Case study: Building assessment

We recently assessed two buildings on a business park in the M3/M4 corridor for a potential occupier. A summary of the main criteria follows.

Services and data:

- services supply feeds;
- supply capacity fit for use;
- reliability and redundancy;
- life cycle costs;
- IT strategy;
- lighting;
- waste and environmental considerations;
- handover and commissioning.

Fabric:

- finishes;
- maintenance.

Space plan:

- size, shape and configuration;
- fit for purpose;
- trial layouts;
- position of major fixes (cores, risers, etc).

External environment and landscaping:

- appearance and image;
- screening;
- maintenance;
- litter.

Envelope:

- cleaning and safety;
- glare and solar gain;
- logistics and lead-in of replacement glazing.

Health and safety:

- fire evacuation routes;
- compliance with legislation;
- first aid.

Security and access:

- positioning of reception;
- image;
- availability of lifts;
- disabled access provision;
- smoking areas;
- goods in and out;
- security strategy.

Staff and business support facilities:

- proximity to local facilities;
- need for staff restaurant.

These form a useful checklist for occupiers taking a lease on any space.

Case study: Flexible build-to-suit

In planning their new 13,000 sq m regional headquarters in Sevenoaks, BT's property team was keen to retain as much flexibility for the business as possible. This has been achieved partly through adopting the predominantly open-plan BT Workstyle standards, making good use of hot-desking, formal and informal meeting spaces.

Figure 5: BT building, Sevenoaks

In addition, to ensure their future options are left open, BT employed Stanhope[1] as a knowledgeable adviser on the potential 'letability' of the building. Stanhope set criteria on the optimal dimensions and aspect ratio of the space and from this flowed many of the design decisions regarding:

- how the space was articulated into three primary bays;
- where cores were located;
- how the entrance was configured.

The result is a building that works very well for BT, and can accommodate a number of future options.

---

1 *See also* German, R and R Harris (2001) *A Review of Small Power Provision and Occupation Densities in Office Buildings,* Stanhope Position Paper.

Figure 6: Auditorium referred to in 'Taking risk' case study

Balancing risk and value

We must never lose sight of what allows clients to spend money on office space in the first place. Profit is the return companies make on the risk they take. Sometimes it seems we forget this basic principle. Often, the design and delivery team tries to manage out the client's risk (and most of ours, if we are honest), spending the client's money in the process. The various traditional forms of contract assign risk to varying degrees between the client and delivery supply chain: they do not tend to promote a collective approach. More balanced contracts incorporate risk sharing, with painshare/gainshare arrangements to encourage a collective approach.
Would you not rather spend your money working with designers and a delivery team to understand, plan and respond to risk on a case-by-case basis? An example of how this process was managed to the benefit of one of our clients is detailed in the case study below.

Case study: Taking risk

Some way through the construction and fitting out of their new headquarters, our client recognised an urgent business need for a world-class auditorium space. The obvious location was on top of the new building. This involved removing the recently-finished roof and building an additional floor for the auditorium.

The risks included water intrusion onto floors lower down the building that were already occupied. Any interruption would cause huge financial losses. The project had to take place over the autumn of 2000, which turned out to be one of the wettest on record. Our client took the advice of their whole project team and gauged that the potential benefits outweighed the risks as long as precautions were taken.

These countermeasures included two levels of weather protection:

- a temporary roof over the area of the new auditorium;
- a watertight membrane above the occupied floors.

These were connected to a carefully thought-out temporary drainage system. In addition to the physical measures, a flexible response process was put in place to react rapidly to a range of possible scenarios.

The outcome was that the structural works were completed, the building is now fully weather tight again, and the auditorium was fitted out without a single interruption to the client's business due to water ingress.

Risk and change

The most common risk is that your business changes substantially during the life of the project:

- you merge with another organisation;
- technology advances quicker than expected;
- a new sector opens up;
- demand reduces dramatically in another sector.

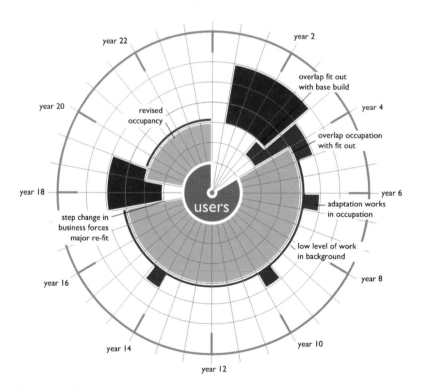

Figure 7: Office lifecycle showing overlaps between construction, fit out and occupation

A building that could not accommodate these changes would be the wrong space for your business. However, to try and build in sufficient flexibility across all areas is uneconomic, and risks failing if there is a lot of change in just a few areas. It would be much better to have a resilient, agile contingency plan for change, and implement change to the right level in the right areas only.

Current view

This presents considerable challenges to the current way commercial offices are designed, procured and delivered. The traditional mindset views change as A Very Bad Thing. It is tolerated with bad humour, and discussions nearly always lead to confrontation and blame. A project should ideally be designed, constructed and handed over without change on the easily-defined practical completion milestone. The client should then take it over and run it as built, all without any change. This works as long as the building life cycle is shorter than the cycle of change affecting the business.

In reality, of course, change is the only certainty and the cycle of change is accelerating. The design needs to evolve continuously in tune with the business, the construction needs to keep up, and once distinct milestones are now less clear-cut. Even after you take occupation, you will probably be involved in an almost continuous churn process. The very simple clock face model needs to be adapted to reflect reality, with overlaps between construction, fit out and occupation to achieve the earliest move date. Regular work will be needed to adapt the space to meet business change, together with low-level maintenance. Some major work will probably be needed to reflect the impact of a step change in business need.

The new thinking

In this environment, any change order process has to be very efficient. It places great emphasis on effective, targeted information flow. It must also be a two-way street, allowing the supply chain to suggest improvements which may lead to business benefits. You will also look to them to provide you with the programme, cost and practical impact assessments on which to base a confident decision. An 'expert client' is often very useful in filtering out change requests that are unnecessary, based on internal politics, or do not fit the core business needs.

The way forward

Finding a way through this confusion of risk and change is actually quite simple: you need to gather a team who will be around for the long run and not just the old model of a single project, and you need to concentrate on the areas of substantive change. Building the right team is covered under 'Managing the supply chain' later in this chapter.

Substantive similarity

Finding the areas of substantive change can be more difficult. If we think about the way offices have worked over the last ten years, some areas remain remarkably constant:

- Each person performs a variety of tasks at their primary workstation, including screen-based work, paper-based work and interaction, face to face or remotely.
- They need an amount of easily-accessible storage – physical and/or electronic.
- Some tasks require privacy.
- A range of meeting spaces encourages interaction.

These areas of substantive similarity can usually be satisfied with a stable, quite generic space solution. If this became more widespread, it would encourage greater standardisation, pre-fabrication and a drive towards higher quality and lower costs.

The effort (or contingency allowance) otherwise used in changing the substantially similar areas could be channelled into those which require substantive change:

- areas of high or specialist technological content, e.g. communications room, auditorium;
- highly branded areas, e.g. reception;
- areas which affect the adaptability of the space, e.g. cores.

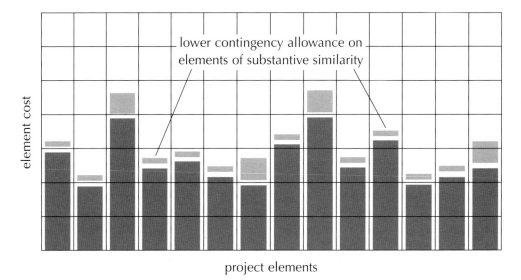

Figure 8: Graph showing areas of substantive similarity

Managing the supply chain

Just as you rely on us not to let you down, we rely on our trades, and they in turn rely on their suppliers. A network of relationships, contractual and informal arrangements leads up to the day you walk into a completed office. We have to communicate the aims, urgency and value imperatives throughout the whole supply chain to make sure the final product matches (and hopefully exceeds) your expectations.

As a best-practice employer, your company probably already has a psychological contract with its staff based on trust, respect and opportunity. It has probably also started to re-evaluate some of its relationships with suppliers of products and services that are key to your business. The car industry is often quoted as an exemplar of the kind of symbiotic, ongoing partnerships between suppliers and business. For many office-based companies, IT is a key business-critical area where long-term alliances are becoming more widely used.

Many companies are also starting to examine the importance of their property portfolio on their business, and the relationships they have with suppliers involved in the provision and care of existing and new property. Term contracts, framework agreements, and partnering arrangements regularly make the news.

Unfortunately, until recently many parts of the sector have not been able to respond to the level of trust and commitment to service expected of them. As an industry, we are criticised (Latham et al) as being short-termist and inefficient.

The sharp end

At the sharp end of service delivery are many specialist sub-contract companies. Often bearing the brunt of the criticism and blame from (as traditionally seen) further up the food chain, they rightly complain that they are given unrealistic targets with little chance to add their input to the process. Recent history has not helped: the rapid move to sub-contracting and the boom-and-bust economy a few years ago tended to produce small supplier companies with owner-directors and little management structure or long-term strategy.

Now, though, the market is maturing, and there are a number of very professional suppliers with long-term strategies and high calibre staff. Examples are often found in the mechanical, electrical, IT and controls trades. These firms are well-placed to work closely with clients and main service providers to develop best value products which work properly first time, and need less maintenance.

In our experience, it is those clients whose business brings them close to their customers – particularly the retail sector – that are most open to partnering with their suppliers. They recognise the very strong link between supplier performance, the quality of their business space, and the revenue it generates.

Benefits

This commitment to development needs investment and has to generate a return for those involved. Setting up a framework or partnership provides a sustained income stream for the suppliers, and makes investing in improvement attractive for them. The client benefits from new products that are:

- appropriate for their intended use;
- consistent in quality;
- durable.

Techniques such as mass production, standardisation and modularity help to deliver these benefits, with lower cost as an attractive spin-off. The transaction costs and administrative overhead of dealing with a reduced supply base are also lower; lead-in and reaction times are faster. Both parties, therefore, share the benefits of a more collaborative approach.

Keeping it fresh

A typical charge levelled at partnering is that it only leads to cosy deals and restrictive practices: it does not encourage the kind of leading-edge solutions that competition produces. Is this true? Poorly set up and run, of course.

The key to being in a successful relationship is communication. Client and supply team have to be clear on what they each want out of the arrangement from the start, and where the areas of common interest lie. By communicating, we find out what makes each other tick, and what motivates us towards high performance. The client, the consultants and the supply team can then structure a simple reward system to encourage constructive behaviour.

Reflection and learning is often missing on many assignments. After each project, there should be a frank, open discussion on how it ran, how the final product works for the business, and what could be improved. There are risks as well as benefits of innovation, and these need to be shared in a blame-free atmosphere. This requires trust.

In return for more commitment and improvement, the client is obliged to run the scheme fairly, listen to suggestions for improvement, and act on suppliers' concerns. If these basic tenets are obeyed, the relationship will continue to grow and the client will reap increasing benefits. The Case study on airport construction profiles an example of good practice in this area.

Case study: Airport construction training alliance

BAA and its suppliers recognised that their airports were seen as difficult, hostile and unwelcoming places for trades to work. Paradoxically, BAA relied on the construction trades to deliver high-quality facilities on time to meet customer needs. They recognised that they needed to start treating the trades as professionals who had a valuable input into making the airports world-class facilities.

As a major client (they currently let around £500 million worth of projects per year), they wanted to secure the best construction workers to deliver high quality projects.

BAA set up a 'Passport to Work' scheme in 1998, and set themselves a target of 2001 for full implementation, with everyone working on a BAA site being able to demonstrate competence to a nationally-recognised level.

BAA invest in its construction workforce, demonstrating commitment through a variety of respect for people initiatives including branded clothing, transport initiatives and it has also fitted out a high-standard central welfare area for construction workers.

Major benefits have been realised since the scheme has been introduced. There has been a:

- drop in the accident frequency rate by almost 50 per cent;
- major increase in trade morale and higher standard of appearance;
- much reduced turnover of construction staff;
- retention of essential airport skills;
- greater pride and ownership of quality.

The 'Passport to Work' scheme, along with the 'One in a Million' safety drive has set BAA apart as a forward thinking construction client.

The IT backbone

Since we were founded in 1989, we have seen the rapid rise in importance of information technology. It has to be considered an integral – and often primary – part of any modern functioning office space.

Then

Until only a few years ago, many IT installations involved simple standalone desktop systems. Most of our clients had only limited reliance on IT for their business functions. Space planning was driven by furniture layout, and the main effort in M&E services was in providing the right environment for the staff. The design, installation and commissioning of the fairly minimal IT infrastructure tended to be a linear process. Historically there was a limited overlap between the client's IT team (if there was one) and the project delivery team.

Now

Nowadays, most clients – particularly financial institutions – rely totally on IT for their business functions. This places greater demand for resilience on the IT systems themselves, and in turn on support M&E services. The importance of IT and complexity of the systems involved has led to a far more integrated design and construction process. It integrates the fundamental drivers of the core business with the day-to-day operation of the facility and the installation enablers. There is now a greatly increased level of communication with the IT team, but barriers and complications still exist.

As a client, you will want confidence that your project team will build in enough flexibility for the changes in the IT infrastructure to be accommodated between the time the project was first thought of to the time it is finished, and further throughout its life cycle.

Communication

A client's internal project team may feel threatened by direct contact between the IT team and the project delivery team. A lack of shared language, comprehension and feedback may also contribute to a lack of dialogue. The situation may be further complicated by long-standing direct links between the IT team and their preferred specialist equipment suppliers. The principal project delivery service provider – construction manager, management contractor or main contractor – needs to have a very good understanding of IT operations, and must be prepared to listen and learn from the client's IT team and the specialist suppliers. The wrong attitude is, 'We've done this a hundred times before; this one's exactly the same as the last one.' It is not.

Perhaps we should turn to the process industries – pharmaceuticals, chemicals – for ideas of how to work better. Here, a client would typically turn to a turnkey provider to design and build a new plant. The brief is a detailed process flow and control diagram showing:

- what the end product is;
- how it is manufactured;
- where the critical controls are needed;
- what the raw materials are.

The turnkey provider then provides an integrated service to deliver the plant to fulfil these process requirements. In the commercial office environment, all parts of the design and delivery would benefit from a clear statement of the client organisation's core business process.

Integration

Future trends in the rapidly-changing IT sector are very hard to predict but a safe bet would be the continued integration of network media: copper wirebased, fibre-optic, and wireless into a seamless, data net in which the different elements are used for the best balance of speed, bandwidth and flexibility in a way that is transparent to the end user.

Data location

The debate between remote or local hosting of data will continue, since it rests largely on psychological not technical grounds. It depends on how the risks are seen and where responsibility lies. On security grounds, it is worth noting that, to the best of our knowledge, there has never been a recorded physical attack on a remote data hosting facility. Much more attention will be paid to the security of the data.

Specification

Current design specifications for power requirements are based largely on a crude area measure. Evidence (BCO/Stanhope Position Paper 2001) shows that the power densities are often around two times too high compared with actual usage. The results include:

- apparent under-supply of energy;
- more demand for power generation;
- environmental impact.

Instead, power demand should be assessed on likely usage (perhaps derived from the client's process diagram) and the processor power needed to satisfy that usage. This is a strong function of data volume and speed. The power demand can then be met by modular units such as switchgear, allowing for simple future expansion if necessary.

Controls

At the moment, controls on building services are a strange combination of the crude and the sophisticated. We still hard wire controls to tailor them to a particular installation instead of using flexible programmable logic controllers, widely used in the process and car industries. We also make little use of the intelligence in the management systems we install. They could be used much more in monitoring efficiency and planning a more efficient use of resources.

Reliability

Currently, a lot of emphasis is placed on 'n+1' (or even '2×n') redundancy in all services supporting the IT installation. In future, we expect that clients will not want this level of risk elimination at any price. Instead, they will look carefully at the impact on their core business of a failure of each component, and will only want back-up on the most critical parts.

On many projects, we have effectively installed miniature individual power stations which sit idle for most of their life. Clever choice of a range of sizes of standby generators could allow a client to run the smallest set regularly to lop the peaks off their power usage. They might even be able to sell surplus power back to the grid.

Operation and maintenance

With an increased reliance on smooth operation of the IT infrastructure comes a need for technical maintenance provision. The installer could be well-placed to offer this service, as they have seen the evolution of the system from the start, and hold all the information and knowledge associated with it.

Furniture

Let us think about the first hour your staff spend in their new office. Over the first week or so they may notice the clever layout of the refreshment areas, and the range of types of interaction spaces available to them. As we have seen earlier in this chapter, there are some elements – such as the services – that your staff should never notice anyway.

But as they sit down at their new workstation to finish that important assignment they started the Friday before, they will evaluate the style and quality of the desk, the colour and comfort of the chair, and the availability of the different types of storage they need. They will discuss how their new furniture compares with the old, and how it measures up to their colleagues in another department.

The paradox is that furniture is at the end of the programme, but is the first thing your staff notice as they start work in the new space. It could be one of the most important factors in staff morale and productivity. It has to be worth doing properly.

Stakeholders

The trouble with furniture is that it is so subjective. A wide range of key people are likely to have a say in the choice of it:

- The chief executive will evaluate against corporate vision, aesthetic and functional criteria.
- The finance director will evaluate against budget and life cycle value criteria.
- The design team will evaluate against aesthetic and functional criteria.

There are many others. There will have been a build-up of expectation regarding the new workplace, and everyone will have formed a wish list for their furniture.

However, furniture is sometimes near the bottom of the priority list, and the wish list is at risk of being pared back to fit in with the overall budget. An expectation gap can form, affecting the perceived success of the entire project.

Advice

It has been the case that furniture providers have served their customers poorly. Clients are confused by volumes of undifferentiated sales material with little clear basis for comparison and not much impartial advice. The business has a reputation, if not for always being late, at least for being very over -optimistic regarding programme. This affects the credibility of the advice given and the trust between client and provider.

There is a real need for an ideal specialist furniture advisor to provide independent, consultative and knowledgeable guidance in this key area.

This person would:

- work closely with the client and designers to interrogate the furniture brief in the light of the wider business needs and space to be delivered;
- be sensitive to the work they may have already done and the choices they may have made while communicating the various options available;
- manage the procurement and selection of the chosen system or systems;
- manage the delivery, installation and commissioning of the furniture;
- train users and maintainers in the operation of the furniture.

Developing a brief and budget

The furniture brief will be based on a combination of an understanding of the client's business and the new space being delivered:

Business:

- image;
- business aims;
- values;
- technology used and likely to use;
- any history relevant to the choice of furniture.

Space:

- floorplate;
- lighting;
- communications;
- adjacencies.

Budget is always vitally important.

Over the last five years, costs have remained remarkably consistent, and a broad-brush banding can be applied for low-, medium- and high-specification workstations. The figures in the table below give an approximate indication of the cost per head for desk, chair and storage.

Low specification	Medium specification	High specification
Less than £1000/head	£1000 to £2000/head	More than £2000/head

In compiling a useful brief, the key thing is to introduce as few constraints as possible, and to interrogate those you do.

Compliance

The standards most relevant to your choice will be the European Community VDT directive on workstation ergonomics, and the British Standard BS 6396 on electrical systems at a workstation.

A Best Practice organisation will also want to ensure that the manufacture and maintenance of their furniture complies with environmental considerations. This includes raw materials from sustainable or re-cycled sources.

Future-proofing

Trends we have seen in furniture since the 1980s include:

- panel-based systems;
- three-way separated cable management for power, voice and data;
- height adjustment.

Most of these have disappeared, either through technical advances or a better understanding of the costs and real benefits of adaptability.

Technology is now fully integrated with nearly all business functions, and the furniture solution has to accommodate current technology and a sensible degree of future change. For example, many companies predicted a rolling change-over programme from cathode ray tube (CRT) monitors to flatscreen technology. In practice, some of our largest customers made a single change as the price of flat screens fell rapidly and the advantages were overwhelming. Flatscreen technology now allows us to depart from the standard L-shaped workstation, designed to accommodate deep CRT monitors.

You often find that all work functions in an organisation can operate effectively from a small range of types of workstation. The key to a durable, long-term furniture solution is to find a range that is modular and uses a small kit of parts to change from one workstation type to another. You also need a furniture supplier who has a smart inventory system and a relationship-based culture to be able to continue to provide you with the parts you need to adapt to your changing business.

Defect-free completion

Why do we work so hard to achieve a high quality end result? Looking back from the end of a project, the last few weeks will be freshest in your mind. The site search and briefing process may have been fascinating; the design phases challenging; and most of the delivery stage very satisfying. But if the last few weeks were characterised by defects that never seemed to get fixed, by blame and counter-blame, then your lasting impression of the project and all involved will be coloured.

What is quality?

Quality is difficult to talk about in abstract. In a car, we can recognise quality as a mix of sensory perceptions: the 'clunk' of the door closing; the feel of the upholstery; the quiet sound of the engine running. Detail is everything: a tiny blemish in the paintwork can affect the perception and enjoyment of the whole.

Built space has analogous quality criteria: the uniformity of fair-faced concrete; the precise line of the facade glazing and internal partitions; the feel of the joinery. The overall perception can be ruined by a lack of attention to a single detail such as a poorly-aligned light switch.

Quality in other areas is unseen and unheard. In a car, you may never open the bonnet to appreciate the logical layout of the engine and ancillaries that make servicing simple and cheap. You will never see the carefully-selected materials and components that enhance reliability and increase the service interval.

Likewise, in a building, you should never hear or feel the services that keep the internal environment at a precise comfort level. You should never notice the power back-up system that kicks in without a flicker of your screen.

Learning from other industries

The car industry has a lot to teach us about how to build a better, more reliable, more consistent and cheaper product:

- Designing for reliability and manufacture.
- Simple and rigorous quality control checks throughout the process.
- Best use of mass production, modularisation and pre-fabrication.

Figure 9: UK Passport Agency

- Supportive relationships with the supply chain based on high service levels and commitment to deliver 'just in time'.
- Two-way communication between shop floor and management to build ownership and reward quality-led innovation.

They do not get it right all the time, as recent recalls show.

Teaming up for quality

It is a fair criticism of the property business that each project is treated as a one-off prototype. It will continue to be this way as long as a fresh team is assembled from scratch each time. By taking initiatives such as framework agreements and supply chain partnering, explored elsewhere in this chapter, we can start to build strong teams that have worked together before, know each other's expectations, and will not repeat old mistakes. Successful partnerships generally only form between people with shared values, so the teams will naturally form around like-minded people from reputable, long-term companies. A readiness to listen will encourage quality-led innovation up and down the supply chain.

Quality has to start early, with an insistence on the highest standards from the beginning. Clear benchmarks showing the standards expected must be set up, and simple performance measures put in place. Procedures have their place, but by gathering a team of compatible people, we can count on each person's pride in doing their best work to produce a high-quality end result, rather than wasting time and effort in more and more bureaucratic quality control processes. Case study 6 details how, together with the client, designers and trades, we delivered a completely snag- and defect-free major project.

Case study: Zero defects

The relocation of the UK Passport Agency to a refurbished 1960s building was initiated by the well-publicised problems associated with the backlog of passport applications in the summer of 1999. With the high public visibility of the project, cost and programme were key concerns for the client. Despite this, we believed that a high-quality end product was achievable within the cost parameters, and with the full commitment and buy-in of our sub-contractors and the client's team we set out to achieve a defect-free phased completion.

Some of the approaches involved value-engineered alternative solutions to give a better end result. The original employer's requirement was to patch, repair and decorate the existing plastered soffit, plastered walls, column finishes and perimeter concrete mullions, with perimeter plastered bulkheads to house fan coil units, ductwork and pipe work. Instead, we introduced:

- all new suspended ceilings with integral services;
- overboarding of existing walls and columns;
- GRG casings to perimeter concrete mullions.

These measures substantially improved the quality of finish, and were economical solutions: for instance, the ceiling system is the least expensive metal ceiling on the market, and gives a much better technical, more durable and aesthetic solution.

Other approaches involved careful sequencing of operations to avoid damage and re-working. For example, we designed a special perimeter casing in which the visible finished elements were fixed as the final operation, after all the services had been installed.

Much of the credit for the result, however, is associated with the human approach adopted. From the outset, the drive to achieve the zero defect standard met with enthusiasm and assistance from the client's team and our trades. This was assisted by a series of long-standing working relationships with many of the companies and individuals involved.

As each trade started work, our senior construction manager explained the high standards required. These standards were carried across every area of the project. A site foremen's meeting was held twice a week to air issues and resolve problems face-to-face. No special incentives were put in place beyond our usual bottle of champagne for Sub-contractor of the Month. Competition for this award became intense.

As a result of these methods, morale on site remained high. Health and safety performance was also exceptional. The entire building was handed over without a single defect being found by the client, design team or our internal quality auditors.

How to get what you want

When you take over a space, there are many items to think about at a time when you are already very busy. If you are at the stage of preparing to sign a lease, you will be also thinking about the design of the space and considering how to get it fitted out or refurbished to your requirements, as well as negotiating favourable terms with the developer or landlord. If the space is complete, you may be deep in the process of moving your staff in and running the building.

Whatever stage you are at, there are a few key questions you can ask to clarify the issues:

- What do I want from the space?
- When can I move in?
- What are the processes for putting right any snags or defects?
- Is my business going to be interrupted by these processes?
- How will I be able to adapt the space later?

In our experience, difficulties are often related to the services, the information on their performance, and the certainty that they comply with relevant standards. This could be overcome simply with a concise building manual, extracted from the full documentation, containing:

- a brief description of scope of installation;
- directory of designers, installers and suppliers;
- certification on key safety or business-critical systems, e.g. electrical, water quality, lifts;
- building regulation approvals.

Some of the situations we have come across, together with suggested ways out, are outlined below.

Table 1: Common issues at handover

Issue	Impact	Suggested mitigation
Incomplete documentation or information on base build systems available at practical completion.	Information on which fit out services are tendered is 1-2 generations behind as-installed with attendant cost and programme risk.	Obtain base build safety file to at least 'B' status prior to practical completion including draft commissioning data and residual risks.

Table 1: Common issues at handover – *continued*

Issue	Impact	Suggested mitigation
Suspect water quality, e.g. pseudomonas bacterium in water circuits.	System needs treating, flushing and re-circulating with attendant cost and programme risk.	Obtain progressive water quality checks prior to handover.
Incomplete validation of very complex systems, e.g. building management system (BMS) and controls.	Delay while systems are understood and tested.	Appoint independent commissioning consultant to validate base build and fit out systems. Appoint controls trade early to understand system.
Restrictive covenants, e.g. noise, environmental health, sub-tenancies, access.	Progress and cost of construction; potential unforeseen impact on use of building.	Question lease agreement rigorously.
Limited terms of due diligence search.	Focus only on quality of installation rather than assessing impact of any partial completion on progress and cost.	Widen scope of report.
No continuity between construction and operation. decisions; impact on	Involvement of facilities or IT team in key early efficiency and effectiveness of space; potentially higher long-term costs in use.	Involve FM team, IT team and key suppliers (such as furniture) at early stage.
No certification on lifts	No weight testing; potentially considerable health and safety risk.	Certify lifts by practical completion.
No provision for maintaining fabric and systems between base build practical completion and first occupation.	Possible invalidation of warranties; potential water quality issues.	Appoint same maintenance service provider who will be maintaining elements when you take occupation.

Table 1: Common issues at handover – *continued*

Issue	Impact	Suggested mitigation
Lease places onerous provisions on tenant.	Progress and cost of fit out.	Agree at negotiation stage on issues including: • access and demise; • rights to inspect progress and quality of base build; • procedures for handing over space and systems and for remedying defects. Appoint independent commissioning consultant to validate base build and fit out systems.

Managing the facility

This is where we look forward, from practical completion, to the continuing operation of the office over its life cycle. How do you ensure it keeps running smoothly?

Whether or not factors such as globalisation and competition are having a greater impact on businesses than the past, they are affecting how business leaders and commentators view the way organisations are run. This affects how they use space. Recent trends include:

- a move away from too much diversification towards a greater concentration on core business;
- impact of e-commerce, producing new organisational models and new ways of working;
- renewed focus on costs – financial and environmental;
- demand for agility and flexibility in all parts of the business.

Core and peripheral functions

Many organisations are moving towards a 'shamrock' pattern[2], with three distinct parts:

- core professional team;
- flexible resource;
- outsourced functions.

2 Handy, C (1993), *Understanding Organisations 4th Edition*, London, Penguin Books.

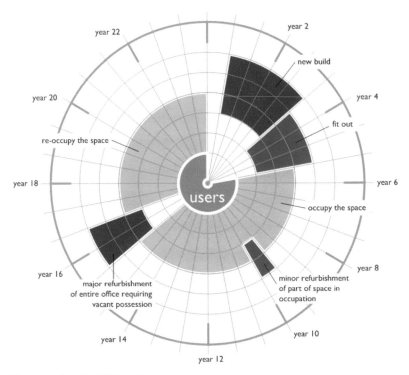

Figure 10: Standard Office lifecycle

As we discussed under the heading 'Build-to-suit solutions' earlier in this chapter, this type of model is driving changes in the way organisations accommodate their staff, choosing from a range of occupancy products such as purpose-built owner-occupied, leasehold, serviced offices and virtual space.

The outsourcing debate

Some organisations are considering a radical new option for providing space and services: outsourcing to a specialist management company. This is often known as 'Corporate PFI' after the government-sector private funding initiative, of which Project Prime, the outsourcing of the DHSS portfolio, is a well-known example.

The main feature of this arrangement in its purest form is the transfer from Company A of the risk associated with owning, leasing and operating its property portfolio to Company B. In return, Company B charges a unitary fee in return for taking some risk for changes in the accommodation requirements and risk on providing the services at an economic rate throughout the period. One of the benefits seen by Company A is a reduced administration overhead on paying this unitary charge rather than separate building-by-building payments for rent, life cycle replacement and facilities management.

So far, most of the private-sector property outsourcing exercises have been primarily financial re-engineering exercises, based upon sale and leaseback principles, without significant outsourcing of services.

The costing models used for these types of solutions are based upon a whole life approach. The consumer – Company A – will calculate how much its accommodation will cost over the period based upon its existing approach, whilst the supplier – Company B – needs to estimate how it can reduce this through innovation and better procurement.

Benefits

The advantages to the consumer (Company A in the example above) are generally:

- Lower accommodation costs – a provider can usually take better advantage of economies of scale and market buying power.
- Greater certainty of costs – the unitary charge and mechanisms for coping with change are built into the PFI deal.
- Better quality of services – a corporate specialist provider should be able to manage better performance.

Depending on the precise structure of the deal and on the interpretation of new accounting procedures, it may be possible to avoid having to capitalise the property charges on the balance sheet.

Flexibility is often cited as a key benefit, although it has to be remembered that flexibility for the consumer results in risk for the provider, and probably a higher unitary charge. The real benefit comes from occupants and specialist providers working together to look at the likely real business need for flexibility and how it might impact on the space requirement and mix.

Setting up the outsourcing deal

The four keys to setting up a successful outsourcing deal are:

- Establishing a common language to describe the service and outcome.
- Clearly defined service performance measures and targets.
- An agreed method of comparing capital costs and revenue over the whole life of the deal.
- A common understanding of the different life cycles of building, occupancy and business unit, and how each is used in the whole life costing model.

The first of these elements should be built into a comprehensive set of property, lease and facilities management data and the occupier's likely business plan for the term of the agreement. There will probably already be some performance measures in place.

This dataset will form the basis of tendering or negotiating the deal. The OPD Total Occupancy Cost Code, with the categorisation and identification of cost elements, is a major contribution to achieving a consistent measurement of occupier performance and ensures that we are all talking the same language.[3]

The provider can then propose how they will deliver the service to meet the occupier's needs over the term, and suggest key performance measures and comparative methods.

At an early stage, occupier and provider need to work together to understand:

- what stage each property in the occupier's portfolio is at on the building life cycle;
- what stage each property is at on the life cycle of the business unit occupying it;
- where the business plan for the occupier's company is likely to take the component business units;
- what effect that has on the property portfolio.

Conclusion

We have now come full circle: we have followed the facility through its full life cycle on the clockface from its conception, construction, fitting out and management. Along the way, we have outlined many of the factors that affect the success of that facility. Many of these issues need to be managed in a complex, parallel process to meet the key milestone dates: this is our art or craft.

---

3 Guscott, F (2001), *Occupier Performance – Assessment of Costs,* Third OPD Conference 2001.

Author profiles

Matthew Giles, Former Group Marketing Director
Interior Services Group

Matthew Giles has followed a career in marketing and research with a number of construction companies including Mace and Schal. In 1997 he co-founded Exterior, the innovative new build sister company to Interior, and went on to become Group Marketing Director.

Dr Alister Harwood, Head of Proposals
Interior Services Group

Alister Harwood joined Ove Arup & Partners as a geotechnical design engineer after graduating. His career has included research and lecturing posts at the universities of Newcastle and Birmingham. He joined Interior in 1997, where his work involves seeking out and disseminating good practice and information across the ISG group of companies.

Interior Services Group offers owners and occupiers a range of occupancy support services to customers across Europe. By providing advisory, management and delivery services for our customers' facilities, we enable them to focus on their core business. Through our core skills Interior Services Group is able to:

- create facilities;
- manage and operate them;
- look after the people who use and invest in them.

Matthew and Alister would like to thank the following individuals for their assistance:
Steve Bagland, Interior plc; Clive Butterfield, Interior plc;
Sam Cassels, ISG Occupancy; Ian Cheetham, Interior Construction GmbH;
Fred Guscott, ISG Occupancy; Robert Harris, ISG Occupancy;
Graeme Horne, ISG Occupancy; and Mike O'Mahony, Interior plc.

Index